OPERA: A H

Christopher Headington is
and writer. He is the author of *The Bodley Head
History of Western Music* and a number of other
books on musical subjects. He taught music at
Oxford University, reviews records for the
Gramophone, is a frequent broadcaster and is well
known as a pianist in many countries.

Roy Westbrook supervises music teaching at the
Department of External Studies at Oxford and is
a frequent writer and reviewer on musical
subjects.

Terry Barfoot is Senior Lecturer in the History
of Music at the South Downs College, lectures at
Oxford and is Chairman of the Music Panel of
Southern Arts.

OPERA
A HISTORY

Christopher Headington
Roy Westbrook
Terry Barfoot

ARROW BOOKS

Arrow Books Limited
20 Vauxhall Bridge Road, London SW1V 2SA

An imprint of the Random Century Group

London Melbourne Sydney Auckland Johannesburg
and agencies throughout the world

First published in Great Britain by The Bodley Head 1987
Arrow edition 1991

© Christopher Headington, Roy Westbrook and Terry Barfoot 1987

Printed and bound in Great Britain by
The Guernsey Press Co. Ltd
Guernsey, C.I.

ISBN 0 09 985150 4

To Kay Bridges, Robert Westbrook
and Philip Barfoot

Contents

Preface

Benjamin Britten called opera 'the most exciting of musical forms'. Yet it is some time since a substantial history appeared in English for the general reader, and this seems a pity since recent years have seen the creation of many new operas and the revival of major classics. There have also been striking developments in musical language and production style. The audience for opera has become ever larger and more enthusiastic, despite the high cost of opera-going associated with persistently rising production expenses.

In this book we have attempted a survey of the various aspects of opera. As regards its music, we discuss composers and their individual works, singers and performing styles, and the development of the orchestra. Stage direction and design provide another important theme, as does finance and the role of the producer-impresario or subsidising body. In addition, we touch on social-political, aesthetic, philosophical and even religious factors where these seem important. In this way we hope to pose, if not always to answer, questions as to the fundamental role of music drama in Western culture from ancient times to our own.

There has seemed no need to depart from the generally accepted chronological approach to history, though there are some cross-references. It is perhaps natural, too, that much of the book is devoted to the nineteenth and twentieth centuries, since the repertory draws so extensively upon this period. However, Chapter 1 does sketch in a background to the first Florentine operas, dealing as it does with the ancient world and with Christian and secular musical plays, and we hope that the following five or six chapters are more informative and stimulating on the rich period 1600–1800 than some earlier histories. Of course many operas of this time remain unfamiliar and once celebrated singers are forgotten, but we cannot overlook them when they have so positively enriched the development of the form. In any case, the most unlikely works have enjoyed revival in recent times and it may be that at least a few of the operas of Vivaldi and Alessandro Scarlatti, together with those of Keiser, Hasse and Jommelli, will one day find their way back to a place in the sun, particularly as recordings today often pave the way for successful restagings.

The matter of nomenclature has been no easier for us than for earlier writers. Broadly speaking, we have tried to use the original title for the first reference to an opera, except where the language is very unfamiliar to English-speaking readers—say Czech, Russian or Hungarian. However, a later reference may use English, and *Die Zauberflöte* become *The Magic Flute*. General usage has it that some titles are almost never translated, such as *Cosi fan tutte, La traviata, Der Rosenkavalier* and *L'heure espagnole*. However, in many cases we have given a translation immediately after the first mention of a title and hope that an occasional literary clumsiness thus caused is outweighed by usefulness. The same applies to our general rule of giving composers and some other persons their dates in the text and providing details of 'where and when' for operatic premières.

As a *troika* or triumvirate of authors, we initially apportioned the various chapters on an equal basis but also decided not to attribute these to ourselves as individuals. Throughout there has been an exchange of views as to content and style, and each of us has contributed something—an idea, a fact, even perhaps some text—to most chapters. We hope that a consistency of approach has resulted. Valuable ideas and practical help have also come from others, and we gratefully acknowledge our indebtedness to Geoff Coleman, Bes Croscombe, Richard Osborne, Dave Billinge and Roderick Swanston—as well as the inventors of word processors. Our heartfelt thanks also to two long-suffering wives. Finally, but far from least, our commissioning editor at The Bodley Head, Jill Black, has brought her considerable skill to the shaping of the final text, and for this—as well as her patience—we are all grateful.

CHRISTOPHER HEADINGTON
March 1987

1

ORIGINS

Music in the Greek and Roman theatre. Medieval Christian drama.
Secular musical plays and the Italian intermedio.

MUSIC IN THE GREEK AND ROMAN THEATRE

Opera tells a story, in an alliance of words, music both sung and played, and stage action. It may be described as sung drama, in which the theatrical force is carried by the music as well as the text. In this form opera goes back some four hundred years to the work of Italian Renaissance musicians and poets around 1600, among whom the chief figure is the composer Monteverdi.

But the idea of presenting drama with and through music was not invented by these Italian artists or the wealthy intellectuals who stimulated and supported their ideas. In fact they did not even think they were creating something new, but instead looked back with a kind of admiring nostalgia to the theatre of the ancient Greeks. The Greek literature accessible to them made many references to musical instruments and also to 'choral lyrics' involving a mix of words, music and dance. There was even an intellectual status to such a form of art, and in his *Poetics* (fourth century BC), the philosopher Aristotle wrote that a play should be an imitation of life 'rendered pleasurable' by ornamentation with melodies and rhythms. The Greeks made music part of general education and used it widely: there was choral singing at public games and ceremonies such as weddings and funerals, and besides this it featured in both tragic and comic plays. Sometimes a play's text was merely spoken in set verse rhythms by an actor or a chorus, but elsewhere a musical element was added—in other words the text was not merely declaimed rhythmically but actually sung. As for instruments, these might include a reed wind instrument called the *aulos*, with a piercing bagpipe-like tone, and perhaps also the stringed lyre called the *kithara*. There is no hard evidence that percussion instruments like drums, castanets (clappers) and cymbals played a part in theatrical performance, but it seems likely that they did on occasion for special effects, since the Greeks possessed them and a Roman mosaic at Pompeii shows cymbals and drum being played in a theatrical comedy.

For the Greeks, words and music were closely identified and indeed dramatists usually devised their own music. Even so, intelligent and questioning as always, the Greeks discussed the question of just how subordinate to the text music should be. Aristotle complained that some dramatists tended to introduce musical choruses having 'no more connection with their subject than with that of any other play, so that they are now separate pieces inserted at will'. Later, Lucian in the second century AD disapproved of a tragic actor 'actually singing his lines and—surely the height of unseemliness—melodising his misfortunes . . . Certainly if he is Andromache or Hecuba his singing may be acceptable, but when he enters as Hercules warbling some ditty a right-minded man must regard this as a solecism.' The debate concerning verisimilitude has been taken up time and again since then, for example, in the eighteenth century by Gluck, when he declared: 'I tried to restrict music to its proper function of serving poetry through expression, following dramatic situations.'

Despite their favourable location, the Renaissance Italians knew little of music theatre in ancient Rome. In fact the Romans had mimed dances as early as the fourth century BC in which the music was played on the *tibia*, a reed instrument similar to the *aulos*. Later, Latin adaptations of Greek plays were given with music, and in time many of the musicians were themselves Greek. The Roman playwright Plautus introduced songs (*cantica*) and ensembles into his comedies, where trumpeters (*tibicines*) were also a feature. Mime or pantomime also provided a light kind of musical entertainment: here dancing and singing might be accompanied by the beat of clappers as well as melodic instruments. In the early centuries AD, under the friendly patronage of emperors such as Hadrian and Diocletian, most theatrical musicians were guild members whose profession enjoyed privileges such as tax immunity, and a few 'star' performers were given civic honours.

But in ancient Rome as in Greece, theatre music remained just one of the many elements that made up a play—dancing, costume and visual effects being others. Together they enhanced a text, but that text itself remained the central vehicle for dramatic meaning. Thus music served a story rather than occupying a primary place. However, the Renaissance intellectuals who met in Florence and elsewhere after about 1570 seem to have been firm in their belief that classical plays were sung throughout, and so they placed the emphasis on vocal and musical aspects above all. From this error arose their fundamental concept of opera, which has, broadly speaking, remained our own.

Religious drama was not invented by the Christian Church. Greek theatre itself had developed from ritual dedicated to the god Dionysus, and the gods themselves continued to play a seen or unseen part in Greek stage events—for example, Dionysus himself appears as a youth in Euripides' *The Bacchae* to destroy King Pentheus for denying his worship. During the so-called dark ages between about the sixth century which saw the end of the Roman Empire in Western Europe and the tenth century, theatrical skills survived in the varied entertainments given by the *joculatores*— itinerant comics, storytellers, jugglers, animal trainers and minstrels— sometimes all these embodied in the one versatile entertainer—whose talents must have included such fundamentals of opera as the ability to create moods and tell stories with the help of music.

The Church was not slow to recognise the effectiveness of drama, and for that matter simple entertainment too, upon an unsophisticated audience. An acted Biblical story was much more compelling and memorable than one which was simply read aloud in church. Thus from the tenth century onwards we find dramatic musical interpolations to church services. One of these is the Easter *Quem quaeritis* that tells of the women's visit to Christ's empty tomb and the angel's announcement to them of the Resurrection: the music here is unison plainchant but laid out as dialogue with a theatrical upward leap at the dramatic climax '*Non est hic*', 'He is not here!' Similarly a Christmas piece has dialogue between the shepherds seeking the Holy Child and the midwives at the manger— the latter roles being invented with an early but astute use of dramatic licence. Other miniature music dramas of this kind include an Annunciation and Assumption featuring the Virgin Mary, and stories of Christ's resurrected appearances to his disciples including Doubting Thomas: these are known from France, England, Switzerland, Spain and Italy and so must have taken place almost everywhere. In England, the cathedral city of Winchester had a tenth-century *Visit to the Tomb* that may have featured its famous 400-pipe organ: this Easter piece belonged to a festive season that with Christmas produced many exuberant musico-dramatic treatments. However, two plays in the thirteenth-century South German manuscript *Carmina burana* also explored the more sombre aspects of the Passion story.

The stage upon which these Christian dramas were enacted was of course normally the local church, which became a kind of theatre in the round where different scenes could take place in different parts of the building. The Stations of the Cross contemplated in solemn procession, as they still are today on Good Friday, as well as the Christmas crib in an aisle or side-chapel, remind us of how a scene could be set to which those present would turn their attention at the right moment. But a small symbolic crib would not have satisfied St Francis of Assisi, who in 1223 used a live ox and ass in a Nativity music play. We do not know if St Francis's Virgin was played by a woman, but it seems more likely that the role would have been taken by a boy or youth. It was rare for the sexes to mix in the cast of a liturgical play, and actors were often priests or monks. As regards costume and visual effects, no one expected an angel actually to fly or even have wings, but verisimilitude was sought for none the less and the performers might be directed to sing 'loudly, as if rejoicing', or to wring their hands, or to act 'as if searching'.

The origin of the music in these church plays was plainchant, a form of rhythmically flexible unison singing known to everyone through its regular use for psalms, hymns and other parts of the church service. Gradually, though, the additional music provided for these little sung plays took on a character of its own. An Easter play of the thirteenth century, the *Ludus paschalis* from Origny-Ste-Benoîte in northern France, has a scene in which the Marys buy spices for Christ's tomb: here, despite the unbarred plainchant notation, the music is in an evident triple time, with French, not Latin, words and a lilting melody no different in style from secular songs of the time—which was that of those courtly singers of love, the troubadours and *trouvères* who flourished in France at this time.

Another French thirteenth-century piece of the first importance is *The Play of Daniel*, from the city of Beauvais with its fine Gothic cathedral. Here students at the theological school devised a Christmas entertainment with a wealth of vivid rhythmical tunes and also instrumental colour, as we know from such directions as 'let drums resound and harpists pluck their strings'. Here we find clues as to the role played by instruments at this time, and it appears that they may have played independently rather than accompanying the voices. This work still has enough dramatic life to engage our attention today, and has been performed and recorded.

The rather earlier *Ordo virtutum* of Abbess Hildegard of Bingen (1098–1179) had marked another historical milestone. Here for the first time we find the name of a creator attached to one of these musical plays. Hildegard was an intellectual religious, a diplomat as well as a mystic, and this morality play devised for her nuns to perform at her monastery in Rupertsberg in the German Rhine Valley has over eighty distinct melodies; its subject is the battle for the human soul, called Anima, between the Devil and the sixteen Virtues.

The story of early Christian drama in Europe in its aspect as a forerunner of modern opera is a rich one. From the Benedictine monastery of Fleury in France there is a twelfth-century *Raising of Lazarus* and a moving *Slaughter of the Innocents*, in which the children still sing after they are dead and so anticipate the improbabilities of opera plots to come. The *Carmina burana* collection, also Benedictine, contains an elaborate Christmas sung play. A fourteenth-century *Plaint of Mary* from the collegiate church of Cividale del Friuli in northern Italy has detailed stage directions to the singer playing the Virgin, who is at appropriate moments instructed to 'turn to the men with arms outstretched', or to 'wring her hands', or 'with her head bowed throw herself at the feet of Christ'. The *Presentation of the Virgin* play (Avignon, 1372), given with papal approval, shows Mary as 'a very beautiful little girl' of three or four climbing the temple steps to an altar in order to be presented to the bishop by her parents Joachim and Anna. There are also in this play 'two youths who shall play gentle instruments', though we do not know what they were— perhaps bells or plucked-string instruments.

Such dramatic-musical inventions as these gave way to the still more elaborate and lengthy mystery plays that date from the fourteenth to sixteenth centuries and so bring us into Renaissance times. Mystery plays characteristically used the vernacular rather than Latin, and, in a significant change of focus, they were organised and presented by the community as a whole and not the Church. The subjects were still religious ones, so naturally the Church remained involved, but now the actors were professionals or local people. The stage was no longer confined to ecclesiastical premises and was removed outdoors. Sometimes it was small, a kind of processional cart that could take the show around a town. But if not mobile in this way, it could be large and set up in a town square, and this permitted all kinds of spectacular effects—angels flying, Lucifer riding a dragon, and even earthquakes. The popularity of such effects inevitably caused their exaggeration, arising from the presenters' natural wish to make this year's performance even more astonishing than the last; and in time additional farcical, crude and even obscene elements came to find their place in the dramas. The Church authorities were not pleased at the increasing dilution and distortion of the plays' original religious message, and at the same time the music also suffered—it was left to a twentieth-century composer, Benjamin Britten, to provide fully developed music for the Chester Miracle Play *Noye's Fludde*. It would seem that although music was used for such events as processions and dances, we have have here already moved away from the real sung liturgical drama which might have been seen as a forerunner of opera.

In France, however, true religious drama continued to flourish, and literary-musical competitions were held. Instruments like trumpets, together with shawms and sackbuts (early forms of oboes and trombones) were a feature of a Montferrand Passion Play of 1577, while tambourine, pipe and tabor (small drum), and dances too, appeared even in this sacred context. Elsewhere these instruments could, after the fall of Lucifer, be required to make 'a great storm'; while on the vocal side, Lucifer could demand a song 'with unmelodious music' in the interests of dramatic truth. Thus the interest in music as such was not lost, although it could take curious forms. In a Rouen *Incarnation* (1474) a young shepherd asks what the art of singing is called. 'Music,' comes the answer. 'What a nasty word!' cries the youth.

SECULAR MUSICAL PLAYS AND THE ITALIAN *INTERMEDIO*

The earliest known play with music that was independent of religious subject-matter and Church patronage was *Le jeu de Robin et de Marion*, written around 1283 by a Frenchman from Arras, Adam de la Halle. This was composed in Italy for Adam's employer Charles d'Anjou, the tenth son of Louis VIII who reigned as King of Sicily from 1264–85, and it was presumably given a fairly lavish production at Charles's court. It is a pastoral play set mostly to music, although there are some spoken passages, and was essentially a light-hearted entertainment. Scholars argue that some of its melodies are of folk origin, but the evidence is circumstantial only; what is important is that they sound as if this were so, having a fresh, secular feeling about them. Adam's talents were those of a melodist in the *trouvère* tradition of northern France, and, as with many opera composers, it is for his tunes above all that he is remembered.

The word '*jeu*' in Adam's title is in itself significant. Music could be played by instruments alone, or serve for singing or dancing, in more or less any combination: even the words *jeu* and *jouer* in French still serve for both acting and the performance of music. Like the ancient Greeks, the players and audiences of the Middle Ages and even the Renaissance were not concerned with separating the arts of music and poetry, nor for that matter dance and scenic effects. Thus we find a use of music in many forms, some of them semi-operatic.

Popular artistic activity was reflected in the highest circles. A love of dance in the French court naturally involved music, and in his production called *Circé ou le Ballet comique de la Reine*, commissioned by Catherine de' Medici and given at the Petit Bourbon Palace in Paris on 15 October 1581, Balthasar de Beaujoyeux (ca 1535–87) added songs to story and dance to produce a convincing artistic balance. The plot told of the destruction of Circe's magic power and the re-establishment of order and harmony. There were solo arias (*airs*) and sections for instruments alone. Beaujoyeux himself did not compose all the music, much of which was by Lambert de Beaulieu and Jacques Salmon, but he co-ordinated the performance and probably played in it as a violinist. He was Italian-born and originally called Baltazarini, and had been led to to France by the Medici family, whose marriage links to the court led to many cultural gains. For example, masquerades, court entertainments of Italian origin which were often danced, became the order of the day. Sometimes, as in a *Ballet des fous* (1596), they were comically grotesque.

In Italy a strong tradition of spoken drama gradually yielded to the characteristically Italian love of music. By 1500 performances of Latin plays, such as the comedies of Plautus and Terence, often had musical interludes or *intermedi* – sometimes also referred to as *intermezzi* – played in the intervals between the usual five acts. The reason initially may have simply been to show the act division, since there was no curtain to fall, but gradually the music of the *intermedi* became more elaborate as time went on. Eventually an *intermedio* could be a staged entertainment whose plot had no connection at all with the spoken drama, though attempts were sometimes made to link them with the main production.

In due course these *intermedi* took on something of a life of their own. At Ferrara in 1499 one dramatic festival featured sixteen of them, and their complement of performers, 144 in all, exceeded those involved in the plays themselves. They were 'peasants, youths, nymphs, buffoons and parasites' who danced and mimed and sang in pastoral, mythological and amorous scenes: the songs, to lute and/or bowed-string accompaniment, mostly helped to explain what passed for a plot. In Urbino in 1513 four *intermedi* given in one performance attempted a linking theme, the triumph of Love, personified by Cupid, over Disharmony, and the whole ended with an invocation to the spirit of love for 'four voices and viols who sang a stanza with a beautiful melody'. A Florentine performance in 1565 told the tale of Cupid and Psyche in *intermedi* by Francesco Corteccia and Alessandro Striggio, with songs, ensemble madrigals and a variety of accompanying instruments including harpsichords, flutes, recorders, trombones, lutes and viols.

By now the *intermedi* often overshadowed the plays for which they were originally intended merely as a foil—'Once *intermedi* were made to serve the play, but now plays are made to serve the *intermedi*,' was a comment made in 1556. As the scholar John Addington Symonds has written in *The Renaissance in Italy* (1882): 'For the majority of the audience the dances and pageants formed the chief attraction. It is therefore no marvel if the drama, considered as a branch of high poetic art, was suffocated by the growth of its mere accessories.'

Once again, the ground was unconsciously being prepared for the fully sung drama of opera. The foundations were also being laid by a series of pastoral plays with music that began with a *Fabula di Orfeo* by Angelo Poliziano (Mantua, ca 1480) and culminated in such works as the poet Guarini's *Il pastor fido* (1584), a cheerful comedy of intrigue having two sets of lovers and a pair of villains which has music by several composers. The purgation of tragic emotion intended by classical dramatists was not for Guarini, who took a much lighter view of his role, stating that his chief aim should be to provide reassuring entertainment, 'the driving-out of melancholy'. Two other such plays were Emilio de' Cavalieri's lost *La disperazione di Fileno* and *Satiro* (both Florence, 1590).

A final Italian forerunner of opera was the so-called madrigal comedy. The madrigal itself was an ensemble vocal piece whose words almost without exception concerned love and nature, often together. It was sometimes adapted in a semi-dramatic way to tell a story. The best-known piece in this form is Orazio Vecchi's *L'Amfiparnaso*, first heard— but probably not acted, since he indicated in its prologue that staging was not intended—in 1594 and described as a 'harmonic comedy'. Here in the course of thirteen scenes the shepherd and shepherdess Lucio and Isabella are separated by a misunderstanding but finally reunited and married. Other characters are the *commedia dell'arte* figure of Pantalone, the courtesan Hortensia, the pompous Dr Gratiano, the boastful Spanish captain Cardone and so on. The whole piece is scored just as a madrigal might be, for five individual voices who tell the story in the sung words. As for the title *Amfiparnaso*, it seems to express Vecchi's view that the summit of Mount Parnassus, sacred to the Muses, was best reached by the skilful combination of the grave with the gay. Another ensemble madrigal comedy was Alessandro Striggio's *Il cicalamento delle donne al bucato* (*The Chattering Washerwomen*, 1567), but this too was probably not staged. However, Vecchi's pupil Adriano Banchieri went further towards opera in his *Prudenze giovenile* (1607), requiring his actors to mime the story while the singers and instrumentalists remained in the background and perhaps invisible.

All these works contributed to the background of opera as we know it. They used music to express moods, pictures and stories in dramatic form. At the same time, during the long gestation period covered by this chapter, European art music came of age as a fully-fledged language with its own laws of structure and syntax. It was now ready to take a role, which hitherto had only been possible in short and simple structures, as an equal partner with words and spectacle in that artistic alliance which we may call opera in the fullest sense.

2

SEVENTEENTH-CENTURY ITALY

The Florentines. Monteverdi. Later Italian opera.

THE FLORENTINES

The imaginative and inventive Renaissance spirit manifested itself in many aspects and places, and it was against the background of social life in the cultivated circles of Florence towards the end of the sixteenth century that the first operas were created. It was here that music drama in the modern sense finally crystallised, establishing a basis for a creative tradition that has extended into our own time.

We have seen how the fundamental elements for opera already existed: the stage presentation of a story, and the use of music that was both sung and played. What was new in the works that emerged in Florence was the recognition that story and music were one artistic whole, and that the drama existed not only in the text and stage actions but also in the music. This was a major achievement, and it is not to detract from the Florentines to add that it was made possible because of important developments that had by now taken place in music itself. There had been a gradual growth of a sense of form, so that music could now sustain its own structure and 'meaning'. The move from the old church modes towards the newer major and minor scales with their rich store of associated harmonies opened up a whole world of expressive resource, so that changes of key or even of chord could now be subtly expressive or vividly dramatic. Varying tone colours, textures and dynamics (the range from soft to loud in volume) were equally important. There was a further stimulus in the much improved range of available instruments, skilfully constructed to sound well alone and in tune when in ensemble, and also in the diversity of tone colour to be drawn from them. It would seem too that the human voice was now being used by singers of education and intelligence with more refinement and imagination than before. Finally, there was a drive towards an expressive force and a seriousness of purpose that were features of the other arts such as literature and painting but were relatively new in secular music, which had often been expected merely to provide agreeable entertainment. The first major composer of opera,

Monteverdi, wrote: 'Contrasts are what move our souls, and this is what all good music aims at,' and during this same Baroque period the English writer Roger North declared that as well as giving pleasure music was intended to 'move the affections or excite passion'.

On the whole these were new ideas. Nevertheless the dramatic plots chosen by the early Italian opera composers were rather stylised and stiff, being well-worn tales from the myths, or sometimes the history, of the ancient world. In this one sense the innovators can be said to have been conservative. Their acknowledged aim was to recreate the style of the Greek theatre and, as the very word Renaissance suggests, this was meant to be a rebirth rather than a new concept, at least initially. However, their ideas were newer than they realised. Since the ancient Greeks restricted music's role in drama, and rarely used such musical notation as they had to record it, we know little of their singing, or of their instrumental and compositional skills. By contrast, the intellectually curious Florentines had skilled singers and players to hand to inspire their imagination and invention; and their performance, unlike Greek plays given in the open air to large numbers, took place before smallish, educated audiences who could respond to delicate effects as well as broad ones. All this produced an art form different indeed from its source of inspiration.

The ideas of the Florentines took shape slowly over a period of nearly thirty years and first emerged among the members of the influential *Camerata* or 'society' which held its meetings between about 1573 and 1592 at the house of the Count of Vernio, Giovanni de' Bardi. According to the account written in 1634 by his son Pietro:

He always had about him the most celebrated men of the city, learned in this profession [music], and inviting them to his house, he formed a sort of delightful and continual academy from which vice and in particular every kind of gambling were absent. To this the young nobility of Florence were attracted with great profit to themselves, passing their time not only in pursuit of music, but also in discussing and receiving instruction in poetry, astrology, and those other areas of knowledge that in turn lent value to this pleasant converse . . . Giulio Caccini, considered a rare singer and a man of taste although very young, was at this time in my father's *Camerata*, and feeling inclined toward this new music he began, solely under my father's instructions, to sing *ariettas* [short songs], sonnets and other poems suitable for declamation, accompanied by a single instrument, in a way that astonished his hearers. Also at this time in Florence was Jacopo Peri . . . like Giulio, he sweetened his style and rendered it capable of moving the passions in a rare manner.

When Count Bardi moved to Rome in 1592 the meeting place of the *Camerata* changed to the house of a much younger man, Jacopo Corsi (1561–1604), who by now was, after the Medici family, the chief among Florentine patrons of music. This gifted connoisseur, we are told, kept his house 'always open, like a public academy, to all who were really interested in the liberal arts—noblemen, men of letters, established poets and musicians', and was 'discontent with all but the superlative'. Here in 1598 was performed what is usually conceded to be the first true opera: *Dafne* by Peri (1561–1633), with a libretto by the poet Ottavio Rinuccini. One account suggests that Corsi also contributed to the music. Based on Greek myth, the story tells how the god Apollo slays the Pythian dragon and boasts about it to Cupid. In order to reduce Apollo's pride and also to show his own power, Cupid makes him fall in love with the river nymph Daphne, while she, to escape his attentions, is transformed into a laurel tree—or perhaps the shrub with scented flowers that still bears her name.

Peri said that he had tried 'to imitate speech in song' in his music and had used 'elegance and graces that cannot be notated', in other words subtleties of tone, rhythm and pitch. He himself played Apollo in *Dafne*, and with his long blond hair and slim build did so with success. According to Pietro Bardi, a group of instruments accompanied the singing. As for the effect overall, Bardi declared, 'I was left speechless with amazement.' *Dafne* was given several performances, but only a few sections of its music have survived. However, the manuscript of Peri's second opera, *Euridice* (1600), was preserved. This tells the Greek story of the minstrel Orpheus and his descent into Hades to seek and regain his lost bride; but whereas in the original tale he loses her again, here the ending is happy and the couple return to their idyllic world of shepherds and nymphs. All this is in keeping with the spirit of a work whose prologue tells us that fear and sorrow must yield to the sweeter emotions evoked by music. *Euridice* features solo recitative, in other words free and declamatory vocal writing, and there are also actual songs, for example in strophic form with succeeding verses sung to the same melody, and choral writing in four or five parts. As for the recitative style, Peri declared in his preface to the opera that he had aimed at 'an intermediate course, lying between the slow and suspended movements of song and the swift and rapid movements of speech . . . I judged that the ancient Greeks and Romans (who in the opinion of many sang their staged tragedies throughout in representing them upon the stage) had used a harmony surpassing that of ordinary speech but falling so far below the melody of song as to take an intermediate form.'

Peri went on to compose several more dramatic works, but most of them have been lost. In the extant *La Flora* (Florence, 1628) he only wrote the music for the principal female character, Clori; but it is clear from her virtuoso aria in Act II that his style had become more free and elaborate in the intervening years, while the instrumental accompaniment is richer also.

Giulio Caccini (1545–1618), already mentioned as a member of the original *Camerata*, seems to have made some contribution to Peri's *Euridice*; and rather confusingly he then set the same text himself. His work was performed at the end of 1602 in the same Florentine mansion, the Palazzo Pitti, as the Peri work. Caccini aimed at a style in which 'men might, as it were, talk in music', and he too wrote quite convincing recitative. But overall the opera is less elaborate than its predecessor, and the gain in intimacy is at the same time a loss in expressive power. Nevertheless, the two men founded an operatic tradition. A singer like Peri, Caccini discussed in his essay on the 'new music' (1602) the principles of vocal ornamentation. Thus the art of opera, beginning perhaps as a mere intellectual speculation of philosophers and theorists, came to flower with practical musicians, while they in some cases became careful scholars.

MONTEVERDI

Claudio Monteverdi (1567–1643) is the first major composer of opera whose work still holds a place in the repertory. The son of a barber-surgeon and apothecary and a mother who died before he was ten, he lived as a boy near the cathedral of his birthplace Cremona and began his musical studies with its *maestro di cappella*, the composer Marc'Antonio Ingegneri (ca 1547–92). The young musician's career as a composer commenced when he was fifteen with the publication in Venice in 1582 of some sacred vocal music set for three voices. It was to be an exceptionally long one, ending sixty years later with the opera *L'Incoronazione di Poppea*.

It was probably in 1590 that Monteverdi was appointed as a string player to the Gonzaga court at Mantua, arriving there with a number of published madrigals and other vocal pieces to his credit. From the first, his work must have included playing in the court orchestra for the ballet performances that were a regular feature there, and also in the various *intermedi* that were presented. We know that there was a performance in 1598 of Guarini's musical pastoral *Il pastor fido* which possibly included some Monteverdi music. In the following year he married, and in 1601 he was able to celebrate the birth of his first son and his appointment as Mantua's *maestro di cappella*.

Monteverdi may have visited Corsi's *Camerata* in Florence, for one account names him there. As a composer of madrigals, he had learned early to write skilfully and expressively for the voice. Indeed his bold and advanced style was criticised by a contemporary theorist called Artusi for its irregularities, to which he replied in 1605 that 'with regard to consonances and dissonances there is yet another consideration different from those usually held, which defends the modern style of composition while satisfying reason and senses'. He also had experience of writing dance music and a letter dated 1604 shows his interest in balletic structure and even choreography. Clearly here was a potential music-dramatist.

Monteverdi's chance to create an opera finally came when he was in his fortieth year, in connection with the carnival festivities in Mantua in February 1607. The Duke of Mantua, Vincenzo I, had seen Peri's *Euridice* in Florence and he and his sons Ferdinando and Francesco decided to mount a similar project at their own court, clearly confident that their *maestro di cappella* could do them honour. For *L'Orfeo, favola in musica* (Mantua, 1607), the tale of Orpheus and Eurydice was again chosen. The opera had the court chancellor Alessandro Striggio as its librettist and the collaborators restored at least part of the original tragic Greek ending: Orpheus loses his wife after a forbidden backward glance as they return from the Underworld, but is then taken up into heaven by Apollo. The singers were mostly Mantuan, though some came from Florence, and the production, probably in the Duke's palace, was a great success. Several performances took place and a new opera was commissioned from the composer for the next carnival. The only sadness of the time was the serious illness of his wife Claudia, who in fact died in September of the same year.

In every way, *Orfeo* was an advance on what had been done by Peri and Caccini. The layout, in a prologue and five acts, was more elaborate and structured, with songs and an 'echo song', choruses and ballets, and an orchestra of some fifteen strings, brass and other wind. There were keyboard and plucked-string *continuo* instruments to provide a 'backing' bass, and this instrumental force was used with variety and above all imagination from the brisk overture onwards, including sections for instruments alone. The writing for voices was sensitive and varied in expressive language, for example in the scene in which Orfeo lulls Charon to sleep with his song before crossing the river Styx. The fame of *Orfeo* spread quickly, and its libretto and, later, the music itself were published.

Monteverdi's second opera was *L'Arianna* (Mantua, 1608). The libretto, by that same Rinuccini who had written for Peri and Caccini, told the Greek story of the young King Theseus and the Cretan princess Ariadne, who after being abandoned by him on an island finally joins the gods as the bride of Dionysus. The court chronicler Federico Follino was one of a larger audience, and wrote in rapturous terms:

This work was very beautiful both because of those taking part, dressed in clothes no less appropriate than splendid, and because of the scenery, showing a wild rocky place among the waves, which in the furthest distance could be seen continually in motion, giving a charming effect. But since to this was joined the force of the music, by Signor Claudio Monteverdi, *maestro di cappella* to the duke, a man whose worth is known to all the world, and who in this work excelled himself, combining with the blend of voices a harmony of the instruments behind the scene which always accompanied the voices, and as the mood of the music changed so was the instrumental sound varied; and as it was acted by men and women who were excellent singers, every part succeeded well and most especially wonderfully in the lament which Ariadne sings on the rock when abandoned by Theseus, acted with much emotion and so piteously that no one hearing it was left unmoved, nor among the ladies was there one who did not shed a few tears at her plaint.

Alas, the music of *L'Arianna* has been lost save for the lament, but in this famous aria the composer showed his ability to 'move the passions'. He liked human characters with whom he and his audience could identify, and once complained in a letter (1616) when commencing work on a sea opera called *Le nozze di Tetide*: 'I see the characters are winds . . . how can I imitate their speech and stir the passions? Ariadne moved the audience because she was a woman, and Orpheus too because he was a man and not a wind . . . I find that this tale doesn't move me at all.' The work was never completed, and what did exist is now lost, as is much that Monteverdi produced for the theatre. Barring a major discovery, we shall never know what kind of music he wrote for a variety of characters who featured in his later stage pieces: Diana, Mercury, Mars, Proserpine and Aeneas. But the dramatic cantata *Il combattimento di Tancredi e Clorinda* (Venice, 1624) shows how his language advanced, not least in the writing for the orchestral strings — for example the use of loud-soft contrasts, and *pizzicato* and *tremolando* effects. This work was not intended to be staged, but it has a lively story from the poet Tasso in which the crusader Tancred fights and mortally wounds Clorinda in man's disguise; when he finds she is a woman he is grief-stricken. The orchestra evokes Tancred's galloping horse and the clashing swords of the fight, and his vocal role in particular allows a fine range of emotion from aggression to tenderness. At this time the composer was working on his theory of emotional expression, derived from Plato's views on the relation between words, notes and rhythms, and we know that he aimed to create operatic figures who could display in turn a whole series of passions, representing the various 'affections'—in other words, emotional states—of the human mind. In the absence of more material, however, we can only speculate on the extent of his success.

However, Monteverdi's two last surviving operas, the second of which was his last work in the form, show a master's touch. In 1613 he had taken up one of the most important posts in Italy, that of *maestro di cappella* at St Mark's Cathedral in Venice. Following upon the opening in 1637 of the first public opera house in Venice, the Teatro San Cassiano, his *L'Arianna* was revived in 1640, and after that he composed three more operas. *Il ritorno d'Ulisse in patria* (San Cassiano, Venice, 1640) does not sound like the work of a septuagenarian. It tells a spectacular and lengthy story from Homer's *Odyssey*, with comic scenes as well as lofty ones involving gods, but it is the moments that are in a quite modern-sounding popular style that are the most remarkable. Monteverdi's next opera, *Le nozze d'Enea con Lavinia* (Venice, 1641), has been lost, but the evident psychological sophistication of *Il ritorno* progressed several stages further in his last opera of all. *L'Incoronazione di Poppea* (Venice, 1642), is about wholly real people and no longer the vague or idealised creatures of legend. Here, as in history itself, Nero and Poppea are neither heroic nor virtuous, but their ruthless and colourful intrigues make for compelling music drama—one feels indeed that some of the doings of their Roman world were perhaps not so different from what could happen in the composer's own Italy. The spoiled and dangerous young Emperor is given brilliant, tense dialogue with his grave tutor Seneca, a fine bass role, whose later enforced suicide in the presence of protesting pupils (*'Non morir, Seneca'*) is equally memorable. The flirtatious page boy Valletto is a worthy predecessor of Mozart's Cherubino in *Le nozze di Figaro*, while the roles of the rejected Empress Octavia (with a fine lament, *'Disprezzata regina'*) and Poppea's husband Ottone are also fully characterised. Nero and Poppea's love music has been called 'voluptuous, incandescent', though the final duet (*'Pur ti miro'*) of this unscrupulous couple is gentle. Perhaps the composer knew that with this work he had crowned his achievement. In the following year he obtained leave to revisit his native Cremona and died shortly after his return to Venice.

In Venice, where Monteverdi spent the latter part of his career, opera ceased to be a private entertainment for the cultured nobility. The citizens of this beautiful, wealthy and influential city-state included well-travelled and educated merchants, professional men such as lawyers and doctors, church dignitaries and, of course, the 'city fathers' or rulers. Venice was renowned—Shakespeare's *The Merchant of Venice* was written in Monteverdi's lifetime—and proud of her fame, while her civic and religious ceremonial was lavish and theatrical. Thus even a procession of holy relics in 1617 was given elaborate decoration, singers and instrumentalists, and a boy actor to play the Virgin. The whole thing cost 800 ducats, nearly three times Monteverdi's annual salary at San Marco. It is not surprising therefore that the spectacle and drama inherent in opera found an immediate response in Venetian society. As we have seen, the first-ever public opera house, the Teatro San Cassiano, opened in Venice in 1637, and this was followed within four years by others including the SS Giovanni e Paolo, San Moïse and the Teatro Novissimo which was especially famous for its spectacular productions. By the end of the century there were twelve opera houses in the city, usually named after the parish in which they were situated. They were built by noble families, but their day-to-day running was entrusted to professional impresarios.

By the end of the seventeenth century, three hundred new operas had been staged in Venice. Despite the number of opera houses, it is clear that normally the run given to a work was short; as was the case with films in the early part of the present century, a presentation was taken off after a limited number of performances to give place to an even newer one. Perhaps this was to some extent mass production for a fairly undiscriminating public, but we should not underestimate the citizens of Venice, who seem to have regarded the arts—architecture, painting and sculpture, drama and music—as central to their lives and not a needless luxury. For a parallel today we may need to look as far afield as the island of Bali. And the new audience for opera demanded new features: characters that were more obviously human, with amours and intrigues and comic escapades, more scene changes and spectacle, and more dramatic tension. There might still be gods and goddesses, or mythical figures such as Hercules, Perseus and Medea, but they had to behave like real people with whom the audience could identify. These were all gains in variety and flexibility, and in human terms. The chorus in Venetian opera became rarer, however, being thought too stiff and stately. The virtuoso singer on the other hand, was a Venetian forte, though audiences came also to appreciate subtle as well as sensational vocal effects.

For the successful opera composer there was money to be earned. Monteverdi's pupil Pietro Francesco Cavalli (1602–76) negotiated a contract with the impresario Mario Faustini which brought him a sum equivalent to the San Marco *maestro di cappella*'s annual salary for composing an opera and supervising its first few performances, though it is probably true that the prestige of the principal musical appointment at San Marco was never matched by a commensurate remuneration. Certainly operatic fame in Venice might come quickly and vanish with equal speed, and so few composers' names from the period are remembered today and even less actual music. However, Cavalli is one survivor. His real name was Caletti, but he took the name of his first patron, the Venetian governor of his birthplace Crema who discovered his gifts as a treble singer and took him to join the San Marco choir in this capacity in 1616. He remained at San Marco for over fifty years, finally becoming *maestro di cappella* in 1668 and holding that post until his death. During his long residence in Venice he composed nearly thirty operas for the city. *La Calisto* (1651) is a sophisticated tale of gods and mortals, while *Giasone* (1649) tells a story of Jason and the Golden Fleece that allowed the composer to show a vigorous and direct style. Cavalli's orchestra was usually of strings only, but he used it effectively, not least in the overtures; choral writing is rare though not unknown, but there are plenty of melodious arias, usually in triple time, which often look forward to the rich *bel canto* style of the early eighteenth century, and duets also that use an imitative style between the voices. Nearly all his operas include a lament in the minor mode, but there are comic arias also, with brisk and vivid rhythms.

Cavalli's contemporaries in Italy accorded him the chief place among the opera composers of his generation, and a hundred years after his death his work was still of interest to scholars. The German critic Johann Adolph Scheibe, writing in 1745, found Cavalli's recitative 'bold and affective', though the English historian Dr Charles Burney, who travelled extensively in Italy during the 1770s, pronounced the arias in his *Erismena* (Venice, ca 1656) 'monotonous and dull . . . deficient in poetical and musical merit'. There have been successful recent revivals of his operas: first *Didone* for the 350th anniversary of his birth (Florence, 1952) and then Raymond Leppard's presentations of three others: *Ormindo*, *Calisto* and *Egisto*, the first two at Glyndebourne.

Antonio Cesti (1623–69) was a native of Arezzo and enjoyed the patronage of the Medici family and the friendship of the painter and writer Salvator Rosa. A Franciscan monk and a tenor singer of skill, he composed at least four operas for Venice (*Genserico*, 1669, being of doubtful authenticity), of which the first, *Orontea* (1649), was then performed in various Italian cities over several decades. Inevitably he found his increasing involvement in the operatic scene to be in conflict with ecclesiastical duties and in 1658 he applied successfully to Rome to be released from his monastic vows, singing on four occasions, as Rosa tells us, to Pope Alexander VII to clinch his argument. He then joined the papal choir, but soon left it to resume his independent career. Evidently he was not popular with all his fellow-musicians in Venice, and some conflict with Cavalli—to whom he was certainly a rival—has been assumed but not proved. As for his death in Florence, one writer in 1717 tells us that he was 'poisoned by his rivals', but this too is unproved.

Cesti's musical style is flowing, lyrical and vocally elegant. He was a master of comedy and created amusing servant characters who delighted the public in such operas as *Orontea* and *Alessandro vincitor de se stesso* (Venice, 1651). His comic vein was also strong in two operas he wrote for Innsbruck in Austria, *La Dori* and *La magnanimità d'Alessandro* (1657, 1662). His *Il pomo d'oro* (Vienna, 1668), based on the story of the judgement of Paris and the golden apple, has plenty of spectacle including dancing, choruses and a big orchestra with flutes, bassoon, cornetts, trumpets and trombones. Besides all this, the use here of five acts instead of the usual three, together with twenty-four sets, made this an especially lavish production which has been called by the scholars David Burrows and Carl Schmidt 'the most notable Baroque court opera in the grand manner'.

However, this last opera, as we see, was not written for Venice, for neither Cesti nor Cavalli restricted their activities to that one city or even to Italy. At the time of *Il pomo d'oro* Cesti enjoyed the title of 'Chaplain of honour and Intendant for theatre music' at the Viennese court where he served the Habsburg family, and he composed other operas for Vienna and Innsbruck. Similarly one of Cavalli's last operas, *Ercole amante* (1662), was written for the Tuileries in Paris. Opera was spreading outwards rapidly from its birthplace in Florence, though on the whole Italy remained its source and provided its language—though not in all cases, as we shall see. In the latter part of the century, the Italian public could see opera in Florence, Rome, Genoa and Bologna. In Rome the Teatro Barberini was inaugurated by *Sant' Alessio* (1632) by Stefano Landi (ca 1586–1639): this told the life of St Alexis in a spectacular way, including a depiction of the flames of hell. Although it dealt with a sacred subject, this opera had human interest too—there is a comic duet and a lament sung by the saint's wife and family upon his death, choruses of servants, angels (in eight parts) and devils (in merely four), dances and the full use of an orchestra. Its overture, with four distinct sections, is a clear precursor of the form of a classical symphony, as its name (*sinfonia*) implies.

It was also for Rome that the first comic operas with contemporary settings were written. The librettist of *Sant'Alessio*, Cardinal Rospigliosi, also provided the text for comedies with names like *Chi soffre, speri* (1639) and *Dal male il bene* (1653) (*Sufferers, take heart*, based on a Spanish story, and *From evil comes good*, taken from Boccaccio). This agreeably worldly prelate went on to become Pope in 1667 and used his supreme office to place Roman opera on a fully established basis. The composers for his comedies—men such as Mazzocchi, Marazzoli and Abbatini, often working in collaboration—are now forgotten or nearly so, but these works look forward to the *opera buffa* of the next century. Ensemble writing, where several characters joined together to sing, was a feature of Roman comic opera: the difference between this and choral writing as such was that they usually had their own words and so preserved their dramatic identities. It was a useful way of ending an act effectively, and of expressing the often tangled situations of the plot, by letting everyone on stage voice his or her thoughts.

Ensembles also featured in a pastoral opera called *La Galatea* (Rome, 1639) by Loreto Vittori (1600–70), but this musician is mentioned here for another reason. As well as being a composer, Vittori was also a celebrated *castrato* soprano singer. Women singers were uncommon in seventeenth-century opera, though not quite unknown—one, the soprano Vittoria Archilei, sang the title role in Peri's *Euridice*—but they were effectively banned from the public stage. Women's roles were therefore allotted to men. The practice of castration, by an operation usually performed by the age of eight, was an ancient one that was not officially recognised in Europe until the sixteenth century. Though it was even then regarded as dishonourable, it nevertheless remained tolerated, and *castrato* voices were employed in the papal choir of the Sistine Chapel and other major musical establishments of the Church. The spread of this type of voice to opera was doubtless inevitable, and the singers themselves quickly found a field in which they could win riches and renown. Thus Vittori was praised as a sorceress in Domenico Mazzocchi's opera *La catena d'Adone* (Rome, 1626) and equally in a church performance as Mary Magdalene lamenting at the feet of Christ. Many *castrati* seem to have enjoyed some kind of sexual life, and the voice and stage personality were capable of virility in all aspects save pitch. The roles of Monteverdi's Nero, Handel's Julius Caesar and even Mozart's Prince Idamante in

Idomeneo were all written for male sopranos or mezzos. Reports of such voices varied: the Frenchman Charles de Brosses (1709–77) found one 'clear and penetrating as that of a choirboy . . . brilliant, light, full of impact', but his compatriot Voltaire disliked the sound.

The practice of castration continued for a long time in music. Mendelssohn heard such singing in the choir of the Sistine Chapel in 1831, and the last known *castrato* in that choir, Alessandro Moreschi, left it as late as 1913, having actually made some early recordings (1902–3) in which the sound of a *castrato* voice may still be heard. (For a further discussion, *see* Chapter 5.)

As well as ensembles, Italian comic opera used a brisk and bustling recitative (*recitativo secco*) for the more prosaic and less important parts of a text and for quick conversational exchanges. It contrasted well with the more spacious and melodious style of word setting used in the arias, and was given the minimum of accompaniment, mainly a series of punctuating chords. This balance and contrast of recitative and aria was just one aspect of the use of musical form in opera. It was by now fully realised that it was not enough to rely wholly upon an operatic libretto for shape and merely to clothe it with appropriate music as it went along. Audiences wanted to hear a variety of specifically musical things, displayed in good proportion: fine voices and memorable tunes in the arias, vivid recitatives and ensembles, and a dramatic use of instrumental colour. In time the sweep of choral melody was also to become a feature, and so, at least in France, was dancing. In the meantime it was known that the right sequencing of recitative and aria could advance the action quickly or halt it for a melodic flowering, while ensembles could form climactic points.

Arias themselves—solo songs—now tended to favour certain standard shapes. The strophic aria had the same melody for each of its stanzas, like a hymn tune, though improvised melodic embellishments and variations called ornaments were expected and were part of a singer's skill. Another shape was the *da capo* form in which two contrasting sections were followed by a repeat of the first in an A,B,A structure, '*da capo*' being the instruction at the end of the second section to return to the start. This return was usually extensively ornamented. Ornaments were left to the performer and thus not notated, but a rare written-out singer's ornamentation of Handel's time, noted by a friend of the composer, shows that three notes in the original have become a sequence of eleven in the return broadly following the same melodic contour. A third category of aria had the voice moving fairly freely over a regular repeated orchestral bass or 'ground'. It was characteristically used for laments, and a famous example is the final aria of Purcell's *Dido and Aeneas* (London, 1689),

'When I am laid in earth'.

The operatic orchestra was by no means standardised, but was based on a body of bowed strings and a keyboard instrument such as the harpsichord—certainly Cesti's *Il pomo d'oro* score was exceptional, with its additional flutes, bassoon, cornetts, trumpets and trombones. Wind instruments were commonly brought in to add a particular colour to certain scenes—for example flutes for pastoral episodes and brass for infernal ones. The orchestra could be used alone, as it was in the overture or *sinfonia*, and also in interludes that could heighten or change a mood or merely fill in time needed for scene-changing. Each act of *Il pomo d'oro*, for example, begins with an instrumental prologue called a *sonata*—this early use of the word, deriving from the Italian verb *suonare*, to play, meaning no more than an instrumental piece in the sense that a *cantata* was a sung one.

Venice remained the chief among Italian operatic centres. Antonio Sartorio (1630–80) held a post in Hanover but often made the long journey to his native city to compose new operas and recruit musicians for the German court whose music he directed. His fondness for heroic themes is symbolised by his arias with trumpet *obbligato*, the *obbligato* being a kind of secondary solo to complement the singer's melodic line. We find arias of this kind in his *L'Adelaide*, *Giulio Cesare in Egitto* and *Antonino e Pompeiano*, produced in the San Salvatore theatre between 1672 and 1677. *L'Adelaide* also had effective crowd scenes in its choruses for quarry workers, and its lament in Act II reminds us that Sartorio also favoured this type of aria, which not surprisingly also occurs in the '*E morta Euridice*' of his *L'Orfeo*, produced in the same year. His writing for voices was bold, and florid arias abound, while at the same time he had a gift for comic scenes which often brought a sharp juxtaposition of the heroic and the lowly.

The mingling of serious and comic moods was evidently to Venetian taste and also occurs in the operas of the priest Giovanni Legrenzi (1626–90), only four of whose seventeen operas survive. Both Sartorio and Legrenzi in turn held the post of vice-*maestro di cappella* at San Marco, a fact that underlines the continued dual allegiance of Venetian musicians to Church and opera house alike, following the examples of Monteverdi and Cavalli. Both artists, of course, wrote sacred music, but their operatic activities must have brought them greater financial rewards. Legrenzi, born in poverty, died a rich man, but not at the expense of his Church duties: indeed, the San Marco authorities were so pleased with his work for them that two years after his promotion to *maestro* in 1685 they granted him a special salary increase for 'the person and not the office'. His operatic arias fall into two main types, one in fast quadruple time and the other using a slow triple metre, the latter obviously expressing more poignant emotions. The use of a repeated bass figure (ground bass) is common. The plot of his *Giustino* (Venice, 1683) tells of a loyal and heroic peasant lad who becomes an emperor, and this story provides a striking contrast with the old *opera seria* tradition in which noble actions and feelings are confined to the nobly born: here again the barriers between lofty and homely styles seem to be in the process of breaking down. This opera had exceptional success and was seen not only in Venice but also in eight other Italian cities.

The operas of Pietro Andrea Ziani (ca 1616–84) and Carlo Pallavicino (ca 1635–88) are still closer to straightforward comedy. Ziani was a priest, but in his *Annibale in Capua* (Venice, 1661) the amorous adventures of the great general feature more prominently than his military exploits. Here, and also in his *La Semiramide* (Venice, 1670), Ziani uses popular song and dance elements and these, together with bustling recitatives, look forward to eighteenth-century *opera buffa*. Similarly, Pallavicino's *Messalina* (Venice, 1679) takes a murderous Roman empress as its protagonist, but we see no crime in the opera worse than her frequent deception of her husband. Indeed, *Messalina* was a satire on Venetian morals in which the real target is underlined by the inclusion of a very Italian carnival scene in masquerade. Marc'Antonio Ziani (ca 1653–1715), the nephew of Pietro Andrea, had a very successful career in Venice until about 1700, when he transferred his prolific operatic activity to Vienna on taking up a court appointment there. His skill in characterisation and the matching of text to music seems to have been exceptional. Besides this, he gave prominent instrumental passages to his orchestra, which incorporated regular wind players and featured solo writing in a way that was advanced for the time, and included solos for the cello, trombone and even a precursor of the clarinet called the chalumeau.

As we have seen, ordinary people could often identify with stage characters during this period, although these might nominally be noble and historical. Possibly the social climate of the time, at least in Italy, was anticipating later fundamental changes in the structure of society, and it produced what may be seen as operatic forerunners of later and more famous social comedies. Thus the Teatro della Pergola in Florence opened in 1657 with *La Tancia* by Jacopo Melani (1623–76), in which the heroine is a country girl loved by a nobleman in a way that at least half anticipates Susanna and the Count in Mozart's *Nozze di Figaro*: this rustic comedy is set to simple strophic arias and brisk recitatives, with added elements of *commedia dell' arte* buffoonery. Similarly, the *Il trespolo tutore* (Genoa, ca 1677) by Alessandro Stradella has a comic bass in the title role, a guardian in love with his ward—a novel situation then but much used later; the title implies a perhaps rickety tutorial support, '*trespolo*' being a trestle. Stradella (1644–82) made a considerable reputation before his early death. He possessed a wit and invention that earned him the admiration of Purcell, who learned to know his work from as far away as England, while he also anticipated the graceful *bel canto* style of the school of composers which was to be led by Alessandro Scarlatti.

Finally, for a composer who represents the sheer exportability of Italian opera, we may cite Antonio Draghi (ca 1635–1700), a native of Rimini who produced the majority of his 170 operas, which featured virtuoso coloratura writing for the voice, in Vienna. Others who worked abroad were Pallavicino in Dresden, Sartorio in Hanover—to which city he seems to have introduced Italian opera in 1672—and Pietro Andrea Ziani in Vienna. Though the composer was not present, one of Ziani's operas inaugurated a new opera house on the Leidsegracht in Amsterdam in 1680. A celebrated later example of this situation was, of course, Handel—a German by birth who composed Italian operas for English audiences.

Though a rich production of Italian operas continued throughout the seventeenth century, few indeed survive save perhaps in the form of scores. The leading composer of the Venetian opera towards the end of the century was perhaps Carlo Francesco Pollarolo (1653–1722), a Legrenzi pupil, but what can modern audiences know of his eighty-five operas, which include *Onorio in Roma* (1692) and *Ottone* (1694), despite the praise given by scholars to his expressive range, formal flexibility, harmonic richness and vocal-instrumental textures? Pollarolo also at times used a divided orchestra, on and off-stage, and echo effects, as well as helping to give the oboe its standard orchestral place. Perhaps his chief historical importance lies in the fact that he laid an increasing emphasis on the kind of ornate vocal style which led to the Neapolitan *bel canto* opera composers of the early eighteenth century. In the meantime we may quote the German musicologist Hellmuth Wolff's tantalising tribute to Pollarolo as 'a daring pioneer of new ideas in Italian opera ... [whose] contribution remains virtually uncharted territory on the map of operatic history'.

Tomaso Albinoni (1671–1751) is known today for his instrumental music, but he too wrote a vast body of now forgotten operas—eighty-one of them, according to the libretto of his penultimate work, *Candalide* (Venice, 1734). Perhaps one day modern audiences will discover what

Albinoni had to say in musical terms about such exotic rulers as *Tigrane, King of Armenia* (1697) and *Primislao I, King of Bohemia* (1698).

We do at least have the accounts of contemporaries who attended some of these Venetian performances. In 1645 John Evelyn wrote of Giovanni Rovetta's new opera *Ercole in Lidia* that it had 'excellent musicians, vocal and instrumental, and machines for flying in the air, and other wonderful motions . . . magnificent and expensive'. The work itself is lost, as is Rovetta's other opera *Argiope* (1649); its composer (1595–1668) was another who divided his energies between Church and opera house, being Monteverdi's successor as *maestro di cappella* at San Marco. In 1680 a French traveller to Venice found 'the theatres large and stately, the decorations noble but very badly lit . . . these operas are long, the ballets or dances between the acts generally so pitiful that they were better omitted . . . [but] the vocal charms amend all imperfections, the beardless men [*castrati*] have silver voices, the women are the best in all Italy'. However not all visitors were so satisfied, and in 1699 another Frenchman found 'a certain confusion and unpleasantness in many aspects of the singing: they dwell many times longer on one quavering than in singing four whole lines, and sometimes run so quickly that it is hard to tell whether they are singing or speaking'.

It is clear that with the opening in 1637 of San Cassiano, the first public opera house, opera entered a new era. Impresarios whose motives were inevitably more commercial than those of the Florentine pioneers catered for a merchant public whose taste for spectacle was satisfied by the elaborate stage designs and machinery of such artists as Giovanni Burnacini, who designed Cesti's *Il pomo d'oro*, and Giacomo Torelli, whose indoor scenes and simultaneous scene changes were admired. The perspective stage had been established in the theatre since the early sixteenth century, but in the seventeenth a further realism was achieved, and although cost was always a consideration, any impresario knew that box office success depended largely on spectacle and budgeted accordingly. The moving cloud scene for the production in Venice's San Salvatore theatre of Legrenzi's *Germanico sul Reno* (1676) was typical: an illustration of the set exists, together with a drawing of the stage machinery involved. Somehow, the difficulty of lighting such elaborate sets, as well as the actors and musicians, was solved. Candles and oil lamps were all that was available, and it is fortunate that few if any catastrophes have been recorded from the period: one can hardly believe that gangways and fire exits ranked highly in the extensive catalogue of an impresario's preoccupations.

As for the audiences, they seem to have looked on opera more as

entertainment than serious art. Charles de Brosses tells us that performances in Rome began at eight or somewhat later and lasted perhaps till
midnight. In this social gathering, 'the pleasure these people take in music
and the theatre is more evidenced by their presence than by the attention
they bestow upon the performance'. The boxes in which fashionable
people sat were well lit so that their occupants could play cards, or other
games. Chess [or possibly draughts], declared de Brosses with tongue in
cheek, 'is marvellously well adapted to filling in the monotony of the
recitatives, while arias are equally good for interrupting a too assiduous
concentration on chess'. Dr Burney mentions the card players indulging
in games of faro at the opera in Milan while another traveller wrote of the
suppers served in the boxes during performances in Florence. As for
Venice, it seems that the pit—the lowlier audience area—was filled with
workmen and gondoliers: 'There is a constant noise of people laughing,
drinking and joking, while sellers of baked goods and fruit cry their wares
aloud from box to box.' It all sounds rather like a modern race meeting,
where people move about, chat and eat and drink until an actual race takes
place—in this case, perhaps an aria sung by a famous singer, or a
spectacular change of scene or stage effect—to provide a high point of
interest. However, it is wrong to imagine that the opera provided merely a
social forum: presumably those wishing merely to play cards and chat, or
to appear socially, could do so more comfortably and cheaply elsewhere,
and the high fees paid to star singers and to popular composers and
designers show that the public was prepared to pay for this kind of
entertainment. The profits of the impresarios were also enough to keep
their active interest. In turn, the star singers, like champion horses, had
their successful trainers: Italian schools of singing were important
establishments serving opera houses at this time, and two of the most
famous were set up by *castrato* singers, Antonio Pistocchi (1659–1726)
and Antonio Bernacchi (ca 1690–1756). Opera had changed substantially since its foundation, but it was healthy and spreading far beyond the
bounds of its native Italy.

3

FRENCH OPERA

*Court beginnings and Italian influence. Lully. From Lully to Rameau. Rameau.
Comic opera and the* guerre des bouffons.

COURT BEGINNINGS AND ITALIAN INFLUENCE

Like American jazz in the twentieth century, Italian opera spread from its
country of origin to become a world style, while undergoing changes in
the process. The conditions in which it could flourish were met in
different ways: a theatre could be private, as at the French court, or
public, as in the rich city of Hamburg, while Purcell's *Dido and Aeneas*
dispensed with a theatre altogether and was performed at a London girls'
school. Musicians and musical scores travelled freely and the Italians'
theatrical and vocal skill was widely appreciated, though with reservations
in some Protestant areas. However, in a religious context the dramatic use
of music was accepted everywhere, and Bach's Passion music and
Handel's oratorios alike owe much to operatic style.

In France, such works as Adam de la Halle's *Le jeu de Robin and de
Marion* and Balthasar de Beaujoyeux's *Ballet comique de la Reine* had been
musical plays for court entertainment. The title of the second of these is
significant. By the seventeenth century dancing was the social skill to
which every French courtier aspired, as did the monarch himself. Its
possession could give an entrée to the highest court circles, and thus an
Italian-born musician of humble origin, the twenty-year-old Jean-Baptiste Lully, danced in 1653 in a *Ballet de la nuit*, partly written by himself,
alongside the boy king Louis XIV. Less than a month later Lully was
appointed *Compositeur de la musique instrumentale du roi*.

French court ballet, called *ballet de cour*, did not require the fine
physique or the rigorous training needed in modern dance theatre.
Essentially it consisted of a series of dances in accepted steps and styles,
performed for the pleasure of the participants as much as that of any
spectators present. But these homely affairs, sometimes just a way of
passing an evening, could be elaborated on special occasions into a
calculated blend of dancing, spectacle and music that was both played and
sung. The Bourbon court of Henri IV enjoyed Italian-style masquerades

37

with titles like *Ballet des fous* (1596) and *Ballet des barbiers* (1598), but with the accession in 1610 of Louis XIII a more ceremonial style emerged. The composer Pierre Guédron (ca 1570–1620) wrote songs for a *Ballet de Monseigneur le duc de Vendôme* (1610) and a *Ballet du Roy, ou Ballet de la délivrance de Renaud* (1617). In a *Ballet de Madame, soeur du Roy* (1613), Guédron enjoyed the collaboration of his son-in-law Antoine Boësset (1586–1643). Boësset was to become *Surintendant de la musique du roi* to Louis XIII in 1623 and the acknowledged master of the court song (*air de cour*) that had by now found its place in the more elaborate ballets. A contemporary declared that Boësset 'laid down the first foundations of *airs* and . . . composed beautiful songs'.

The alliance of drama and music was also strengthened in plays that required sung sections. France now had such master dramatists as Corneille, Molière and Racine, but there were many others who also contributed to a diverse picture. Myths, love stories and pastoral tales were staged in public theatres, and some lent themselves to the use of music. For example, plays about the minstrel Orpheus and the Homeric hero Ulysses (including the sirens' song) presented in the 1640s had sung music, and so did Corneille's *The Golden Fleece* (*La Toison d'Or*, 1660)—the latter being a spectacular piece written in honour of Louis XIV's marriage to the Infanta Maria Theresa. However, Corneille did have reservations about the use of music, and wrote: 'I have taken good care to have nothing sung that is necessary to the understanding of the play, since as a rule sung words are imperfectly heard by the audience.' Claude Boyer's *Loves of Jupiter and Semele* (*Les amours de Jupiter et Sémélé*, 1666) had music, probably by Louis de Mollier (ca 1615–88), for flutes and oboes, trumpets, viols and a drum: here there was a 'symphony fit for the appearance of Apollo', a series of songs praising art, and finally a scene of 'the heavens burning to the sound of music'. The French public learned to accept music as part of theatre and to value it beyond its function for entertainment and dancing.

The earliest true operas given in France were, not surprisingly, Italian. The Italian-born statesman and churchman Cardinal Mazarin was influential in matters of fashion and taste, and it was probably he who introduced an unidentified Italian pastoral to the court in 1645. This was quickly followed by *La finta pazza* (*The Pretended Fool*) by Francesco Sacrati (ca 1605–50), first heard in Venice in 1641 and now with additional ballets to satisfy French taste. In 1646 Cavalli's *Egisto* was performed and in the following year an audience in the Palais Royal saw the spectacular *Orfeo* by Luigi Rossi (ca 1597–1653). Corneille attacked its vocal extravagance, but the essayist Saint-Évremond wrote in praise of its charm and lyrical feeling, and *La Gazette*, the first French newspaper, with Mazarin as its patron, declared that the singing and the instrumental writing together 'attracted the soul through the ear'. The boy king Louis XIV went three times to see it.

Mazarin's political opponents criticised the cost of operatic productions at a time of widespread poverty in France. Even so, more Italian operas made their way to Paris and one, *Le nozze di Peleo e di Teti* by Carlo Caproli (ca 1615–92), had some nine performances in 1654 in the Petit Bourbon Theatre. The King himself danced in its ballets, and invited the public to attend the last two performances. Both French and Italian singers took part, and Caproli was awarded the position of *Maître de la musique du cabinet du Roy.*

We should never underestimate the influence of Louis XIV himself, the *Roi soleil* whose radiance was supposed to contribute to the splendour of France. For one thing, his reign was very long— 1643–1715. As a child he loved music and formed a small string group; he also showed skill as a lutenist, guitarist and harpsichordist, and danced without embarrassment alongside professionals before court and public. Music was heard in his apartments when he rose or retired to bed, during dinner, while he was walking or even boating, and during visits of church or state dignitaries. The royal Mass was always sung, not said, and on every evening except Saturdays music was played in his quarters. It was he who chose the subjects for ballets and later for Lully's operas. He insisted that his children learn music and formed an Académie de Musique in 1669. His court musicians amounted to about 150—some ninety singers and four organists for the royal chapel, some fifty military and ceremonial players including wind instruments for hunting parties, and the string orchestra called the *vingt-quatre violons du roi* which played for ballets. The writer Madame de Sévigné described him as one almost obsessed with music.

During his reign French interest in Italian opera continued. Audiences already knew Cavalli's *Egisto* and *Xerse*, and now the same composer's *Ercole amante* was specially composed for Paris and given there on 7 February 1662. The King and Queen themselves both danced in the ballets specially composed for this new opera (as had been those in *Xerse*) by Lully. The *Gazette* praised the production, but it seems to have left Cavalli rather disillusioned, perhaps because the inflation of his score by the interpolated ballet material brought the running time to six hours. Besides this, the Tuileries Theatre acoustics seem to have been unsatisfactory—the Venetian ambassador reported that the music was 'fine and fitting [but] could not be enjoyed because of the vastness of the theatre'.

LULLY

In 1669, with the necessary royal approval, the composer Robert Cambert (ca 1627–77) and his librettist Pierre Perrin established a theatre in Paris 'to sing plays in public', and so laid the foundation of French opera. The two men were not novices. Cambert, who served in the household of the Queen Mother, Anne of Austria, described his beginnings: 'Having always thought of introducing musical plays as in Italy, I began to compose an elegy in 1658 for three voices in dialogue form . . . Monsieur Perrin, having heard this composition, wished to create a little pastoral play.' This, called *La pastorale*, claimed on its title page to be the 'first French play to music' and it was performed before the King and Cardinal Mazarin in 1659. Following on the Cardinal's suggestion that it should have a successor, *Ariane, ou Le mariage de Bacchus* was quickly written by the same artists and given some semi-public performances; its lament for Ariadne earned the praise of the influential Saint-Évremond.

After the grant of the royal licence to present French opera 'in Paris and the other cities of the Kingdom', Cambert and Perrin produced *Pomone* (Paris, 1671), yet another pastoral, with much success. Their aim was described by Perrin as the creation of a style that would convey feeling without excessive embellishment, length and exaggeration. Pomona's first air, '*Passons nos jours dans ces vergers loin des amours et des bergers*', is elegantly flowing and simple, with a Gallic lightness, wit and intelligence. Saint-Évremond 'listened to the singing with delight [in this] first French opera to be staged'. A 'heroic pastoral' called *Les peines et les plaisirs de l'amour* (Paris, 1671) soon followed. But by now Perrin, possibly betrayed by unscrupulous business associates, was in a debtor's prison, and to escape from this predicament, sold his royal licence on 13 March 1672 to Lully. Two weeks later the licence was revoked. Perrin died in 1675, and Cambert, after an unsuccessful attempt to interest England in his operas, was to die in London. On 13 August 1672 the royal licence for French opera was formally granted by the King to '*nostre cher et bien amé Jean-Baptiste Lully*'.

Thus the somewhat shadowy figure of Lully (1632–87), the violinist, harpsichordist, dancer and composer whose name has been woven with increasing importance into this story, now emerges clearly as the undisputed leading figure of seventeenth-century French opera. Between 1672 and his death he produced an opera almost once a year, and it was said by a contemporary that 'since M. Lully has taken upon himself the organisation of these musical productions, we have seen that perfection which can only be achieved by art, knowledge, genius and long experience'. Lully established a large-scale French operatic style, and not only in France. His *Cadmus et Hermione* (Paris, 1673) reached London and Amsterdam, *Thésée* (Paris, 1675) was seen in Brussels and The Hague, while the heroic pastoral *Acis et Galatée* (Anet, Eure-et-Loir, 1686) was performed in Hamburg and *Armide* (Paris, 1686) in Rome.

Lully, as we have seen, was not French but Italian. Born in Florence as the son of a miller named Lulli, he was brought to France by a travelling nobleman at the age of thirteen and entered the service of Louis XIII's niece, the young Duchesse de Montpensier. There he continued to improve an already remarkable musical talent, especially for the violin: later in life he said he 'had never learned more about music than he knew at seventeen but worked all his life to perfect that knowledge'. At twenty he left her Tuileries court for the royal household and, as we have seen, was already at twenty a court composer. Now his star rose rapidly. 'Baptiste', as he was called, was praised, for example by Jean Loret in 1657: 'For dance and song, I must say that Baptiste is an admirable fellow.' But the friendly comment is exceptional. As a man, Lully has had a bad press. Among contemporaries, La Fontaine called him 'lewd and evil-minded' and Boileau labelled him 'a hateful court jester'. Small and short-sighted, with a dark complexion that suggested his Italian birth, his ambition was great and he guarded his near-monopoly of French opera with ruthless cunning. On the whole, though, he enjoyed royal favour throughout his many years of court service. In 1661 he was naturalised a Frenchman, and a year later was made *Maître de la musique de la famille royale*. In that same year he married, and the King did him the honour of witnessing the marriage contract.

Lully learned his stagecraft largely in ballet, a form which attracted him throughout his career. One of his collaborators was Molière, for example in the *comédie-ballet Le bourgeois gentilhomme* (Château de Chambord, 1670). Such pieces had airs as well as dances, and the drinking song *'Buvons, chers amis'* in Act IV of this Molière play was apparently Lully's own favourite among his songs. If some of this early music suggests comic opera, a *tragédie-ballet* on the theme of the human soul called *Psyché* (Paris, 1671) points the way to an operatic style and the genre of *tragédie lyrique*, this being the designation he gave to most of his mature operas.

These *tragédies* form the first repertory of opera outside Italy. They consist characteristically of a prologue and five acts and are mostly on Greek mythological subjects. Lully's chosen librettist was Philippe Quinault (1635–88), a wealthy poet who joined the court circle in 1668 and collaborated with Molière and Corneille in the text of *Psyché*. The series of *tragédies lyriques* began with *Cadmus et Hermione* (Paris, 1673) and their principal works, all of which were first seen in or near Paris, number eleven. Of these only *Alceste* (1674) and *Armide* (1686) are regularly staged today. Quinault received four thousand *livres* for each of his libretti, which drew on myth or chivalrous legend to tell of gods and lovers, duty and glory, in a way not very different from the conventions of Italian opera.

Quinault's libretti could stand alone as dramatic poetry, and Lully learned to match them with music. He studied the declamation of actors in order to find a way of setting French that flowed naturally yet expressively, whether in lyrical recitative or melodious air, and which could be accompanied merely by a keyboard *continuo* or by the whole orchestra. His method was more generally flexible than that of the Italians with their clearer-cut division of sections and styles. A master of dramatic timing, Lully could be memorably forceful, as in Armide's air *'Le perfide Renaud me fuit'*, where changes of time signature unusual for the period suggest her agitation. His command of a folk-like idiom, as in Act V of *Alceste* with its sung dances, made some of his melodies into actual popular songs. The author of a *Comparison between Italian and French Music* (1705), Le Cerf de la Viéville, wrote: 'When I heard the air from *Amadis* [1684], *'Amour, que veux-tu de moi'*, sung by every French kitchen maid, I was right to think . . . that this tune had captured the esteem of all, learned and unlearned . . . I concluded that it must be beautiful indeed, natural and fully expressive, to have moved so many different hearts.' The Abbé Raguenet (1702) agreed: 'There are so many things in which French music is better than Italian . . . our operas are much better composed: nothing could be more lively and natural than their dialogues: gods are caused to speak with suitable dignity, nymphs and shepherds with gentleness and innocent merriment . . . the French, in their airs, aim at the gentle, easy, flowing and coherent . . . [while] Italian recitative is too contained and simple and similar throughout, not really singing at all.'

Though the plots of Lully's operas nominally concerned gods or lofty persons, there were thus also homely and lively aspects to them. The *castrato* voice was disliked in France and thus not featured, but the bass was, and to advantage. The village wedding in Act IV of *Roland* (Versailles, 1685) counterpoints with choruses and dances of joyful shepherds and shepherdesses the despair of the protagonist, who has discovered that his beloved is another's bride. Choral sections often shape and punctuate the overall musical and dramatic form. Another device is the use of a repeated ground bass under developing music, and in Act V of *Armide* a bass of this kind links a series of numbers including a dance and choruses. Duets are frequent, but larger ensembles less so, though there is a trio of Fates in *Isis* (Saint-Germain, 1677).

Lully's use of the orchestra, though, is unremarkable, and this may reflect his habit of writing at the keyboard with, at least initially, just a vocal line and a figured bass to indicate harmony. The foundation of his orchestra was a body of strings, and wind instruments like flutes, oboes and bassoons often merely doubled them in the appropriate registers. However, he did divide the orchestra into a large general body and a smaller group of about ten players who might accompany solo airs. Instrumental scene-painting as such was thus limited, though there is a quietly flowing sleep scene in *Atys* (Saint-Germain, 1676) and in *Armide* one gentle recitative (*'Plus j'observe ces lieux'*) has the orchestral strings muted. Possibly some dances had sections just for wind, perhaps two oboes and bassoon.

'The father of our beautiful French music', as Lully was once called, met a strange death. He was conducting a performance of his *Te Deum* to celebrate the King's recovery from an operation, and 'in the heat of the moment' he struck his foot with the cane or *baton* with which he beat time. Gangrene set in and, refusing the amputation of the toe advised by his doctor, he died a few weeks later. He left a large fortune — and three sons who all became professional musicians.

FROM LULLY TO RAMEAU

The basic style of French opera that Lully established remained unchanged well into the eighteenth century. The political and literary journal *Le Mercure galant* was doubtless right when it declared in 1683 that 'Paris should not be reduced to having just a single opera each year', for Lully's influence limited the natural development that occurs when several artists are working simultaneously in the same field. Still, musical establishments now proliferated and created a climate in which change was at least possible. As Louis XIV's immensely long reign drew to its end and royal interest and enterprise diminished, new musical plays were being performed in noble houses. In the more modern rococo or Regency climate, pomp and ceremony gave way to a prettier and more intimate style. The idealised shepherds and shepherdesses of Watteau's paintings and the delicately ornamented harpsichord music of Couperin symbolise this new atmosphere, as did the outdoor *fêtes-galantes* and pastorals that brought fresh air and open skies to what had become an increasingly enclosed court ambiance. At the same time, the *opéra-ballets* such as *L'Europe galante* (1697) by André Campra (1660–1744) — a composer regarded by Le Cerf de la Viéville as chief among Lully's successors — tended to restore dancing to its central position in French theatre, and the drama suffered. But although *L'Europe galante* moved away from the Lully–Quinault tradition, it left that tradition unchanged because its aims were different. Between 1697 and another famous *opéra-ballet*, Rameau's *Les Indes galantes* in 1735, Paris saw some forty new works in this genre, though Lully's operas too held the stage.

It may be noted that not all Frenchmen approved of opera generally. Boileau complained on religious grounds about the 'pagan stories', and Voltaire said, probably in joke, that all those who were Christians when at Mass were 'pagans at the opera'. La Fontaine and Saint-Évremond felt that in such a mingling of poetry and music neither art could shine unobstructed. On the other hand, others felt that this was a legitimate art form offering delight that was *sui generis*, and the normally incisive critic La Bruyère declared that opera should 'hold the mind, eye and ear in an equal enchantment'.

The *opéra-ballet* emphasised spectacle, and Campra was accused of 'drowning the story in mere *divertissement*', but there were composers who pursued a more traditional and Lullian course. The *tragédie lyrique Omphale* (Paris, 1701) of André Destouches (1672–1749) has been praised for its touching and imaginative style of recitative. The last stage work of this gifted composer was a *ballet héroique* called *Les stratagèmes de l'amour* (Paris, 1726) which claimed to be a 'noble comedy having the character of antiquity' and thus aimed perhaps at the best of all possible worlds.

Besides Destouches' *Omphale* and his five other 'lyrical tragedies', there were other serious operas produced in the period between Lully and the next major figure in French opera, Rameau, whose *Hippolyte et Aricie* dates from 1733. Two by Marc-Antoine Charpentier (ca 1650–1704) are *David et Jonathas* (*sic*, 1688) and *Médée* (1693), based on Thomas Corneille's tragedy. Charpentier is currently undergoing a rediscovery, and *Médée* was rapturously received in a 1984 Paris production. Thomas Corneille was the younger brother of the more famous dramatist, and this '*tragédie mise en musique*' tells of the encounter at Corinth of Jason and the sorceress who gives the opera its name. Thwarted in her love for the hero, Medea wreaks her vengeance: Creon the King is compelled to suicide, Jason's beloved Creusa is murdered with a poisoned robe, and Jason himself is cruelly taunted. Finally this dangerous lady leaves Corinth in flames as she departs on her winged dragon. Her character is given powerful and vehement music, and needs a skilled actress-soprano, while Jason's heroic but tragic role is a high-lying tenor. Many warlike choruses also feature and so do demonic ensembles. Charpentier's orchestra has woodwind, trumpet, large lute, strings and drums, and he uses it with an imagination and energy in keeping with an eventful plot. Another operatic work by this composer, the pastoral in six scenes called *Actéon* (1685), in which the tale of the huntsman who is punished by death for observing the goddess Diana bathing, is given a surprisingly light-hearted and even boisterous treatment.

Campra, mentioned above for his innovations and use of a lighter style, also wrote in the serious genre in his *Tancrède* (1702), which includes an earthquake scene, and *Idomenée* (1712), with its scene of shipwreck. This composer with a taste for colourful subjects also composed some scenes for an unfinished *Iphigénie en Tauride* (1704) by Henri Desmarets (1661–1741), which has a storm scene and, says the scholar James R. Anthony, 'a more expanded harmonic language, more sophisticated orchestration and more flexible, singing recitative than is found in Lully's operas'. There is also the *Alcione* of Marin Marais (1656–1728)—another composer with a taste for storm music who, in one instrumental work, went so far as to depict an operation upon himself for the removal of a stone in the bladder. It is doubtless true that while some of these works broadly followed the Lully tradition, they did not merely imitate him. A greater flexibility of form, vocal writing, harmony and texture, and instrumentation were now entering the operatic language.

RAMEAU

Le Cerf de la Viéville had written in 1705 that the setting of words to music should be 'natural, expressive and harmonious . . . not loaded with ornamentation . . . notes so aptly chosen that the poet's verses are lost in the music yet live again through it'. Few would disagree, but how to achieve this was a problem each composer had in turn to solve, and perhaps differently if he was to sound a personal voice. When Jean-Philippe Rameau (1683–1764) turned to opera for the first time at the age of fifty, in 1733, he learned and profited from what had gone before. Campra saluted the new master who composed *Hippolyte et Aricie* as 'one who will eclipse us all'.

It may be that Rameau succeeded in opera partly because he waited until he was middle-aged and experienced before venturing into the field. A provincial from Dijon, he held various posts as an organist and published his first keyboard music in 1706. In 1722 he produced a treatise on harmony that had few precedents and showed a keen analytical intelligence, but his careful account of the basis of musical language also stressed the necessity for what he called 'the ear's judgement' and he pointed out the actual need for dissonance in the interests of vitality and variety. He seems to have been a man of independent views, and not always an easy one: he had a 'thunderous voice' and a bent and bony figure. He was not a courtier and only after sixty did he gain official recognition as a royal musician. On the other hand, his marriage at forty-two to a girl of nineteen seems to have been very happy, and they had four children.

'I followed the theatre from the age of twelve,' Rameau said, 'but I did not work in the opera till I was fifty, for till then I didn't feel capable of it.' Oddly enough it was just after he married that operatic ambitions began to surface. In 1727 he asked the poet Houdar de la Motte for a libretto, but on receiving a discouraging answer replied with some heat, perhaps feeling his talents were misunderstood:

> Those who speak of a 'learned musician' usually mean a man knowing everything about combining notes, but also so absorbed in them that he sacrifices all — feeling, common sense, wit and reason. Such a one is merely an academic . . . I have not devoted myself to note-combining so far as to forget their intimate connection with natural beauty . . . I try to use the art that conceals art, considering only people of taste and learned men not at all.

Rameau next approached Voltaire, and they began work on a Samson and Delilah opera only to find that this Biblical subject was considered unsuitable for the stage. However, he now met and collaborated with the dramatist Abbé Simon-Joseph Pellegrin. Their opera *Hippolyte et Aricie*, played privately in July 1733 at the house of a wealthy friend and connoisseur, Le Riche de la Pouplinière, reached the Paris Opéra three months later.

The first public production of *Hippolyte et Aricie* was initially only fairly successful. For some, its style inspired a mere guarded respect, and it was said that the composer had 'substituted harmonic speculations for the ear's delight'. But the tide turned. In its first season the opera was given over thirty times, and it was revived with some alterations in 1742, 1757 and, after the composer's death, 1767. In the meantime Rameau had gone on to write over twenty more stage works, among them opera-ballets and the 'lyric comedy' *Platée*, celebrating the Dauphin's wedding in 1745. *Castor et Pollux* (1737) and *Dardanus* (1739) are five-act *tragédies* on the broad Lullian pattern, but a glance at Rameau's stage catalogue gives the impression of a gradual lightening of subject-matter that may reflect both public taste and a change in the composer himself. *Les surprises de l'Amour, divertissement* (Versailles, 1748) and *Le procureur dupé sans le savoir, opéra-comique en vaudevilles* (private performance, 1759) hardly sound like the works of an elderly scholar. *Platée* in particular has a sharp frivolity and sense of caricature, the imitation of animal noises, and much laughter.

Rameau's style of word-setting in *Hippolyte et Aricie* was flexible. Melody was a strong element, and at the same time the expressive depiction of emotions was never forgotten—as Diderot put it, no composer before him had so distinguished 'the tender from the voluptuous, the voluptuous from the passionate'. This music could give psychological depth to a character such as King Theseus, and there were recitatives, *petits airs* or florid *ariettes*, *airs tendres* in dialogue and full-scale arias in *da capo* form such as Phaedra's complaint to Venus at the start of Act III. Continuity was a feature too: and at least two scholars have suggested that Rameau, perhaps through Gluck later in the century, helped to pave the way for Wagner's through-composed operatic style. Duets—sometimes euphonious, elsewhere in vivid dialogue—are effectively used. But trios are rare, and indeed one for the Fates, modulating mysteriously in chords, was omitted as too difficult in the first production. There are no larger ensembles, and in fact the only Rameau quartet is in *Les Indes galantes*. However, he used the chorus to great effect: like that of Greek tragedy his chorus both participates in the action and comments upon it.

The dance *divertissements* in *Hippolyte et Aricie* are perhaps the stylistic area in which even Rameau was unable to change French taste for ballet in the interests of dramatic tension and verisimilitude. Even so, he adapted them carefully to the story and made them characterise a situation. While using the dances of the time—minuet, *chaconne*, *gavotte*, *tambourin* and the like—he could at least choose and adapt them to the action, as in a 'dance for the lovers following Bellona' in *Les Indes galantes* and the perhaps ironic high-leaping *tambourin* given in the presence of the brooding Theseus in Act III of *Hippolyte*, as well as the rather ambiguous *musette* in seven-bar phrases near the end of the same opera.

Mention of irregular phrases reminds us that the rigid patterns of formal dances were now beginning to give way to a less formal style with an increasing use of mime. By 1770 we find a description of 'ballets almost without dance steps and made up of demonstrative gestures, in other words acting without speech'. Among the outstanding dancers of this era were Marie-Anne de Camargo (1710–70), noted for her agility and brilliance, and Marie Salle (1707–56), tall and romantic and, according to Voltaire, 'an excellent dancer who conveys the passions'. There can be little doubt that Rameau's revitalisation of dance music paralleled developments in dance itself.

Rameau's use of the operatic orchestra was one of his strongest features. The players were around forty in number and consisted of strings, flutes, oboes and bassoons. A drum would play at times, for example in the *tambourin* dances, and occasional extra instruments included horns, clarinets (in *Zoroastre*, 1749) and even cannon for the fireworks scene in *Acante et Céphise* (1751). Details abound showing the composer's interest in instrumental sound, for example an instruction in his handwriting in the score of *Hippolyte et Aricie* for bassoons to play 'with full tone, not separating the notes'. In the same opera the zephyrs have a *pizzicato* string accompaniment, and there is an orchestral stormy sea in Act III as well as birdsong imitations in Act V contrasting with the stark music for Theseus' journey to Hades. A contemporary, Hugues Maret, said of Rameau: 'Sometimes with a vigorous, virile touch he conjured up dread and dismay, elsewhere with the sweetest and most caressing sounds he moved us to tears.'

In Rameau's operas we also find quite elaborate orchestral passages existing in their own right. The overture to *Zoroastre*, with its three sections (fast, slow, fast), was intended to suggest the main elements of the stage action that was to follow, and besides the programmatic element here the relation between this musical form and the emerging symphony—introduced from Germany into France around 1755—repays study. Among descriptive orchestral interludes are an earthquake and sea storm in *Les Indes galantes* and a sunrise in *Zoroastre*, besides the passages already mentioned in *Hippolyte et Aricie*. Even the short prelude to a Rameau *air* may create a mood—there is an example in Hippolytus' '*Ah! faut-il en un jour perdre tout ce que j'aime?*' with its thirteen-bar orchestral introduction, and another in the '*Cruels tyrans*' monologue in *Zoroastre*.

The staging of the Rameau operas was often remarkable, though the Opéra itself, in the Palais-Royal in the Rue St Honoré, was surprisingly small, with an auditorium only sixty-five feet across. But that at least made it easier to light, and details of costumes and scenery were visible to all. The style was rich, and the painter François Boucher worked there as a designer from 1737–48, creating fine landscapes and *fêtes-galantes*. Professor Brian Trowell has vividly described productions during the mid-eighteenth century at the Palais-Royal:

The stage machinery must have followed the usual arrangement of sliding shutters and screens, with plentiful trapdoors, and cloud-machines suspended from the fly-gallery. Such equipment could handle the most complicated transformations in a flash, and part of the audience's enjoyment lay in watching the invisibly-propelled alterations of scene. The main house curtain was raised at the beginning of the performance, but not lowered again until the very end. The lighting seems to have been remarkably flexible. Though many auditorium lamps were kept burning, the main central chandelier could be winched up into the roof. There are directions for a total blackout as early as the seventeenth century. Footlights were also in use at that time, and are still called 'floats' in the profession—a reminder that they were once oil or tallow lamps which floated in a long trough of water: if less light were needed, the water was run off and the lamps sank deeper into the trough. One reads of galaxies of candles behind the scenes. Fades were arranged by closing lantern-shutters. Sunrises and spectacular changes of colour could be managed with the aid of glass bowls containing coloured fluids which were placed in front of the lights. Gauzes were known, with their peculiar properties of becoming solid or transparent at will . . . the costumes of the Opéra were by every account extremely impressive. Paris even then led world fashions in dress, and the French actors wore the court costume of their day, whether in opera or in Racine. There was little attempt at realism or local colour . . . Serious attempts to reconstruct the true dress of classical times did not become the rule until the generation of Gluck.

COMIC OPERA AND THE *GUERRE DES BOUFFONS*

Musical history is never as simple as historians make it. The famous *guerre* or *querelle des bouffons*, or 'comics' controversy' of 1753 was a storm in a teacup fought on slogans and minor issues, and although passions may have run high in a few cases it is hard to believe it was of profound significance or historical impact. Nevertheless no history of opera is complete without it and it provides some amusing anecdotes.

The chief figures in this dispute over French music, Grimm and Rousseau, were respectively German and Swiss. Friedrich Grimm (1723–1807) was a young German diplomat living in Paris since 1749, a friend of the intellectual encyclopédiste circle that included Rousseau and Diderot. His first essay at music criticism was an attack in the *Mercure de France* in 1752 on Destouches's *Omphale*, which at the time was being revived, in which he ridiculed classical opera although praising Rameau. In the same year, at Fontainebleau, the first production was seen of *Le devin du village* (*The Village Soothsayer*), called an '*intermède*' but in essence a comic opera, by Jean-Jacques Rousseau (1712–78), a young intellectual and largely self-taught musician: its success and royal approval brought it to the Paris Opéra within five months.

For Grimm, the natural simplicity and wit of his friend Rousseau's work were a revelation. He now, in 1753, published in the journal *Correspondance littéraire* a satirical tract in which he represented himself as a Bohemian musician miraculously transported to Paris and dropped into a theatre. Here the conductor seemed to him a mere woodchopper beating a stick, 'but though it was beaten most forcibly, the musicians were never together'. He was pleased by some voices, but not that of an elderly singer 'who gargled at the public'. This kind of opera was 'the laughing-stock of Europe . . . you have chosen a Florentine for your idol, whom you call M. de Lully . . . and I saw that they called this in France an opera, and was very content to see the curtain fall'. A further prong to Grimm's attack on classical opera came in his praise of an Italian comic opera, Pergolesi's *La serva padrona*, which had been put on successfully in Paris in 1752.

Rousseau himself also went into print with a violent attack, probably written with his tongue in cheek, but in which his shafts were skilfully sharpened and thrown. Quarrels, he said, were alien to him, and this was a time for calm reason: he would state his opinion frankly, without fear of giving offence. Having thus disarmed the reader, he then launched a swingeing assault. 'The Italians claim our melody to be flat and tuneless, and all non-aligned nations confirm this judgement.' French operatic songs and monologues were 'insipid little ditties [and] tedious lamentations'. His conclusion was: 'I think I have shown that there is neither measure nor melody in French music, because the language is incapable of them; that French singing is a continual squalling, insupportable to an unprejudiced ear; that its harmony is crude and devoid of expression and suggests only the padding of a pupil; that French "airs" are not airs; that French recitative is not recitative. From this I conclude that the French have no music and cannot have any; or that if they ever have, it will be so much the worse for them.'

Rousseau's tirade produced a violent reaction, although some must have seen the element of teasing in it. People even made an effigy of him and hanged and burned it. The French court itself became somewhat involved in the *querelle*. Officially it defended the classical French style despite the King's enjoyment of *Le devin du village*, but unofficially the Queen seems to have supported the intellectuals led by Rousseau and Diderot, and to have liked the fresh simplicity of Pergolesi and Rousseau, artists who offered stories about ordinary people set to lively music and were amusing without being empty-headed.

Today we can see that Rousseau's position was an odd one. After all, three years previously in a letter to Grimm he had compared French and Italian opera and reached a conclusion mainly in favour of France: it would have embarrassed him if this document had been produced at the time of the *guerre*. He was himself the composer of a successful French opera, and was in due course to contribute to another, *Pygmalion* (Lyon, 1770). Probably he recognised the inconsistencies in his attack on French music, and in his *Confessions* completed in that same year he admitted that he had 'wished to be regarded as a composer so as to show his superiority to the other philosophers'. We may note also that, together with Grimm, Rousseau recognised the genius of Gluck's French operas in the 1770s.

The lighter kind of opera which is exemplified in Rousseau's work had very mixed antecedents that included the Italian *commedia dell' arte* and its French equivalent the *sotie* or *sottie*. This was a satirical entertainment in which the characters were supposed to be mad, and performances were mostly in street theatre at fairs and similar occasions. Even royalty, including Louis XIV himself, would sometimes mingle unnoticed with the crowds at the great Paris fairs like the Foire St Germain held in Lent, despite an atmosphere described by the historian Auguste Font as having 'excitement and gaiety [but also being] a sink of iniquity, a vast sewer, the scene of quarrels and fights, and this explains the quality of the amusements provided, the licence and salaciousness of their tone and the frank brutality of the subject matter'.

Lighter musical shows in the theatre were called variously *comédies à vaudevilles* and *comédies à ariettes*, the one using popular *airs* and the other specially composed ones. The term *opéra comique* occurs first in 1715, and the dramatist Charles-Simon Favart directed a theatre presenting such pieces which actually had that name from 1780. Spoken dialogue was always a feature, just as it is in modern musical comedy. Voltaire praised Favart for 'first making a decent and ingenious amusement out of a form which, before you, did not concern polite society. Thanks to you, it has become the delight of all decent folk.'

Among the composers who set Favart's libretti were François Philidor (1726–95), a pupil of Campra, with his *L'amant déguisé, ou Le jardinier supposé* (Paris, 1769) and Pierre-Alexandre Monsigny (1729–1817) in *La belle Arsène* (Fontainebleau, 1773). But neither of them confined himself to comic opera pure and simple. Philidor based his *Tom Jones* (Paris, 1765) on Fielding's picaresque novel. Monsigny's best known opera is one which he called a *drame*, *Le déserteur* (Paris, 1769), a work of force and some pathos based on an episode in a Flemish war. But such works as these belong already to a period of music remote indeed from Lully and Rameau. The *querelle des bouffons* marked a step along a road leading from *tragédie lyrique* to *Tom Jones* and beyond, from gods and heroes and sorceresses to picaresque adventurers and their ladies. From the 1750s onwards French comic opera travelled with success to the courts and theatres of other European countries including England, and Rousseau's *Le devin du village*, through Favart's adaptation called *Les amours de Bastien et Bastienne*, was to provide the inspiration for Mozart's *Bastien und Bastienne* (Vienna, 1768). As for the subject-matter of comic opera, it became more broadly popular, in keeping with the climate of social change that was to be violently demonstrated in the events of the French Revolution.

4

ENGLAND AND GERMANY

The Masque. Blow and Purcell. German Opera. Handel.

THE MASQUE

The tradition of spoken drama was strong in England, but music had a place in the English theatre during the middle years of the seventeenth century in the masque. This was not unlike the French *ballet de cour*, in that it was a lavish court entertainment. It had reached England from France and Italy by 1512, when according to Hall's *Chronicle* Henry VIII took part, disguised, in 'a maske, a thynge not seen afore in Englande'. The subjects were usually mythological, and presented through a combination of poetry, singing, music, dancing, acting and sheer spectacle. The masque therefore differed from the Italian opera in that music was not pre-eminent, but was mixed with spoken dialogue, and usually accompanied dancing, the traditional court diversion. Variety of entertainment was the main objective; the story was less important.

The masque in England escaped from triviality through the theatrical involvement of some of the best poets of the time. In 1605 Ben Jonson collaborated in *The Masque of Blackness*, which had rapid scene changes that showed the influence of contemporary Italian stage techniques. Five years later his *Masque of Queens* was the first attempt to introduce an element of burlesque into the form, while his *Lovers Made Men* (1617) had music by Nicholas Lanier (1588–1666), who later became Master of the King's Musick. The poet described its style as 'after the Italian manner, *stylo recitativo*'. Although little music from these masques has survived, what we do have indicates that no specifically operatic forms were used. Instead, the songs were lute-songs and 'ayres', and the dances simple in structure and in the style of Elizabethan consort music. Thus the early masque composers, Thomas Campion, John Coprario, John Ferrabosco, Nathaniel Giles and Robert Johnson, largely maintained the approach and forms in which they were trained, although Ferrabosco's father had emigrated from Italy, and Coprario visited Italy around 1600, after which he had changed his name from Cooper to Coprario.

Traditionally, masques were richly produced, and the English

Puritans were less than enthusiastic about such extravagance. The pamphleteer George Wither wrote in 1641 that 'Scurrilous and obscene songs are impudently sung, without respecting the reverend presence of Matrons, Virgins, Magistrates, or Divines.' Yet not all masques were condemned. *Comus* (1634) was the work of John Milton, himself a Puritan, and its high moral tone took the masque in a direction which kept it alive during the difficult years of the Civil War and the Commonwealth. In *Comus*, Milton collaborated with the composer Henry Lawes (1596–1662), whom he praised in the highest terms:

> Harry whose tuneful and well measur'd Song
> First taught our English Musick how to span
> Words with just note and accent, not to scan
> With Midas ears, committing short and long;
> Thy worth and skill exempts thee from the throng,
> With praise enough for envy to look wan;
> To after age though shalt be writ the man,
> That with smooth ayre couldst humor best our tongue.
> Thou honour'st Verse, and Verse must lend her wing
> To honour thee, the Priest of Phoebus' Quire
> That tun'st their happiest lines in Hymn, or Story.
> Dante shall give Fame leave to set thee higher
> Than his Casella, whom he woo'd to sing
> Met in the milder shades of Purgatory.

Henry Lawes was a member of a new generation of composers, along with his brother William (1602–45), and Nicholas Lanier, Christopher Gibbons (1615–76) and Matthew Locke (1630–77). In 1656 Lawes was the main, but by no means the only, contributor to *The Siege of Rhodes*, an entertainment devised by the then Poet Laureate, Sir William Davenant, who described it as 'a Story sung in Recitative Musick, unpractised here, though of great reputation among other nations'. The diarist Samuel Pepys referred to Davenant's London theatre as 'the opera'.

By this time the new Italian style was clearly extending an influence, through travel and cultural exchange of the kind recorded by the young John Evelyn when he went to Venice in 1645 towards the end of the Civil War. Evelyn wrote in his Diary:

> This night, having with my Lord Bruce taken our places before, we went to the Opera, where comedies and other plays are represented in recitative music by the most excellent musicians, vocal and instrumental, with variety of scenes painted and contrived with no

less art of perspective, and machines for flying in the air, and other wonderful notions; taken together, it is one of the most magnificent and expensive diversions the wit of man can invent.

The very popular cantata *Hero and Leander* by Lanier confirmed this Italian influence with its closer links between text and music. As time went on, composers used masques increasingly to experiment with their craft, so that after the restricted activities of the Commonwealth years, there was a musical potential ready to flower with the restoration of the monarchy in 1660.

BLOW AND PURCELL

With the accession of Charles II, English musical life changed dramatically. The King's years of exile in France had evidently made their mark, for he was immediately anxious to create a musical climate like that at the court of Louis XIV. Among the chief composers of the period were Locke and John Blow (1649–1708), both of whom were aware of the developments in music theatre on the Continent. Locke's masque *Orpheus and Euridice* has music closely integrated with the plot, whilst Blow's *Venus and Adonis* (1682) goes further in this direction and is almost an opera, though the composer himself called it a masque—for by that time the title of masque was given to any court entertainment which was staged and had both music and dancing.

Venus and Adonis was written for private performance before the King. Its chief significance lies in the way that it combines so many different elements: the mythological story of the masque and operatic traditions, tragedy mixed with comedy according to the dictates of the plot after the later manner of Monteverdi, and the use of dances as in Lully's French operas. There are three short acts, and the music is strongly Italianate, but the deployment of chorus and instrumental dances shows a link with the masque style. As Adonis dies, he sings a fine lament, and the work ends with a funeral chorus, 'Mourn for thy Servant', that maintains the mood. The score demands four-part strings, recorders (perhaps doubling oboes), and continuo. *Venus and Adonis* is a work of stature, both for its own qualities and because of its influence on what was to come.

In 1685, John Dryden defined opera as 'a poetical tale, or fiction, represented by vocal or instrumental music, adorned with scenes, machines, and dancing'. Dryden collaborated with the French composer Louis Grabu (ca 1635–94) in *Albion and Albanius* (1685), an allegory on the restoration of the British monarchy which failed artistically and economically because of the mediocre music and a production coinciding with the Monmouth rebellion. In his preface to the work, Dryden admitted that he had to overcome a reluctance to have his words set to music, and he made a similar point in 1691 over a more famous collaboration, *King Arthur*, with music by Henry Purcell: 'In many places, I have been obliged to cramp my verses, and make them ragged to the reader, that they may be harmonious to the hearer.' Clearly his reference to the qualities of the music reflects acceptance of the emphases of opera proper as opposed to those of the masque.

Perhaps such acceptance was inevitable. Composers had been increasingly interested in the theatre since the Restoration, and none more so than Henry Purcell (1659–95), who was trained at the Chapel Royal and wrote his first music for the stage as early as 1680. A continuing interest in drama inevitably drew him towards opera, and in 1689 he received an unusual commission which allowed that term to be applied without reservation for the first time to an English work.

Josias Priest kept a 'School for Young Gentlewomen' in Chelsea, and he invited Purcell to write an entertainment for performance there. The result was *Dido and Aeneas* (1689). The libretto was by Nahum Tate, whose immediate source was his play *Brutus of Alba*, or *The Enchanted Lovers*, based on Virgil and completed some ten years earlier. The new text was designed to compress the plot and to enable Priest's pupils to be seen and heard to advantage. Thus not the least remarkable thing about *Dido and Aeneas* was that its virtues arose out of necessities. It required little or no staging, to the extent that the focus of attention was thrown onto the music. The opera lasts about an hour, and Purcell included numerous dances to take account of Priest's talents as a dancing master. With the obvious exception of Aeneas (baritone), together with a minor part for a sailor, all the solo roles were female. The small chorus was drawn from Priest's girls, and from youths who attended Louis Maidwell's school in Hatton Garden. Originally there was an elaborate Prologue, but this has been lost, and it is not even certain that Purcell provided any music for this introduction with characters that included gods, nymphs, and shepherdesses. It seems likely that the orchestra consisted of strings, harpsichord, and guitars; although the guitar music has not survived, some recent performances have inserted appropriate items in the interests of authenticity.

Given Purcell's training at the Chapel Royal, where he was taught by Blow and Pelham Humfrey (1647–74), it is hardly surprising that he had been influenced by the taste of Charles II himself, and turned for his model to French opera as it had been established by Lully—both

Humfrey and the King had visited Versailles. It is in the overture and some of the dances that the French influence on *Dido and Aeneas* is most strongly felt. However, the arias dominate the recitatives, a procedure more Italian than French, while several of the dances suggest an English style, for example the hornpipe in Act III.

A mood of seriousness permeates *Dido and Aeneas*, and this is because Dido is the character who dominates the opera. Her moving final lament, 'When I am laid in earth', is constructed on a ground bass (*see* Chapter 2). The outline of this recurring theme, above which the Queen sings her lament, conveys the mood of gravity: it starts with an octave leap, before descending step by step as if to emphasise the tragic inevitability of Dido's death. This bass is repeated ten times, and over it appears the theme in a binary (two-part) form, the second half beginning with the words 'Remember me'. It is typical of Purcell that the orchestra frames the aria, both preparing and maintaining its atmosphere. The concluding chorus is hardly less fine. It owes much to John Blow's *Venus and Adonis* in musical terms, and also fulfils the role of the Greek chorus by commenting on the action.

These aspects of *Dido and Aeneas* are undeniably great achievements, with Purcell reaching the very height of his powers. But no opera can maintain such intensity throughout, and there are sections that reflect the traditions of the period rather than the timeless quality of genius. For example, Purcell was following the masque tradition in the full use he made of witches and the supernatural, and through their intervention the action can leap ahead and the abiding emphasis on fate can be reinforced. The character of Aeneas, unlike that of Dido, is given a low profile. His relationship with her is left somewhat undeveloped, although this weakness does result in the positive virtue of throwing the focus of attention firmly towards Dido and, especially, her personal tragedy.

It might seem strange that Purcell did not follow this masterpiece with other operas, but instead turned to a hybrid form known as the 'semi-opera'. The reason was a practical one. The composer stood at the crossroads of a noticeable shift in English taste: while *Dido and Aeneas* looked forward, his other stage works satisfied more traditional demands. They were written for the professional stage, to which Purcell had a lifelong commitment. In the five years after 1690 he composed music for some forty plays, and it is in five of these that his contribution was substantial enough to merit the term 'semi-opera'. This may be defined as a drama in spoken dialogue, but containing sizeable musical portions: overtures, interludes, ballets, and other scenes. The chief works of the genre were *Dioclesian* (1690), *King Arthur* (1691), *The Fairy Queen* (1692),

The Indian Queen (1695), and *The Tempest* (1695). In all these works the chorus is important, but most of the music is instrumental: apart from a few *arioso* passages (i.e. between recitative and aria), speech prevails. In *The Fairy Queen*, a free adaptation of *A Midsummer Night's Dream*, the point is emphasised by the fact that Purcell set none of the verses from the original Shakespeare play. Nevertheless these works contain some of the composer's finest music: *Dioclesian*, for instance, so impressed John Dryden that the poet was moved to collaborate on *King Arthur*, the only one of the 'semi-operas' that does not adapt an earlier play. The depth of Purcell's stage experience is reflected in the last two of these works, *The Indian Queen* and *The Tempest*. Here Italian influence is to be found in the vocal numbers and French in the instrumental ones, thus confirming the trend that began with *Dido and Aeneas*. However, Purcell's strength is that he absorbs the devices of others rather than imitates them, and some of his technical solutions, especially his use of dissonance, are very much his own. Furthermore, although he was fond of employing *arioso* technique, he seldom used the fully developed Italian *da capo* aria. Even though practical circumstances restricted him in the field of opera, he thus remains a figure of major importance.

As it was, English musical taste had by about 1700 developed sufficiently to allow the ready acceptance of foreign imports. Even before the turn of the century Italian singers were becoming popular in London, and soon adaptations of Venetian operas were appearing in translation, with Italian singers alongside their English counterparts (*see* Chapter 5), so that performances sometimes used a mixture of the two languages. Handel's *Rinaldo*, when it was produced in 1711, was one of the first all-Italian operas the capital had seen, with the full deployment of the classical opera style. That it was written by a German whose experience of Italy was fresh reveals that this had now become an international language, and that this style, called *opera seria*, and not the masque or the 'semi-opera', was to become the accepted form of music drama in England (see also pp. 67–8 and 73).

GERMAN OPERA

No better example of the influence of Italian music throughout Europe during the seventeenth century could be cited than the career of Heinrich Schütz (1585–1672), who as a young man went for three years to study in Venice with Giovanni Gabrieli. The visit was paid for by the Landgrave of Marburg, in whose chapel choir Schütz had sung as a boy, and who evidently felt that Italy was the place to develop the talents of a budding composer. Schütz kept in touch with Italian musical developments, and in 1628 went to Venice once more specially to meet Monteverdi, whom he greatly admired. Yet through his long life Schütz worked in the north of Europe, first in Copenhagen and then at the Saxon court at Dresden. It was in 1627, the year before his second Italian visit, that Schütz produced his only opera, *Dafne*, the music for which is now lost. The text was by Ottavio Rinuccini, and had been set by Peri when he created the very first opera (*see* Chapter 2). *Dafne* was translated into German and the language adapted towards a more lyrical style by the poet Martin Opitz. What this would actually have meant in terms of musical experience must, however, remain a mystery.

It is surely one of the frustrations of music's history that the Thirty Years War stifled the development of German culture, and created conditions unsuitable for the establishment and growth of opera. Even though Sigmund Staden of Nuremberg published his *Seelewig* in 1644 — a pastoral morality set to music 'in the Italian style', as the composer put it — a truly German opera was still a long way off. The Italian style dominated, and major cities in Germany imported operas from across the Alps.

Apart from London and Hamburg, the main centres of Italian opera outside Italy were Dresden, Vienna, Hanover, and Munich. At Munich the skilful work of Agostino Steffani (1654–1728) was admired, but he spent the last forty years of his life at Hanover, where his *Henrico Leone* (1689) was written for the opening of the Italian opera house. His other successful operas included *Servio Tullio* (Munich, 1685), *La superbia d'Alessandro* (Hanover, 1690), and *I trionfi del Fato* (Hanover, 1695).

Inevitably the influence of the courts of many German rulers had been weakened by the Thirty Years War, and the towns were beginning to take a more active role in musical life as the expanding merchant classes joined the traditional patrons of music, the Church and the aristocracy. In university towns schools of music became focal points; the most celebrated was the Leipzig Collegium Musicum, founded by Telemann and directed by J. S. Bach from 1729. It is in the music of Bach that we can most clearly observe the fusion of Italian melody and counterpoint with French expressiveness and colour; for at no time before or since has German music been so affected by that of other nations. Nevertheless the use of full polyphonic textures was already a national trait, and the German style continued to develop through the assimilation of the foreign idioms. In instrumental music, Georg Muffat (1645–1740) was largely responsible for establishing the suite of dance movements and for incorporating the sophisticated orchestral colours of Lully. The orthodox Lutheran Church favoured using full musical resources in worship, the main forms being the cantata and, on a larger scale, the Passion. The summit was reached in all these non-operatic forms in the music of Bach, while in opera itself the foreign influences were at their most direct.

There were many composers of Italian opera at work in Germany and Italy, but the German Johann Adolf Hasse (1699–1783) eclipses all save Handel. Hasse was a pupil of Nicola Porpora and Alessandro Scarlatti (*see* Chapter 5), and married the famous soprano Faustina Bordoni. He was based at Dresden, although his operas were performed all over Europe — in 1734 he visited London, where his *Artaserse* was offered as a counter-attraction to Handel. His thirty years in Dresden established Italian opera there, and in such works as *Demofoonte* (1748) and *Selimano* (1753) his graceful arias anticipate the rococo *style galant*, and the orchestra matches the music to the drama. Hasse was the favourite composer of the poet Pietro Metastasio, each of whose librettos he set at least once.

By the 1760s Hasse's style had come to seem old-fashioned to his contemporaries in the wake of the reforms of Gluck — the Vienna version of Gluck's *Orfeo ed Euridice* dates from 1762. That is not to belittle Hasse's achievement, however, for within the conventional pattern of *opera seria*, which he more than anyone established in German musical life, Hasse managed a considerable range of expression. His scoring, employing strings plus woodwind and brass, is often transparent, and his use of the aria, whilst closer to Italian models than to other styles, allows his melodic elegance to come to the fore. Besides being a composer, Hasse was a producer and performer of the music of others, and he brought many of Handel's London operas to Dresden.

Other centres of German opera included the courts of Brunswick and Weissenfels, and Hamburg, a self-governing free municipality whose city fathers and musicians had founded the first German opera company in 1678. This was done in the face of Church opposition, and in order to appease the clergy the early productions dealt exclusively with Biblical subjects. However, Church influence gradually declined and social fashion came to favour 'the public and popular opera theatre'. The company gave regular seasons, mostly in German, until the growing taste for Italian opera brought its eventual demise in 1738. The high point of the Hamburg Opera was the work of Reinhard Keiser (1674–1739), who from 1695 composed over fifty operas, some of them in a comic vein. His position there extended into the 1730s, and his best works, for instance *Croesus* (1711) and *Fredegunda* (1715), represent a fusion of styles: his arias are often brilliant, although his liking for expressive profundity in slower music led him away from Italian melody towards a more Germanic polyphonic texture.

Most striking of all in this balance of styles, however, was the fact that Keiser refused to mould his arias in the traditional Italian *da capo* (ABA) form, preferring to use a more flexible *arioso* approach and thus make a stronger impression on the listener. Such innovations inspired the young Handel, as well as Georg Philipp Telemann (1681–1767), whose *Pimpinone* (Hamburg, 1725), with only two characters, was a German predecessor of Pergolesi's comic *La serva padrona* (*The Maid as Mistress*). Around 1700, the Germans adopted the word *Singspiel* (that is a play with singing) for popular comic opera, and as time went by, this new form developed a pattern of spoken dialogue linking the musical numbers. Perhaps the nature of the German language contributed to the initial failure of the *Singspiel* to establish a foothold, let alone a firm place, in the international repertory: only much later, with two mature operas of Mozart, *Die Entführung aus dem Serail* and *Die Zauberflöte*, followed by the work of Weber and his contemporaries, was this achieved.

Carl Heinrich Graun (1704–59) wrote Italian operas for Brunswick before moving to Berlin in 1740 to become Court *Kapellmeister*. There he continued to compose in the conventional manner, depending especially on virtuoso coloratura in arias. Two of his operas, *Silla* (Berlin, 1753) and *Montezuma* (Berlin, 1755), were written to texts by his employer, Frederick the Great.

HANDEL

The outstanding opera composer during the long period between Monteverdi and Mozart was George Frideric Handel (1685–1759). His reputation rested until after the Second World War on only a part of his huge output, for not one of his operas was staged between 1754 and 1920: the full nature of his achievement has therefore only recently and gradually become apparent.

At the age of eighteen, Handel left his native Halle for Hamburg, where he played violin and harpsichord in the opera orchestra. Within two years he presented his first opera, *Almira* (Hamburg, 1704), whose style reflected that of Keiser, the leading local composer at that time. *Almira* was intended for the north German public; the recitatives were given in the vernacular with the arias in Italian, which was considered more appropriate for singing.

Such was Handel's determination to learn his craft that Hamburg soon failed to satisfy him, and in 1706 he set off for Italy. In Florence he met Alessandro Scarlatti and completed a new opera called *Rodrigo*, then visited Rome, Naples and Venice, composing oratorios and cantatas. His opera *Agrippina* was written for the Venice Carnival of 1709, and its success there brought him enormous public acclaim: its initial run of twenty-seven performances was a record he would never match later in his career. The result was that Handel left Italy a famous man, whose talents were sought in Germany and in England too.

He accepted a salaried post as Steffani's successor at the court of Hanover, but almost immediately left for London, arriving there towards the end of 1710. A few weeks later, early in 1711, he achieved a notable triumph with *Rinaldo*. The splendour of the production, which caused a sensation during Almirena's 'Bird Song' when a flock of live sparrows was released, and the singing of the *castrato* Nicolini enhanced the qualities of Handel's music. This, like most of his later operas, was staged in Europe too, reaching Dublin in 1711, Hamburg in 1715, and Milan in 1718.

Through the production of *Rinaldo* Handel had learned enough about the London musical scene to make him want to return there. He did so the following year, and this time he stayed for good. None of the operas he produced at the King's Theatre in the Haymarket during the next few seasons, *Il pastor fido* (1712), *Teseo* and *Silla* (both 1713), and *Amadigi* (1715), achieved remotely the success of *Rinaldo*, although they did secure Handel's position in London society. The accession of his former employer, the Elector George Ludwig, to the English throne in 1714 as George I could possibly have made matters difficult for him, but the new king's liking for his music, matched as it was by the admiration of the public, prevented any rift. By basing himself in London, Handel was committing himself to a career in the professional theatre; even though royalty and the aristocracy supported him, he usually had to rely on the box office to maintain his operations. In this relationship with the theatre there is a link with Purcell, whom he revered. When he was at the height of his fame, a friend pointed out that a certain passage of his sounded rather like Purcell, and Handel retorted, 'If Purcell had lived, he would have produced better music than this.'

Between 1715 and 1720 Handel wrote no operas, since he was employed by the Duke of Chandos and had no connections with the theatre. However, at the end of that period, he took over the direction of the Royal Academy of Music, a company established and financed by members of the nobility for the presentation of Italian opera. The Academy's stocks were listed at the Stock Exchange, and some investors subscribed for speculative rather than musical reasons. By February 1720 nearly £20,000 had been raised, and the Earl of Shaftesbury, one of Handel's aristocratic patrons, wrote in his memoirs:

The method of subscription was for each Subscriber to sign a Bond for £200, which Sum was to answer all calls that might be made upon the Subscribers for expenses in carrying on the Operas exceeding the sums collected each night at the House. And a set of Directors were Elected for carrying on the Affairs of the Academy, which was incorporated by a Charter. The Directors were for the most part Persons of Distinction.

The composer was closely involved in the running of the Academy, which was based in the King's Theatre. He attended board meetings and played an active part in the administration, the engagement of singers, the scenery and staging, the programming and the rehearsals. The most successful Academy season resulted in the payment of a dividend of seven per cent to the shareholders in February 1723.

The next few years were to see some of Handel's greatest creations, and London became for a time the operatic capital of Europe. His operas were often inspired by the qualities of the singers he found during talent-spotting European tours, and the main attractions were the *castrato* Francesco Bernardi, who took the stage name Senesino from his birth-place Siena, and the soprano Francesca Cuzzoni. It was Senesino who created the title role in *Giulio Cesare* (1724), while Cuzzoni caused the sensation of the London year with her performance in *Ottone* in 1723. *Tamerlano* (1724) is one of the most remarkable of all Handel's operas, and at its first performance Cuzzoni and Senesino were apparently outsung by a new tenor, Francesco Borosini. It was actually very rare for Handel to have a tenor to write for, but the part he created in this opera for the Emperor Bajazet shows that he relished the opportunity. The dramatic characterisation he achieved here is unique in *opera seria*, for a noble character dies on stage to a *recitativo accompagnato* that mingles with *arioso* to bring the utmost realism.

The London opera audience came from the wealthy sectors of the community, the merchant and landowning classes, since for the vast majority of the city's population, which was quite without education and material wealth, intellectual pursuits were out of the question. Furthermore, only the rich could afford the London 'season', of which opera formed a fashionable part.

Performances began at around five or six p.m. after dinner had been eaten during the afternoon. Audience etiquette in the theatres of Hanoverian London was less rigid than it was in the royal courts of Europe: audiences tended to be noisy and singers acquired fanatical followings. During the première of Handel's *Admeto* (1727), a member of the audience shouted, 'Damn her! She has got a nest of nightingales in her belly,' as Francesca Cuzzoni performed.

The theatres were lit with oil lamps and candles, and those in the auditorium remained in use during the performance. The wicks needed constant attention, and onstage a uniformed attendant or even a member of the orchestra assumed this responsibility. Though the subjects of *opera seria* were from classical Greece and Rome, only the monumental sets, which relied on a keen sense of perspective, emphasised this. The costumes were basically contemporary—the elaborate dress of the rich who were flattered to see themselves mirrored on the stage. Only a few details, such as a helmet and plumes on top of a fashionable wig, or an added Roman tunic, acknowledged the period of the plot. The star singers usually brought their own costumes with them, while the theatres merely provided the trimmings.

Handel's audience supported him sufficiently well to allow the expected structure and virtuosity of *opera seria* to be moulded into a musical language of truly human dimensions: the emotions to be found in Handel's characters are real. And yet maintaining the interest of the opera audience was not always easy, and sometimes Handel failed to avoid mistakes. One of them was to allow an artificial rivalry to be created between himself and another composer, Giovanni Bononcini (1670–1747). Then in 1726 the Academy engaged a second prima donna, the soprano Faustina Bordoni from Venice, Hasse's wife. The *London Journal* plainly announced: 'A famous lady (Faustina) is coming over to rival Signora Cuzzoni.' The inevitable result occurred in 1727, during a performance of Bononcini's *Astianatte* attended by the Princess of Wales, when brawls in the auditorium spread to Cuzzoni and Bordoni on the stage. The *British Journal* of 10 June reported:

> A great disturbance happened at the Opera, occasioned by the Partisans of the Two Celebrated Rival Ladies, Cuzzoni and Faustina. The Contention at first was only carried on by Hissing on one Side, and Clapping on the other; but proceeded at length to Catcalls and other great indecencies. And notwithstanding the Princess Caroline was present, no regards were of Force to restrain the Rudeness of the Opponents.

Such absurdities hastened the demise of the Academy, which went bankrupt shortly afterwards.

Another contributory cause of this collapse was the enormous success at the time of *The Beggar's Opera* (1728), a pastiche work arranged by the poet and dramatist John Gay (1685–1732) and Johann Christoph Pepusch

(1667–1752), a minor composer who did little more than add a bass to the popular pieces that were gathered together, and compose an overture. The material used possibly resulted from a comment made to Gay by Jonathan Swift, that an opera set in a prison 'would make an odd pretty sort of thing', a direct contrast to the traditionally noble settings of *opera seria*. The deliberately satirical approach also applied to the music, for this ballad opera used spoken dialogue to link the musical numbers, all in English, and the collection was then linked to a story involving London's low life. Although much of the original material used by Gay and Pepusch was by established composers like Handel, in its new context it was very different from the style of Italian opera. The story was up-to-date and homely, the tunes were attractive, Italian opera was caricatured and the government satirised: all in all, a good recipe for success.

In fact both Gay and Pepusch were friends of Handel and they certainly did not seek to kill the Italian opera. The actor-dramatist John Rich (1682–1761), who put on *The Beggar's Opera* at the Lincoln's Inn Fields Theatre, a success which, it was said, 'Made Gay rich and Rich gay', in 1730 began subscriptions to build the Covent Garden Theatre, which was completed in 1732. The very next year, at Lincoln's Inn, Rich decided to begin the promotion of Italian opera, a fact that puts the supposed rivalry into its proper perspective.

After its initial success, however, ballad opera failed to establish itself, although it enjoyed a brief revival with *Love in a Village* (London, 1762) by Thomas Arne (1710–78), the only distinguished English composer during the middle years of the century. Arne's *Artaxerxes* (1762) was a popular opera in the Italian style, based on an English translation of Metastasio, but when he composed *Olimpiade* (1764), a Metastasian opera in Italian, he met with failure.

As early as 1729, Handel was already back in business with a new company recruited during a tour of Italy, but his soprano Anna Maria Strada and, especially, his *castrato* Antonio Bernacci failed to capture public support. In 1733 some of King George II's political enemies, including the Prince of Wales and several other aristocrats, set up a rival Italian company, their involvement giving it the title 'Opera of the Nobility'. This only added to the complications, for the next year Handel broke off his relationship with the King's Theatre and the impresario John Jacob Heidegger, selling his lease to his rivals. He then made an arrangement with John Rich at Covent Garden for the alternate production of Italian opera and English drama.

Although after the success of his English oratorio *Esther* in 1732 Handel gradually moved away from opera and towards oratorio, the operas he produced over the following years were of comparable quality with their predecessors: *Orlando* (1733), with its celebrated 'mad scene', *Alcina* (1735) and *Ariodante* (1735) are all among his finest works. Of the very last operas, the most important is probably *Serse* (1738), which was written specifically to show off the talents of Caffarelli (his real name was Gaetano Majorano), yet another star *castrato*, and which brilliantly balances tragedy with comedy. During these years fashions were changing. Italian opera was becoming less popular and Handel responded by developing a new type of work for the theatre, while still trying to keep the opera alive. The advantages of the oratorio in English on biblical themes were clear: he could save the very high costs incurred by costumes and sets and star singers, and tap the new mood of patriotism by presenting a very English type of work.

Handel had developed his ideas about opera with his close friend at Hamburg, Johann Mattheson (1681–1764). Their differing ideas about the *continuo* accompaniment in Mattheson's opera *Cleopatra* (Hamburg, 1705) even led to a duel in which Handel's waistcoat button is said to have saved his life; but after this incident the two became firm friends. In later life Mattheson turned from composition to writing, and his views on how opera can express states of emotion must have been formulated with Handel particularly in mind:

> One can find in operas a conflux of all of music's beauties. For in them a composer has excellent opportunity to give free reign to his powers of invention. In them he can imitate very naturally, with grace, and with thousands of variations, Love, Jealousy, Hatred, Gentleness, Impatience, Desire, Lethargy, Fear, Revenge, Valour, Timidity, Magnanimity, Terror, Dignity, Baseness, Pomp, Poverty, Pride, Meekness, Happiness, Laughter, Crying, Pleasure, Pain, Bliss, Despair, Storm, Calm,—yes, even Heaven, Earth, Sea, Hell, and all of the human activities associated with these passions— especially if our eyes are willing to give just a little aid to our ears.

Bold claims indeed, but Handel achieved maturity early and from 1709 onwards they are truly met in his operas. Like all the greatest composers, he unerringly selected the material appropriate to the need of the plot and then deployed it in such a way that it seemed inevitable as well as varied and memorable.

From the time of *Agrippina* in 1709, Handel never ceased to assimilate new influences, but in fact he maintained certain features of style. He most frequently wrote heroic operas with plots from Roman or Greek history or from mythology. In *Siroe* (1728), *Poro* (1731) and *Ezio* (1732) he set texts by Metastasio, but his finest achievements in this field are the masterpieces of 1724–5, *Giulio Cesare*, *Tamerlano* and *Rodelinda*. Scenes of sorcery and witchcraft are found in the five 'magic operas', the best of this genre being *Orlando* (1733) and *Alcina* (1735), whose music is of the highest order throughout. Some operas are even anti-heroic, with parodies of *opera seria* included in the mixture of the comic and the serious, of which *Flavio* (1723), *Partenope* (1730) and *Serse* (1738) are examples. Handel thus encompassed the full range of mood and drama, always writing with the talents and needs of particular singers in mind, the sopranos and *castrati* the public wanted to hear.

In *opera seria* the singers were entertainers who related directly to their audience. They treated arias as concert pieces removed from the flow of the drama, as opportunities to display their virtuosity. When operas were revived, the original parts would be altered to suit the new singers. Handel responded to this challenge with the greatest ingenuity, his music allowing a range of approaches from virtuoso coloratura to deeply felt expression. However, his frustrations were noted by Sir John Hawkins: 'In his comparison of the merits of a composer and those of a singer, Handel estimated the latter at a very low rate.' Handel's biographer John Mainwaring tells how the composer became so frustrated with the antics of the soprano Cuzzoni during a rehearsal that 'he swore he would fling her out of the window'.

During this period professional opera stars rose to prominence for the first time, commanding huge fees because of their international reputations. Technically singers were trained in the Italian manner which subsequently became known as *bel canto*, based on an understanding and control of vocal style. The fact that virtuosity ranked higher than dramatic intensity represents a fundamentally different priority from that of later opera.

From about the third decade of the century Italian *opera seria* was governed by conventions which determined the nature of both music and plot. The reforms of Zeno and Metastasio (*see* Chapter 5) were helpful to composers in that they sought to construct libretti which would permit more unity between plot and music, allowing the development of formal devices which dominated the structure of both. But a rule of order was the dominant feature: the dramatist Goldoni records in his memoirs that his libretto *Amalasunta* was refused by a Milanese opera company in 1733 because it did not conform to the conventions. One of the company's directors explained what was required:

... the three principals ought to sing five airs each, two in the first act, two in the second, and one in the third. The second soprano can have only three, and the inferior characters must be satisfied with a single air each, or two at the most. Take care that two pathetic airs do not succeed each other; distribute with the same caution the bravura airs, the airs of action. Above all, avoid giving impassioned airs or bravura airs to inferior characters.

There were other conventions besides. Characters were to exist upon completion of an aria, the plot had to concern a tragic or heroic event, either classical or historical, and display the high moral actions which flattered the aristocratic patrons. Unhappy endings were rare. In an *opera seria* six main characters were expected, and the issues concerned were political and amorous, that is, public and private, conflicts. The motives involved were to become the fundamental tensions of all opera: inclination versus duty, temptation versus loyalty, courage versus compliance, and as such they appealed to the audience of the day as they were to continue to do when they were adapted within later styles. The story was told through a sequence of *recitativo secco* (voice with harpsichord and string bass), alternating with arias in which solos were accompanied by the orchestra. This procedure was not entirely rigid, however, for occasionally there were sections of *recitativo accompagnato* in which the orchestra was used, or of *arioso*, a fragment of singing in the manner of an aria. Ensembles and choruses were altogether rare. All the musical attention tended to be directed towards the arias, soliloquies in which characters reacted to the situations in which they found themselves. These were in a *da capo* (ABA) form: a first section followed by a middle section of contrasting character, and then a decorated repeat of the first section.

The conventions provided strengths as well as weaknesses, as we can see from Handel's achievements in the field of the *da capo* aria. His development of character is done chiefly through his arias, which prove to be suitably adaptable for the purpose. His *Giulio Cesare* gives us, in the character of Cleopatra, an example of how a succession of solo arias can together portray a fully rounded character, and one in whose fate the audience consequently must take an interest. She teases her tyrannical brother, Ptolemy, with staccato repeated notes and laughing runs; she rejoices in her beauty's power over Caesar and charms him with a love song, '*V'adoro pupille*', in which the accompaniment is provided by an unusual instrumental group including theorbo (a large lute) and harp. Her aria '*Piangerò la sorte mia*' is one of Handel's great melodies. It shows her in mourning and contemplating her misfortunes in its slow outer sections, whereas the middle section brings a complete change of mood and of musical style, as she vows, in more virtuoso music, to haunt Ptolemy after her death.

The *da capo* aria is clearly the mainstay of Handel's operatic style. Yet there are numerous occasions when his formal flexibility transcends the conventions of *opera seria* and looks forward to the later reforms of Gluck. One of the most outstanding examples is the sequence which brings the second act of *Tamerlano* to its close. *Recitativo accompagnato* provides its basis, but there is also, most unusually, a trio for three leading singers, Bajazet (tenor), Andronicus (male alto), and Irene (soprano), who then have fragments of *arioso* before the aria for Asteria (soprano) which closes the act. Such complexities of contrast provide an extended finale which has its own compelling sense of dramatic motion.

The range of music in Handel's *da capo* arias is wide indeed, as befits the emotions the characters portray. Yet the very quantity of them makes complete fidelity in performance difficult: most Handel operas, if performed uncut and with two intervals, would last well over four hours. The pace of life in eighteenth-century London was much slower than it is two centuries later, and performances today need to be carefully pruned if they are to find a new audience. There seems no excuse, however, for the all too frequent practice of cuts in recorded performances.

Ariosos and *ariettas* exist as well as full arias. Their presence gave flexibility to Handel in varying the dramatic situations he explored in his recitatives, in some of which the orchestra is deployed, *ritornello* fashion, as in the use of *tremolando* strings to express the hero's shock at being called a traitor in *Ottone*. The role of the orchestra is often much more than mere accompaniment—some singers, indeed, objected that Handel's instrumental writing took the public's attention away from the vocal line. The textures of Handel's orchestra were dominated by the strings, and the use of wind instruments was sparing, but perhaps consequently more effective. The intervention of a recorder or an oboe or brass instrument lends a special flavour to a scene, for instance Caesar's aria with horn *obbligato* in Act I of *Giulio Cesare*. There is no better example in Handel of his awareness of the potential of the orchestra than the death aria in the final act of *Tolomeo* (1728). At the final repetition of the phrase '*la morte a chiamar*', the composer omits the last notes of the vocal line, allowing the orchestra alone to provide the resolution of melody and harmony.

While the textual language of Handel's operas was Italian, his overtures were of the French type, with a solemn slow introduction followed by a lively rhythmic *allegro*, generally contrapuntal-fugal. The issue for him was merely how he could employ the most suitable material. He had become aware of French models during his years in London, to some extent through his reverence for Purcell, and the weightier French overture was more appropriate than the brilliant Italian *sinfonia* as an introduction to dramas of noble heroism. Although the overtures are not thematically linked to their operas their music is certainly strong enough for them to be able to stand in their own right as concert pieces.

Why did Handel's operas fall into neglect? It seems clear that the chief reason was the subsequent success of his oratorios and instrumental music. This neglect has only been overcome during the twentieth century: as more of these operas have been performed or recorded, so the appropriate staging and performing styles have been developed and a proper awareness of Handel's stature in this field has grown. Casting remains difficult because few singers are capable of the elaborate virtuosity required, and the important *castrato* roles have either to be transposed or sung by a woman or a counter-tenor. However, producers and musicians have found that the static *opera seria* approach can still hold the stage and that these works can display great musical and dramatic diversity. Handel was a composer whose command of the late Baroque style was matched only by Bach, but in opera he was without peer.

5

ITALIAN HIGH BAROQUE AND GLUCK'S REFORMS

Naples and Venice. Opera buffa. *The* castrato. *The Metastasian libretto. The reform of* opera seria.

NAPLES AND VENICE

Opera came late to Naples. This was the Mediterranean city where the Emperor Nero liked to sing, considering it to be 'almost Greek'. Here, according to the French traveller J. J. Lalande, 'the membranes of the eardrum are more taut, more harmonious, more sonorous than elsewhere in Europe [and] the whole nation sings'. However, there was almost no operatic activity there before 1650, when Cavalli's *Didone* may have been performed, to be followed in 1651 by Monteverdi's *L'incoronazione di Poppea* under the title of *Il Nerone*. During the next thirty years, opera was usually imported from Venice, although there was some contribution from local composers. Francesco Provenzale (ca 1626–1704) wrote eight or nine operas for Naples, but only two survive in complete form dating respectively from 1671 and 1678: *Il schiavo di sua moglie* (*His Wife's Slave*) and *Difendere l'offensore* (*The Attacker Defended*). Provenzale used a variety of aria forms in a way that reminds us that *da capo* structure was not yet obligatory. His genial tunes, often dancelike and popular in character, and the close connection between drama and music, make him the first important Neapolitan composer. He was also esteemed as a teacher, and in his time Naples with its four conservatories became a principal centre of musical education.

Opera was largely under the patronage of the successive Spanish viceroys who governed the Kingdom of Naples. They had private theatres at their palace and summer residence, and took a close interest in the public theatres, of which the most important was the Teatro San Bartolomeo. The viceregal *maestro di cappella* also directed the music at San Bartolomeo, and when this post fell vacant in 1684 Provenzale expected to gain it. However, the Viceroy appointed instead a young Sicilian musician, Alessandro Scarlatti.

Scarlatti (1660–1725) studied in Rome. He married in 1678, having by this time acquired the support and protection of important persons, among whom was Queen Christina of Sweden, a patron of the arts who resided in the Palazzo Farnese in Rome from 1655, founded an academy of arts and constructed a private opera house. Scarlatti was only eighteen when he attracted her attention with his first opera, *Gli equivoci nel sembiante* (*Misunderstandings and Appearances*, Rome, 1679), and it was she, together with two cardinals, who defended Scarlatti and other opera composers when Pope Innocent XI decided to discourage public opera performances. She commissioned from the young Scarlatti his second opera, *L'honestà negli amori* (*Sincerity in Love*, Rome, 1680), and he became her *maestro di cappella* until 1684, when the Spanish ambassador to the Vatican, the Marquis de Carpio, became Viceroy of Naples and took Scarlatti there with him.

With Scarlatti, Neapolitan opera gained a new prominence. He had two periods as *maestro di cappella*, from 1684–1702 and 1708–25, and the first of these was especially prolific: indeed more than half the new operas heard in the city were his. He claimed that *Lucio Manlio l'imperioso* (Florence, 1705) was his eighty-eighth opera. His work travelled widely in Italy and abroad: thus *Il Pirro e Demetrio* (Naples, 1694) was to be staged within a few years in Rome, Siena, Florence, Milan, Brunswick (first in Italian, then in German), Leipzig and London, where it ran in a part-English translation for over sixty performances. Such an international success was rare, but it brought no additional income. Scarlatti seems to have been overworked and underpaid in the Neapolitan court — he had to provide other music besides opera, such as serenades and church music, and his salary was usually in arrears — and he may have been discontented with the limitations imposed on him by a court taste that demanded comic scenes even in serious operas. Eventually he decided to leave his post in Naples in search of independent work in other centres, Florence, Venice and Rome. All these cities were glad to commission work from him, but no important permanent post was offered, and he seems to have been relieved to become the assistant *maestro di cappella* at the church of Santa Maria Maggiore in Rome. He wrote to one of his patrons, Prince Ferdinando de' Medici, that 'Rome has no shelter for music, which lives here as a beggar'.

In 1707 the Kingdom of Naples passed from the Spanish court to the Habsburg Empire, and Scarlatti was invited to return to serve the new Austrian viceroy, Cardinal Grimani. Of his later Neapolitan operas, *Il Tigrane* (1715) was the most successful, while *Il trionfo dell'onore* (1718) was his only mature comic opera and *Il Cambise* (1719) his last for the city. He returned to Rome to supervise his *Telemaco* (Rome, 1718), and his

Marco Attilio Regolo followed (Rome, 1719). His last opera, *La Griselda* (Rome, 1721), was commissioned by his Roman patrons and according to his own tally brought his total to 114.

Scarlatti's career established all the main features of *opera seria*, the genre of serious opera that dominates the first half of the eighteenth century in Italy and elsewhere. Handel knew Scarlatti both personally and through his music, and seems to have been influenced by him, notably by the opera *Il Mitridate Eupatore* (Venice, 1707), which is unusual in its degree of detailed craftsmanship, in being called a *tragedia per musica*, and in its use of five acts rather than the usual three. Most of Scarlatti's operas have the designation *dramma per musica*, but it is music and not drama that dominates. Plots concern rulers and their loves and responsibilities together with their attempts to bring about a happy outcome to events. Aria forms are varied in his early work but are increasingly dominated by the *da capo*, while florid vocal writing is designed to display the skill of the *bel canto* masters in the company. Duets, ensembles and choruses are to be found, but are much rarer than solo arias, of which a single opera can have between forty and sixty. Such was the general style of *opera seria* until the time of Gluck's reforms.

A fine example of Scarlatti's vocal writing occurs in the number '*Idolo mio, ti chiamo*' in his *Tito Sempronio Gracco* (Naples, 1702). This is a *siciliano*, a gently flowing melody in a lilting 12/8 rhythm that the composer brought to opera from his native Sicily. It is also an ensemble, marked *aria a quattro*, and more a *da capo* aria for four voices than a quartet with four independent vocal lines. In his later works Scarlatti often closed each act with such an ensemble, and this became common practice after him. Another feature of *Tito* is the orchestration, with its two independent oboe parts. To a basic string group Scarlatti occasionally added extra instruments, such as these oboes, the horns in *Tigrane*, *Telemaco* and *Marco Attilio Regolo*, and the flutes in *Cambise* and *La Griselda*. The early arias have mostly only continuo accompaniment, but later orchestral accompaniments of much contrapuntal interest become the norm. The overture (*sinfonia*) is from about 1695 standardised into a three-section pattern of fast, slow, fast. A short *sinfonia* or interlude may also occur, usually to introduce a particularly grand scene. Numbers are linked mainly by *secco* unadorned recitative, the more elaborate accompanied recitative being reserved for moments of special tension.

By the end of his life, Scarlatti was probably regarded as old-fashioned, for during his last seven years no opera of his was played in Naples. Like J. S. Bach in other realms of music, he was perhaps not primarily an innovator, but rather a creator who sums up an age by consolidating its prevailing genres and providing their best examples. The epitaph on his tomb, possibly by his patron Cardinal Ottoboni, calls him the greatest 'renewer' of music.

Scarlatti's successors in Naples included Leonardo Vinci (ca 1690–1730), of whom the English music historian Dr Burney wrote: 'Vinci seems to have been the first opera composer who . . . without degrading his art, rendered it the friend, though not the slave, of poetry, by simplifying and polishing melody, and calling the attention of the audience chiefly to the voice part, by disentangling it from fugue, complication, and laboured contrivance.' As Burney suggests, Vinci developed vocal writing that is closely responsive to the text, and often intensely expressive in its use of *appoggiaturas* and dotted rhythms. Many of Vinci's *opere serie* texts were by Metastasio, for example *Siroe, Re di Persia* (Venice, 1726), *Alessandro nell'Indie* (Rome, 1729), and *Artaserse* (Rome, 1730). Of his thirty-five operas, eleven were written for other centres than Naples, though his eleven comic operas all had Neapolitan premières. His early death came from 'a sudden colic pain' that carried him off before he even had time to make his confession: perhaps in Italy it was inevitable that some thought him to have been poisoned following upon 'the indiscretions of an amorous intrigue', though a caricature of the time by Pier Leone Ghezzi shows not a charming young gallant but a rather unhandsome figure, squat and hook-nosed. Vinci's reputation did not die with him. *Artaserse* was given in Naples eight years after his death, and the same opera was selected to inaugurate a new Dresden opera house in 1746.

Leonardo Leo (1694–1744) was to become *maestro di cappella* of the Neapolitan court chapel and composed sacred music as well as being a distinguished teacher. Although a slow worker he also wrote over fifty operas—even though a guard once had to be posted outside his door to make him finish an opera on time. He made effective use of the chorus in the 1742–3 revivals of his operas *Il Ciro riconosciuto* (Turin, 1739) and *Olimpiade* (Naples, 1737). *Il Ciro* contains an aria, *'Non so con dolce moto'*, which as late as 1782 was described by the German composer and writer Johann Friedrich Reichardt as 'sublime, irresistible' in its portrayal of the tears of 'a resolute father faced with the suffering of his innocent child'. *Andromaca* (Naples, 1742) takes the story of Andromache, the wife of the Trojan Hector whose son was put to death by the victorious Greeks. Several scenes go some way towards matching the dramatic power of Euripides and Racine in their treatment of the story, and this *opera seria* may be among the finer achievements in the genre.

The life of Giovanni Battista Pergolesi (1710–36) was even shorter than that of Vinci, and Ghezzi's caricature of him is no more flattering. He was the son of a surveyor, a delicate child who grew up with a limp and perhaps a deformed left leg, and went to Naples at about the age of twelve, where Vinci was among his teachers. As a gifted choirboy and violinist, he was soon noticed and finally he made his mark in 1631 by composing a 'sacred drama' on the life of St William of Aquitaine which was given in the monastery of San Agnello Maggiore. The surprising feature about such a work as this was that it was expected to contain comic scenes, and Pergolesi's is no exception. Posterity has judged that his skill lay especially in comedy, though his life was no laughing matter: he seems to have been dogged by illness, possibly tuberculosis, and he died in a monastery at twenty-six. In *opera seria* he could not match the achievements of his more mature predecessors, but he composed four: *Salustia* (Naples, 1732), *Il prigioner superbo* (Naples 1733), *Adriano in Siria* (Naples, 1734) and *L'Olimpiade* (Rome, 1735). Of these, the last two have Metastasio texts, while *Il prigioner superbo* was the opera to accompany which he wrote the comic intermezzo *La serva padrona* (*The Maid as Mistress*) upon which his fame today chiefly rests. (*See* also below and Chapter 3). Another comic opera was his *Lo frate 'nnamorato* (*The Amorous Friar*, Naples, 1732), which achieved such success that following a long run it was 'sung in the city streets for twenty years'. Not all Pergolesi's operas succeeded at first, but after his death fame came rapidly. Queen Maria Amalia, the ruler of Naples in 1738, demanded that *La serva padrona* and another intermezzo called *La contadina astuta* (*The Cunning Peasant Woman*, Rome, 1734) should be performed, saying 'this composer is dead, but he was a great man,' and the French writer Charles de Brosses called Pergolesi his favourite composer, '*mon auteur d'affection*'.

Despite the growing importance of Naples, Venice nevertheless remained the major operatic centre in Italy. By the end of the eighteenth century there were nineteen opera houses there, which commissioned new works each season, while Naples by contrast saw a mere three or four new operas a year. When the writer and adventurer Casanova was short of money, he turned to the one form of employment easily obtained in Venice, playing in theatre orchestras. Each Venetian theatre, as we have already seen in Chapter 2, was owned by one or more noblemen, who did not always make money from the enterprise: one contemporary called them 'rich people who by banding together bring honour on themselves through making sacrifices for their compatriots' entertainment'. The fees demanded by singers, especially the *castrati*, kept costs high, and these were more again if a chorus, ballet, or extra singers—say for an intermezzo—were needed. Composers in Venice came more cheaply, but there was little chance of increasing box office revenue since competition between theatres kept the ticket prices very low. The chief operatic season was Carnival, the period from 26 December to Shrove Tuesday when Venetians wore masks. The preceding autumn season, from early October to mid-December, was usually devoted to spoken comedy, though an occasional opera was given. Private operatic performances in the gardens and palaces of the aristocracy continued throughout the year.

To supply such a demand for music—besides opera, sacred and instrumental music abounded—there was a host of talented composers, who were doubtless more prolific than profound as the situation demanded, concerned to make a living rather than earn immortality. Such men as Luca Antonio Predieri, Antonio Zanettini, Giovanni Maria Ruggieri, Fortunato Chelleri and Giuseppe Maria Orlandini are now remembered by their names only, if even that. However, more lasting fame was earned by three other composers: Gasparini, Lotti and Vivaldi.

Francesco Gasparini (1668–1727) wrote over sixty stage works, comic and serious, twenty-four of them in Venice before 1713, in which year the composer moved to Rome. He was one of the first Italians to have operas performed in London, including his Hamlet opera *Ambleto* (Venice 1705, London 1712). Gasparini's style is essentially seventeenth-century Venetian, with arias accompanied by *continuo* bass and, at least in his earlier operas, in *da capo* form; more elaborate string accompaniments occur in his *Tamerlano* (Venice, 1710).

Antonio Lotti (1667–1740) continued the style of his teacher Legrenzi, and began his operatic career in Venice with his *opera seria Il trionfo dell'innocenza* (Venice, 1692). In 1717 he was invited to the Dresden court, where two of his operas—*Giove in Argo* and *Ascanio*—were given (1717, 1718) and his *Teofane* opened the Neues Opernhaus (1719). In the autumn of the same year he returned to Venice and, for reasons that are not clear, abandoned opera in favour of sacred music.

The forty-odd operas of Antonio Vivaldi (1678–1741) were written between 1713 and 1739, mostly for his native Venice. About half of them survive in score, even if sometimes incomplete, but they are still virtually unknown to the public despite the composer's popularity in other fields of music. The scholar Michael Talbot writes in his book on the composer (1978):

> Despite their many beautiful moments, Vivaldi's operas cannot lay claim to the historical importance of his concertos. Yet the vigour, complexity and variety of their instrumental writing, especially in the works of the first decade (1713–23), set a fashion for his older

contemporaries. Had he begun to write his operas earlier, or had the rise of the Neapolitans occurred later, their orchestra-dominated style might have established itself more firmly. Though he continued after the critical period around 1725 to produce innovations, these never became consolidated into a 'late-period' style. A work like *Catone in Utica* betrays a self-consciousness foreign to the early operas . . . the malaise of a composer whose ambition has outlasted his capacity for self-renewal.

However, recent recordings may well presage a revival. *Orlando furioso* (Venice, 1727) has been restaged and recorded, and recordings are also available of *L'Incoronazione di Dario* (Venice, 1717) and *Catone in Utica* (Verona, 1737).

OPERA BUFFA

Venetian opera in the seventeenth century featured an interweaving of comic and serious elements. As the century drew to a close, the comic scenes became more independent, developing into true *intermezzi* or interludes that could be performed apart from the rest. Serious characters gradually came to be omitted from the final scene of an act in such a way that comic servants had it to themselves and it became a kind of contrasting entr'acte. Eventually these entr'actes, often composed by a different musician from the main work, separated altogether to form a brief independent comedy. At the same time, opera librettists led by the Venetian intellectual Apostolo Zeno (1668–1750) were aiming to exclude comedy altogether from their libretti. Comic scenes tended to take the characters and conventions of *opera seria* as their target, and the high-minded Arcadian movement (*see* below) had no place for this. A separate but analogous development took place in Naples in 1709, with a first season of operatic comedies in local dialect that reflected the lives of ordinary people. The *intermezzi* performed between the acts of serious opera were not in dialect, however, and so were more acceptable in other centres. Thus Pergolesi's non-dialect *La serva padrona* had an international success that was denied to his dialect *buffo* operas.

A principal influence on the development of *opera buffa* was the *commedia dell'arte* or 'artisan comedy', also known as 'comedy of masks' and 'improvised comedy'. It flourished in Italy, especially Venice and Naples, from the early sixteenth century until the latter part of the eighteenth, and spread from Venice all over Europe, influencing even Shakespeare and Molière among other playwrights. In Italy, however, the literary establishment regarded it with a certain disdain as a mere improvised entertainment for unlettered working people. The *commedia* players, descendants of the Roman street entertainers called *joculatores*, were professional actors relying on skill, wit and the fact that the characters and situations they portrayed were always the same and well-known to the audience. The characters were masked and their gestures, costumes and accessories stylised. The action was fast and based on a short scenario with everyone either improvising the lines or using stock expected responses. Topical issues were brought in, jokes were coarse, and there were songs, dances and acrobatics. At its vital best, *commedia dell'arte* was superb theatre. Its stock characters included Pantalone, a lecherous old merchant who dotes on an only daughter Columbina, the learned but gullible Doctor Graziano in academic garb speaking pompous absurdities, the boastful Scaramuccia, the clown Pedrolino and the *zanni* or lowly and 'zany' characters—the male servants Arlecchino and Pulcinella. Their descendants can be recognised in the few *opere buffe* that are performed today, such as those which Mozart and Rossini based on Beaumarchais, *The Marriage of Figaro* and *The Barber of Seville*, and in modern Punch (that is, Pulcinella) and Judy shows and pantomimes.

The original *commedia dell'arte* was reformed and refined in the eighteenth century by the Venetian playwright Carlo Goldoni (1707–93), who in the late 1740s persuaded some of its actors to relinquish their masks and let him provide them with written dialogue. Goldoni also wrote libretti for *opere buffe* such as Galuppi's *Il mondo della luna* (*The World of the Moon*) and thus brought the vigorous spirit of the *commedia* into the opera house. His texts provided simplicity and directness of plot, a diminution of mere recitative in favour of more set musical 'numbers' including songs (arias and *ariettas*, the latter lacking *da capo* repeats), and lovers' duets and big final ensembles. That this was due to Goldoni rather than any composer is borne out by a contemporary Italian's description of him as 'the foremost inventor of finales'. Goldoni also made provision for fine and elaborate scenery and choreography. This newly independent Italian comic opera dispensed with spoken dialogue, which distinguishes it from English ballad opera and French *opéra comique*, and it was *secco* recitative rather than speech that separated the more elaborate numbers. The pace of the *commedia* tradition and the ability of the Italian language to communicate at speed, punctuated only by a few harpsichord chords, made *opera buffa* the dominant type of comic music theatre for a century, until the death of Donizetti in 1848. Between 1749 and 1761 Venice saw nearly seventy new comic operas, and during the century nearly 2,000 such works were presented in Italy.

Several of Goldoni's libretti were set by Baldassare Galuppi (1706–85), a pupil of Lotti and the finest of the Venetian comic opera composers. Like Goldoni's stage plays, they dealt with lower and middle-class life and guyed the aristocracy. But though Goldoni's plays are acknowledged masterpieces, the modern view of the Galuppi operas based on them is not very sympathetic, finding them musically thin (*see* page 85) though Dr Burney admired the man—'intelligent and agreeable . . . very much the look of a gentleman'—and the music. Besides earning artistic admiration from Burney and fellow composers such as C. P. E. Bach and Salieri, Galuppi won riches and renown, and his *Il filosofo di campagna* (*The Country Philosopher*, Venice, 1754), with its Goldoni libretto, achieved such a success that a modern scholar has called it 'the world's first full-length hit show'. In fact Galuppi also composed serious operas including an *Idomeneo* (Rome, 1756) and an *Ifigenia in Tauride* (St Petersburg, 1768)—the latter written when he obtained leave from his post as *maestro di cappella* at St Mark's in Venice to work for three years as *maestro* for the chapel of the Empress Catherine the Great in St Petersburg, staging other Italian works besides his own and thus reminding us of opera's ability to spread far and wide. But it is on his comedies that his importance rests. *Il mondo della luna* (Venice, 1750) was widely known, and its Goldoni libretto was later used by others including Paisiello and Haydn. In *opera buffa* a composer was freer to experiment than in serious opera, and Galuppi and Piccinni (*see* Chapter 6) were among the first to compose the extended multi-section ensemble that closed an act. Such finales gradually came to embrace more and more of the material that would normally have been set in recitative, thus demanding a more sophisticated musical organisation. A convincing scenario such as Goldoni provided was essential, bringing all the characters on stage for the composer to have several different vocal types to work with.

Opera buffa had one great musical advantage over *opera seria*: the latter was largely music for virtuoso high voices, but the former, with no *castrato* roles, and with singers usually less skilled, had to develop musical interest by combining voices and using extended forms. Since lower voices were much used, a full range of vocal types was employed and—though arias were not neglected—the heart of *opera buffa* was ensemble singing.

THE *CASTRATO*

The performance of *opera seria* centred on the *castrati*, male singers whose vocation was irrevocably chosen, but for whom the rewards for an early sacrifice not of their choosing might be great. Their training was thorough and rigorous. At a conservatory in Venice or Naples, the regime typically consisted not only of singing exercises but also of acting, diction, music theory and composition. An opera composer could trust the finest *castrati* to embellish his music convincingly with ornaments—runs, trills and the like—in the repeat of a *da capo* aria, and might well seek technical advice from a leading singer for whom he was writing a role.

A *castrato* voice had the purity of a boy's allied to the power of a man's. Its volume was not arrested by the operation performed in early boyhood, but grew, and exercises increased lung capacity so that its owner could sustain notes longer than most men. Of the *castrato* Pauluccio an observer wrote: 'Besides that his voice was higher than anyone else's, it has all the warblings of a nightingale, but with only this difference, that it was much finer; and did not a man know to the contrary, he would believe it impossible such a tone could proceed from the throat of anything that was human.' Castration affected not only the voice: these singers typically became both taller and broader than other men. They were able to enjoy some aspects of erotic life and a number of them married, despite a Church ban on such unions. In the theatre a *castrato* could look splendid in the role of a hero or ruler. However, in some cases the condition also produced a physical awkwardness. As one London observer remarked of Farinelli (1705–82):

> What a pipe! What modulation! What ecstasy to the ear! But heavens, what clumsiness ... If thou art within the environs of St James thou must have observed in the park with what ease and agility a cow, heavy with calf, has arose up at the command of a milk-woman's foot: thus from the mossy bank sprang up the divine Farinelli.

But musically there was only praise, and another London critic wrote in 1734: 'Farinelli was a revelation to me, for I realised that till I had heard him I had heard only a small part of what human song can achieve.' His portrait painted in the same year by Bartolomeo Nazzari shows a sensitive face and handsome well-dressed figure. It was Farinelli who sang for King Philip V of Spain, who was suffering from depression. 'Philip appeared at first surprised, then moved,' wrote Dr Burney, and 'asked him how he could sufficiently reward such talents, assuring him that he would refuse him nothing. Farinelli ... only begged that His Majesty would permit his attendants to shave and dress him, and that he would endeavour to appear in council as usual. From that time the king's disease gave way to medicine, and the singer had all the honour of the cure.' In his retirement Farinelli was visited by such celebrities as Gluck, Mozart, Casanova and the Austrian Emperor Joseph II, and he died rich and universally honoured.

The wealth and prestige of another *castrato*, Nicolini (ca 1673–1732), is symbolised by his salary in London, where he signed a three-year contract in 1709 for an annual income of 800 guineas plus £150 for each opera he adapted for the English stage, a sum corresponding to some £100,000 in today's currency. Burney called Nicolini 'this great singer, and still greater actor', and the *Tatler* correspondent declared that 'every Limb, and every Finger, contributes to the part he acts'. Joseph Addison wrote in the *Spectator* that this was 'the greatest performer in dramatic Music that is now living, or that perhaps ever appeared on a stage'. A contemporary caricature shows Nicolini as grossly obese, but Handel composed the title roles of *Rinaldo* and *Amadigi di Gaula* for him.

The very nature of the *castrato* voice affected the course of operatic history. The fabulous agility of the best of these singers led composers to write in a brilliant, florid style that was expected by the artist and audience alike. Beyond this, the ability of a good *castrato* to improvise led to the *da capo* aria becoming standard, with the reprise of the first section providing him with the opportunity for spontaneous and sensational vocal display. As for the written musical text, if a star singer found that not to his liking he could make the composer alter or replace it. Indeed the composer was often a humbler person in the operatic firmament than a singer, or indeed an impresario, rather as the author of a play or film may be obscured today when his work becomes a showcase for star actors. Thus the mezzo-soprano Faustina Bordoni received a fee twice as much as that of her husband, the composer Hasse, when his opera *Cleofide* (Dresden, 1731) was first performed—a performance, incidentally, which J. S. Bach probably attended.

Women's roles in *opera seria*, however, were mostly taken by young *castrati*, while leading male roles alike used the same type of voice. No fashionable present-day search for authenticity can restore this particular sound—barring drastic measures that not even musicologists seriously contemplate!—and for that reason modern performances of Baroque *opera seria* must miss a central feature of its former glory. Conversely, the other types of voice were neglected. Standard male registers including the tenor, and women singers, where women were used at all, were usually confined to minor roles. Vocal treatises in the eighteenth century mostly deal with the instruction of '*un soprano*', in other words the *castrato* voice. Only a very few outstanding female singers like Faustina Bordoni (1700–

81) could be heard in principal roles, for example in her husband's operas performed at the Dresden court between 1731 and 1751. However, one gifted contralto, Vittoria Tesi (1700–75), became renowned in both female and male roles—such as that of Achilles in Jommelli's *Achille in Sciro* (Vienna, 1749)—thus completing the sexual confusion of *opera seria*. Later in life she was a teacher, was visited by Mozart and Casanova, and received the title of *virtuosa della corte imperiale* to the Austrian court.

THE METASTASIAN LIBRETTO

A Baroque opera libretto had a life independent of any one musical setting of it, and the best texts were set many times. In the seventeenth century, the heroic opera libretti by such popular writers as Nicolò Minato and Silvio Stampigli often had complex plots, but at the end of the century a new simplicity came into vogue, largely as a result of the so-called Arcadian movement. 'Arcadia' suggests a pastoral idyll, and societies with this name were founded in Rome in 1690 and then in other Italian cities dedicated to the revitalisation of Italian vernacular poetry. The movement was taken seriously, and was durable. Before leaving Rome in 1753 for a post in Stuttgart, the successful and well-established composer Nicolò Jommelli became a member of an Arcadian Academy in Rome under the improbably 'pastoral' name of Anfione Eteoclide. It may be regarded as part of a process of reform towards simplicity that was taking place and in which Jommelli himself was to play a part, as we shall see. Many aspects of *opera seria* at this time derive from the movement, in particular the heroic and pastoral settings and a dignity owing as much to the French classical drama of Corneille and Racine as to the Greek tragedians.

The librettist's role was given a new status by the work of Apostolo Zeno (1668–1750), whose first opera text, *Gl'inganni felici* (*The Fortunate Deceptions*), appeared in 1695 and was set by Pollarolo. Zeno was a Venetian and from 1718 to 1729 he was court poet to the Emperor Charles VI in Vienna. As an historian, he was familiar with the works of Thucydides and Herodotus and based several of his plots on them. As Corneille did in France, Zeno provided situations in which his contemporaries could find models of aristocratic behaviour, and at the imperial and princely courts *opera seria* became an elaborate artistic sycophancy as some Roman emperor or the great Alexander showed superhuman qualities of courage, loyalty and clemency. Zeno reduced the number of characters in opera and excluded comic scenes. The drama is always one of character rather than situation, the story being carried forward in *secco* recitative with the personalities explored in solo arias.

Although the arias were fewer than before, solo vocal numbers still remain more numerous than duets and ensembles. Fifteen of Zeno's thirty-five libretti were written with a collaborator, Pietro Pariati, who seems to have exercised a skill in versification while Zeno constructed the narrative.

Zeno was succeeded as Viennese court poet in 1729 by Pietro Trapassi (1698–1782), known as Metastasio, the adopted son of a Roman jurist and scholar who inherited sufficient wealth to abandon his legal studies and become a poet. He moved into opera in his mid-twenties and soon produced his first original libretto, for Domenico Sarro's *Didone abbandonata* (Naples, 1724). His genuine interest in music was a strength and he actually composed his libretti seated at a keyboard; for a later writer, Stendhal, 'he never conceived his poetry save in the context of music'. At the same time, Italians still consider him one of the great figures in literature. Metastasio was enormously popular among composers, and some of his texts were set sixty times or more, sometimes more than once by the same composer. We have already seen in Chapter 4 how strict the conventions of *opera seria* became, with a kind of 'pecking order' of exit arias arranged to reflect the relative importance of the singers. Metastasio's skill lay in creating drama which observed all these conventions but could still move an audience. He also flouted convention on occasion: thus his version of Queen Dido's story mentioned above has a tragic ending, as does *Catone in Utica* – an opera set not only by Vivaldi (*see* above) but also, among others, by Vinci, Leo, Hasse, Rinaldo da Capua, Graun, Jommelli, Johann Christian Bach and Paisiello. The Metastasio libretti, twenty-seven in all, are without exception in three acts. Mozart was to set two of them, compressed into a two-act form: *Il rè pastore* and *La clemenza di Tito*.

Metastasio's recitative is mostly in unrhymed lines of varying metre, with turns of phrase as stereotyped as the plots. It is in the arias that we can see why he was the leading poet of his day. These are commonly in two short-lined quatrains, just enough text for the *da capo* form. A favourite type was the 'simile aria', where a person compares his situation to some natural phenomenon. In *Ezio*—to be set by Hasse, Handel and Gluck among others—a man confronting his fate is compared to a ship breasting the waves:

Finche un zeffiro soave	As long as a gentle breeze
Tien del mar l'ira placata	Placates the angry ocean
Ogni nave e fortunata	Every ship is fortunate
E felice ogni nocchier	And each pilot is happy.

E ben prova di coraggio	It is a great test of courage
Incontrar l'onde funeste	To confront the deadly waves
Navigar fra le tempeste	To sail through the tempests
E non perdere il sentier	And not stray from one's path.

The rigidity of the *opera seria* conventions, and the vapidity of some of the music and words hastily written by lesser artists, attracted criticism. Benedetto Marcello's celebrated satire on eighteenth-century opera, *Il teatro alla moda* (1720), has a Swiftian mixture of absurdity and deadly accuracy, yet the effect is not savage but essentially tolerant and even affectionate. In this 'safe and easy Method of properly composing and producing Italian Operas according to modern practice', advice is first given to a poet, who is counselled to 'write the whole opera without formulating any plot', so that the public may remain curious to the end. In treating with impresarios, he must not inquire into the merits of the actors, but ask instead 'if the impresario will have a good bear, a good lion, a good nightingale, good thunderbolts, earthquakes, lightning flashes etc'. Furthermore, if an author finds nothing to praise in his dedicatee, he will say that he is silent 'in order not to offend the modesty of his patron, but that Fame with her hundred sonorous trumpets will sound his immortal name from pole to pole. Finally he will end by saying, in token of his most profound veneration, that he kisses the jumps of the fleas on the feet on His Excellency's dog.' He must not allow a singer to leave the stage 'without singing the customary *canzonetta*, especially when by a vicissitude of the drama the latter must go out to die, commit suicide, drink poison etc.' Similarly, 'if a husband and wife should be in prison and one of them should go out to die, the other must inevitably stay behind to sing an *arietta*. The words of this should be lively, to relieve the sadness of the audience and make them understand that it is all in fun.'

As for the composer of opera, Marcello tells us that 'he will have little facility in reading and still less in writing, [and] will take care never to read the whole opera to avoid getting confused, but will set it line by line'. He should ensure that the arias are alternately lively and pathetic without regard to the words. To keep singers in tune, *ariettas* should be accompanied by unison violins; as for duets or choruses, he will contrive to have them omitted. 'In walking with singers, especially *castrati*, the composer will always place himself at their left and keep one step behind, hat in hand, remembering that the lowest of them is in the operas at least a general . . .' He will 'make use of old arias composed in other countries'. If in spite of all these precautions an impresario should complain about his music, the composer must protest that his opera 'took almost fifty hours to compose'.

The pertinence of Marcello's observations seems reflected in the view the English critic Lionel Salter took in 1982 of Galuppi's comic opera *L'Arcadia in Brenta* (Venice, 1749). He found it 'depressingly thin musically, with interminable stretches of recitative, practically all the arias primitively scored with the violins perpetually in unison with the voice . . .'

Joking aside, much Italian Baroque opera may be inaccessible to modern taste because we now tend to regard quality and individuality of the music as the chief claims on our attention. Marcello's satire tells us that such craft and individuality was far less common than simple conformity to the requirements of public taste. Music was only one element in the operatic show and might be little more than a routine provision. Singers' skills in vocal display, text, costumes and scenery were as important as the written notes and at times more so. Because today the history of opera has largely been taken over by historians of music, it is often forgotten that people might go mainly to enjoy the latest Metastasio text, to admire the vocal art of Farinelli or Bordoni, to marvel at animals, or intricate machinery, or a stage design by Ferdinando Galli-Bibiena that featured his device of *scena per angolo* or angular perspective. But at the Viennese court where Metastasio and the Galli-Bibiena brothers Ferdinando and Francesco worked, opera did at least aim at a high level of quality in all its elements, music included, and foreshadowed the bringing together of all the arts that was to be summed up in Wagner's ideal of the *Gesamtkunstwerk*. However, while in Wagner's vision all contributed to a total effect of drama, Baroque opera was only rarely more than the sum of its parts—at least until the coming of Gluck.

THE REFORM OF *OPERA SERIA*

Marcello's satire on opera was one of the first manifestations of a movement towards reform that gathered momentum during the middle years of the eighteenth century. Francesco Algarotti's *Saggio sopra l'opera in musica* (*Essay upon Opera*) was published in 1755 and translated into English, German and French—an indication of the international character of opera and of a widespread feeling that change was needed. Algarotti wrote that music had 'degenerated from its former dignity . . . through a distempered passion for novelty'. He deplored the musical and dramatic poverty of the *secco* recitative of *opera seria* and urged musicians to return to the expressive monody of Peri and the other founders of opera, using an orchestral accompaniment to the voice. Decorative features of vocal ornamentation in arias, 'sober and judicious' in Scarlatti, were now excessive and 'all bounds of discretion are wantonly overleapt'. The 'skirmishing of voices and instruments' in arias with *obbligato* oboe or trumpet might earn 'peals of applause [but was] very displeasing to the judicious part of the audience'. There was a need, Algarotti concluded, to associate with 'all the gracefulness and charms of the modern the chaste correctness of the old music'.

Musicians were deaf to this plea, because Italian audiences did not share the views of the reformers. Significantly, the first two Italian composers to pursue a new approach in *opera seria* did so in foreign centres. Nicolò Jommelli (1714–74) trained in Naples but did his important work for the Duke of Württemberg's court at Stuttgart, where he wrote twenty *opere serie*, including several Metastasio settings. The Duke had developed a taste for opera in Paris, and a fine new theatre was completed at Stuttgart in 1750. His *Ober-Kapellmeister* was able to attract the best singers, players, dancers and designers, and his orchestra grew in time to nearly fifty in number, with double woodwind, brass and percussion—as well as, rather anachronistically, a lute. In Jommelli's operas arias still predominate, but in *Pelope* and *Enea nel Lazio* (both 1755) there are also richly accompanied recitatives, numerous vivid ensembles—the quintet in *Enea* has been especially praised—and spectacular finales. By the time of his last Stuttgart operas, *Vologeso* (1766) and *Fetonte* (a second setting of the same plot, though with a new libretto, 1768), little of the old *secco* recitative remains, and the same is true of his last of four settings of *Demofoonte* (Naples, 1770). But such a style was not to Neapolitan taste; interestingly, even Mozart at the age of fourteen found Jommelli's *Armida abbandonata*, also produced in the San Carlo theatre in the same year, 'beautiful, but much too clever and old-fashioned for the theatre'. In the same letter to his sister he added that the singing was fine and the theatre beautiful, but the dances 'wretchedly pompous'.

In his later operas, Jommelli broke the domination of *da capo* form in arias in favour of freer structures, some in a two-part form, in other words without a repeat section. No longer is an aria confined to a single 'affection' or mood. Shorter *arietta* numbers break up recitative and intensify emotion. The final trio of the later setting of *Fetonte*, writes the scholar Marita Petzoldt McClymonds, 'is the most extensive spectacle scene in all Jommelli's work: an action ensemble of a type usually found only in comic opera, it combines *obbligato* recitative, *arioso* [a style between recitative and aria], ensemble and chorus with a programmatic orchestral representation of a catastrophe'.

Tommaso Traetta (1727–79) studied like Jommelli in Naples but did his main work elsewhere: at the Bourbon court of the duchy of Parma from 1758, where he first encountered reformist ideas, and later for other centres such as Mannheim, Vienna, St Petersburg and London—writing his *Germondo* (1776) for the English capital. In Parma the Intendant Guillaume du Tillot wished to unite features of French *tragédie lyrique* with Italian *opera seria* and had Rameau's *Hippolyte et Aricie* translated and reset by Traetta as *Ippolito ed Aricia* (Parma, 1759). Traetta had access to Rameau's score, and the new work was judged epoch-making by Algarotti, who attended the performances. Similarly, *I Tintaridi* (Parma, 1760) was based on Rameau's *Castor et Pollux*. Here and later, Traetta showed an ability to innovate—at least in terms of Italian *opera seria*—in instrumentation, structure, the use of ensemble and chorus, and key sequences such as the flat keys that give way to E minor in *Antigone* (St Petersburg, 1772). His overture to *Sofonisba* (Mannheim, 1762) fore-shadows the drama in mood and even uses a theme that recurs in the quintet closing the final Act III.

In his *Ifigenia in Tauride* (Vienna, 1763), Traetta also shows his debt to Gluck, whose *Orfeo ed Euridice* had been written for the same city in the previous year. There were further links between the two men: the *castrato* Gaetano Guadagni sang Gluck's role of Orfeo and Traetta's Orestes, and Gluck himself conducted *Ifigenia* in Florence in 1767. In *Antigone*, the protagonist's lament and invocation of the Furies in Act II owes much to Gluck, while in a later *buffo* piece, *Il cavaliero errante* (place of première unknown, 1778), he actually parodied the famous *Orfeo* aria '*Che farò*'. In *Ifigenia* the influence of Rameau is also evident in the '*O come presto a sera*' in Act II expressing the people's compassion for Orestes. The graceful and flowing '*Non piangete*' aria in Act III of *Antigone* has its ornamentation written out, in other words it was no longer left to the singer, and has rightly been described by Professor Grout as 'distinctly Mozartean'. In the funeral lament in Act II of the same opera, Traetta rose to the challenge of providing music worthy not only of Euripides' tragedy but also of the chorus of the St Petersburg Imperial Chapel.

Gian Francesco Majo (1732–70) set texts by Zeno and Metastasio, and also by the reformer Marco Coltellini who provided the text for Traetta's *Antigone*. Coltellini had succeeded Metastasio as court poet in Vienna, where the reform movement was now centred, and he provided the libretto for the opera *Alcide negli orti Esperidi* (*Alcide in the Hesperides*, Vienna, 1764). Majo also composed an *Ifigenia in Tauride* (Mannheim, 1764) and an *Antigono* (Venice, 1767). Confusingly, he also wrote an *Antigona* (Rome, 1768), and the three spellings listed above for the name of this strong-willed daughter of King Oedipus—Antigone in French and English—are those which were used by the respective librettists. In *Ifigenia in Tauride* Majo relates the overture programmatically with what is to follow in a way that was now becoming standard. There are many ensembles and choruses, and his arias feature little coloratura display. Yet they are flexible and chromatic in a way that may have influenced Mozart, who called Majo's last opera *Eumene* (unfinished and completed by Giacomo Insanguine and Pasquale Errichelli, Naples, 1771) '*bellissimo*' in a letter to his sister.

Christoph Willibald Gluck (1714–87), the chief figure among the operatic reformers of the eighteenth century, began his career in the conventional Metastasian manner. He was born in Bohemia of German stock and had a patchy musical education in Prague. He then went to Vienna at about the age of twenty and a year or so later became a violinist in Prince Antonio Melzi's orchestra in Milan, where he may have studied with the composer Giovanni Battista Sammartini. He made his operatic debut with *Artaserse* (Milan, 1741) to a Metastasio libretto, and then pursued a nomadic career for some years, writing fifteen more operas by 1752. In that year, now married to a banker's daughter, he settled in Vienna, obtaining directorships of the Burgtheater and Kärntnertor Theater and later a post in the household of the Imperial field-marshal, the Prince of Saxe-Hildburghausen, with whom he seems to have enjoyed a genuine friendship. French *opéra comique* was imported to the Burgtheater under Gluck's auspices and as a result of the enthusiasm of Count Giacomo Durazzo, the official Viennese 'director of spectacles' from 1754, and Gluck himself produced a first Viennese *opéra comique* in *La fausse esclave* (*The Pretended Slave*, Vienna, 1758), following it with others. Durazzo, a Genoese, led an anti-Metastasio faction at the court, desiring a more natural blend of music and drama than *opera seria* allowed, and others of like mind included the ballet master Gaspero Angiolini and the stage engineer Giovanni Maria Quaglio. Angiolini choreographed the first work of this group, Gluck's ballet *Don Juan, ou le festin de pierre* (*Don Juan, or The Stone Banquet*, Vienna, 1761), with its sets by Quaglio, and the same two men collaborated in Gluck's opera *Orfeo ed Euridice* (Vienna, 1762).

Orfeo, described as an *azione teatrale per musica*, was a milestone in the movement towards reform, and its subject was surely a deliberate choice in its aptness. The librettist was Raniero de Calzabigi, a poet and, according to Casanova, 'a great lover of women' who before departing from Vienna in 1772 in the wake of an amorous scandal provided Gluck with the texts of his three major reform operas, the others being *Alceste* (Vienna, 1767) and *Paride ed Elena* (Vienna, 1770). In some ways *Orfeo ed*

Euridice was a cautious beginning. The overture is a conventional curtain-raiser and the main role was written for a *castrato*—though Guadagni was an exceptional one who had studied acting with David Garrick. However, Calzabigi's libretto concentrates on emotions and avoids stereotypes. The action is stripped of superfluities and the ballets and choruses are dramatically relevant. While Jommelli's *Fetonte* had had up to ten scenes in an act, Calzabigi's concentration on essentials reduced the number to two. A certain static feeling in these great tableau-like scenes is perhaps a tribute also to the Viennese audience, who it was felt could dispense with regular virtuoso diversions and could absorb themselves in the passions depicted.

The *Orfeo* score has clear and radical features. Because the dominance of the aria has gone, each of the long scenes tends towards greater musical unity. There is little vocal coloratura, for melodies are strong enough to stand in unadorned simplicity—not least the famous lament '*Che farò senza Euridice*' sung by Orpheus after the loss of his wife. The heart is touched where perhaps before the ear was merely tickled; and the same may be said of the serene flute solo in the 'Dance of the blessed spirits' in the Elysian Fields. The chorus is involved in the drama and blossoms as a consequence. Recitative, as Algarotti recommended, is always accompanied by the orchestra, which is itself given a new significance with tone colour a fundamental device. Thus there is the sound of Orpheus's harp, the colour of the flute with its antique associations, and the trombones to lend authority and mystery to supernatural scenes.

What we call Gluck's reforms are more fairly to be described as the fruit of collaboration rather than his work alone. He was a professional composer who provided music in the style appropriate to circumstances, and his next operas were again more conventional, as in the Metastasian *Il trionfo di Clelia* (Bologna, 1763) and the *comédie mêlée d'ariettes La rencontre imprévue* (*The Unforeseen Meeting*, Vienna, 1764). It was five years before he again collaborated with Calzabigi in *Alceste* (Vienna, 1767). When it was published two years later, it was given a preface by the composer, in which Calzabigi may have had a hand, which is a major statement of reform:

> I have striven to restrict music to its true office of serving poetry by means of expression and by following the situations of a story, without interrupting the action or stifling it with a useless superfluity of ornaments; . . . thus I did not wish to arrest an actor in the greatest heat of dialogue in order to wait for a tiresome *ritornello* . . . nor to make a display of the agility of his fine voice in some lengthy passage, nor to wait while the orchestra gives him time to recover his breath

for a cadenza. I did not think it my duty to pass quickly over the second section of an aria of which the words are perhaps the most impassioned and important, in order to repeat regularly four times over those of the first part . . . in short, I have tried to abolish all the abuses against which good sense and reason have long cried out in vain.

Gluck felt that an overture 'ought to apprise the spectators of the nature of the action to be represented', and in this respect *Alceste* is an advance on *Orfeo*, with an overture foreshadowing the drama and leading into the first scene. The gravity of this scene in which an oracle announces that Admetus, King of Thessaly, will die unless a voluntary human sacrifice is made gave Mozart a hint for the solemnities of *Die Zauberflöte*, and it is only one of many passages achieving what Gluck called his aim of 'beautiful simplicity'. The phrase echoes that of the art historian Winckelmann, whose *History of the Art of the Ancients* (1764) stated that the essential quality of Greek art was a 'noble simplicity and calm grandeur'. The neo-classical movement of this time influenced all the arts, and Gluck's statuesque musical manner seems the operatic counterpart of some antique ceremony in a temple on the Aegean shore. *Orfeo ed Euridice* retains traces of the old *opera seria* conventions, and *Paride ed Elena* makes some compromise with it—the lighter story of Paris's wooing of Helen perhaps leads to an excess of ballet and recitative, and a *castrato* Paris is hardly reformist. It is above all *Alceste* that remains the noblest testament to the ideas of Algarotti, Durazzo, Gluck and Calzabigi.

Reform of this kind owed much to French operatic practice. In France, at least since Rameau, music already consciously served the drama, while there was little or no place for dry recitative and conventional display arias, and the overture was already fairly well integrated into the whole. Yet there remained differences, and arguably Gluck brought a specially natural quality to this most artificial and elaborate of art forms. The *castrato* roles in Gluck could not have existed in Paris, and for the production there of *Orfeo* in 1774 a high tenor (*haute-contre* – *see* below) was used for the *castrato* Orpheus role. Similarly, *Alceste* was not to French taste at first and the ever-practical composer made revisions and left others to a collaborator, Gossec: indeed, revisions to both these operas make them less chaste than they were originally. Yet he had met the French tradition halfway, and he now moved in 1773 to Paris in time for the production of his *Iphigénie en Aulide* at the Académie Royale in the following year. Productions of *Orphée et Euridice* and *Alceste* followed. Next came the *drame héroïque Armide* (Paris, 1777), *Iphigénie en Tauride* (1779) and the *drame lyrique Echo et Narcisse* (1779). The popular and admired high tenor Joseph Legros, already well-known in Rameau's operas, played other Gluck roles besides Orpheus, such as Achilles in *Iphigénie en Aulide*, Admetus in *Alceste*, Renaud in *Armide*, Pylades in *Iphigénie en Tauride* and Cynire in *Echo et Narcisse* – with his name, it seems sadly appropriate that Legros had to retire early from the stage 'because of obesity'! His type of voice is rare today but not quite extinct as is the *castrato* – Shostakovich wrote the role of the police inspector for a *haute-contre* in his opera *The Nose*. But the casting of Orpheus in Gluck's opera almost always involves compromise today, whether of sex, pitch or timbre.

The greatness of Gluck's finest opera, *Iphigénie en Tauride*, lies in the addition of an even deeper musical substance to the noble, heroic style he had already evolved. The orchestral writing has vigour right from the outset, where the overture depicts a calm seascape that is to be swiftly disturbed by a storm, drawing us immediately into the tempest which rages within Iphigenia herself, an innocent caught by the curse that pursues the house of Atreus. There is variety and rhythmic interest in orchestral accompaniments such as that to Thoas's aria '*De noirs pressenti-ments*', in which the King's forebodings are suggested by the agitated figure in the strings. In the rapidly moving Act II aria for Orestes, '*Dieux qui me poursuivez*', the strings almost impersonate the pursuing gods. Most remarkable of all is Orestes' other Act II aria, '*Le calme rentre dans mon coeur*', in which the vocal line suggests the returning calm in long notes while the complex, palpitating accompaniment tells us that the Furies' hostility is unabated. There are many such beauties in this rich score, and Gluck is always at his most affecting where the fate of individuals is concerned—whether in Iphigenia's music or Pylades' exquisite Act II aria of friendship for Orestes, '*Unis dès la plus tendre enfance*'.

Despite the great musical wealth of Gluck's Paris operas, the range—if not the depth—of his music has been called into question. His plain homophonic (chordal) style does indeed have the beautiful simplicity which he sought, as if in response to Beaumarchais's complaint that there was 'too much music in theatre music'. Musicians, however, have regretted a certain subordination of purely musical interest, though Handel's reported remark that his cook Waltz knew as much counterpoint as Gluck relates to the very early date of 1745 and, if indeed made at all, was probably in jest, a joke complicated by the fact that Waltz was actually a musician, a bass who sang the title role in the first performance of Handel's oratorio *Saul*. But fugues and canons are hardly essential to the theatre in which Gluck worked all his life. His gifts suited the urgent need of his time, at least in Italian opera, to redress the balance between music and drama. We can hardly regard as less than a fine music-dramatist a composer who was admired by, and influenced, Mozart, Wagner and Berlioz. If the praises of Gluck's operas are sung more often than the works themselves, this may be because of difficulties in presenting them which include a lack of the voices for which they were conceived. When they are staged, audiences usually concur with Berlioz's view of *Iphigénie en Tauride*: that 'with its classical colouring, its solemn accents, its melody and accompaniment so full of noble despair, [it] recalls Homer's sublime poetry, the simple greatness of the heroic age, and fills the heart with that fathomless nostalgia which is always awakened by the evocation of a glorious past'.

MOZART AND HIS CONTEMPORARIES

The young Mozart. Neapolitan composers. Salieri and Haydn. Mozart in Vienna and Prague. The last year.

THE YOUNG MOZART

Although Johann Sebastian Bach wrote no operas, his son, Johann Christian (1735–82), devoted much of his career to the form. J. C. Bach went to Italy in 1754, and there he composed three operas. The success of *Artaserse* (Turin, 1760) brought a commission from the Teatro San Carlo in Naples, where *Catone in Utica* (1761) was triumphantly received: it proved to be his most widely performed opera, with revivals in Milan and Brunswick (1762, 1768). When his next opera, *Alessandro nell' Indie* (Naples, 1762), was performed, it brought an offer from England, so that after this effective beginning he moved on to London in 1762, where his *Orione* (London, 1763) impressed a King's Theatre audience that included George III and Queen Charlotte. The musicologist Dr Burney was there too, and he declared that here 'every judge of Music perceived the emanations of genius'. Burney also observed that Bach no longer regularly used the *da capo* aria, and that his orchestra, which included the then relatively unknown clarinets, was 'most effectively deployed'. *Orione* was soon followed by *Zanaida* (London, 1763) and other operas. Bach was aware of current fashions, and even wrote additional material for the London productions of Piccinni's *Olimpiade* and Gluck's *Orfeo*. He also accepted commissions from other European cities: *Temistocle* (Mannheim, 1772), *Lucio Silla* (Mannheim, 1776), which was admired by Mozart, and *Amadis de Gaule* (Paris, 1779). All his operas use tragic themes, but he was not content merely to follow the received Baroque style. In particular his orchestral mastery, noted by Burney, much impressed the boy Mozart when they met in the 1760s.

The later operas of Wolfgang Amadeus Mozart (1756–1791) are among the greatest in the repertory. But his capacities only emerged from the thorough training and wide experience which he gained during his youthful travels, and *Idomeneo* (Munich, 1781), his first opera of unmistakable genius, was his thirteenth stage work. His first operas were written for the Archbishop's court in his native Salzburg. *La finta semplice* (*The Pretended Fool*, Salzburg, 1768) was his first *opera buffa*, but his first *Singspiel, Bastien und Bastienne* (Salzburg, 1768), based upon Rousseau's *Le devin du village*, is of more interest as he himself contributed to the libretto. Although a slight work, it was a remarkable achievement for a twelve-year-old, containing some lively features, such as the effective imitation of country bagpipes.

Milan then became the focus of Mozart's attention, and he paid the city an annual visit for the next three years, producing major works there. The Austrian Governor-General of Lombardy, Count Firmian, commissioned the first of them, a new *opera seria, Mitridate, Re di Ponto* (Milan, 1770), a full-scale work in traditional style, with roles for three *castrati*. Since most of the singers arrived only just before the first performance, Mozart delayed writing the display arias as long as he could. He knew well enough that he would not win disputes with star singers, who might if they chose replace what had been written with favourite arias of their own that broadly depicted the same emotions, and, taking no risks, he wrote in a conventional way that appealed both to singers and audiences.

Mozart's next opera, *Ascanio in Alba* (Milan, 1771), was commissioned for the wedding celebrations of the Archduke Ferdinand, third son of the Empress Maria Theresa. She also ordered another new opera for the occasion. This was *Il Ruggiero ovvero L'eroica gratitudine* (*Ruggiero, or Heroic Gratitude*, Milan, 1771), the last opera by the septuagenarian Johann Adolf Hasse, and it was followed next day by Mozart's 'dramatic serenade'. *Ascanio in Alba* consists of fifteen arias, three trios, and eight choruses, and offers a charming variety of music — *recitativo accompagnato*, coloratura arias, and choruses of nymphs and shepherds which include dancing as well as singing. It quite eclipsed Hasse's opera, and the older composer generously prophesied that 'This boy will cause us all to be forgotten.'

When Mozart returned to Salzburg one of his first tasks was to compose a new stage piece to a Metastasio libretto for the coronation of a new Archbishop, Hieronymus Colloredo. But the one-act *Il sogno di Scipione* (Salzburg, 1772) is merely a decorative serenade in comparison with the *opera seria Lucio Silla* which was commissioned for Milan in the same year. This time Mozart's contract actually stated that arias were to be written in consultation with the singers. But despite its success — it ran for twenty-six performances — this was the last opera Mozart was invited to write for Italy. Fate determined that his career would develop further north.

It was the Elector of Bavaria who commissioned Mozart's *opera buffa La finta giardiniera* (*The Pretended Gardener*, Munich, 1775), which he completed just before his nineteenth birthday. He was delighted with his work, and wrote to his father, 'My opera was staged yesterday, and was such a success that I cannot possibly describe the tumultuous applause.' Nevertheless the opera suffers from a weak libretto which prevents the music from having a cumulative effect. It is only in the finales to the three acts that there are hints of the Mozart to come, but these alone make *La finta giardiniera* a milestone in his development. *Il re pastore* (Salzburg, 1775) is another Metastasian serenade, this time in two acts, and features graceful arias and a new and inventive use of *obbligato* instruments. The overture is Mozart's first in one movement at a single tempo; in other words it does not retain the traditional Italian *sinfonia* layout of three sections.

In 1779 Mozart began work on a *Singspiel* called *Zaide* for Vienna, which was never finished. When the Empress Maria Theresa died in 1780 Mozart's father informed him that 'the theatres are closed . . . it is better to let things be as the music is not finished'. By that time all the opera lacked was the overture and the final chorus, and it was complete enough to be performed in Salzburg that year. The story, with its Turkish associations—it even includes an Osmin and a Sultan—anticipates *Die Entführung aus dem Serail* (*The Abduction from the Seraglio*), and so does the attractive music. The lyrical soprano aria '*Ruhe sanft, mein holdes Leben*' is especially memorable.

For several years now Mozart had longed for a prestigious opera commission, and early in 1780 one arrived from the Munich court for a full-scale *opera seria*. The circumstances were favourable: he already knew the principal singers, and the librettist Giambattista Varesco was court chaplain at Salzburg. It was also in the political interests of Mozart's employer, the Archbishop of Salzburg, to keep on good terms with his Bavarian neighbours by releasing his court composer to fulfil the commission. The story, taken from a Parisian *opéra-ballet* called *Idomenée* by André Campra, had to be changed in one vital respect, though: since the commission had come from the Elector of Bavaria, the ending needed to ensure that King Idomeneo, a ruler with whom he might be identified, suffered neither death nor disgrace, and Mozart and Varesco changed the plot so that the king abdicated. The change is typical of the freedom with which eighteenth-century librettists treated their classical texts, and in this case, although a conventional tragic ending is averted, the opera remains a work of vivid and direct emotions.

To prepare *Idomeneo* Mozart lived in Munich for many weeks, while Varesco remained in Salzburg, and the resulting correspondence reveals the composer's commitment. His demands were more exact than ever before, for instance: 'For the march in the second act, which is heard from afar, I need mutes for the trumpets and horns of a type that is not available here.' During these crucial weeks of preparation Mozart tailored his music to his singers, fusing their abilities and demands with his own developing ideas. The leading male roles are the Prince, Idamante (*castrato* soprano), and King Idomeneo (tenor), the latter being created by the sixty-six-year-old Anton Raaff, of whom Mozart wrote to his father:

> Raaff is the best and most faithful fellow in the world, but he is so set in his old routines that it would make your blood boil. As a result, it's very difficult to compose for him, though it's easy if you're willing to write conventional arias, as for instance his first one, '*Vedrommi intorno*'. Raaff is too fond of chopped noodles [display pieces] and pays no attention to expression.

Idomeneo is Mozart's first mature opera. Its unity is achieved through the imaginative and flexible deployment of traditional techniques. In recitatives, *secco* style can merge into richer and more dramatic *accompagnato* delivery, or 'orchestral *recitativo*', which in turn develops into arias or ensembles; and this can still be true at the end of set pieces when recitative returns. At the end of Act II, Idomeneo has an accompanied recitative rather than an aria in order to maintain the tension that has been built during the preceding storm scene. Yet though the formal freedom is daring, *opera seria* is here adapted and not rejected. For instance, Electra sings a brilliant formal 'rage aria' when she is spurned by Idamante, and its stature is worthy of the future Queen of the Night in *Zauberflöte*. The Act III quartet in which Prince Idamante bids his farewell before fighting the sea monster, '*Andrò, ramingo e solo*', has been described by Edward Dent as 'perhaps the most beautiful ensemble ever composed for the stage'.

The role of the orchestra in *Idomeneo* is important too, partly because of the use of the famous Mannheim band, whose soloists, like those on the stage, expected opportunities to shine. The orchestra adds to the dramatic atmosphere throughout the work, and takes over the limelight in interludes and ballet music. Thus in its vocal and instrumental writing alike, *Idomeneo* represents a crucial stage in the development and growing flexibility of operatic form, so that characterisation and expression are given increasing importance. Finally, as Mozart himself wrote: 'Where trios and quartets are concerned, the composer must be allowed a free hand.' The ensemble opera had arrived.

In the middle years of the eighteenth century Naples remained a major operatic centre. The career of Niccolò Piccinni (1728–1800) began there with the comic opera *Le donne dispettose* (*The Spiteful Women*, 1754), and two years later he produced his first *opera seria*, *Zenobia*, to a Metastasian libretto. Successful in both genres, within ten years he had become a major figure. Yet the rivalries of the Italian operatic scene displeased him, and he spent the years from 1776 to 1791 in Paris, where he was compared with Gluck and then with Sacchini. Piccinni impressed Dr Burney as 'among the most fertile, spirited and original of composers . . . having a vigour, variety, and especially a new grace, a brilliant and animated style'. His subtle and varied deployment of voice and orchestra brought a new orchestral independence, and he probably invented the multi-section finale, in which the music and mood continually change according to the plot, in his most famous opera, *La buona figliuola* (Rome, 1760), on a Goldoni libretto after Richardson's novel *Pamela*.

Giovanni Paisiello (1740–1816) was another product of Naples, with an output of more than eighty operas during an international career. Having left Naples to spend the years 1776 to 1784 in the employment of Catherine II of Russia, he was from 1802–4 in Paris, where his music was admired by Napoleon. These locations all affected his style: in St Petersburg, for instance, some of his skills in melody and orchestration emerged out of a need to speed up the action, because few people there understood Italian.

The Barber of Seville (St Petersburg, 1782) remains Paisiello's most famous opera. Though it predates Mozart's *Nozze di Figaro* by some years, the score reveals in its vivacity and characterisation that he already knew and admired Mozart's style. Metastasio was another famous figure whom Paisiello admired, and in the final stage of his career Metastasio's was the influence that led him to concentrate on *opera seria*. Here he introduced some flexibility: for instance, *Pirro* (Naples, 1787) employs ensemble finales of the type hitherto reserved for *opera buffa*. But probably his qualities were best suited to the comic genre, since his style relies chiefly upon repetitive accompaniment figures and simple harmonies, and today only *The Barber of Seville* has maintained its position in the repertory. In its own day it became so popular that when Rossini brought out his *Barber* in 1816 he had great difficulty in overcoming the public prejudice in favour of Paisiello's version.

Domenico Cimarosa (1749–1801) studied in Naples, but had by 1780 established an international reputation for comic opera. Indeed, his '*intermezzo in musica*' *I due baroni di Rocca Azzurra* (*The Two Barons of Blue Rock*, Rome, 1783) was produced in Vienna six years later with an extra aria provided by Mozart. Following in the steps of Paisiello, Cimarosa went to St Petersburg, where he directed the opera for four years from 1787. He next moved on to Austria, where he composed his most famous opera, the *dramma giocoso Il matrimonio segreto* (Vienna, 1792). *The Secret Marriage* ranks as one of the best of classical comic operas, for it is brilliantly paced with music that is by turns elegant and infectiously vivacious. The Emperor Leopold II certainly enjoyed it, and after the first performance he ordered supper for the entire cast so that he could hear it again.

None of Cimarosa's later operas has matched the lasting success of *Il matrimonio segreto*, and doubtless his chief skill lay in *buffo* style. But his *tragedia per musica Gli Orazi ed i Curiazi* (Venice, 1797), a tale of opposing political factions set in Roman times, is interesting for its use of a male-voice chorus and textures and accompaniments characteristically relying on short rhythmic figures and a lively alternation of staccato and legato. Though he lacked Mozart's depth of feeling and structural skill, he could and did match his dramatic urgency. His natural theatrical sense and the pacing of dramatic humour in his ensembles reveals him indeed as the ancestor of Rossini.

Pietro Alessandro Guglielmi (1728–1804) remains less well known than his contemporaries, although he composed many operas in both serious and comic genres. His comic opera *La lanterna di Diogene* (Naples, 1794) has a flexible structure with ensemble scenes used as much as arias. By the time he composed his serious opera *La morte di Cleopatra* (Naples, 1796), Guglielmi had incorporated many progressive features into his style, among them a two-act design with the chorus playing its part in the swiftly moving plot and a skilful use of ensembles.

SALIERI AND HAYDN

For all Mozart's genius, during the 1780s Viennese musical life was dominated by the Italian composer Antonio Salieri (1750–1825), now notorious through the dramatisation of his relationship with Mozart, firstly in a Pushkin play and its operatic adaptation by Rimsky-Korsakov, and then more recently in Peter Shaffer's play *Amadeus*, now a popular film. Though Salieri did not poison Mozart, and no derogatory remark is even recorded, the two were certainly rivals, and the older man may have used his influence to block the progress of Mozart's career. He must have realised that his talent could never match the other's genius, a point which

Shaffer makes brilliantly as Salieri reveals his feelings on hearing the Serenade for Thirteen Wind Instruments:

> That night changed my life . . . A solemn *Adagio* in E flat—it started simply enough, just a pulse in the lowest register . . . The slowness gave it . . . a sort of serenity, and then suddenly high above it sounded a single note on an oboe. It hung there, unwavering, piercing me through 'til breath could hold it no longer and a clarinet withdrew it out of me, and softened it and sweetened it to a phrase of such delight it had me trembling . . . I called up to my sharp old God: 'What is this? What?' I was suddenly frightened. It seemed to me that I had heard a voice of God, and that it issued from a creature whose voice I had also heard.

Salieri composed his first opera at eighteen and in fact had genuine gifts which were fully recognised by the time he was twenty-four, when he was appointed a court composer and conductor of Italian opera in Vienna: at thirty-eight he was Court *Kapellmeister*. His chosen librettist was often Lorenzo Da Ponte (1749–1838), their first collaboration being on the *opera buffa Il ricco d'un giorno* (*Rich for a Day*, Vienna, 1784).

Salieri's fame went beyond Vienna: following his lifelong friend Gluck, he became a central figure in Parisian musical life from around 1784, producing operas to satisfy French taste and scoring his greatest triumph with the five-act *Tarare* (Paris 1787). The libretto here was provided by Beaumarchais, and when Da Ponte made an Italian version of the text, it was then styled an *opera tragicomica* and retitled *Axur, Re d'Ormus* (Vienna, 1788)*.

The preface to *Axur, Re d'Ormus*, by Beaumarchais, is a lively defence of the librettist's role, and Salieri too was acutely aware of the importance of the librettist, sufficiently so to make the composer-librettist relationship the basis of an opera. His one-act operetta *Prima la musica e poi le parole* (*First the Music, then the Words*, Vienna, 1786), first presented in Schönbrunn Palace Orangery in a double bill with Mozart's *Der Schauspieldirektor* (*The Impresario*), deals with the problems that follow when a composer informs a poet that their employer the Count has commissioned an opera that must be ready in just four days. This satire on singers, styles, and methods reveals Salieri's realistic understanding of the theatre. In all he wrote more than forty operas, including the first setting of *Falstaff* (Vienna, 1799). His international career was remarkably successful, but after 1788—although still under forty—his influence

---

*Salieri must have had a sense of humour: among his other inventive designations are an *opera filosofico-buffa* and an *opera eroico-comica*.

declined, as his works began to seem old-fashioned in comparison to the Mozartian ensemble opera.

Salieri gradually retired from composition and turned to teaching, counting both Beethoven and Schubert among his pupils. He never really changed his preference for the older, more formal types of Italian opera, and became disillusioned with the new developments. Later, he explained his retirement from opera composition: 'Musical taste is gradually changing to a sort completely contrary to that of my own times; extravagance and confusion of styles have replaced rationality and majestic simplicity.'

Joseph Haydn (1732–1809) ranked opera high among his interests; indeed, it held as central a place in his musical life as it did generally in the musical world. When the Palace at Eszterháza was completed in 1766, it included an opera house with a seating capacity of four hundred, as well as a little puppet theatre, and during his long years of service there he is known to have composed fifteen Italian operas and six German puppet operas. Apart from his own operas, he also arranged and conducted more than seventy by other composers, and this involved revisions and rescoring. The years 1777 to 1782 were especially productive, for during them Haydn actually made opera his priority at the expense of his instrumental output. All this gave him a wide experience of the form, allowing him to approach it with an awareness of its potential, and we must therefore question the received view that his operas are unimportant.

Haydn's centrality to a history of opera can perhaps best be explained through the example of his three-act 'heroicomic drama' *Orlando paladino* (Eszterháza, 1782), which enjoyed a huge success in other centres, including Vienna and Prague. The famous *Orlando furioso* of Ariosto had previously been set by both Lully and Handel, but Haydn's source was more recent, a semi-humorous adaptation to which Prince Eszterházy's director of opera, Nunzio Porta, had contributed.

The possibilities of mixing the conventions of *opera seria* with those of *opera buffa* had already been tried by Haydn in *Lo speziale*, or *The Apothecary* (Eszterháza, 1768), but in his later operas they are developed still further. In *Orlando paladino* there are dramatic accompanied recitatives and dazzling arias, together with the comic characterisation of the bluff squire Pasquino, who even has a patter catalogue aria. Since Haydn's opera was performed in Vienna, and Da Ponte borrowed one of its duets in his libretto for an *opera buffa* called *L'arbore di Diana* by Martin y Soler (1787), this must surely be ranked as the forerunner of Leporello's famous catalogue aria in *Don Giovanni*, the libretto of which he was actually writing at the time. Haydn seldom used the regular *da capo* aria form, and generally preferred flexible ensembles to formal set pieces. His orchestral experience was an asset, and not just in the expected situations such as military scenes with trumpets and drums, for he even wrote a comedy aria in *Orlando paladino* in which the singer imitates the instruments of the orchestra. *La vera costanza* (*True Constancy*) and *La fedeltà premiata* (*Loyalty Rewarded*, Eszterháza, 1778 and 1780) also mixed serious and comic elements, and their well-constructed finales may have influenced Mozart.

Haydn's last two operas were serious: these were the 'heroic drama' *Armida* (Eszterháza, 1784) and an Orpheus treatment called *L'anima del filosofo* (*The Philosopher's Spirit*, London, 1791), the latter being the only opera he wrote away from Eszterháza. Haydn's London engagements, when he went there with the impresario Salomon, included a contract for an *opera seria*, but the weak libretto of *L'anima del filosofo* led to its failure, though some of the choral writing, probably inspired by Gluck, is fine and anticipates that of his oratorios *The Creation* and *The Seasons*. This final opera really stands apart from the rest of Haydn's output, and not only because of the circumstances of its composition. In 1787 the practical composer had declined an invitation to write an opera for Prague on the grounds that he was not familiar with the conditions there. But it does appear that he had in fact lost his appetite for opera, for, as he said, 'scarcely any man could stand comparison with the great Mozart'. Writing to a friend who had recently seen the new production of *Don Giovanni*, Haydn added: 'For if I could convince every music lover—and especially those in high positions—of the inimitable works of Mozart; if they would judge them, as I do, seriously and with musical understanding; if they would let his music touch their souls as it does my own . . . I am furious that this unique Mozart has not yet been taken into the service of an imperial or royal court.'

In the 1780s the two composers had become friends, playing chamber music together and belonging to the same freemasons' lodge in Vienna, and to Mozart's father Leopold Haydn said: 'I say to you before God, and as an honest man, that your son is the greatest composer I know, either personally or by repute: he has taste and the greatest craftsmanship in composition.'

MOZART IN VIENNA AND PRAGUE

And so we return, rightly and inevitably, to Mozart, for posterity has decided that the operas he composed during the last decade of his life far surpass those by his contemporaries.

The first of these was a *Singspiel, Die Entführung aus dem Serail* (*The Abduction from the Seraglio*, Vienna, 1782). It had been commissioned by Gottlieb Stephanie, an actor-dramatist who was the director of the National-Singspiel, a short-lived institution set up by the Emperor Joseph II in the hope of promoting German opera. The music was composed at the time when Mozart was acclimatising himself to a freelance existence in Vienna, and he learned much from the experience, though the postponement of the première by ten months must have been frustrating. Even so, the new work proved popular with the public, and was admired by Gluck, who requested an extra performance, and during Mozart's lifetime it was performed more often than any of his other operas. After the first performance the Emperor made his famous remark, 'Too many notes, my dear Mozart,' to which the composer replied, 'Only as many as are needed, Your Majesty.' The average *Singspiel*, with which Joseph II was making his comparison, was little more than a popular play, a sort of pantomime, interspersed with songs: the form was in fact closely related to the French *opéra comique* and the English ballad opera. But Mozart, with *Idomeneo* behind him, explored the plot of *Die Entführung* in a musical language that is far wider-ranging both vocally and orchestrally than its predecessors in the tradition.

The plot of *Die Entführung aus dem Serail* combines a popular Turkish setting—the Austrians loved to poke fun at the Ottoman Empire—with an attempted rescue motivated by love and a resolution brought about by the generosity of the powerful Turkish pasha. In this way the ideals of the Enlightenment add a deeper dimension, the balanced story allowing the serious to blend with the comic.

The overture to *Die Entführung* shows why Mozart's opera orchestra is larger than his concert orchestra: the Turkish aspect is provided by *forte* statements of the opening theme scored for the full band, including piccolo, triangle, cymbals and bass drum. Every effort is made to explore the possibilities of the drama in terms of its instrumentation. Although a *Singspiel, Die Entführung* shows an Italian influence in that the opera is vocally demanding and can only be performed by the finest singers. A worthy successor to *Idomeneo*, it was valuable to the composer's development because it was in a very different genre. The later comment of Weber is pertinent here: 'In *Die Entführung*, Mozart's artistic experience reached its maturity; it was only his worldly experience which was to develop later. The world was justified in expecting from him more operas like *Figaro* or *Don Giovanni*, but with the best will in the world he could not have written another *Entführung*.'

During Mozart's Viennese years he remained committed to opera and continually looked for new ways to broaden his style. Two *buffo* works were begun and abandoned (*L'oca del Cairo* and *Lo sposo deluso*), and though the reasons for this remain unclear, we can still acknowledge their positions as points in Mozart's operatic career. The chief thrust of this so far had indicated a need for flexibility of language, and it was this, together with the *buffo* style and the work of a fine librettist, which presented the opportunity for his next major step forward.

Buffo style attracted Mozart because it dealt with real people and gave him the chance to treat character and action with freedom and ingenuity. It also allowed him to concentrate on ensembles rather than arias. He knew Paisiello's *The Barber of Seville*, and it may have been his admiration for that opera that induced him to take an interest in the next of Beaumarchais's plays, *The Marriage of Figaro*, which takes up the story where *The Barber* leaves off. Equally, he may have known this play through his friend Emanuel Schikaneder, the future librettist of *The Magic Flute*, who had made a German translation of it. At any rate, the idea for *Le nozze di Figaro* came from Mozart rather than his librettist Da Ponte.

Lorenzo Da Ponte was a favourite of the Austrian Emperor's, and this may have been why he managed to overcome the vigorous official opposition towards the play with its openly anti-aristocratic stance, while his libretto also omitted or toned down the more inflammatory aspects. When *Figaro* was first performed as an opera, the original play was still paradoxically banned on the grounds that it was subversive. This must be understood in terms of the time: there were now major changes in the social climate, as the aristocracy knew to their disquiet, while the French Revolution was only three years in the future.

Le nozze di Figaro (Vienna, 1786) has the subtitle *La folle journée* because the entire action takes place on a country estate near Seville on the day of the valet Figaro's marriage to the maid Susanna, with whom Count Almaviva wishes first to exercise his *droit du seigneur*, the lord's by now obsolete right to make love to his 'subject' before her wedding. The plot is developed around this basic conflict, which inevitably stresses social distinctions, but the libretto had to shorten the original as well as amending it. Da Ponte in his preface to the libretto explained why operas so seldom follow plays exactly: the music prolongs the time-scale.

The duration prescribed for a stage performance by general usage, and the given number of roles to which one is confined by the same, as well as several other considerations of prudence, of costume, place, and public constituted the reasons for which I have not made a translation of that excellent Beaumarchais comedy, but rather an imitation, or let us say an extract. For these reasons I was compelled to reduce the sixteen original characters to eleven, two of which can be played by a single actor, and to omit in addition to one whole act many effective scenes. For these I have had to substitute *canzonette*, arias, choruses, and other thoughts and words susceptible of being set to music. In spite, however, of all the zeal and care on the part of both the composer and myself to be brief, the opera will not be one of the shortest that has been performed on our stages. We hope that our excuse will be the variety of development of this drama, the length and scope of the same, the number of musical pieces necessary in order not to keep the performers idle, to avoid the boredom and monotony of long recitatives, to paint faithfully and in full colour the various passions that are aroused, and to realise our special purpose, which was to offer a new type of spectacle, as it were, to a public of such refined taste and such assured understanding.

For Mozart and Da Ponte, *Le nozze di Figaro* represented a natural development, the combination of their talents to create a range of characters of a depth and subtlety hitherto unknown in opera. A splendid example occurs in the opening *duettino* ('little duet') for Figaro and Susanna, where he measures their new room while she tries on a hat. Each has an individual melodic line and style, and the strength of Susanna's personality is such that by the end of this *duettino* her music is sung by Figaro too.

Mozart's musical style was in many respects similar in both his vocal and instrumental works, and the influence worked both ways—it is possible, for instance, to recognise the *buffo* element in the first movement of the 'Jupiter' Symphony. This is hardly surprising if we consider how the classical sonata principle was a recipe for drama in music: an exposition to set out the characters with the situation and then a development to propel the plot forward. In opera this process is followed by resolution rather than recapitulation. *Le nozze di Figaro* depends mainly on ensembles, and it was in the act-finales and set pieces such as the Act III sextet that Mozart was at the height of his powers, because the libretto allowed him to build large musical structures. Da Ponte himself described an operatic finale as '. . . the great occasion for showing off the genius of the composer, the ability of the singers, and the most effective "situation" of the drama. Recitative is excluded from it; everything is sung, and every style of singing must find a place in it: *adagio, allegro, andante, amabile, armonioso* . . . It is a dogma of theatrical theology that all the singers should appear on the stage, even if there were three hundred of them . . .'

The Act II finale of *Figaro* comprises about two thirds of all the music in the act. The tension builds as characters enter: at first the Count is alone with the Countess and then they are joined by Susanna and, later, by Figaro. The gardener Antonio arrives but does not stay, and lastly Marcellina, Basilio and Bartolo appear as the music moves to its vivid climax. Despite all this diversity Mozart maintains the musical unity as in an instrumental movement. However, the Irish tenor Michael Kelly, who sang in the first performance, testified forty years later in his memoirs that Mozart's own favourite part of the opera was the sextet near the end of Act III. This is indeed a triumph; the characters' thoughts and emotions as they respond to the revelation of Figaro's true identity are captured perfectly by the structure and pacing of the music.

Mozart's act-finales really look forward to the through-composed structures of later operas, since they are made from separate numbers that run from one to the next to become a complete unit, gathering together and resolving the strands of the drama. By the time we reach the Act II finale of *Figaro*, for example, we know about the characters from the preceding ensembles and through solo items like the Countess's poignant '*Porgi amor*', so that the dramatic and musical tensions are considerable, their resolution the more climactic. But this opera provides wonderful entertainment in its every aspect. Its complex plot remains clear and its tensions allow scope for both wit and tenderness; although a comedy it has serious comments to make about human nature, such as the effect of the Count's infidelities on his wife, or the apprehensions of the servant Barbarina as she searches for the pin she has lost. Stendhal declared: 'All the characters are turned towards the tender or the passionate. Mozart's opera is a sublime blend of wit and melancholy which is without any parallel.'

Le nozze di Figaro enjoyed more success in Prague than in Vienna, where despite initial enthusiasm it was dropped after nine performances. Mozart was invited to Prague to conduct it and became a popular hero there. He wrote to his father:

I looked on with the greatest pleasure while all these people flew about in sheer delight to the music of my *Figaro*, arranged for quadrilles and waltzes. For here they talk about nothing but *Figaro*. No opera is pulling the crowds like *Figaro*. Nothing, nothing but *Figaro*. Certainly a great honour for me.

A new opera was quickly commissioned for Prague, and this, at the suggestion of Da Ponte, was based on the famous Don Juan legend. Mozart called *Don Giovanni* (Prague, 1787) an *opera buffa*, but it points a serious moral: that of the 'dissolute man punished' as the original full title (*Il dissoluto punito, ossia Il Don Giovanni*) tells us. Once more the ethical position of the aristocrat, and perhaps the *man* (in the sexist sense) is at the heart of the opera. The overture, which was written last of all as was Mozart's practice, displays the two moods and dimensions which pervade the work. The slow introduction evokes the serious scenes with the Commendatore's ghost, while the rest of the overture is a bustling *allegro* pointing towards the vivacity, humour and pace of the drama. Although Don Giovanni (baritone) himself appears mainly in ensembles, and is actually given less solo work than the other major characters, the action always relates to him, and in this way Mozart points the way to later 'psychological' operas such as Bartók's *Bluebeard's Castle* and Berg's *Wozzeck*. Despite his reputation as a womaniser, outlined in the catalogue aria in Act I in which Leporello lists his master's conquests to Donna Elvira, Don Giovanni is wholly unsuccessful during the course of the opera, where his attempted seductions are repeatedly foiled. Even so, in the end he is visited by the Commendatore's ghost, avenging his daughter Donna Anna's reputation and his own death and, still refusing to repent, he is consumed by the flames of hell. This image appealed to the Romantics, and the nineteenth-century tradition was to end the opera at the point when Don Giovanni disappears and before the final *buffo* sextet begins. The musical language of *Don Giovanni* is very advanced: the ball scene in Act I has three different on-stage orchestras playing simultaneously, while in Act II Mozart quotes both from *Figaro* and from Martin y Soler's popular *Una cosa rara* (Vienna, 1786), while the final scene with the ghost features an off-stage chorus of demons. Thus this operatic fusion of all the elements, tragic and comic, of eighteenth-century practice looks forward too, both dramatically and musically.

After the popularity of *Don Giovanni* in Prague, Mozart enjoyed some success during 1789 when the opera had a run of fifteen performances in Vienna, for which he composed some new material including the splendid soprano aria '*Mi tradi*' for Donna Elvira. Later that year *Figaro* was revived too, but since a composer received a fee for a commission but not for revivals, the rewards were only artistic. The Viennese theatres were run under the auspices of the court, and only special benefit performances allowed a composer any extra income. His 'reward' for success, therefore, would normally only be in the form of the new commissions he might attract. For example, Pasquale Bondini, the theatre manager who staged the 1787 Prague production of *Figaro*, commissioned Mozart to write *Don Giovanni* for a fee of one hundred *gulden*.

Perhaps the 1789 revival of *Figaro* in Vienna led to the commissioning of the third of Mozart's operas with a Da Ponte libretto, *Così fan tutte* (Vienna, 1790). This was by Imperial command, and rumour had it that the story was the invention of the Emperor himself, and prompted by a current Viennese scandal: Don Alfonso, an old cynic, makes a wager with two young officers, Ferrando and Guglielmo, that their lovers, Dorabella and Fiordiligi, will not remain faithful in their absence. The two men appear disguised as Albanians and each proceeds to seduce the other's partner. The *buffo* theme was that 'all women behave this way', hence the opera's title. The strength of this seemingly limited plot was its emotional range, that spanned humour, rage and pathos. Even without the two finales, ensembles again outnumber arias, and the warm and sensuous Mediterranean atmosphere is unique in Mozart's output. The mood is lightly handled but not lightweight, and the vocal music is demanding; the soprano role of Fiordiligi, for instance, is as taxing as any Mozart wrote.

Soon after the first performance of *Così fan tutte* the Emperor Joseph II died, and all the theatres were closed. Consequently the opera had little chance to claim an immediate place in the repertory, and it is really only in the twentieth century that it has joined the other Da Ponte operas in the Mozart canon.

From 1788 onwards Mozart's life was never far from crisis. His Vienna subscription concerts failed, and among his musical associates only Baron Gottfried van Swieten remained consistently loyal. He repeatedly had to borrow money during these years, and often asked for the help of Michael Puchberg, a wealthy merchant and fellow Freemason. One letter, for instance, suggested 'a year or two with one or two thousand *gulden*, at a suitable rate of interest'. At the time of his death, his debts amounted to some three thousand *gulden*, and even though Puchberg had frequently sent sums to alleviate immediate needs, he was probably never repaid.

Mozart's only appointment at this time was that of an Imperial court composer, a minor post which brought a nominal salary and required only the writing of occasional dance music. Yet he did receive an offer to travel to London in 1790 from a British impresario called O'Reilly who was promoting Italian opera there, and the invitation was for six months' work involving 'at least two operas' for the quite large fee of £300. Since this coincided with Johann Salomon's successful bid to bring Haydn to the English capital, where Da Ponte now lived, Mozart's refusal is surprising. Perhaps he was too emotionally attached to his native Austria and to Vienna, and believed that his future lay there.

THE LAST YEAR

Mozart's last year was undoubtedly one of his busiest, for the major works alone included two operas, the E flat major String Quintet, the Clarinet Concerto, and the Requiem. The pressures of having to keep to schedule must have contributed to his poor health, and of course there were always the pressing financial needs of his family. He had married Constanze Weber in 1782, and they had had six children, four of whom died in infancy.

La clemenza di Tito (Prague, 1791) was a commission for the coronation of Leopold II as King of Bohemia, and the composer was instructed to use a Metastasio text of 1734. This was his first *opera seria* since *Idomeneo*, and he had to write it quickly. Caterino Mazzola, who adapted the libretto, wrote of the work he undertook: 'The three acts of the original are condensed into two, the endless *secco* recitatives are shortened, many of the old arias are replaced by others, newly written, and finally all the ensemble pieces—the three duets, the three trios, the final quintet of the first act, and the final sextet of the second act—are added.'

Thus Mozart did not merely set a traditional *opera seria* libretto, as he had earlier in his career. His mature style was hardly suited to a chain of 'exit arias' joined by *secco* recitatives, and in *La clemenza di Tito* the music offers some of the dignity associated with the character of Sarastro in *Die Zauberflöte*. The opera has never achieved a regular place in the Mozart canon, but since it contains excellent music it hardly deserves the relative obscurity to which it is currently confined.

The *Clemenza* commission had arrived in July 1791, and by then Mozart was well advanced with the music of *Die Zauberflöte* (Vienna, 1791). The composer had known the impresario Emanuel Schikaneder for some years, and by 1791 Schikaneder's company had become established at the Theater auf der Wieden in the Viennese suburbs with a series of popular and spectacular productions. Schikaneder asked Mozart to write a *Singspiel* for which he would provide the libretto himself. The production had a large budget and was aimed at a wide audience, so that none of Mozart's previous genres was appropriate. The result was the widest range of musical styles that had ever until then been put into a single opera, with popular songs for Papageno (a part first taken by Schikaneder himself), vehement *opera seria* coloratura for the Queen of the Night, deeply felt and noble utterances for Prince Tamino, and the solemn profundities of the priest Sarastro and his disciples. There was much else besides, but these were the essential contrasts.

Mozart employs a large orchestra in *Die Zauberflöte*, with trombones which are used to emphasise the solemn mood whenever Sarastro is present. An example of this special colour is Sarastro's aria with the chorus of priests at the beginning of Act II, when the orchestration comprises pairs of horns and bassoons with three trombones, and divided violas and cellos.

As Freemasons, Mozart and Schikaneder filled *Die Zauberflöte* with Masonic symbols. One such is the constant stress of the number three: the overture begins with three loud chords, the characters include three ladies and three boys, the serpent in the opening scene is cut into three pieces, and there are three doors on which Tamino must knock. The central feature of the plot is Tamino's quest to achieve nobility and acceptance into the higher order of humanity ruled by Sarastro. All this points to the allegory so convincingly suggested by Wilfred Mellers in his *Man and his Music*:

> First there are the Masonic beings who represent Progress and Enlightenment. Tamino is the Emperor Joseph II, Pamina the Austrian people, and Sarastro Ignaz von Born, a Masonic prophet, half mystical, half rational. Then there is the realm of the Queen of the Night—what seemed to Masonic Enlightenment the effete Catholic world of sorcery, superstition, and seduction. The Queen is Maria Theresa, Monostatos (a semi-comic creature of lust and vengeance) is the clergy, and in particular the Jesuits. Finally, there is the world inhabited by those incapable of the heights of humanism: Papageno being, in his innocence, a kind of comic Parsifal.

But Tamino and Pamina go far beyond mere symbolic existence and breathe life as real people, and their achievement of a spiritually noble status becomes the triumph of light over darkness, of good over evil, a universalised condition propounded by the final chorus: 'Strength is the victor! In glory be crowned, in wisdom and beauty for ever abound.' These words might serve as Mozart's own epitaph.

The Magic Flute was received with great enthusiasm by audiences at the Theater auf der Wieden, and this gave hope to Mozart, who attended numerous performances during the last two months of his life. On one occasion, which he recalled in a letter to his wife, he shared a box with Salieri, who 'listened and watched most attentively, and from the overture to the last chorus there was not a single number that did not call forth from him a *bravo* or a *bello*'. But during this time Mozart's health was declining: he was constantly weary and depressed, and suffered from fainting fits which were caused, the latest research suggests, by rheumatic fever. His death became an obsession as he worked at the setting of the Requiem he would never complete.

For all his financial troubles, the obituary notices prove that Mozart was held in high esteem at the time of his death. Had he enjoyed a normal lifespan, he would still have been active well into the next century, and since he died at thirty-five it is misleading to apply the term 'late' to any of his works. He brought a new enlightenment and humanistic spirit to opera, as well as providing the form with some of its most magnificent music. Indeed, in him eighteenth-century opera reaches its summit. His infinite attention to detail means that he is the earliest composer whose operas feature fully rounded characters, their humanity wholly at one with the drama and the music alike.

Haydn recognised that in Mozart all musical trends seemed to meet, and wrote in 1791 that 'the world will not see such a talent again in a hundred years'. Unlike Beethoven and Haydn, the two other outstanding exponents of the Viennese classical style, Mozart worked in every current medium. He was—and remains—the most universal of composers. His style combines sureness of form with melodic beauty and richness of harmony and texture, and in his operas the subtlety of characterisation is enhanced by lively recitative and inventive orchestral writing. These elements are most clearly represented in his finales, in which there is a full tonal and symphonic control of long spans of dramatic music. His successors understood this, and it was from him that later generations drew their inspiration. E. T. A. Hoffmann's words provide an appropriate tribute: 'Mozart's music is the mysterious language of a distant spiritual kingdom, whose marvellous accents echo in our inner being and arouse a higher, intensive life.'

7

HEROIC AND LYRICAL OPERAS IN PARIS
1760–1875

Opéra comique. *The Revolution and rescue opera. French Romanticism and
grand opera. From Berlioz to Bizet.*

OPÉRA COMIQUE

French comic opera in the mid-eighteenth century was represented by
the *vaudeville* and the *comédie mêlée d'ariettes*, a play with songs which often
parodied more serious entertainments and in which the music was largely
made up of adaptations of popular tunes. The impact on Paris of Italian
opera buffa in the 1750s (*see* Chapter 3) prompted the development of this
type of play-with-songs into the *opéra comique*, in which music played a
greater part than before but which retained spoken dialogue. Thus from
the mid-eighteenth century, French opera had two streams; the lofty,
serious style, derived from Lully, with sung recitative, and the *opéra
comique* with its spoken dialogue. The latter, although the literal meaning
of the term is 'comic opera', also came to treat serious subjects, so that
eventually it denoted little more than the use of dialogue to separate
musical numbers, as in the German *Singspiel* and the English ballad
opera.

A further confusion over the term *opéra comique* can arise from its use
for three different things: a type of opera, the company which performed
it, and the theatres where they performed. The Opéra-Comique company was set up in 1715, and in 1762 it joined forces with another, the
Comédie-Italienne. Despite the merger, and the fact that it occupied the
Théâtre-Italien, only French works were performed. In 1783 they moved
to the Salle Favart, and in 1791 a rival organisation began playing a similar
repertoire at the Théâtre Feydeau. After a decade of intense competition
the two amalgamated in 1801, and occupied various theatres before
settling in the Théâtre Feydeau in 1805. In 1807 the company was given
official status as the Théâtre National de l'Opéra-Comique, and was
usually called simply the Opéra-Comique thereafter.

Many successful works of the period had libretti by Charles-Simon
Favart (1710–92), whose pastoral idylls were sentimental in tone, often

with a native heroine (or *ingénue*) whose tendency to weep led to the genre being called *comédie larmoyante*. The texts were less crude than the older parodies, and Voltaire wrote to Favart in 1775, 'You are the first to have made a decent and ingenious amusement out of a form which before you did not concern polite society. Thanks to you it has become the delight of all decent folk.' The composers who set Favart's libretti included the masters of the pre-Revolutionary *opéra comique*, Monsigny, Philidor, and Grétry. These three also set texts by Favart's follower, Michel Sedaine (1719–97), who brought greater realism to the plots and incidents, reduced the comic element and increased the *larmoyant* aspect.

Sedaine provided the libretto of one of the period's most enduring successes, *Le déserteur* (Paris, 1769), the music of which is by Pierre-Alexandre Monsigny (1729–1817). All but one of Monsigny's seventeen stage works are *opéras comiques*. Such pieces as *Le roy et le fermier* (Paris, 1762) and *Rose et Colas* (Paris, 1764), also both with Sedaine, were well received, but *Le déserteur* was the first major success of the developing genre and held the stage for over a hundred years. The plot concerns Alexis, whose love for his village sweetheart Louise is cruelly tested. He abandons his regiment, is caught and imprisoned, but is eventually reunited with Louise and pardoned by the King. Clearly this is not a comic scenario, but it shows Sedaine's penchant for placing characters *in extremis* and then providing opportunities for expressions of tearful regret. One such is Alexis's Act III aria in which he laments the lost kisses of his girl: 'It would have been so sweet to kiss you,' he sings, and the slightly cloying sentiment is matched by Monsigny's high tenor writing, the pauses, stammers, and sighs being affecting if hardly profound. His fellow-composer Grétry called Monsigny 'the most tuneful of all musicians'.

François-André Philidor (1726–95) produced eleven of his twenty-four *opéras comiques* between 1759 and 1765. After *Le sorcier* (Paris, 1764) he became probably the first composer to be given a curtain call, but his *Tom Jones* (Paris, 1765) was initially less successful, until Sedaine revised Poinsinet's unsatisfactory libretto. Philidor had many links with England, including a friendship with Dr Johnson, and *Tom Jones* is based on Fielding's picaresque novel. The score is ingenious and includes a septet, a duet in two simultaneous metres, and opera's first unaccompanied quartet. Philidor enjoyed illustrative touches; in *Le maréchal ferrant* (Paris, 1761) there is a number in which village bells are suggested by *pizzicato* scales in the strings and 'ding-dong' octaves in the vocal line, and another in which the blacksmith of the title, anticipating Wagner's *Siegfried*, accompanies himself on the anvil.

André Grétry (1741–1813) came from Liège, studied in Rome and worked in Paris. Armed with a recommendation from Voltaire, he soon found favour in France, and he wrote fifty operas in thirty-five years. As he wrote in his memoirs, he had 'the gift of appropriate melody', but lacked skill in 'strict and complicated harmony': but then in true Enlightenment fashion he regarded the voice as the only perfect instrument because it was the natural one, declaring that the relationship of voice and orchestra was that of a statue and its pedestal. The most important of all his works is the *opéra comique Richard Coeur de Lion* (Paris, 1784), which tells of the search by the minstrel Blondel for the imprisoned King Richard I of England. One forward-looking feature of the score is the use of Blondel's air '*Une fièvre brulante*' as a 'reminiscence motif', a recurrent theme used nine times in all in various transformations. Each appearance has some dramatic purpose, and the success of Grétry's idea made reminiscence motifs a feature of *opéra comique*.

In the 1780s the most popular composer of *opéras comiques* was Nicolas Dalayrac (1753–1809). His *Nina, ou La folle par amour* (Paris, 1786) introduced a new operatic situation, for Nina loses her mind when her father prevents her from seeing her lover, and is cured on his return. The touching situation of the heroine, who enters in Act I with 'her hair unpowdered and loose, dressed in a white frock, with a bunch of flowers in her hand, her gait unsteady', is one forerunner of the mad scenes beloved of later Italian Romantic opera (*see* Chapter 9). *Les deux petits Savoyards* (Paris, 1789) was Dalayrac's last success before the Revolution imparted a new character to the *opéra comique*.

During the *ancien régime*, when native composers were creating such a vital tradition of *opéra comique*, the older genre of the *tragédie lyrique* was kept alive mainly by foreign artists. Rameau had died in 1764, and in the 1770s the mantle passed to Gluck, whose Parisian works include his greatest music (*see* Chapter 5). The performance of *tragédie* was still the sole prerogative of the Académie Royale de Musique (known simply as 'the Opéra'), and its form had changed little since Lully's day; there were five acts, much ballet, and recitative rather than spoken dialogue. With less room for experiment than in *opéra comique*, Gluck's successors broadly followed his lead. They were the Italians Piccinni, Salieri (*see also* Chapter 6), and Antonio Sacchini (1730–86). Piccinni had been pushed into an unwanted rivalry with Gluck in Paris, and continued to write operas there after Gluck's departure. His *Didon* (Fontainebleau, 1783), like Purcell's earlier and Berlioz's later treatment of the same Virgilian subject, has a noble heroine who retains authority even when humiliated. Salieri's *Les Danaïdes* (Paris, 1784) was advertised as a work of Gluck's in which he was 'assisted by his pupil Salieri', because Gluck's name ensured a respectful hearing, but when the work was successful, Gluck confessed Salieri's sole authorship. Sacchini worked in London in the 1770s and came to Paris in 1783, and in the following year he produced his *Dardanus*, to the same libretto Rameau had set in 1739. His *Oedipe à Colone* (Versailles, 1786) perhaps shows a conscious desire to imitate Gluck, and the choral passages achieve a Gluckian sublimity at times: this opera remained in the French repertory until 1844.

THE REVOLUTION AND RESCUE OPERA

The Revolutionary and Napoleonic era that began in 1789 deeply affected French musical life. The great outdoor celebrations of events in the Revolutionary calendar, involving vast numbers of performers, were to influence Spontini's grand operas and much of Berlioz's music. Open-air music was most effective with bodies of wind instruments, which by now were better made and played. A desire for brilliance and power led to a raising of pitch. Instruments used outdoors now found their way into the operatic orchestra, such as the tamtam (gong) used in a 1790 revival of Salieri's *Tarare* (1787). The Opéra became a propaganda house, first for Republican and then for Imperial ends. Typical of the works staged at that time was *Le triomphe de la République* (1793), a *divertissement* or entertainment by François Gossec (1734–1829).

However, *opéra comique* thrived. Unlike the *tragédie lyrique*, it was not damned by association with the court, and its spoken dialogue enabled political and social sentiments to come across clearly. Several of the pre-Revolutionary composers switched their attentions to subjects appropriate to the time; thus Grétry's *Guillaume Tell* (1791) put the Swiss revolutionary leader on the stage long before Rossini's opera (1829) and even Schiller's play of 1804. Dalayrac served the fashion for Gothic romances, setting *Camille* (Paris, 1791) in an abandoned convent, where a jealous duke keeps his wife in an underground vault. She is too loyal to respond to her rescuer's advances, and is then reunited with her husband.

Camille is also an example of a 'rescue opera', a type of plot in which the imprisoned or endangered hero or heroine is rescued at the last by a lover, spouse or other agent. It was not new to *opéra comique*, for both Monsigny's *Le déserteur* and Grétry's *Richard Coeur de Lion* have this theme, and a resolution by a *deus ex machina* was almost as old as opera itself. But during the Revolution, and particularly during the Terror of 1793–94, the theme touched the lives of many more people. It also gave an opportunity to express popular ideals of the period such as fidelity, selfless heroism, and married love and to assure the spectator that freedom would always triumph over tyranny. Henri-Montan Berton (1767–1844) produced a pioneering marriage of rescue opera and topical anti-clericalism in his *Les rigueurs du cloître* (Paris, 1790), in which the heroine Lucille is rescued from a convent by an officer of the Republic, and all the nuns are sent out into the world to rear families. The officer tells us that 'The most perfect being in the eyes of the Divinity is he who worthily fulfils his duties as a man, a citizen, a husband, a father, and a friend.' However, this male chauvinism is at odds with the active and heroic roles assigned to women in many rescue operas, including the greatest of them and the only one to survive — Beethoven's *Fidelio*.

Of the figures who came to prominence in the Revolutionary period in Paris it was Luigi Cherubini (1760–1842) who most impressed his contemporaries. Beethoven considered him the finest dramatic composer of his time, and Schubert, Weber and Mendelssohn all shared this view. A Florentine, Cherubini wrote thirteen Italian operas and worked in London before coming to Paris in 1786. His first French work was a classical tragedy for the Opera, *Démophon* (Paris, 1788); but this was in fact a false start, and his principal work was all done in the *opéra comique* form, beginning with the rescue opera *Lodoïska* (1791). The eponymous heroine is imprisoned in a castle by Dourlinski, who wants to marry her, but she is rescued by her lover as the Tartars make a timely attack on the fortress. The final conflagration, in which Dourlinski's castle collapses, was typical of the period's love of stage spectacle, and the dramatic characterisation of the villain was especially influential: thus Dourlinski is the ancestor both of Pizarro in Beethoven's *Fidelio* and Caspar in Weber's *Der Freischütz*. Cherubini's next work, *Eliza* (Paris, 1794), is again on the theme of rescue, and this time the spectacle is provided by an avalanche.

The most powerful of Cherubini's dramas is *Médée* (Paris, 1797). The libretto by François Benoit Hoffman follows Euripides' tragedy *Medea*, and tells of the sorceress whose vengeance on her faithless lover Jason involves murdering his new bride and her own two children by him. Despite the Greek source and tragic ending, the work is technically an *opéra comique*, and thus provides a striking indication of how far the genre had changed by this time. In fact we now find much more than the simple separation of musical numbers by speech. In the finale to Act II, Jason's wedding is taking place at the back of the stage, accompanied by music for chorus and wind, but at the front of the stage Medea prowls angrily, and as her rage increases she moves from unaccompanied speech to *mélodrame* (accompanied speech), then to recitative supported by a few strings, and finally, as her passion becomes ungovernable, to an outburst with full orchestral accompaniment. Cherubini here created a role which offers rewards to a great singing actress, as Maria Callas demonstrated when the work was revived for the Florence Festival of 1953.

With *Les deux journées* (Paris, 1800) Cherubini returned to rescue opera with a tale of persecuted aristocrats in seventeenth-century France who try to escape their pursuers in the barrels of a water-carrier—in England the opera was once known as *The Water-carrier*. The libretto is by Jean-Nicolas Bouilly, whose *Léonore* was to be set by Mayr, Paer, and—in *Fidelio*—Beethoven. The score of *Les deux journées* is remarkable for the dramatic use of *mélodrame* and reminiscence motifs, and has a high proportion of ensembles.

Although Cherubini continued to write for the stage, his most influential work was now done. In *Médée* and the three rescue operas the *opéra comique* had touched new dramatic heights. The sweeping, symphonic style of these works, whose finales have long stretches of music held together by rhythmic drive and harmonic control, profoundly influenced Beethoven. If Cherubini's melodic invention had matched his other musical gifts, his operas would surely still hold the stage today. In his later years he turned also to sacred music and to teaching. He was from 1822–42 the director of the Paris Conservatoire, where he plagued Berlioz and other students with a severe conservatism.

After Cherubini, the major figures of the so-called 'Revolution school' are Méhul and Lesueur. Étienne-Nicolas Méhul (1763–1817) wrote mainly *opéras comiques*, such as *Le jeune Henri* (Paris, 1797), *Ariodant* (Paris, 1799), *Héléna* (Paris, 1803), *Uthal* (Paris, 1806), and *Joseph* (Paris, 1807). The last of these, which has a story taken from the Old Testament, is the only work of Méhul's which survived into the twentieth century, and it was once widely performed. But it is the earlier operas which are historically important for the influence of their demonic atmosphere on Romantic opera. *Uthal* is based on Ossian, the spurious Gaelic bard 'rediscovered' (actually invented) in the 1760s and a favourite source of operatic subjects. To suggest the brooding Northern gloom, Méhul darkens his score by omitting the violins, and this is only one of his many imaginative uses of the orchestra; in addition, its overture is almost without themes and definable form. The overture to *Le jeune Henri* depicts a hunting scene in a forest, while that to *Héléna* is interrupted by a trumpet call—another influence on *Fidelio*, or rather on the overtures to Beethoven's opera. Even when Méhul's operas failed as staged productions, their overtures were often successful.

Jean-François Lesueur, or Le Sueur (1760–1837), made his operatic debut with *La caverne* (Paris, 1793), an *opéra comique* centred on a band of robbers which ends with the siege and collapse of their cave. This was the first 'brigand opera', its theme reflected in Auber's *Fra Diavolo* and Hérold's *Zampa* nearly forty years later. Lesueur had a penchant for special instrumental colour and extravagant demands, such as the ten harps for *Ossian, ou les bardes* (Paris, 1804), written for the Opéra with its larger resources, and many of his more grandiose ideas were later taken up by his pupil Berlioz. The subject of *Ossian* was suggested by Napoleon, to whom the score is dedicated, and was the first production given at the Opéra under its new name of Académie Impériale de Musique.

The first Parisian works of Gasparo Spontini (1774–1851) were *opéras comiques*, which were badly received. But when he wrote for the Opéra, he found his true métier and restored the fortunes of that institution. His first work there was the *tragédie lyrique La vestale* (Paris, 1807), which has a libretto by Étienne Jouy. As librettist at the Opéra, Jouy was a key figure in the development of grand opera, preparing libretti for Cherubini, Méhul, and Rossini (*Guillaume Tell*). His libretti show a fine understanding of where Spontini's particular talents lay, and provided various spectacular *coups de théâtre*. The onstage cavalry charge in Spontini's *Fernand Cortez, ou La conquête du Mexique* (Paris, 1809) was put in on the legitimate dramatic ground that the astonishment the audience would experience would match that of the Aztecs on first seeing horses. Napoleon himself had suggested this subject, apparently in the hope that an opera on the conquest of Mexico would reconcile the French public to his Spanish campaign. The other major Spontini opera is *Olimpie* (Paris, 1819), based on Voltaire's tragedy concerning the thwarted marriage plans of the daughter of Alexander the Great. But it failed with the Parisian public, and after this the composer moved in 1820 to Berlin, where a new version of the opera succeeded in the following year.

Spontini's operas are full of ritual ceremonies and imposing stage tableaux with large choral groupings, battles, conflagrations and the like. He was also, as his complex textures and large forces required him to be, one of the first great opera conductors, and in this role he greatly impressed Wagner, who prepared a production of *La vestale* for Dresden which Spontini conducted. As a composer, Spontini has had no more eloquent advocate than Berlioz, who was naturally drawn to this artist in the tradition of Gluck and the *tragédie lyrique*. The thirteenth of Berlioz's *Evenings in the Orchestra* is a piece of musical appreciation so fine as to make us regret all the more the neglect into which Spontini's music has fallen:

Spontini's orchestration . . . has no antecedents. Its special colour is achieved by a use of wind instruments which, even if not very expert technically, contrasts skilfully with that of the strings. The new and important part the composer gives to the violas ... sometimes dividing them into first and seconds like the violins, is another important characteristic of his instrumentation. The frequent stressing of weak beats, dissonances whose resolution is transplanted ... into a different part, bass figures sweepingly arpeggioed in all manner of forms, rising and falling majestically beneath the bulk of the orchestra, the sparing but ingenious use of trombones, trumpets, horns, and timpani, the almost total exclusion of the very top register of piccolos, oboes, and clarinets—all this gives to the orchestra in Spontini's great works a grandiose character, an incomparable power and energy, and often a poetic melancholy.

As for modulations, Spontini was the first to introduce into dramatic music those supposedly foreign to the main key ... [but] ... they are always motivated and presented with wonderful art. He is not like those restless, uninspired composers, who, tired of uselessly worrying one key without result, shift to another in the hope of better luck. Some of Spontini's modulations are flashes of genius. [There] ... is the sudden transition from E flat to D flat in the soldiers' chorus in *Cortez*: 'Let us leave these shores, Spain summons us.' This unexpected change of key strikes the listener so forcibly that his imagination leaps across an immense distance, flies as it were from one hemisphere to the other.

It was also Spontini who invented the colossal crescendo ... [such as] that in the second act of *La vestale* ... an amazing invention whose full effect is felt only on the stage ...

Spontini would have been gratified to know that a younger genius remembered him for the quality of his music rather than for the spectacle of an onstage cavalry charge.

FRENCH ROMANTICISM AND GRAND OPERA

Romanticism had its roots in the mid-eighteenth century, was fertilised by the French Revolution's irreversible break with the past, and flowered in the early nineteenth century. The new age was characterised by its emphasis on instinct and feeling, first encountered in German writers. In his *Sokratische Denkwürdigkeiten* of 1759—at the height of the 'age of reason'—J. G. Hamann said reason could not be trusted, while Herder twenty years later declared, 'The true knowledge is love, is human feeling.'

Goethe's *Faust* (Part I, 1801) took as its theme man's restless search for self-knowledge, and this restlessness also dominates the work of the Frenchman Victor Hugo, whose passionate and eventful dramas supplied many opera plots in the nineteenth century, including Verdi's *Rigoletto* and *Ernani*. British writers were in vogue also, and Ossian, Scott, Byron and Shakespeare all provided operatic source material. Rousseau's philosophy, with its stress on sentiment and identification with nature, was yet another influence. But nature and the other Romantic enthusiasms did not bring inner peace, nor was this sought: thus Shakespeare's plays, like Beethoven's music, were valued above all for their ability to stir and even disturb. Berlioz was 'ravaged day and night by my love of Shakespeare, which the discovery of Beethoven's music, so far from alleviating, seemed only to make more painfully intense . . .'

During the Empire period of 1804–15 the most popular *opéras comiques* were written by Nicolas Isouard and Adrien Boieldieu. The Maltese-born Isouard (1775–1818) is now virtually forgotten, but his *Cendrillon* (Paris, 1810), started a vogue for fairy-tale operas and held the stage all over Europe until Rossini's Cinderella opera *La Cenerentola* (Paris, 1817) eclipsed it. Boieldieu (1775–1834) possessed a more substantial talent, and after early successes in Paris became court composer at St Petersburg (1804–10). His return to Paris saw a gradual increase in his skill, culminating in one of the most enduring of all *opéras comiques*, *La dame blanche* (Paris, 1825). The story is taken from Scott and tells of a soldier who gains his inheritance with the assistance of a pretended ghost, the 'white lady' of the title. Although he has been called the French Mozart, Boieldieu himself admitted that his range was limited, saying he could respond only to happy subjects. A modern French scholar has called him 'one of the most charming musicians France has ever produced', and it is that quality that has kept *La dame blanche* in the repertory.

Daniel Auber (1782–1871) wrote his first *opéra comique* in 1805 and his last in 1869, and having once found a formula that pleased the public, he repeated it again and again. Of Auber's forty-seven operas, thirty-eight have libretti by Eugène Scribe (1791–1861), whose vast output of texts for most of the French and Italian composers of the day provoked references to 'the Scribe factory'. *Fra Diavolo* (Paris, 1830) is the one Auber work that has lasted. Its plot, in which the villain Fra Diavolo tries to steal some jewels and compromises an innkeeper's daughter (Zerlina) in the process, has a mildly *risqué* flavour. The aria in which Zerlina undresses on stage disturbed the young and prudish Mendelssohn, but he was already a severe critic of Auber's incorrigibly chirpy manner; indeed, of *Léocadie*

(Paris, 1824) he complained in terms that might be applied to many of the weaker *opéras comiques* of the time:

> I will not even mention that there is no fire, no substance, no life, no originality to be found in the opera; nor that it is pasted together out of reminiscences, alternately of Cherubini and Rossini; nor will I say that there is not the slightest seriousness nor a single spark of passion in it; nor even that at the most critical moments the singers have to perform gurgles, trills, and florid passages. But ... a pupil of Cherubini and the darling of the public ought at least to be able to orchestrate ... But not even that. In the entire opera, full as it is of set pieces ... there are perhaps three in which the piccolo does not play the principal part! This little instrument serves to illustrate the fury of the brother, the pain of the lover, the joy of the peasant girl; in short, the whole opera might be excellently transcribed for two flutes and a Jew's harp *ad libitum*.

However, it is worth remembering that Rossini called Auber a 'great musician' and that Wagner also praised him. Of his works for the Opéra, the most significant was *La muette de Portici* (Paris, 1828). This tale of a seventeenth-century Neapolitan rebellion, with its crowd scenes, local colour, and volcanic eruption, began the vogue for grand opera on historical subjects. The mute heroine of the title expresses herself entirely in dance and mime. A performance of this work, and in particular the rousing vengeance duet in Act I, sparked off the rebellion in Brussels in 1830 that led to Belgian independence. Paradoxically, the composer himself, a man of diminutive stature, was so timid he could not attend performances of his own music.

Ferdinand Hérold (1791–1833) is remembered today largely for the overture to *Zampa* (Paris, 1831), even though this work and his *Le pré aux clercs* (1832) have sufficient quality for his early death to be regarded as a blow to French opera. In his final illness he lamented, 'I was just beginning to understand the stage.' The stagecraft of the French-Jewish composer Fromental Halévy (1799–1862) is amply demonstrated in *La Juive* (Paris, 1835). This has a libretto by Scribe which tells of the persecution of the Jews in fifteenth-century Constance, but that did not deter the anti-semitic Wagner from bracketing Halévy's *La Juive* and *La Reine de Chypre* (Paris, 1841) as 'two monuments in the history of musical art'. No such claim has been made for the works of Adolphe Adam (1803–56), although his *opéra comique Le postillon de Longjumeau* (Paris, 1836) was once popular. But today, when the repertory outside France is dominated by Italian and German operas, all we hear from this whole group of artists, apart from a rare revival of *La dame blanche* or *Fra Diavolo*, is an aria from *La Juive*, the overture to *Zampa* and, most frequently of all, Adam's ballet *Giselle*.

A more striking and influential figure was Giacomo Meyerbeer (1791–1864). Jakob Liebmann Beer, to give him his real name, was born into a rich Jewish banking family. He grew up in Berlin, was for a time one of Weber's circle, and then went to Italy (1817–24) where, like everyone else, he wrote operas that were largely Rossini imitations. Meyerbeer came to Paris in 1826, where Rossini had offered to stage the last of his six Italian operas, *Il crociato in Egitto* (*The Crusader in Egypt*, Venice, 1824). While in Paris, Meyerbeer—who added 'Meyer' to his surname at the request of an uncle whose fortune he had inherited, and now called himself Giacomo to signal the musical conversion he had undergone in Italy—set up a collaboration with Scribe. Together they produced the grandest of grand operas and the most influential works for the stage between Rossini and Wagner. These are *Robert le diable* (Paris, 1831), *Les Huguenots* (Paris, 1836), which treats the St Bartholomew Massacre of 1572, *Le prophète* (Paris, 1849), which deals with the sixteenth-century Anabaptist rising in Holland, and *L'Africaine*, which Meyerbeer began in 1838 but had not quite finished when he died in 1864. *L'Africaine* (Paris, 1865) vies with *Les Huguenots* as Meyerbeer's most successful opera. Perhaps because it was twenty-five years in the making, *L'Africaine* is one of the longest operas ever written, with more than six hours of music. It is therefore rarely performed uncut, but no one has ever been known to complain about the loss. One who might have done so was Rossini, who was fond of Meyerbeer and wrote a funeral piece in his memory. It is no less typical of the Italian composer that, when Meyerbeer's nephew played him a piece *he* had written in memory of his uncle, Rossini remarked—according to Verdi, who liked telling the story—'Yes, but wouldn't it have been better if you had died and your uncle had written the music?'

Meyerbeer also had an important spell as *Generalmusikdirektor* in Berlin (1842–9) where he promoted Wagner's music as well as his own, only to be repaid later with the scorn of Wagner's article *Das Judentum in der Musik* (*Jewry in Music*). Apart from his grand operas, he wrote two *opéras comiques* for Paris, *L'étoile du nord* (*The Star of the North*, Paris 1854), which was partly based on an earlier work, and *Dinorah, ou le pardon de Ploërmel* (Paris, 1859). But despite the success of these pieces, his reputation rests on the operas he wrote with Scribe.

Les Huguenots is perhaps the essential Meyerbeer opera. Berlioz considered the score to contain enough material for ten operas, and it is all expertly organised to provide contrast both within and between the five acts. Thus the opening act is largely concerned with the male characters, and the second introduces us to the main female roles, while Act III is given mainly to chorus, orchestra and the *corps de ballet*. Act IV contains the finest music, including the tremendous scene of 'the blessing of the swords' as Catholics prepare to slaughter Protestants in an extended ensemble of fanatical ferocity. Then the Protestant hero Raoul sings a once famous love duet with the Catholic Valentine, '*Tu l'as dit*'. Raoul is a high tenor (*haute-contre*) role, and the stratospheric *tessitura* of the part makes it difficult to cast today. In fact there are seven demanding principal roles, and performances in New York at the turn of the century were dubbed 'Nights of the Seven Stars'. Like all Meyerbeer's operas, *Les Huguenots* has been neglected in more recent times but not entirely eclipsed. Indeed each decade seems to bring a major revival of one of the Scribe-Meyerbeer pieces somewhere in the world. However, apart from the casting and production challenges of these huge scores, Meyerbeer's music itself has been denigrated, for example for an often short-winded melodic inspiration and melodies that are rhythmically too stiff. Yet his orchestration and harmony are often fine, and he generates great tension in large ensembles, so that it is easy to imagine the excitement such scenes once inspired, and why they were a key factor in raising the status of the Paris Opéra to new heights.

After the July Revolution of 1830, Louis Véron (1798–1867) became Director of the Paris Opéra, and he began to provide for the new bourgeois and cosmopolitan audience the spectacle it craved. But Meyerbeer's music and Scribe's words were only two elements in this programme, for spectacle was a vital aspect also. The stage sets were by the greatest of French stage designers, Pierre Cicéri (1782–1868) or, later, by his pupils. Cicéri designed the two productions which set the fashion for grand opera, Auber's *La muette de Portici* and Rossini's *Guillaume Tell*, and specialised in scenery that seemed three-dimensional. He laid down new standards of historical accuracy for the scenery and costumes of works set in the medieval or Renaissance periods, and for *Robert le diable* he built a cloister constructed on three sides, introducing a panorama to suggest a passing landscape. For special effects and new lighting techniques, the Opéra had the services of the pioneer of photography, Louis Daguerre (1787–1851), who could create an illusion of moving clouds, sudden shafts of moonlight, and objects throwing shadows as the sun came out. The Opéra, which had first used gaslight (and how appropriately!) for Isouard's *Aladin ou La lampe merveilleuse* in 1822, first used electric lighting for Meyerbeer's *Le prophète* in 1849. Nor was the spectacle confined to music and staging, for ballet was still obligatory and at this period was led by Marie Taglioni and Fanny Elssler. There was a new generation of distinguished singers, some of whom had been trained by Rossini. Meyerbeer was wealthy enough to pay for a good reception from the *claque* (the part of the audience literally hired to applaud) and also from the press. He is said to have invented the press conference and also to have paid people to fall asleep during performances of works by his rivals. He often paid for extra rehearsals too, so that preparation of his productions was very protracted.

Not everyone admired Véron's directorship of the Opéra. Heine said: 'He has adorned the temple of the goddess but shown the goddess herself the door. Nothing could surpass the luxury that rules at the Opéra, which is now the paradise of the hard-of-hearing.' Later, Verdi was to say that he had 'attended hundreds of shows at this theatre, but never a good musical performance', and Mendelssohn considered that Meyerbeer provided every means to hold the attention of a musically uneducated public, but little to engage the heart. Doubtless Scribe's characters are two-dimensional, and his dramas concerned with situation rather than character. Yet his invention of the spectacular is inexhaustible—*Le prophète* has a coronation, a skating ballet, and an explosion—and in his turn Meyerbeer has been skilful in deploying vast choruses and as many as six solo parts in the huge tableaux. If Meyerbeer's critical stock has fallen dramatically since his death, it is not because his music is worthless, but because it was inextricably allied to an operatic form and a corresponding set of artistic values which seem no longer valid.

FROM BERLIOZ TO BIZET

Hector Berlioz (1803–69) wrote four operas, but of the first of them, *Les francs-juges* (1826, unperformed), only a few fragments and the splendid overture remain. Of the three complete Berlioz operas, *Benvenuto Cellini* (Paris, 1838) is the most problematical because the composer did not leave a definitive version of the work. Originally conceived as an *opéra comique*, it was converted for the Opéra (where the spoken dialogue of the *opéra comique* was still not permitted), and revised in 1852 for the performances given by Liszt at Weimar. In recent years performances have tended to be a mixture of these versions, but usually with dialogue.

But whichever version is used, *Benvenuto Cellini* is one of Berlioz's most dazzling works. The libretto, by Léon de Wailly and Auguste Barbier, draws on the *Life* of the sixteenth-century sculptor Benvenuto Cellini and adds some stock situations and characters from the *opéra comique* tradition. The action culminates in the casting of Cellini's famous statue of

Perseus, and is at times a manifesto for Berlioz himself and for all artists who struggle against misunderstanding and officialdom. Its scoring, an area in which Berlioz was an acknowledged master, is colourful even by his standards, especially in the overture and the scene of the Roman carnival. Indeed, the carnival scene has a pace and vivacity that Berlioz never attempted to equal in any later score, and the contrast with the static and monumental quality of some Meyerbeer crowd scenes is striking. The rhythm is especially ingenious, as in the passage near the end of the scene where the brass are in triple time against the rest of the orchestra and chorus in quadruple time. There is also room for tender lyricism and for comedy. Berlioz wrote in his *Memoirs*: 'I have just re-read my poor score carefully and with the strictest impartiality, and I cannot help recognizing that it contains a variety of ideas, an energy and exuberance and a brilliance of colour such as I may perhaps never find again, and which deserved a better fate.' That fate—the work failed its première— was partly due to the technical difficulty of the score, both for the orchestra and the singers—the tenor role of Cellini being especially taxing in its high *tessitura*. Even today, *Benvenuto Cellini* is a work for a virtuoso company.

The failure of *Cellini* effectively closed the doors of the Opéra to Berlioz's operatic masterpiece taken from Virgil, *Les Troyens* (*The Trojans*). This five-act grand opera with ballets was intended for the Paris Opéra, the only French theatre then capable of performing it. Berlioz wrote the text and music in two years (1856–8), and then for five years he waited for the Opéra to agree to stage it before allowing the ill-equipped Théâtre Lyrique, who thought it too long, to divide it in two. In the event they performed only the second part, *Les Troyens à Carthage*, Acts III, IV, and V of *Les Troyens* with a new prelude. Berlioz never heard the first two acts or *La prise de Troie* (*The Fall of Troy*), and a definitive score of the whole work was published only in 1969, one hundred years after the composer's death. Now, mainly thanks to British productions, we can see that *Les Troyens* is a single work, and since its uncut length is about four hours it should always be performed complete and in a single evening.

Berlioz put more of himself into *Les Troyens* than into any other of his works. He had a lifelong love of Virgil's *Aeneid* and dedicated his score 'to the divine Virgil'. As a boy he was overcome when he encountered, under his father's tuition, the story of Queen Dido. As a man writing *Les Troyens* he again had 'fallen in love with this Queen of Carthage [and] passed my life with this race of demi-gods; it seems they must have known me, so well do I know them'. The rejection of this work, which the composer knew to be his best, was a mortal blow to him. As Gounod remarked,

'Berlioz, like his namesake Hector, died beneath the walls of Troy.'

The poet Heine once called Berlioz 'a colossal nightingale, a lark the size of an eagle', and *Les Troyens* blends the intimate and the epic in a synthesis of tragic grandeur. The Trojan acts and the Carthaginian ones complement each other in colour and atmosphere, as the scholar David Cairns has said: 'the contrast in the Trojan and Carthaginian scenes is a contrast in the whole quality of sound—the one austere, electric, possessed, the other lyrical, sensuous, sundrenched, starladen'. As the inexorable destiny of a nation tramples over the fate of individuals, Berlioz records the cost of warfare in personal terms. In Troy there is the affecting scene of Andromache, Hector's widow, who silently leads her son to receive Priam's blessing while a long clarinet melody sings her grief. In Carthage there is the lovely song of Hylas, about which Berlioz wrote to his son, Louis, himself a sailor, 'I thought of you, dear Louis, when I wrote it . . . It is night, the Trojan ships lie at anchor in the port. Hylas, a young Phrygian sailor, sings as he rocks at the masthead . . .' This song, '*Vallon sonore*', creates an intense nostalgia for the 'echoing vales' where Hylas used to wander, and which he will never see again, yet it was cut from the 1863 production of *Les Troyens à Carthage*, as was the great orchestral set-piece of the score, the *Royal Hunt and Storm*, one of Berlioz's most stirring inspirations. Of the many remarkable features of Acts I and II, two stand out—the characterisation of Cassandra and the role of the chorus. Berlioz holds back the strings from the opening to give their authority to Cassandra's entrance, when they introduce her with music throbbing, fateful, and portentous. Her despair increases as the drama unfolds and her prophecies go unheeded by her people, and reaches tragic heights in Act II when she leads the Trojan women to their terrible self-destruction. But no solo role can completely dominate what is essentially a story of nationhood, and it is the chorus which truly animates the drama. From the frenetic celebration of the end of the long siege to the frozen horror at the news of Laocoön's death, the range of the choral writing encompasses all the communal emotions of a race destined for destruction and rebirth.

The later acts offer respite from the din of battle and reach a peak of serenity in the lovely sequence of quintet, septet, and duet which closes Act IV. Indeed, if one has to single out a particular number from *Les Troyens*, perhaps it should be the Act IV duet between Dido and Aeneas, the first music for the opera that Berlioz composed. '*Nuit d'ivresse et d'extase infinie*' ('Night of boundless ecstasy and rapture') is cast in G flat, a favourite key for love duets since Meyerbeer's '*Tu l'as dit*' in *Les Huguenots*, and the text borrows from Shakespeare's *The Merchant of*

Venice ('In such a night as this, when the sweet wind did gently kiss the trees'). The words have a detachment born of the numerous classical allusions, and Dido and Aeneas do not declare their love or discuss each other's merits. Yet Eros is certainly present in such detailed symbolism as the intertwining of the lovers' voices at the first refrain. Here as elsewhere, Belioz can only in a qualified sense be called a Romantic composer, for there is a chastity even about his love music as if his idol Gluck were looking over his shoulder as he wrote. In the musician as in the man, there was always a certain *hauteur*. This gives *Les Troyens* its unique flavour, for classical mythology is put on to the operatic stage without any loss of its cathartic power. The scholar Donald Tovey called *Les Troyens* 'one of the most gigantic and convincing masterpieces of music drama'.

Berlioz's last opera, *Béatrice et Bénédict* (Baden-Baden, 1862), is inevitably a lesser achievement. This two-act *opéra comique* draws on Shakespeare's comedy *Much Ado About Nothing*, and is at its best in the duo-nocturne that closes Act I, which returns us to the balmy Mediterranean night of Act IV of *Les Troyens*, bathing the listener in its warm serenity. '*Il faut méditerraniser la musique*' demanded Nietzsche—'music must be Mediterraneanised'. The philosopher could have been satisfied in this respect by Berlioz.

After Shakespeare and Virgil, the writer Berlioz most admired was Goethe, and his 'dramatic legend' *La damnation de Faust* (1846) is sometimes staged. But for a genuinely operatic *Faust* the world has long settled on Gounod's opera, one of the most widely performed of all French stage works. Charles Gounod (1818–93) made his operatic debut with the somewhat Gluckian *Sapho* (Paris, 1851), written for the Opéra, but it did not succeed. His first *opéra comique* was the Molière adaptation *Le médecin malgré lui* (Paris, 1858), a good-humoured and tuneful work which also proved his first real success. However, the triumph of *Faust* (Paris, 1859) has been remarkable: 1,000 Paris performances by 1894, and 2,000 by 1934, and translated into twenty-five languages. Yet *Faust* was Gounod's artistic undoing. A true *opéra comique*, more engaging in its many lighter moments than in its only mildly Goethean high drama, within ten years of its original production it had acquired sung recitatives and a ballet and had become the quasi-grand opera we know today. Perhaps because it is thus a hybrid, *Faust* broke out of the Meyerbeerian mould of grand opera in its reduction of spectacle and its creation of believable characters. Gounod wisely confines the plot to Part I of Goethe's drama, concentrating on the love of Faust and Marguerite and reducing the philosophical side of Faust's nature to little more than hedonism tempered by feelings of guilt. The pious mood of some moments, especially the final bars when an angelic choir hymns Marguerite's salvation, can seem unctuous today, and the composer rarely conveys more than the surface of emotion— Wagner referred to Gounod's 'face-powder music'. But if *Faust* is less popular now than in earlier generations, its wealth of memorable tunes will ensure that it never leaves the repertory. Perhaps the most surprising melodic inspiration comes in the last scene when Marguerite calls upon the '*Anges purs, anges radieux*' to carry her soul up to heaven. Instead of the *religioso* treatment we might expect Gounod to give such words, he writes a march tune to depict the heroine's crazed defiance of the forces of darkness. No less famous are such numbers as Méphistophélès' *couplets* on 'The Golden Calf', Marguerite's 'Jewel Song', the 'Soldiers' Chorus', and Valentin's Act II *cavatina* with its tender theme taken from the prelude to the opera. The score holds surprises for anyone who thinks he has never heard it, for its fund of melody makes *Faust* the operatic equivalent of *Hamlet*—it is full of quotations.

Two later works of Gounod survive in the French repertory. *Mireille* (Paris, 1864) suffered at first from an unwieldy libretto, and had to be reduced from five acts to three. In the five-act original Mireille, whose love for Vincent is opposed by her father, dies; but at the close of the three-act version she and her lover are happily united. The opera is set in Provence, and features the local dance called the *farandole*. *Roméo et Juliette* (Paris, 1867) is unusually close to Shakespeare, even including the prologue, the passage where we hear of the 'pair of star-crossed lovers' who 'with their death bury their parents' strife'. This is set as an overture with choral participation, the curtain rising to show the chorus and principals who sing lines equivalent to Shakespeare's introductory sonnet. The subject allowed Gounod to write love music in such pieces as Roméo's '*O nuit divine*' in Act II or '*Nuit d'hyménée, o douce nuit d'amour*' in Act IV. Though he is not a profound artist, Wagner's charge of superficiality is unfair, and his lyric gift was to influence both his pupil Bizet and Massenet in their operas.

From the works of Ambroise Thomas (1811–96), only two operas are now performed, *Mignon* (Paris, 1866) and *Hamlet* (Paris, 1868). The former was played over a thousand times at the Opéra-Comique between 1866–94 and both were once performed outside France. From *Hamlet*, Ophelia's mad scene survives as a coloratura display piece, but Thomas is musically unequal to the subject and his general tunefulness lacks character. Perhaps this comment is reflected in Chabrier's somewhat cryptic remark, 'There are three kinds of music— good music, bad music, and the music of Ambroise Thomas.'

More representative of Second Empire Paris is the music of Jacques Offenbach (1819–80), who set up his own company at the theatre he called the Bouffes-Parisiens in 1855. There he produced a string of hugely successful musical stage works he termed either *opéras bouffes*, *opéras comiques*, or *opérettes*. All have spoken dialogue and are witty, brilliant satires on classical subjects as in *Orphée aux enfers* (Paris, 1858) or *La belle Hélène* (Paris, 1864), or on contemporary society as in *La vie Parisienne* (Paris, 1867). Although in English these works are usually called light operas or operettas this does not mean the scores are trivial; their irrepressible gaiety and melodiousness is maintained with skill and the wit is often *risqué* and sharply pointed. There was some prudish resistance to such an art in France, summed up in Saint-Saëns's observation that operetta was 'A daughter of *opéra comique*, but a daughter who has gone to the bad.' But when Offenbach took his music to America there was a stronger reaction and the *New York Times* considered that 'the *opéra bouffe* is simply the sexual instinct expressed in melody . . . priapism is put on a level with music.' Offenbach's last work, *Les contes d'Hoffmann* (Paris, 1881), was unfinished at his death, and is no longer an *opéra bouffe*. But the essential Offenbach remains in those works, with their vivid comedy, which influenced Johann Strauss as well as Sullivan, and which led Rossini to dub their composer 'the Mozart of the Champs-Elysées'.

A satirical bite in Offenbach gave his works a dimension that had once belonged to *vaudeville* and *opéra comique*, but by the 1860s the latter form retained little of its former vitality and invention. The repertory at the Opéra-Comique, although often reviving perennial favourites such as Boieldieu's *La dame blanche* and Hérold's *Le pré aux clercs*, did at least regularly include new works, even if these were written in the old way. At the Opéra between 1860 and 1875 barely a dozen new operas were performed, and they included the work of Wagner (*Tannhäuser*) and Verdi (*Don Carlos*). Of course the French stage had a long history of foreign domination, from Lully through Gluck to Rossini and Meyerbeer, and at this period it was unfortunately especially reluctant to recognise the finest native product, as the history of Berlioz's *Les Troyens* indicates. Two companies were insufficient for Paris, and as a government minister said, 'Between the Conservatoire, which is a school, and the Opéra, which is a museum, a single intermediary—the Opéra-Comique—is not enough.' A third company, the Théâtre-Lyrique, did do much to fill the gap in the 1850s and 1860s, when under the directorship of Leon Carvalho it produced Berlioz's *Les Troyens à Carthage* as well as Gounod's best operas, but it did not survive the Franco-Prussian war of 1870. In the event, French opera was to be rescued from its potentially moribund condition largely by a single masterpiece—Bizet's *Carmen*.

In 1869 Georges Bizet (1838–75) wrote to the Director of the Opéra-Comique, Camille du Locle, 'I shall be delighted to . . . try to change the genre of *opéra comique*. Down with *La dame blanche*!' Bizet had written a number of operas by this date, of which *Les pêcheurs de perles* (*The Pearl Fishers*, Paris, 1863) and *La jolie fille de Perth* (Paris, 1867) based on Scott, are the best known. *Les pêcheurs de perles* received the last review Berlioz wrote before resigning his job as a music critic, in which he said that the opera 'does M. Bizet the greatest honour'. The tenor-baritone duet from the first scene, '*Au fond du temple saint*', is a fine example of Bizet's lyrical gift.

But these works have never matched the universal popularity of Bizet's last and best opera, *Carmen* (Paris, 1875). Based on a story by Prosper Mérimée, set in Seville, *Carmen* tells of the alluring gypsy who gives her name to the opera, and the fatal attraction she has for Don José, the corporal who deserts from the army to follow her. The first performance of *Carmen* at the Opéra-Comique on 3 March 1875 was a failure. Bizet died three months later, and there is a romantic myth that he died never knowing that *Carmen* would soon be recognised as a masterpiece. But from the outset the work had champions, who recognised its quality and importance. The tragic passion of Carmen and Don José, ending in a final scene in which José stabs Carmen to death onstage, was the departure point for the *verismo* movement. 'All men kill the thing they love,' observed Oscar Wilde, and this side of *Carmen* appealed even to the fastidious Nietzsche:

> Finally, love . . . but love as *fatum*, as fatality, cynical, innocent, cruel—and precisely in this a piece of nature. That love which is war in its means, and at bottom the deadly hatred of the sexes! I know no case where the tragic joke that constitutes the essence of love is expressed so strictly, translated with equal terror into a formula, as in Don José's last cry, which concludes the work:
>
> > Yes I have killed her,
> > I—my adored Carmen!
>
> Such a conception of love (the only one worthy of a philosopher) is rare: it raises a work of art above thousands.

Musicians have always admired *Carmen* for its orchestration, the last example of the characteristic French *clarté* before Bizet's successors in France became besotted with Wagner and until Ravel restored classical values in scoring. Richard Strauss's advice to young composers was, 'If you want to learn how to orchestrate, don't study Wagner's scores, study the score of *Carmen*. What wonderful economy, and how every note and every rest is in its proper place.'

There are some familiar *opéra comique* features in *Carmen*, notably Escamillo the Toreador with his '*Votre toast*' and Micaëla, the traditional 'sweet girl'. The first act has an *opéra comique* lightness, with lengthy dialogue separating the set pieces. But as the plot unfolds in later acts the seriousness increases, as does the proportion of music, and Bizet is especially skilful in using snatches of music within the spoken passages to maintain continuity. All this is lost in the version with recitatives added after Bizet's death by the composer Ernest Guiraud. Yet this was the most familiar version of *Carmen* until recent performances which attempt to return to Bizet's original conception and which reveal the innovatory aspects of his work. The dialogue has important points of plot exposition and characterisation, and portrays Mérimée's low-life characters in a way that shows how little *Carmen* has to do with the patronising handling of such figures in *opéra comique*. But then, and paradoxically, *Carmen*, which Bizet intended to reform the *opéra comique* genre, ended up in abolishing it. After such a musical and dramatic *tour de force*, both the heroic posturings of grand opera and the sentimentalities of *opéra comique* seem irrelevant, and in time both were to be replaced in France by the intermediate form of lyrical opera represented by Massenet.

Opera in Paris during the first two-thirds of the nineteenth century became increasingly dominated by the distinct repertory of two theatres, the Opéra and the Opéra-Comique. In the last third it was the latter which was to produce the important new works, while the Opéra produced old favourites or major foreign works, though even in this respect it often lagged far behind its more adventurous rival, first giving *La traviata* for instance in 1926, after it had been in the repertory of the Opéra-Comique for sixty years. The Opéra of the 1870s had hardly changed since the 1830s, when Heine remarked on its increasingly bourgeois and philistine audience: 'The Opéra has become reconciled with the enemies of music, and the well-to-do citizen class has made its way into the *Académie de Musique* as into the Tuileries, while high society has quitted the field.' In 1860, Wagner's *Tannhäuser* fell foul of the Jockey Club, that young, rich and fashionable section of the audience who were accustomed to dine first, then come to the Opéra for the second act of whatever was being performed, when they expected to be able to watch their favourite ballerinas. Wagner refused to put a ballet in the second act, and provoked a riot. But most of the audience no longer summoned carriages, but caught trains back to the suburbs, and the modern opera-goer will have some sympathy with the Opéra management insisting in 1867 on cuts in Verdi's *Don Carlos* so that people would not miss the last train home. But putting the needs of the audience first was not always the way to run a great opera house. Verdi and Wagner, the two giants of the age, were to have their final and greatest triumphs in their own countries, and Paris ceased to be the operatic capital of the world. Ironically, this pre-eminence passed away more or less at the time when the company entered its present, splendid home. The Paris Opéra, still the world's largest theatre, at least in acreage, opened in 1875. All too predictably, the opening programme was largely devoted to its great past, and the overtures to *Guillaume Tell* and *La muette de Portici*, two acts from *La Juive* and a scene from *Les Huguenots* were prepared. The composers of these pieces were all dead, and so was the era they dominated.

8

GERMAN ROMANTIC OPERA

Attempts at vernacular opera. Beethoven's Fidelio. *German Romanticism.*
Weber. Marschner to Schumann. Wagner to Lohengrin.

ATTEMPTS AT VERNACULAR OPERA

By the beginning of the nineteenth century, German-language opera still
enjoyed a lesser status than its Italian and French counterparts. In the
multitude of German states, large and small, princes and public alike
preferred foreign opera, and permanent Italian companies existed in
Berlin until 1806, Munich until 1826 and Dresden until 1832, while
Vienna had state-subsidised Italian opera. In the Austrian capital lively
German *Singspiele* had their place alongside the Italian imports, but other
performances in German were often of French *opéra comique* and Italian
opera buffa in translation.

The reasons for this were largely historical. New operatic traditions
were not easily established, and three of the best German-speaking opera
composers in the eighteenth century—Handel, Hasse and Gluck—had
never used German, while even Mozart wrote only two major operas in
the *Singspiel* tradition, *Die Entführung aus dem Serail* and *Die Zauberflöte*.
Thus German-language poets were unpractised in writing libretti, while
German composers had not yet established an effective vocal style for
their own language.

The *Singspiel* was originally a homely type of comedy, and a good
example is *Doktor und Apotheker* (Vienna, 1786), by Karl Ditters von
Dittersdorf (1739–99), with a domestic setting, a stock *buffo* plot and
characters and lively ensembles. Yet the *Singspiel* existed in another form,
that of spectacular pantomime, and here it could blossom into romantic
expression and mystery, even magic, as it did in the case of *The Magic
Flute*. The same Schikaneder who was both impresario and librettist for
Mozart's work commissioned a sequel to it which used many of the same
characters, the 'heroic-comic opera' *Das Labyrinth oder Der Kampf mit den
Elementen* (*The Labyrinth, or The War with the Elements*, Vienna, 1798), by
the German composer Peter Winter (1754–1825). In a longish career of
some forty years as an operatic composer, Winter had intermittent

successes, and his *Das unterbrochene Opferfest* (*The Interrupted Sacrifice*, Vienna, 1796), a semi-serious work with an English hero set in Peru, is arguably the most convincing German opera between *The Magic Flute* and Weber's *Der Freischütz* (1821). It mixes the genres of *Singspiel*, serious opera and French rescue opera, and Weber liked it enough to conduct it at Dresden. On the other hand, *Colmal* (Munich, 1809), a heroic opera inspired by the Gaelic poems of 'Ossian', did not succeed although Winter thought it his best work. This prolific composer also wrote Italian *opera seria* and *buffa* for Italian audiences, a French *La mort d'Orphée et d'Euridice* (place of première unknown, 1792) and, after Voltaire, *Tamerlan* (Paris, 1802) and several *Singspiele*. *Der Sturm* (Munich, 1798) is a comic opera, but its 'storm' title, after Shakespeare's *The Tempest*, anticipates the romantic treatments of Nature which were to come in the nineteenth century.

Winter was no genius—his melodic and rhythmic invention was very limited and his often florid writing for solo voice frankly bad, while an example of misjudged word setting in Act I of *The Interrupted Sacrifice* gives the soprano Elvira fifteen bars of decoration on one syllable of the word *verzehren*, 'consume'. Beyond this, a weakness of characterisation and structure is evident in his ensembles and finales, although he did show some feeling for the stage. His heterogeneous operatic output in fact reflected the situation of his time, when German opera was a meeting-point of all the current operatic genres.

Winter's *Das Labyrinth* seems to have tried to outdo Mozart's *Zauberflöte*, and such a contest may suggest the limitations of the *Singspiel* and the need for new ideas and directions. These came with the new 'French' operas that Vienna heard in 1802–3, among which were those by Cherubini, a French composer by adoption, such as *Lodoïska*, *Les deux journées* and *Médée* (*see* Chapter 7). The same composer's *Faniska* (Vienna, 1806) impressed both Haydn and Beethoven, who were already his admirers. *Les deux journées* had a text by Jean-Nicholas Bouilly (1763–1842) and the same writer's 'old French libretto', as Beethoven called it, *Léonore, ou L'amour conjugal*, had been used in 1798 for an *opéra comique* of the same title by the French composer Pierre Gaveaux (1760–1825). It told of a true incident that had occurred at Tours during the Reign of Terror: a woman gains entry to a prison where her husband is held by a political enemy, intervening with a pistol when he is about to be murdered. A trumpet call announces the arrival of the Minister, who releases the prisoner. Bouilly, who had himself been the 'Minister' in the real incident, transferred the action to Spain so as to avoid identifying the persons involved. His libretto, after many vicissitudes, became that of Beethoven's opera *Fidelio*.

Fidelio was not quite Beethoven's first operatic venture, for he had worked briefly in 1803 on a Schikaneder libretto, *Vestas Feuer*, an intrigue set in ancient Rome. But he was not particularly excited by a text which contained, as he put it, 'language and verses such as could proceed only out of the mouths of our Viennese apple-women', and he soon abandoned it for the new *Fidelio* project. The opera exists in three versions and has no fewer than four overtures associated with it. The first version (under the title of *Fidelio oder Die eheliche Liebe*, Vienna, 1805) has a libretto by Joseph Sonnleithner, which was revised and reduced from three acts to two by Stephan von Breuning in the following year. The original overture is now confusingly called 'No 2' and was replaced by 'No 3' in the 1806 version; while the *Leonore* Overture 'No 1' was composed a few months later, possibly for a planned production in Prague. The opera finally took shape as we know it today as *Fidelio* (Vienna, 1814), with a libretto revised, with Sonnleithner's permission, by Georg Friedrich Treitschke: the overture now used was named *Fidelio* in the usual way. The composer seems to have been surprised by the revival of interest, and wrote to Treitschke: 'I could compose something new much more quickly than patching up the old . . . I have to think out the whole work again . . . this opera will win me a martyr's crown.' From then on, however, *Fidelio* was a success. Recent revivals of the original version show that some fine music was lost in the revision which the composer reluctantly undertook after complaints that it was 'ineffective and repetitious', but the tightening up of the drama in the final version and its greater concentration on the principals, the imprisoned Florestan and his devoted wife Leonore (disguised as the young man Fidelio), make it the most satisfactory form of the work. It was an especial favourite of the composer's. He told his biographer Anton Schindler, 'Of all the children of my spirit, this one is the dearest to me, because it was the most difficult to bring into the world.'

Beethoven was not deterred by the existence of earlier settings of Bouilly's libretto, of which there were two others besides that of Gaveaux: by Paer (Dresden, 1804) and Mayr (Padua, 1805). There is no evidence that he knew Mayr's one-act *L'amor coniugale*, but he possessed a score of Paer's *Leonora, ossia L'amore conjugale*. He seems also to have known the Gaveaux score, which has several echoes in his own, the most striking of which is the treatment of the prisoners' chorus with its long-held bass notes and gradual rise in pitch and volume as the men emerge from their cells into the light of day. The whole ethos of French revolutionary opera meant much to him, and the fact that Bouilly called the story *'fait historique'* must have moved him especially. Musically he shows a clear debt to Cherubini, and the opera's serious and dramatic elements reflect that composer's energy and noble pathos, while *Singspiel* style has influenced such lighter scenes as those with the jailor's daughter Marzelline and her suitor Jacquino. However, Beethoven transforms and surpasses his models, and the opera is among the noblest in the repertory, with a high moral tone that finds a counterpart in the music itself.

Ethically, *Fidelio* is central to Beethoven's output. The prisoners' chorus itself seems to speak and plead for any oppressed community. Florestan and the other prisoners trust in Heaven for their deliverance, and when it comes his phrase 'your reward awaits in a better world' has an affecting simplicity. Beethoven makes us believe in his essential goodness and that of his wife Leonore, and the opera is an affirmation of his faith in humanity—although the villainous governor Pizarro shows its darker side also—and in a benevolent deity. There is a parallel here with his Ninth Symphony and its choral finale. For those who are not disturbed by the one-dimensional and perhaps naïve C major rejoicings at the end, *Fidelio* can offer one of the most ennobling of all operatic experiences.

The power of this, Beethoven's only opera, comes not simply from the music but also from certain symbolic resonances in the whole scenario. On one level *Fidelio* is a simple rescue opera raised to unusual heights of eloquence and musical drama. But there is another dimension in the composer's identification with Florestan, in that his growing deafness corresponded to prison walls shutting him off from society. Beyond this, according to Maynard Solomon in his *Beethoven*, Leonore's male disguise permits him some 'feelings of feminine identification ... while the nobility of [her] actions assuaged whatever anxiety might otherwise attach to such feelings'. The bachelor Beethoven had closer relationships with men than with the various women in his life. We may consider also the religious symbolism of Act II of *Fidelio*, moving from a Stygian F minor introduction to a blazingly sunlit C major conclusion in one of the theatre's great darkness-to-light pieces. We have already learned from a phrase in the prisoners' chorus that 'the dungeon is a tomb', and the liberation of Florestan is as much a resurrection as a rescue. The frequent references to God's justice underline this aspect of the opera, as does Florestan's vision of Leonore as 'an angel who leads me to Heavenly freedom'.

GERMAN ROMANTICISM

Romanticism, said the French writer Madame de Staël, should achieve 'sublimity of spirit, feeling and action'. For the German novelist Jean Paul it was 'beauty without bounds', while another German writer of the time, E. T. A. Hoffmann, declared that Beethoven's music awakened 'that infinite longing which is the essence of Romanticism'. The events of the French Revolution had deeply impressed German intellectuals and artists. They too sought for social change and, in addition, a sense of national unity and identity. The composer Johann Gottlieb Naumann (1741–1801) cried: 'I and all patriots wish that a good German operatic theatre existed.' A more popular and realistic form of opera might replace the old-fashioned *opera seria* with its court associations, and such rescue operas as *Fidelio* and Winter's *Das unterbrochene Opferfest* did just that, as did the more down-to-earth *Singspiel*—a form to which even Beethoven contributed a couple of finales, one called *Germania*, to works produced in Vienna in 1814–15. A new imaginative interest in folksongs, ballads and fairy tales was yet another aspect of national feeling. The *Kinder-* and *Hausmärchen* fairy tales collected by the Brothers Grimm (1812–14) testified to what has been called 'the timeless components of national consciousness'. Romantic love and longing—the German word *Sehnsucht*—was summed up in the poet Novalis's concept and symbol (1802) of the *blaue Blume* or 'blue flower'. Opera had a special role to play in this movement. As Winton Dean has written, here was 'an art-form perfectly suited to explore the recesses of the subconscious mind, since its use of a double means of expression—words and notes, dramatic action and musical development—enabled it not only to say two or more things at once but to draw on music's hitherto scarcely exploited power to evoke memories and verbal concepts and to suggest what is not explicitly stated. When words failed, the orchestra could take over.'

In German music, attempts to define new expressive areas produced a new feeling of national consciousness. The work of Franz Schubert (1797–1828) is little known in the field of opera, though this was not for lack of trying. Always interested in the stage, his awareness of current intellectual tastes and preoccupations led him to compose several *Singspiele*. The one-act *Die Verschworenen* (*The Conspirators*, 1823, produced Vienna, 1861) takes the Aristophanes *Lysistrata* tale of sexual strike by a group of wives and transfers it to the Crusades in tuneful and colourful music. There were abandoned projects too before the completion of his operas *Alfonso und Estrella* (Vienna, 1822, performed Weimar under Liszt, 1854) and *Fierabras* (1823, performed Karlsruhe, 1897).

The first of these two, sometimes known as *The Magic Harp*, follows the Mozart–Schikaneder *Magic Flute* in its lavish demands for scenic effects. But Schubert did not follow the *Singspiel* tradition of using spoken dialogue—which was also dispensed with in Spohr's *Jessonda* and Weber's *Euryanthe* (*see* below). The libretto of *Alfonso und Estrella* is romantic in feeling and has links with rescue opera: it features choruses for knights, equerries and troubadours as well as a fine duet for the protagonists and a strong E flat minor aria for the villain Adolfo in Act II. It is said to have been Schubert's own favourite among his operas and has skilful and vivid orchestral effects such as the opening dawn scene depicted by a gentle instrumentation of flute, oboe and strings.

Schubert's last opera, *Fierabras*, was intended for the Kärntnertor Theatre and was composed during 1823. However, the failure of Weber's *Euryanthe* earlier in the same year discouraged the management from staging another German opera, and the production was cancelled. This opera set in Spain tells how love overcomes a German-Moorish rivalry in a style and story giving scope for national and romantic feeling. There are good solo numbers and duets—effective arias for Fierabras and Florinda, a duet for Florinda and Maragond and another scene in which Eginhard serenades the King's daughter Emma with clarinet and *pizzicato* strings. Choruses are another feature, and one unaccompanied chorus has the words '*O teures Vaterland*', 'O dear Fatherland'. *Fierabras* deserves to be better known than it is, for although some have doubted its dramatic effectiveness, the scholar Maurice Brown declares of its music that 'page after page reveals the greater Schubert'.

E. T. A. Hoffmann (1776–1822) is better known as a writer than as a composer, but his music with its strong element of fantasy was influential and admired in its time. He produced a number of stage works including a *Singspiel* on a Spanish story called *Liebe und Eifersucht* (*Love and Jealousy*, 1807), a 'romantic opera' called *Der Trank der Unsterblichkeit* (*The Cup of Immortality*, 1808) on the theme of eternal life, and a 'heroic opera' called *Aurora* (1812). But his best known opera is *Undine* (Berlin, 1816), which deals with the love of a water-spirit and a mortal, Hugo. The work was called a 'magic opera', but is in fact a kind of *Singspiel* which includes spoken dialogue and an elaborate finale. There are songs and choruses, and a certain seriousness of tone that may owe something to Gluck, Cherubini and Mozart—whom Hoffmann called 'the inimitable creator of Romantic opera'. The action moves quite swiftly, however, though in this 'number' opera some critics noted a tendency to end sections abruptly. Among those critics was Weber, himself to become a major figure of Romantic opera, though in general he was highly enthusiastic, and in 1817 wrote of *Undine*, 'I thought the music full of character and effect. It is the opera Germans want, a self-contained work of art in which all elements, contributed by the related arts in collaboration, merge into one another and are absorbed in various ways so as to create a new world.' Here was a reference forward to what Wagner was to call the *Gesamtkunstwerk* or artistic union that was to be the ideal of German opera, while the story of an attempted union between a supernatural creature and a mortal symbolised a romantic wish to achieve union with Nature. The story was to be treated again by Lortzing (*see* below) in 1845.

Ludwig Spohr (1784–1859) made his name with *Faust* (Prague, 1816), which for some is the first fully Romantic opera. Again we may quote Weber, who conducted its première, and admired the way in which the composer used 'a few melodies, carefully and felicitously devised, which weave through the work like delicate threads, holding it together intellectually'. Another feature Weber especially admired was the way in which themes of the opera were foreshadowed in the overture. Spohr revised it much later, in 1852, and added recitatives: but more important was his addition of 'reminiscences . . . harmonies of then and now' that look forward to Wagnerian *leitmotif* technique. The supernatural element belongs in the new Romantic tradition, as does the 'beauty and the beast' fairy story of Spohr's *Zemire und Azor* (Frankfurt, 1819), while the theme of redemption through love anticipates Wagner, as does the atmospheric instrumentation. But the composer's major operatic success was in his *Jessonda* (Kassel, 1823). Set in India, this tells of the Rajah's widow Jessonda, who must die on her husband's funeral pyre according to custom: she is helped by a young Brahmin priest and a former lover who rescues her. Spohr's naturally chromatic style was given full rein in this opera, in which he also broke down the 'number' element into a kind of continuous *arioso*, thus yet again paving the way for Wagner, who was to adopt such 'through-composed' methods in his own works. Possibly Spohr allowed lyricism to dominate over action too far for his operas to have held the stage, but *Jessonda* is still to be seen occasionally. Wagner paid him a fine tribute when he later called him 'an old man worthy of the highest honour . . . whose youthful spirit is still illuminated by the radiant sunlight of Mozart'.

WEBER

Carl Maria von Weber (1786–1826) was the son of a theatre director, a musician who married a singer. He thus grew up with music and the stage in his blood. He composed his first *Singspiel* at the age of eleven, and this was followed by a 'romantic-comic opera' called *Das Waldmädchen* (*The Forest Maiden*, Freiberg, Saxony, 1800), later revised as the 'romantic opera' *Silvana* (Frankfurt, 1810), about a knight, Rudolf, and his love for a girl of the woodland. A two-act opera on a contemporary novel featuring Nature, the power of coincidence and a holy man, *Peter Schmoll und seine Nachbarn* (Augsburg, ca 1803), was successful enough to secure for him the post of *Kapellmeister* at Breslau at the precocious age of seventeen. There he was to upset many people in the theatre by such demands for reform as 'the rearrangement of the orchestra's seating plan, the revision of the repertory to exclude feeble but popular works, and the superannuation of elderly singers'. He seems to have been an early example of a modern whiz kid, unpopular though respected for the quality of his work. A strange accident—drinking engraving acid he mistook for wine—put him out of action for two months during which his reforms were undone, and Breslau may have been relieved when he resigned in pique.

Such talent and energy were not unrecognised, however. Weber's career proceeded apace, and in 1813 he took up a major appointment as Director of the Prague Opera. Here, he recruited singers for their ensemble abilities and ability to be part of a team rather than their star quality. He revised rehearsal schedules, and held discussions with designers and costumiers, even learning Czech to facilitate his work. Despite some resistance and controversy, he seems to have been happy: 'I had the splendid feeling that I could express myself as perfectly through my orchestra as though I were sitting alone at the piano.' His repertory included not only his own operas but also those of Cherubini and Spontini, Gluck and Mozart, and *Fidelio* – though Beethoven's opera was little appreciated when he performed it in 1814.

Weber never enjoyed good health—a damaged right hip gave him a permanent limp, and he died young of tuberculosis—and the pressures of work took their inevitable toll. The time available for composing remained limited when he moved on from Prague in 1816 to become Royal Saxon *Kapellmeister* at Dresden. There his repertory had to be planned to take account of the flourishing Italian Opera which was in competition and supported by the court, but he nevertheless decided to make Dresden a springboard for German opera and worked hard to improve standards, extending his interest to matters of lighting and staging and elaborate rehearsal schedules that began with a reading of the text of a new opera to enable the singers to understand its subtleties. Here too he established a fine repertory, and staged *Fidelio*, five Mozart works, Spohr's *Jessonda*, Winter's *Das unterbrochene Opferfest* and—in time—his own *Der Freischütz* and *Euryanthe*.

The story of *Der Freischütz* first came to Weber's attention in 1810, but before turning to it he first completed the lively *Singspiel Abu Hassan* (Munich, 1811), in which Abu and his wife Fatima try to rid themselves of debt by indulging in intrigues from which the Caliph finally rescues them: the vivacious overture gives the flavour of the plot. An unfinished comic opera called *Die drei Pintos* (1821) only reached the stage when Mahler completed it for a production in 1888. However, the 'romantic opera' *Der Freischütz* (Berlin, 1821) was given over thirty performances within a year in various German cities and became the acknowledged model of a new kind of German opera that had an immediate relevance to real life. Its title translates only clumsily into English: *The Magic Bullet* is sometimes used. The story, set in the seventeenth century, is drawn from a series of ghost stories called *Gespensterbuch* (*Collected Ghost Stories*, 1810–17) by Johann August Apel and Friedrich Laun. It tells of a young forester called Max who, frustrated after failing in a shooting test, is persuaded to cast magic bullets with the aid of the evil forester Caspar and his familiar spirit Samiel. In the competition on which his future depends, he astonishes all with his skill at first, but the last bullet then strikes down his beloved Agathe. However, she and Max (who confesses his fault) are saved upon the intercession of a good and wise hermit.

'No German opera has ever been taken up so widely and so rapidly,' writes the scholar John Warrack, and the immediate success of *Der Freischütz* is not hard to understand. Plot, characters and style were all typical of a now prevailing fashion in which ordinary people confronted wild and mysterious forces of good and evil. In this number opera, certain pieces had a wide appeal—a Huntsmen's Chorus and Bridesmaids' Chorus use a folk idiom, while the Wolf's Glen scene where the magic bullets are cast is attractively eerie, using speech as well as music and set in a forest with a waterfall, thunderstorms and a mountain background. Such fashionable Gothic horrors could only please with an agreeable *frisson*, and if any single operatic scene can be said to represent this aspect of German Romanticism, the Wolf's Glen is the one. Its music features the mysteriously rootless chord of the diminished seventh which is associated with the devilish 'wild huntsman' Samiel, together with sinister horns and drums emphasising the bass register, while a big climax is reached with the moulding of the bullets.

When a Viennese impresario, Barbaia, asked Weber for a new opera 'in the style of *Der Freischütz*, he decided instead to offer a grand opera, something new rather than a mere reworking of an earlier vein. His 'grand heroic-romantic opera' *Euryanthe* (Vienna, 1823) is an ambitious work with a complex plot of love and intrigue. Though he was now famous and the friend of Beethoven and Schubert, Weber's uncertain health had deteriorated and he worried about the new work and its awkward libretto by the poetess Helmine von Chezy. The cast liked the new opera, but Schubert had doubts—and Weber was rather irritated to learn of his opinion, though he tried to put on the younger composer's *Alfonso und Estrella* at Dresden later. The cuts that were made by the conductor after Weber's departure for Dresden eleven days after the première did not help matters, and the opera was not successful. Yet in *Euryanthe* Weber had not rested on his laurels: he had cut out spoken dialogue in favour of continuous music and intensified expression through subtle techniques such as bold harmonies and modulations, for example at the start of Act III, and the use of a sinuous *leitmotif* for the evilly scheming Eglantine. He described such motivic writing as a useful device that provided 'the threads in the fabric of an opera'—again an anticipation of Wagner's method. He must have been pleased that *Euryanthe* was rather more liked by the Dresden audience when he presented it there in 1824, and it was later admired by Schumann, Liszt and Wagner.

In the summer of 1824 Weber was asked to compose a new opera for London's Covent Garden Theatre. His health had now worsened to the point when his doctor told him that tuberculosis would inevitably kill him within a few years, and it seems to have been partly for the sake of his family's financial future that he accepted the London offer. *Oberon* (London, 1826) is almost a pantomime, with a story taken from a poem of chivalry and magic by Christoph Martin Wieland (1780) set in the thirteenth century and beginning with the line 'Ride out into an old romantic land!' Here the true love of Sir Hüon of Bordeaux and the Sultan's daughter Reiza is tested by adversity in locations as exotic as Baghdad and Tunis. As well as the Emperor Charlemagne, Haroun el Rashid, pirates and mermaids, the characters include Oberon, Titania and Puck, although there is no real connection with Shakespeare's *A Midsummer Night's Dream*. Today *Oberon* is best remembered for its overture, music of great delicacy and atmosphere, and Reiza's evocative soprano aria 'Ocean! thou mighty monster'.

Travelling via Paris, where he called on Cherubini and Rossini, Weber reached London in March 1826 and conducted the première of *Oberon* on 12 April. He then became seriously ill, although his departure for home was fixed for 6 June. On the morning of the 5th he was found dead in his bedroom. He was buried in England, but in 1844 his successor at Dresden, Wagner, arranged that the coffin should return to that city. When the ship bearing it docked at Hamburg, other vessels in port dipped their colours in salute, and an oration was delivered at the reburial by Wagner himself, who also composed a choral piece for the occasion.

MARSCHNER TO SCHUMANN

Heinrich Marschner (1795–1861) was one of Weber's disciples, and when Weber produced Marschner's opera *Heinrich IV und d'Aubigné* at Dresden in 1820, the younger man made his home there soon after. Here he called publicly for the establishment of a national German opera, produced a *Singspiel, Der Holzdieb* (*The Outlaw*, Dresden, 1823), and in time gained a permanent appointment in the city. But when Weber died Marschner was not appointed to succeed him and he sought his fortune elsewhere, settling in Leipzig and remaining there for many years in association with the Stadttheater. His Leipzig *Der Vampyr* and *Der Templer und die Jüdin* (*The Templar and the Jewess*, 1828, 1829) were alike styled 'Romantic operas'. So was his best-known work, *Hans Heiling* (Berlin, 1833), a psychological drama set in no defined place that has as its title the name of the underworld spirit king whose unsuccessful attempts to court a mortal girl, Anna, provide the plot. Marschner tends to emphasise characters rather than atmosphere, and though not wholly successful he thus provided a valuable dimension beyond Weber's own achievement. His characters are more complex and modern-seeming, and even the central character of *Der Vampyr*, the Lord Ruthven who must sacrifice three girls to placate Satan, is one divided against himself and not wholly villainous. In *Der Templer und die Jüdin*, based on Scott's *Ivanhoe*, Wagner admired the mixture of good and evil in the flawed hero Sir Brian de Bois-Guilbert, who has killed but repents as a Knight Templar, calling his big *scena 'Mich zu verschmähen'* 'a creation of the greatest originality and feeling'. As for *Hans Heiling*, its story looks forward to Wagner's *Der Fliegende Holländer* (*The Flying Dutchman*), and the opera has been called by the scholar Volkmar Köhler 'the definitive expression of the spirit of his age . . . if musical romanticism ever re-created *Don Giovanni* in its own terms, it was in *Hans Heiling*'. On the other hand, in his one comic opera, *Der Bäbu* (Hanover, 1838), Marschner seems to have been less at ease. Structurally, he tried to move away from number opera and to make opera flexible, but did not find an effective through-composed form until his last work, *Sangeskönig Hiarne, oder Das Tyringsschwert* (*Hiarne the Singer-King or The Thuringian Sword*, 1858, produced Frankfurt, 1863). But perhaps his work is neglected today because its music is not strong enough. The music of opera, as we have seen, cannot be merely incidental to the text. Wagner evidently learned from Marschner in the realm of plot and mood, and even probably music, but he added a vital dimension of symphonic development and musical-dramatic cohesion of his own.

The career of Albert Lortzing (1801–51) was almost wholly in opera. This actor's son was a composer, librettist, conductor, producer and tenor singer who wrote operas on a variety of subjects, including *Hans Sachs* (Leipzig, 1840), *Casanova* (Leipzig, 1841) and *Undine* (Magdeburg, 1845), the first two designated 'comic operas' and the last a 'romantic magic opera'. As with Hoffmann, *Undine* has magic to the fore, especially at the end, where Lortzing foreshadows Wagner's *Götterdämmerung* with a palace disintegrating amid rising waters. But his two most impressive operas are the comedies *Zar und Zimmermann* (*Tsar and Carpenter*, Leipzig, 1837) and *Der Wildschütz* (*The Poacher*, Leipzig, 1842). Here he deals with misunderstandings—in the first, originally called *The Two Peters*, they surround Tsar Peter the Great of Russia and his shipyard friend Peter Ivanov, and in the second they involve Baroness Freimann disguised as the poacher-schoolmaster Baculus's fiancée Gretchen. Such easy-going romantic comedies suited Lortzing admirably, and in them he produced tuneful arias and substantial finales. The writing for chorus reveals Weber's influence, not least in the hunting music in Act I of *Der Wildschütz*, and the use of the orchestra is effective with appropriate though seldom sparkling colours. Marschner and Lortzing provide a contrast, the former excelling in serious work and the latter's gift being mainly for comedy: thus in Lortzing's one serious 'revolutionary opera' *Regina* (1848, produced Berlin, 1899), the absence of comedy deprives the music of real life. Lortzing's view of his own gifts was modest: 'I would be happy for a few of my works to give a number of honest souls some agreeable hours.'

Otto Nicolai (1810–49) trained in Berlin and then went in 1833 to work for some years in Italy. Later he was to say: 'Had I never left Germany, I should never have written as I do. You have to have German schooling, and then add Italian facility. That is how Mozart came to be.' He composed five operas in all. Only the last of these, *Die lustigen Weiber von Windsor* (*The Merry Wives of Windsor*, Berlin, 1850) is to a German text, and it is for this work only that he is remembered now. This 'comic-fantastic opera' after Shakespeare has become a well-loved repertory work and represents a triumph for a composer whose mixed German and Italian background was not always easy for him to integrate, and who once said, 'I have more intellect than imagination, and so composition is harder for me than for others—people like Donizetti write continuously without self-criticism.' Nicolai knew the *buffo* and lyrical styles well, and admired Rossini and Bellini among the Italian composers of his day. Eventually his search for a libretto without 'eternal raging, bloodletting, insults, beating and murder' brought him to *The Merry Wives of Windsor*, although with typical modesty he at first hesitated to set it, feeling that only Mozart could have done it justice. Here he produced the harmonious balance of styles that he sought, with Italian grace allied to vigorous *Singspiel* comedy. The plot is similar to that of Verdi's *Falstaff*, which was the name used when it was performed in London in 1864, but Alice Ford and Meg Page are called Frau Fluth and Frau Reich. In the view of the scholar Thomas-M. Langner, Nicolai 'brought to a peak the bourgeois romantic comic opera' in a work rich in melody, neat ensembles, feeling and pace. Sadly, two months after its première this 'small, blond and affable man' was dead of a stroke at thirty-eight.

Hardly any German composer could refrain in the first half of the nineteenth century from writing opera. Friedrich von Flotow (1812--83) composed eighteen, but only the graceful and charming *Martha* (Vienna, 1847), set in the England of Queen Anne, has endured. Among greater figures we rarely think of Mendelssohn and Schumann in this connection, but both attempted it. Felix Mendelssohn (1809–47) composed six before he was twenty-one, considered Shakespeare's *Tempest* as a subject in 1831 and briefly worked on another, *Die Loreley*, two years before his death. As a boy he drew on the *Singspiel* tradition, writing music of great skill and character as early as *Die Soldatenliebschaft* (*The Soldier's Love*, 1820) and *Die beiden Pädagogen* (*The Two Pedagogues*, 1821): doubtless the model was Mozart in both of these. *Die Hochzeit des Camacho* (*The Camacho Wedding*, Berlin, 1827) was a more ambitious opera on a tale drawn from Cervantes' *Don Quixote*. It must have been an unusual and saddening experience for this brilliant youth to see it fail at its première, when there were even demonstrations against it. The reasons are still unclear: perhaps the audience disliked the social criticism in the plot, in which the champions of wealth are defeated by Cupid's warriors, or the way in which the pretended death of one of the main characters was not set to music at all. The one-act *Liederspiel* or 'song-play' *Die Heimkehr aus der Fremde* (*The Return from Abroad*, Berlin, 1829) seems to have been very simply melodious: its overture survives today under the alternative name *Son and Stranger*.

Robert Schumann (1810–56) once wrote that German opera was his 'artistic morning and evening prayer' and yet despite his strong literary background and interests he only composed one, *Genoveva* (Leipzig, 1850). He had considered many operatic subjects including *Hamlet* and *The Tempest*, the Nibelung saga, *Till Eulenspiegel*, Schiller's *Maria Stuart*, King Arthur and the *Odyssey*, and then worked on a *Scenes from Goethe's*

Faust during 1844–53, when the original operatic form changed to that of a cantata. *Manfred* (1849), based on Byron, exists only as incidental music rather than sung drama, while *Paradies und die Peri* (1843) is a 'secular oratorio'.

Genoveva reached completion and production as a four-act work based on a tragedy by Friedrich Hebbel set in the Middle Ages, itself derived from a French legend. A wife, Genoveva, is left in the care of the knight Golo while her husband Siegfried goes on a crusade: Golo attempts to win her, but she remains faithful. Schumann found the story difficult to set and altered the libretto provided for him by Robert Reinick, who then disowned it. Having approached Hebbel himself without success, the composer then showed his text to Wagner. But the younger man was uneasy: 'I have grave misgivings [and] called his attention to some grave defects, suggesting the changes needed . . . [but] he deeply resented any interference, so that I let it alone.' The opera's lack of real success was a disappointment. Yet it was not a complete failure either: Schumann and his wife found 'a growing enthusiasm in the audience'. Does it deserve its neglect? The critic Joan Chissell feels that 'all the characters sing the same sort of music . . . that fails to capture their several kinds of emotional storm and stress', while Gerald Abraham has found the work's lack of dramatic skill a 'mortal weakness':

> The score of *Genoveva* has many beauties and is written in a convention little less advanced than Wagner's at the same period, with continuous texture and almost complete absence of bare recitative, but suffers from lyrical expansiveness and feeble characterisation. *Genoveva* employs thematic reminiscence—particularly in association with the villain Golo—quite as much as *Tannhäuser* or *Lohengrin* (Wagner himself had not yet arrived at the true symphonic *leitmotif*), but it is characteristic of Schumann's lack of theatre sense that his points are made so unobtrusively that they have often passed unnoticed, whereas Wagner's are driven home with the necessary emphasis.

It may be unwise to write *Genoveva* off as wholly unworthy of revival: after all, we are talking of a major work by a major composer. Perhaps the right kind of production would at least bring a partial rehabilitation, and in the meantime, substantial excerpts have been recorded.

WAGNER TO *LOHENGRIN*

Whatever the stature of the composers discussed in this chapter so far, they must be viewed above all in relation to Richard Wagner (1813–83), the towering figure in German opera during the latter part of the nineteenth century. His rise to prominence was beset by problems, but by the middle of the century he had written opera of real stature and was moving towards the new operatic concepts of his mature years. This journey can be traced in the events of his life and in his stubborn belief in his own abilities and vocation, especially as the tribulations of his early career directly influenced his compositions.

His father died when he was six months old and his mother married an actor and poet called Ludwig Geyer. Richard's interest in the theatre began on the literary side, and at fourteen he wrote a tragedy which he said was 'constructed out of *Hamlet* and *King Lear* . . . forty-two people died in the course of this piece, and I saw myself compelled as it developed to call most of them back as ghosts, otherwise I should have been short of characters for my final act'. The experience of writing this play led him to music: as he realised, 'My work could only be rightly judged when set to the music I had resolved to write for it, which I intended to start composing immediately.' At this time his musical studies were haphazard, aided by a study of Beethoven's symphonies and a couple of textbooks, followed by some harmony lessons with a teacher called Christian Gottlieb Müller. 'I am letting everything else go and doing nothing but music,' he wrote at this time. In February 1831 he enrolled as a music student at Leipzig University.

The young Wagner admitted three main influences—E. T. A. Hoffmann on the literary side, Weber and Beethoven on the musical. Hoffmann's works excited him because this writer's dream-like images 'seemed to take on living form and reveal their powerful meaning'. Live music thrilled him also, as he remembered forty years later in his memoirs:

The mysterious joy I felt in hearing an orchestra play close to me remains one of my most pleasant memories. The mere tuning up of the instruments put me in a state of mystic excitement; even the sounding of fifths on the violin seemed to me like a greeting from the spirit world, the sound of these fifths was closely associated in my mind with ghosts and spirits. The long-drawn A of the oboe, which seemed like a call from the dead to arouse the other instruments, never failed to raise all my nerves to a feverish pitch of tension and the swelling C in the overture to *Der Freischütz* told me that I had stepped with both feet, as it were, into the magic realm of awe.

When he heard a Beethoven symphony for the first time in the Leipzig

Gewandhaus, his emotional response was typical of the Romantic age: 'The effect on me was indescribable; I conceived an image of him in my mind as a sublime and unique supernatural being. This image was associated in my brain with that of Shakespeare; in ecstatic dreams I met them both and spoke to them, and on awakening I found myself bathed in tears.'

The young composer set about acquiring the technique that would allow him to emulate his idols: 'What I wanted in my youth was not fame but the ability to write one theme that was my own rather than remodelled Beethoven or Weber.'

In the summer of 1832, aged nineteen, Wagner set to work on his first opera. *Die Hochzeit* (*The Marriage*) was 'a nocturnal piece of darkest hue' which had conventional dramatic elements of love versus duty; but he only wrote part of the music. Possibly he lost interest after gaining fresh experience in a répétiteur-chorusmaster's post at Würzburg, the first of several theatrical appointments held in these years of apprenticeship. Early in 1834 he completed a 'romantic opera' called *Die Feen* (*The Fairies*, produced Munich, 1888). It was in the tradition of Weber and Marschner, and though he never heard it performed its completion gave him confidence. By this time, too, he knew that all libretto texts must be his own. In the same year, the first of his many essays, *Die deutsche Oper*, presented a case for a 'cosmopolitan' operatic style. *Das Liebesverbot* (Magdeburg, 1836) is a two-act comedy after Shakespeare's *Measure for Measure* that owes more to Donizetti and Auber, and perhaps Rossini also, than German models. It seems that he learned his craft in part by studying a variety of styles, but though the melodious Italianate style of this opera pleased the Magdeburg audience, he failed to get it presented in the more important centres of Leipzig and Berlin.

Marrying in 1836, Wagner moved to a new post as musical director of the theatre at Riga in the following year. His experience as a répétiteur and conductor already included *Fidelio* and *Don Giovanni*, as well as operas by Cherubini, Meyerbeer, Auber, Rossini, Marschner, Bellini, Hérold, Weber and Spohr; now he added *Figaro*, *The Magic Flute* and Bellini's *Norma* to them. Few opera composers have been better informed and practised in the styles of his own and earlier generations, and Wagner was convinced that he could match the masters of his day and that recognition must come. In the meantime his luxurious style of living ran up large debts, and when his contract in Riga expired in 1839 he and his wife Minna had to leave secretly so as to avoid their creditors. They made their way first to London and then to Paris, where Meyerbeer had promised him an introduction to the Opéra management and he hoped to have his new opera, *Rienzi* (Dresden, 1842), produced. But all his hopes foundered: even an attempt to join the chorus at the Opéra failed and months of grinding hack-work in journalism and making piano arrangements of other men's operas did not save him from actually spending some time in a debtors' prison.

The failure to mount *Rienzi* was especially disappointing in that the opera marked a real advance on its predecessors. Bulwer Lytton's novel of a real-life fourteenth-century Roman tribune who rescued the citizens from a corrupt patriciate is here given a rich treatment with chorus, ballet and spectacle. It perhaps also reveals that Wagner saw himself as a hero who would rescue opera itself from tired and trivial traditions. At this stage his ideal was to go beyond them, intending 'not only to imitate but, with reckless extravagance, to surpass all that had gone before'. Later, he would abandon those same earlier methods and replace them with something entirely new.

The often rough sea voyage from Riga had reminded him of the legend of the ghostly Flying Dutchman, and this was to provide him with the libretto of his next opera, *Der fliegende Holländer* (Dresden, 1843). In the meantime, Paris afforded new musical experiences: a fine performance of Beethoven's Ninth Symphony, with its 'most touching and heavenly melodies', and Berlioz's *Roméo et Juliette* and *Symphonie fantastique*, while a fellow-German introduced him to the legends of Lohengrin and Tannhäuser. In 1841 he completed *The Flying Dutchman* and in the following April he moved to Dresden, where in 1843 he became the conductor of the Opera. There the first performance of *Rienzi* was a useful experience though the work lasted over six hours and cuts had to be made to the score.

Der fliegende Holländer represented a further step towards Wagner's mature style, with its strong human drama allied to supernatural elements and the vast forces of Nature, while its theme of redemption through love was to continue to preoccupy him. The plot, as told by Heine in a story dated 1831, is of a sea captain who has invoked the Devil and is condemned to sail the seas until a good woman's love redeems him: in the end this is done by Senta, and the two are finally seen ascending to Heaven. The composer had at first conceived it in one great sweep without intervals, though he sensibly changed his mind before the performances. Nevertheless, even the revised three-act version makes considerable demands on the singers, who must act convincingly as well as being vocally strong. Stormy sea music and shanty-like rhythms pervade the score, and its wild atmosphere must also be conveyed by the production. The conductor Franz Lachner said once that 'The wind blows out at you whenever you open the score,' and nowhere is this truer than in the overture, a symphonic poem in its own right built around the music of the Dutchman, Senta and the solo in Act II called 'Senta's Ballad' in which the young girl recounts the Dutchman's story while spinning with her friends in her father Daland's house. This ballad was written first and, said the composer, contained 'the thematic seed of all the music . . . the poetically condensed image of the whole drama as it was in my mind's eye'. But the première of what he called his 'storm-swept ballad' was fairly coolly received, although the famous soprano Wilhelmine Schröder-Devrient sang the role of Senta, and a year later two performances which he conducted at the Berlin Opera brought sharp press hostility.

Wagner had by now become convinced that legend and medieval poetry must be the source of his operatic material, and the knightly tale of *Tannhäuser* (Dresden, 1845) reflects a new confidence and artistic conviction. He finished his texts in verse form, originally called *Der Venusberg*, during 1843, but the Dresden production of this 'great Romantic opera' was only of its first version, for a new one with added ballet and other changes was prepared for Paris in 1861. Here 'number' opera was left behind once and for all, and the composer wrote more continuously, as he put it, 'to turn away from operatic diffuseness'. There was a new involvement with the psychological states of the characters, that is strikingly illustrated in the scene of the knight Tannhäuser's return from the worldly pleaures of the Venusberg. The solo line here is flexible and semi-declamatory in a way that stems from *arioso* style and from the German language itself, while the orchestra enhances the mood. Against this we may contrast a number of big set pieces like the singers' tournament and the choruses of pilgrims which arise plausibly from the plot. To allow his flawed hero Tannhäuser to carry the expressive burden of his role and dominate the ensembles, Wagner needed a new breed of tenor singer, the heroic tenor or *Heldentenor*, with a voice heavier than its Italian counterpart, and henceforth this voice would be important to all his work.

In *Lohengrin* (Weimar, 1850), Wagner again sought to let plot and characters evolve in a way that was dramatically convincing and musically cohesive, and he relied increasingly on the *leitmotif* technique in which musical ideas are identified with individuals and dramatic features and recur throughout the opera. Here the mood is one of expressive longing as befits the story of the knight of the Holy Grail, Parsifal's son, who descends from Montsalvat to seek the earthly love — 'a woman who would believe in him [and] love him as he was', said the composer — from which his divine nature has excluded him and who is only invincible while his true identity remains unknown. Once again the plot deals with the conflict between spiritual and carnal desires, and redemption through sacrifice. Orchestral textures are at once fuller and more subdued than before, and musically unified scenes tend to gain in length, with solo voices and choral writing well integrated. Tonality (the use of key) signals the approach of the mature Wagner: Lohengrin's characteristic key is a clear and bright A major, while his beloved, Elsa, is given a 'softer' and more feminine A flat or E flat, and the forces of evil are generally placed in F sharp minor. Thus the music parallels the drama, which proceeds at a dignified pace that matches the nobility of the principals, much of it indeed being rather static in feeling. The melodic vocal line still dominates, so that *Lohengrin* remains in essence a series of recitatives, *ariosos* and choruses, although there is now a superbly sustained lyricism. Despite the skilful linking of scenes, however, we still lack the unique feature of the later Wagner, a cumulative symphonic power, although he had written in 1851: 'The new form of dramatic music must have a musical shape and to do that it must display the unity of a symphonic movement . . . in the closest association with the drama.'

That Wagner should move forward so purposefully in these years is a reflection of the relative security he found in Dresden. His salary was still not enough for his lifestyle, and he resented having to spend much time performing, especially at court functions where his status was only that of the King of Saxony's skilled servant. His report on performing conditions tells us that he thought singers were overpaid and orchestral musicians the opposite, and that the principal players were as important as the star singers. At that time the conductor was placed between the stage and the orchestra, with his back to them, a situation Wagner felt should be changed 'because he cannot communicate his intentions to the players as he would like [while as they look towards the stage] much of their tone is lost to the audience'.

In 1848 Wagner became involved in the revolutionary politics that were spreading through Germany, going so far as to contemplate a dramatic work on the story of Jesus which made the founder of Christianity a revolutionary, and reading a fiery socialist speech at a public gathering. At the same time he also began work on a poem called *Siegfrieds Tod* (*The Death of Siegfried*), in which his hero would overturn an old and corrupt order. His motives were in part a desire for a new and more artistically fruitful order and in part a general support for German nationalism and unification, but such sentiments were of course hostile to the Saxon court where he worked and his actions meant that he had to flee the city, where a warrant for his arrest had been issued. Seven years later the King of Saxony was to say that had he not fled, he would probably have been sentenced to death.

Once again the years of pilgrimage were resumed. Wagner went first to Weimar where Liszt was making preparations for productions of both *Tannhäuser* and *Lohengrin*. From Weimar, where he remained only briefly, he continued, via Paris, to Switzerland where he settled in July 1849.

9

ITALY IN THE *PRIMO OTTOCENTO*

Interregnum—Paer, Mayr, and others. Operatic conditions. Rossini in Italy. Rossini in France. Donizetti and the rossiniani. *Bellini, Romani, and Romanticism.*

INTERREGNUM — PAER, MAYR AND OTHERS

In his *Life of Rossini* (Paris, 1824) Stendhal called the first decade of the nineteenth century an 'interregnum' in the history of Italian opera. Cimarosa had died in 1801 and Paisiello had retired soon after, so that no single figure dominated the scene. But of the many operatic composers at work, two who enjoyed international success stand out—Paer and Mayr. Ferdinando Paer (1771–1839) was director of the Kärntnertor Theatre in Vienna from 1797 to 1801, worked in Dresden for the next five years, and moved to Paris in 1807 where he became Napoleon's *maître de chapelle*. Appropriately enough, his most successful work for Paris was an *opéra comique* called *Le maître de chapelle* (1821). He became director of the Opéra-Comique and, from 1812, of the Théâtre-Italien. Rossini co-directed with him at the Italien in 1824, and an uneasy collaboration ended with Paer's dismissal in 1827. He stayed on in Paris, enhancing his already considerable fame as a singing teacher.

Paer produced much of his most characteristic music in the fashionable form of *opera semiseria*, which, as the term suggests, mixed comic and serious elements. This genre dates back as far as Piccinni's *La buona figliuola* of 1760, but Da Ponte's libretti for Mozart and the French *comédie larmoyante* gave impetus to its development. In Paer, the sentimental aspects of the plots increasingly took precedence over the often perfunctory comic scenes or characters. In *Griselda* (Parma, 1798), based on the last of the hundred tales that constitute Boccaccio's *Decameron*, a marquis marries a peasant girl and subjects her to a series of humiliations culminating in his pretence that he has killed their child, while she, Griselda, nobly endures all and remains loyal. Another ill-treated wife, in this case threatened with starvation, is the heroine of *Camilla* (Vienna, 1799). Paer gives an important role to Camilla's son, Adolfo, which the seven-year-old Rossini was to sing in Bologna in 1805.

Paer's career shows how at this period the initiative in creating new forms and fashions in opera had passed from Italy to France. He took not only *Camilla* but also *Sargino* (Dresden, 1803) from texts already set by Dalayrac, and made an important setting of Bouilly's *Léonore* libretto (*see* Chapter 8). Paer's *Leonora* (Dresden, 1804) has long solos for both hero and heroine, much longer than in Beethoven's *Fidelio*, and consisting of several linked sections. But these are less impressive than the telling moments of intimacy or pathos, such as the exquisite *arietta* '*Deh, per pietade*', in which Florestano begs for water and which achieves great lyrical beauty in just nineteen bars. *Leonora* was revived and recorded in the 1970s.

Johannes Simon (or Giovanni Simone) Mayr (1763–1845) was Bavarian, but trained and worked in Italy. In the words of one German scholar, 'Germany gave England a Handel, France a Gluck, Italy a Simone Mayr', and the conjunction of Mayr's name with two such distinguished predecessors shows the eminence he once had. After a comparatively late start in opera with *Saffo* (Venice, 1794) he was in such demand that he produced sixty-one operas in the next thirty years. Almost all were for Italian cities, but several were also heard abroad, in New York, London, Dublin, Berlin, Warsaw, and even Corfu. He declined several offers of appointments in European capitals and remained devoted to his adopted town of Bergamo in Northern Italy, where he founded a conservatory in 1805. With the rise of Rossini around 1813 Mayr's work was less in demand and he gave more time to his teaching. His most famous pupil was Donizetti.

Mayr wrote in all the prevailing operatic genres. In comedy he followed the *buffo* manner of his time, as in *Le finte rivali* (Milan, 1803), which has pairs of lovers, Eastern disguises, and a baron seeking the most lucrative match for his daughters. He wrote more individual music in his *opere semiserie*, which like Paer he often took from French sources. *La Lodoiska* (Venice, 1796), *I due giornate* (Milan, 1801) and *Elisa* (Venice, 1804) were all treated earlier by Cherubini, and there is even a Mayr version of *Léonore*, called *L'amor coniugale* (Padua, 1805)—but its distance from the original is shown by the elimination of any political content and the designation of this one-act piece as a *dramma giocoso*. Even his 'heroic melodrama' *La rosa bianca e la rosa rossa* (Genoa, 1813), although obviously set in England during the Wars of the Roses, derives from a French libretto. This was one of Mayr's greatest successes, and the first libretto of the writer who was to become the finest Italian librettist of his day, Felice Romani. To complete the range of the composer's *oeuvre*, there are genuinely tragic subjects, at a time when most serious operas still ended happily. *Fedra* (Milan, 1820) is quite a faithful rendering of Racine's *Phèdre* (1677), except that the librettist Luigi Romanelli has Phaedra, having taken poison, leave the stage to die. *Medea in Corinto* (Naples, 1813) owes something to Cherubini's *Médée*, but then Mayr's contract specified that the work should be written 'in the French manner'. In practice this meant that *secco* recitative was abandoned in favour of declamatory recitative accompanied by the orchestra. In this respect *Medea in Corinto* anticipated Rossini's *Elisabetta* by two years, and was probably the first Italian opera to employ the orchestra throughout in this way. This opera is Mayr's finest, and has been recorded.

Mayr was admired by his contemporaries, and even ten years after his death Rossini declared that 'If the composers of our day were to study the operas of Mayr, who is always dramatic . . . and ever melodic, they would find all that they are looking for', though he added that perhaps his chief skills lay in drama. Of his melodic vein there is no more engaging example than the *romanza 'Ov'è la bella virgine?'* from another opera with an English setting, *Alfredo il grande* (Bergamo, 1819). This ballad allowed the composer to use one of his favourite instruments, the harp, which he popularised as an orchestral instrument. A small ensemble of six solo instruments also weaves expressive filigree around the vocal line, an idea perhaps suggested by Mozart—Mayr was regarded as a 'learned' composer because of his scholarly interest in the masters of German music as well as the fashionable French composers. Today the music of 'the immortal Mayr' is largely forgotten, and he is remembered more as a teacher and for his importance in the history of the orchestra—the music historian Paul Henry Lang goes so far as to assert, 'The supposed inventor of the modern orchestra, Berlioz, owes him the lion's share.' Yet of all the composers of the period who are now neglected, it is he perhaps who most merits revival.

There was a host of lesser composers. Niccolò Zingarelli (1752–1837) was one of the last to write conventional *opere serie* on mythological subjects, but he did also compose a *Giulietta e Romeo* (Milan, 1796), complete with a typical *opera seria* happy ending. By contrast, Valentino Fioravanti (1764–1837) was mainly a composer of *opere buffe*, of which the most lasting has been *Le cantatrici villane* (*The Boorish Singers*, Naples, 1799), still sometimes played in Germany as *Die Dorfsängerinnen*. Pietro Generali (1773–1832) made his name with a version of Goldoni's libretto *La buona figliuola* called *Pamela nubile* (Venice, 1804). Generali's lively style and orchestral flair partly anticipate Rossini, whose success led to the eclipse of these artists in the theatre, after which all three, like Mayr, turned increasingly to church music. For Stendhal in 1824 such figures, even Mayr, were mere precursors awaiting the messianic rise of his hero Rossini, so his judgement is often harsh; but perhaps his comment on their decline has some substance: '. . . sudden annihilation is the ultimate fate of all aesthetic artificiality, for, one fine day, the eye will light upon *natural* beauty, and be astonished that the opposite has managed to deceive it for so long'.

OPERATIC CONDITIONS

For much of the *primo ottocento* (roughly the first half of the nineteenth century in Italy) opera composers worked within a system which throws much light on the works themselves. In particular these conditions explain why many artists were noted for craftsmanship rather than inspiration, and for the number rather than the memorability of their operas.

Italian opera houses were not like modern ones, showplaces for a few frequently revived masterpieces. They required new works for each season, and although favourite works were revived, many of the operas were either commissioned by the theatre or had not been heard there before. An impresario would first engage the singers, who were frequently more important than either composer or librettist and better paid. Singers' fees were often the subject of elaborate negotiation. When the impresario at Genoa asked Maria Barbieri Nini to perform at his theatre, she replied that she would restrict her fee to 20,000 francs 'for the sake of the pleasure of singing at the Teatro Carlo Felice and the beautiful views of Genoa'. The impresario replied that he could not afford such a fee but would be happy to send her a picture of the view. Having engaged his company, the impresario needed a new work by a fashionable composer to open his season. He in turn was provided by the local poet with a libretto on a well-known theme.

At this stage the composer might be a month away from the opening night. Typically his contract required him to write his score (tailored to the particular singers engaged), rehearse it, and direct the first few performances. He did not have the whole of the month for composition, since the singers needed time to learn their parts. Thus the overture was usually written last, as it had then only to be copied and distributed to the players, and the recitative sometimes left to a collaborator, as happened in the case of several Rossini operas including *Il barbiere di Siviglia*. If especially pressed, the composer could insert numbers from another of his operas—few scores were printed and an opera written for one city was unlikely to be familiar in another. Indeed, in later years Rossini was alarmed by the proposal of his publisher Ricordi to bring out an edition of his works, and wrote to him, 'The edition you are bringing out will lead to much (justified) criticism, for the same pieces of music will be found in several different operas; the time and money allowed me for my compositions were so paltry that I scarcely had leisure to read the so-called poem I was to set to music.' In view of other aspects of opera at this time, such as the *aria del sorbetto*, the 'sorbet aria' assigned to a minor character and giving the audience the chance to take some refreshment, or the *aria di baule*, the 'suitcase aria' which singers carried with them to insert into any opera, we may wonder that composers took trouble over their work. In such circumstances self-borrowing can be understood, and it is remarkable that a system aimed principally at rapid production also produced much fine music.

The operatic year was divided into seasons, the most important being Carnival, which ran usually from 26th December to Shrove Tuesday. It was during Carnival that an opera house would present its major works and new productions. During Lent the governments of the various Italian states would allow only 'sacred drama', hence the various operas written on Biblical themes such as Rossini's *Mosè in Egitto*. *Opera seria* remained the most prestigious genre, with star singers, splendid sets and costumes, a more aristocratic audience and higher prices—although prices generally were extremely low, to the wonder of tourists. People paid simply to enter the building (*ingresso*), whether or not intending to see the opera; the opera house was the centre of social life in Italian towns and the locals paid *ingresso* just to meet friends, drink, or join the gambling that went on in the foyer. In older theatres an extra payment was necessary to enter the stalls, and sometimes another fee was demanded if the patron wished to enter a box or have a stalls seat unlocked. Typically the stalls area was a standing one with a few benches and some fixed, locked seats, but there was a gradual tendency towards the fixed and numbered seating we know today.

The local audience struck non-Italians as noisy even though no European audience was really silent at this period. The chatter would abate for a favourite singer or aria, and a particularly fine phrase or flight of virtuosity would be met by shouts of approval. If a new work or singer was considered bad, the hostility of the audience could degenerate into a riot. The characteristic storm of whistling feared by all impresarios was actually banned in many places, and armed soldiers might be called in to arrest the worst offenders. Sometimes a new opera greeted thus was hastily replaced by an old favourite, the singers pulling out their *arie di baule* and hoping to survive the setback. In extreme cases, the impresario might be obliged to spend a few days in prison to pacify the public and, perhaps, for his own protection. It is difficult not to feel, as we settle into our seats in a dark modern theatre, that something of the colour has gone out of opera-going.

The singers worked hard. Although there were usually only two operas in a season, they had to learn the second while performing the first five nights a week, and the dress rehearsal could be held on the day of the first performance. One observer tells us of 'the singers tired and hoarse, the orchestra stumbling, costumes held together with pins, paint on the scenery still wet, carpenters still hammering amid the singers' roulades'.

New types of singer came into prominence as the *castrati* gradually disappeared. The tenor voice was increasingly allotted major roles, such as those Rossini wrote for Giovanni David (1790–1864) in Naples. A still more significant associate of Rossini's was the Spanish tenor Manuel Garcia (1775–1832), who apart from his work as interpreter and later impresario was also the father of the Manuel Garcia (1805–1906) who became the finest of the nineteenth-century singing teachers, and of the two great mezzo sopranos, Pauline Viardot (1821–1910) and Maria Malibran (1808–36). Malibran was described by Chopin as 'miraculous, marvellous', and she and the sopranos Isabella Colbran (1785–1845) and Giuditta Pasta (1797–1865) represented a new and influential breed of singing actress, whose compelling stage performances were as important perhaps in moulding early nineteenth-century music as were Chopin's development of the pianoforte and the violin playing of Paganini. Pasta, apart from her beauty of voice and person, had such dramatic gifts that one critic wrote of her 'magical and fearful Medea — a part musically and dramatically composed by herself out of the faded book and correct music of Simone Mayr's opera'. In her short life Malibran, who worked in New York, Paris, London and Italy, had an even more remarkable impact. Her compass was exceptional and her histrionic style moved all who heard her and brought the opera singer into the Romantic age. One follower on hearing her in Paris in 1827 wrote, 'Until that time, music had been for me an amiable art, compounded of graciousness and spirit. Now, suddenly, it became the purest and most dramatic expression of poetry, of love and of pain. A new world was revealed to me.'

ROSSINI IN ITALY

The brilliant career of Gioachino Rossini (1792–1868) falls into three phases: the period from his earliest works up to *Tancredi* in 1813; his time at Naples which produced *opere serie* of great influence as well as comic masterpieces for other cities; and the Parisian period when he revised two earlier works and wrote three new operas. From the 1820s he was one of the most famous men in Europe, but he abandoned operatic composition at the age of thirty-seven, having written thirty-nine operas in nineteen years.

Rossini's first opera to be performed was *La cambiale di matrimonio* (*The Marriage Contract*, Venice, 1810), a one-act *farsa* for the Teatro San Moisè. Rossini later recalled this as a fortunate way to pass an apprenticeship, since 'the expenses of the impresario were minimal, because except for a good company of singers (without chorus), they were limited to a single set for each *farsa*, a modest staging, and a few days of rehearsals. From this it is evident that everything tended to facilitate the debut of a novice composer . . .' Of Rossini's first nine operas five were similar one-act comedies for the same theatre, culminating in *Il Signor Bruschino* (1813).

The previous year had shown how much in demand the young composer had become in such a short time. He had five new operas performed in Milan, Venice and Ferrara, but among those produced a work of the quality of *La pietra del paragone* (*The Touchstone*) for La Scala, Milan. Another of these five, *Demetrio e Polibio*, had been composed much earlier, before 1809, and was thus the first of all Rossini's operas to be written. Yet even in his mid-teens, as this work shows, Rossini had a special gift; the melody of the duet '*Questo cor ti giura amore*' is particularly fine, as Rossini himself evidently thought since he re-used it in five later operas!

1813 was the *annus mirabilis* in Rossini's early career. In that year he produced operas which revitalised both *opera buffa* (*L'italiana in Algeri*) and the *opera seria* (*Tancredi*). The former is still a favourite at many opera houses, while the latter is less often heard, although it was Rossini's first international success, and yielded the hit tune of the day, '*Di tanti palpiti*', the *cabaletta* of Tancredi's *cavatina*. Stendhal declared that *Tancredi* went round the world in four years, and wondered whether it was possible in the whole of Europe to find someone who did not know '*Di tanti palpiti*'.

The formal elements of Rossini's style are already established in *Tancredi*. The arias are usually in two movements, the first section slow and expressive, the second section (or *cabaletta*) fast and brilliant, providing an opportunity for the singer to display his or her technique. The *cabaletta*'s livelier music is often justified dramatically by new information or a sudden resolve. Duets are also in several sections, the soloists rivalling each other with contrasting and then shared musical material, moving from slow expressiveness to brilliance. The 'singing contest' element is never far away, and it is given dramatic point by the duettists being rivals, or lovers temporarily at odds. However, political accord and joyous reunions may use the same structure and similar music. Arias and duets may involve the chorus; the first-act finale almost invariably does. This extended structure for all the singers often has two main sections which freeze the action, and intervening passages which carry it forward to a fast concluding section (or *stretta*), corresponding to the *cabaletta* of the aria and duet.

These structures became the essential building blocks for any Italian opera of the period. Indeed so pervasive was this influence that Julian Budden has called it the 'Code Rossini', a procedure which dictated the course of events in European opera as the Code Napoleon did in the courts. Budden has also pointed out that in Rossini's hands these forms are not rigid stereotypes, but rather 'Platonic forms', a series of examples from which the 'ideal form' can be deduced.

As an example of one aria from *Tancredi* in its dramatic context, Argirio's '*Ah! segnar invano io tento*' in Act II offers a classic *opera seria* situation. Argirio is leader of the Senate. His daughter, Amenaide, has been found guilty of treason, and Argirio must now sign her death warrant. After an introductory section of free declamation in which Argirio appeals to his 'cruel god', the first section of the aria begins slowly and expressively, 'I try in vain to sign my name'. Then he receives conflicting advice from two halves of the chorus, one imploring him to ask mercy for his daughter, the other advising him to serve his country. This provokes a repeat of the first section, before he suddenly resolves that justice shall triumph ('*Sì, virtù trionfi omai*') and launches into the *cabaletta* as he signs the document. 'Let every traitor to our land perish with my daughter,' he declares to music of virtuoso fire and wide leaps. The chorus, backed by bellicose trumpet fanfares, assures him that 'The people will always revere you as father of our glorious country'. He then repeats his *cabaletta* but now expresses grief over the loss of his daughter. In a brilliant coda the chorus consoles Argirio with the thought that virtue and honour will reward him for his sorrow.

Here musical form and dramatic needs are—with one exception—well matched. Argirio's progress from misgiving to resolution is neatly portrayed in the progress of the bipartite aria. But when he briefly weakens towards the end of the piece, and his earlier uncertainty returns, his earlier music does not. The exigencies of musical form here dictate that the *cabaletta* must be repeated, so we are given contrasting sentiments to identical music, an example of what Berlioz meant by Rossini's 'melodic cynicism'. For Rossini an opera was a large dramatic structure made up of separate musical units with their own internal rules. This means that whenever there is conflict between dramatic propriety and the integrity of the independent musical form, Rossini gives precedence to the latter. The later nineteenth century reversed that precedence, and condemned Rossini's practice. The proper appreciation of Rossini partly depends upon our ability to empathise with his aesthetic rather than the one which has replaced it.

The most controversial aspect of modern Rossini performance concerns the nature, placing, and quantity of 'flowery' decoration (*fioritura*) which singers should add to the melodic line. Rossini often had virtuoso performers available for his works, and the public came principally to hear them. The logical place for vocal fireworks was at the end of a piece, in the repeat of the *cabaletta*, to ensure maximum applause. From Rossini's coloratura passages we can see that the essential melodic line should always be clear. Rossini once reproached the celebrated soprano Adelina Patti after an over-decorated performance of Rosina's '*Una voce poco fa*' from *Il barbiere di Siviglia*. 'Charming, my dear,' said the composer, 'but tell us, who wrote the music you have just sung?' Rossini's style increases in floridity through the Naples years, when he had singers renowned for vocal agility, and reached a peak in his last opera for Italy, *Semiramide* (1823). Modern revivals of this grandest of *opere serie* have shown the validity of its style, when a singer of the calibre of Marilyn Horne sings the male role of Arsace. Hearing this music sung as it can be is to realise that the runs, roulades, trills and leaps are not merely an opportunity for virtuoso display but a pre-Romantic way of conveying intensity and fullness of emotion. Rossini's music held sway over his contemporaries not only because they were dazzled by it, but also because they were moved by it.

Rossini's coloratura writing may derive partly from his early memories of the singing of the *castrati*, of whom he wrote in later years, 'I have never forgotten them. The purity, the miraculous flexibility of those voices and, above all, their profoundly penetrating accent—all that moved and fascinated me more than I can tell.' But these singers were now in decline. Mayr had written for them in several works, but Rossini wrote only one operatic role for a *castrato*, that of Arsace in *Aureliano in Palmira* (Milan, 1813). This was for Giovanni Battista Velluti (1781–1861), the last great male soprano in opera, whose last major role was in Meyerbeer's *Il crociato in Egitto* (Venice, 1824). As we have seen, the tenor was becoming more important, basses were no longer confined to *buffo* roles, and the rising generation of virtuoso female singers included Isabella Colbran. She was Mayr's Medea in *Medea in Corinto* and her dramatic gifts made her especially suited to the powerful ladies of *opera seria*. Rossini wrote a string of such roles for her in his operas for Naples, and she became his first wife. But his favourite female voice was, he said, the contralto, and he wrote some of his finest music in this register, such as the breeches roles of Arsace in *Semiramide* and the eponymous hero of *Tancredi*.

In 1815 Rossini signed a contract to produce two operas a year for Naples. The impresario who had succeeded in capturing this most sought-after composer was Domenico Barbaia (1778–1841), the Diaghilev of the *primo ottocento*. He was at different times in charge of the San Carlo theatre in Naples, the Kärntnertor in Vienna, and La Scala, Milan, and besides working with Rossini he was influential in the careers of Weber and Donizetti.

The San Carlo theatre, and the company which performed there, were among the most splendid in Europe. In 1770, Charles Burney noted that, 'The stage, the scenes, dresses, and decorations were extremely magnificent, and this theatre is superior, I think in these particulars as well as in the music, to that of the great French opera at Paris. It surpasses all that poetry and romance have painted.' The orchestra was large — seventy players in 1810; Rossini's *Maometto Secondo* (Naples, 1820), in addition to a full complement of strings and woodwind, requires four horns, two trumpets, three trombones, percussion, harp, and a stage band. The principal singers included Colbran and several fine tenors — the three tenor parts in Rossini's *Otello* (Naples, 1816) makes it difficult to cast today. These artists were given annual contracts, an unusual stability in their profession at that time, and Barbaia could be relied upon to pay — how rare this is we can see from Stendhal's remark that, 'If there is one thing in all Italy which passes for a miracle, it is an impresario who fails to go bankrupt, and who observes some regularity in the payment of salaries ...'

Rossini's contract did not tie him to Naples exclusively but allowed him to accept some commissions elsewhere. He took advantage of this to write two of his finest comic operas, both for Rome: *Il barbiere di Siviglia* (1816) and *La Cenerentola* (1817). In consequence the Neapolitan period, which lasted from 1815 to 1822, can be seen as the zenith of Rossini's career; the *opere serie* for Naples and the *buffo* works for Rome are surpassed only by his last opera, *Guillaume Tell* (Paris, 1829).

Rossini's first opera for Naples was *Elisabetta, regina d'Inghilterra* (1815). This shows an advance on *Tancredi* in one respect only — the recitative is accompanied by strings, not harpsichord. This had become the norm during the second decade of the century in Italy, since the new Napoleonic regime had brought the spectacular works of Spontini and Méhul to Naples, with their *recitativo accompagnato*.

A more substantial musical development occurs with *Otello* (1816). For the first two of its three acts, the plot bears little resemblance to Shakespeare: 'They are crucifying *Othello* into an opera,' wrote Byron when he saw it, but the third act is a dramatic and musical *tour de force* – perhaps Rossini himself had taken a hand in shaping the libretto at this stage. Desdemona and her maid Emilia are in the bedroom where at the end Otello will kill his wife. To set the mood of foreboding, the act opens with a passing gondolier singing lines from Dante's *Inferno*;

> *Nessun maggior dolore*
> *Che ricordarsi del tempo felice*
> *Nella miseria.*

Desdemona is moved by the apposite sentiment—'There is no greater woe than to recall past happiness while in distress'—as we too are by the superb folk-like invention of the melodic line. Her 'willow song' is ostensibly strophic, but the subtle developments introduced for each verse mirror her growing anxiety, and she is unable to complete her song, a rare example of the composer putting the drama before musical manners. The haunting orchestral writing for this scene, especially for the woodwind, reminds us that Rossini, like Verdi, can obtain his most powerful effects with reduced forces. *Otello* held the stage in the nineteenth century almost up to the time of Verdi's masterpiece, for which, at least in Act III, it served as a model.

There are many such musical and dramatic innovations in Rossini's Neapolitan *opere serie*, and they are historically important even if they do not always add up to an experience which makes them worthy of more than an occasional revival. Knowing his theatre and artists, the composer could expand his formal and expressive range. There is the majestic opening to *Mosè in Egitto* (1818), which has no overture, but opens with the 'Plague of Darkness' chorus, which evokes the despair of a captive people as the soloists' cries draw us into a personal drama. *La donna del lago* (1819), based on Scott's poem *The Lady of the Lake*, also has no overture. The brief orchestral preamble is followed by a lively chorus, with the sound of hunting horns on and off stage. The scale and integration of this opening indicate Rossini's growing interest in the expansion of the musical units which had hitherto formed the basis of his operas. This is followed up in *Maometto Secondo* (1820), whose '*terzettone*' ('a big, fat trio') fills more than a third of Act I and welds various musical sections and dramatic events into a single continuous structure. Our knowledge of these scores is still developing, but already we can see that ignorance of them has distorted our view of opera in the nineteenth century, placing certain 'innovations' later and in the works of others. Thus a book on Berlioz published in 1982 can still describe the absence of an overture to that composer's *Les Troyens* as 'an innovation in the history of opera'.

However, despite the historical importance of his *opere serie*, Rossini's chief claim on the affections of opera lovers remains with his comic operas. *L'italiana in Algeri* (Venice, 1813) was written in twenty-seven days, although so tight a deadline meant that others composed the recitatives and some minor numbers. The libretto by Angelo Anelli (1761–1820) had already been set in 1808 by Luigi Mosca: to compare Mosca's setting of the Act I duet '*Ai capricci della sorte*' with Rossini's is to see how the common musical coin of the day could be turned into gold by a finer artist. Where Mosca spins notes attractively enough, Rossini has Isabella silence her suitor Taddeo with her insistence upon a formal recapitulation. The sense of Isabella cutting Taddeo off with an air of 'Enough of that—now, as I was saying,' is witty because it allies musical form to dramatic sense.

The most celebrated part of *L'italiana* is the great Act I finale, which ends with the most riotous of all Rossini's *strette*. The characters, all in a delirious state, utter the sounds that fill their heads with only an approximate onomatopoeia. The women hear bells going 'din din', Lindoro's hammer sounds 'tac tac', Taddeo's crow sings 'cra cra' and Mustafà's cannon booms 'bum bum' in a riot of dizzying invention. On one level we are invited to laugh; on a deeper one we are disturbed that events are spinning out of control. Perhaps it is the response of the artist to a militaristic age. In Richard Osborne's words, 'Rossini's sense of the unstoppable whirl of human endeavour, something induced in part perhaps by his sense of the often frantic and disordered state in which Europe found itself in these years, becomes one of the central images of his art.'

In 1898 Verdi wrote: '. . . *Il barbiere di Siviglia*, with its comic verve and its truthful declamation, is the most beautiful *opera buffa* in existence.' Although the first performance of the work at the Teatro Argentina in Rome on 20 February 1816 failed, *Il barbiere* has held the world stage continuously ever since. The universal familiarity of this score makes it difficult to appreciate that after Paisiello's decorous version of Beaumarchais's play Rossini's *Barber* was found radical and disturbing.

Figaro's *cavatina*, the famous '*Largo al factotum*', with its hectically exciting orchestral introduction, is perhaps the greatest operatic entry before Verdi's *Otello*. The heady virility of this hedonistic outburst, at times frankly sexual ('Then there are the perks of the trade with the young ladies'), is both defined and controlled by Rossini's peerless mastery of *buffo* rhythms. Again musical form points the comedy, or provides ironic comment upon it. To underline the pedantic character of Dr Bartolo, the *allegro vivace* section of his *cavatina* is in sonata form. In Don Basilio's aria '*La calunnia*' the spreading calumny is depicted by a favourite device of Rossini's, the crescendo—the increasing growth of rumour mirrored in the swelling dynamic level. A delightful use of the incongruity of musical form and dramatic sense occurs in the trio '*Ah! quel colpo inaspettato*'. Rosina, having discovered her lover's true identity, now needs to make her escape with him. She and the Count celebrate their new-found good fortune, but Figaro is anxious to complete the elopement. Musical form demands a *cabaletta* here, duly sung to such words as 'let's get out quickly by the ladder from the balcony'. While they sing the necessary repeat of the *cabaletta*, the ladder is removed and the escape thwarted by the correctness of their own musical manners. When *Il barbiere di Siviglia* was first performed in London in 1818, Thomas Love Peacock wrote, 'We saw at once that there was a great revolution in dramatic music. Rossini burst on the stage like a torrent . . .' Although some Rossini admirers feel that the music is less inspired in Act II than in Act I, *The Barber* seems unlikely to be dislodged from its position as its composer's most performed score.

In *La Cenerentola* (Rome, 1817) Rossini turned away from true *buffo* style. Don Magnifico and his valet Dandini are typical *buffo* roles and they share a fine *buffo* duet in Act II, '*Un segreto d'importanza*'. But Cinderella herself and her prince, Don Ramiro, are sentimental rather than comic, and Cinderella's rags-to-riches story is reflected in the opera's subtitle '*La bontà in trionfo*'—Goodness Triumphant.

La gazza ladra (Milan, 1817) tells of a servant girl who is convicted of theft, and only as she is on her way to execution is the real culprit discovered—the thieving magpie of the title. Here Rossini carries the hybrid style further, into true *opera semiseria*. Whether because his experience in Naples led him to prefer serious subjects, or because he felt he had exhausted the comic genre in *L'italiana* and *Il barbiere*, he wrote no more *opere buffe* after 1817. There is one more comic opera in 1828, but as its title—*Le Comte Ory*—indicates, the focus of Rossini's activities had by then moved to Paris.

ROSSINI IN FRANCE

In 1824 Rossini became co-director with Paer of the Théâtre-Italien, the house where Parisians could hear the latest Italian operas. With a fine company at his disposal, he presented his own music as well as that of other composers, including Donizetti and Bellini. This was a vintage period for the theatre, as we can see from a letter Chopin wrote in 1831: 'Never have I heard the *Barber* as last week with Lablache, Rubini, and Malibran (Garcia), or *Otello* as with Rubini, Pasta, and Lablache; or again, *Italiana in Algeri* as with Rubini, Lablache, and Mme. Raimbeaux. Now, if ever, I have everything in Paris!'

Rossini still composed after he moved to France, but not at the frantic pace of earlier years. In 1825, for the coronation of Charles X, he produced *Il viaggio a Reims* (*The Journey to Reims*). As soon as it had served its role as a *pièce d'occasion*, he took it off and later raided parts of the score for *Le Comte Ory* (1828). The original was found only in 1979, and the production mounted in the composer's birthplace of Pesaro in 1984 proved that this was one of the happiest of twentieth-century rediscoveries. He also provided for the Paris Opéra revisions of two of his Neapolitan *opere serie*; in 1826, *Maometto Secondo* became *Le siège de Corinthe*, and the following year saw *Mosè in Egitto* become *Moïse et Pharaon*. Now that the Neapolitan versions of these works are becoming more familiar, it can be seen that the changes made for Paris are not all gain, and that the original versions are by no means eclipsed. But in the process of revising the two operas Rossini had acquired a knowledge of the Paris Opéra and of the technique of setting French that made possible his final operatic masterpiece, *Guillaume Tell* (1829).

Schiller's *Wilhelm Tell* fares much better in Rossini's treatment than Shakespeare's *Othello* had done. The three librettists, Jouy, Bis and Marrast, seem to have benefited from Rossini's own guidance in some respects. The overture is a large-scale piece whose four sections have more to do with the symphonic poem than with a curtain-raiser for the audience to chatter over. The opening for five solo cellos assumes an audience that will listen, the *ranz des vaches* for solo cor anglais is the first of several pastoral evocations in the score, the storm is appropriately thunderous, the final galop rhythmically irresistible. Act I sets the scale of the work, with bucolic choruses and a familiar set of dances, but it is Act II which launches the central drama. 'The first and last acts were written by Rossini,' said Donizetti, 'but the second act was written by God.' The first act has its critics, but the second would not involve us so if Rossini had not used the opening act to establish Switzerland as a land both lovely and beloved. The second act opens with yet another chorus, this time with evocative horn writing—*Tell* is the work of Rossini's with the boldest *tinta* (or characteristic colour), one of pastoral oboes, Arcadian harps and horn calls across Alpine valleys. Mathilde's aria '*Sombre forêt*' and the ensuing duet with Arnold are cast in forms long established by Rossini, but filled with a feeling that is proto-Romantic. The vocal style which he developed for setting French is much less florid, either because he felt the need for artistic change or as a concession to singers who would have paled before the score of *Semiramide*. The great trio in Act II '*Quand l'Helvétie est un champ de supplices*' won the admiration of both Wagner and Verdi, the latter declaring, 'He (Rossini) possessed a quality that is now lost, that none of us now have: he knew how to write for the voice. Look at the trio from *Guillaume Tell*!'

The third act contains the scene where Tell must shoot an apple from his son's head, and tells the boy to be still in the aria, '*Sois immobile*'. When Wagner met Rossini in 1860, he praised this aria in particular. Rossini explained: '. . . the feeling which moved me most in my life was the love I had for my mother and father, and they repaid it at a usurer's rate of interest, I'm happy to tell you. It was there that I found the note I needed for this scene of the apple in *Guillaume Tell*.' At the end of the work, the storm clouds depart from the newly liberated land, which thus appears in the eyes of Tell and his countrymen like paradise regained. In a transcendent finale horns, harps, and voices unite in praise of the most radiant of all dawns—the dawn of freedom. From its celebrated overture to its incandescent close, *Guillaume Tell* is Rossini's greatest work.

Despite its high quality and subsequent influence on the development of grand opera in France, *Guillaume Tell* did not have an easy path. The tenor role of Arnold is notoriously taxing, and the first singer of the part, Adolphe Nourrit, soon omitted the big Act IV aria '*Asile héréditaire*' from his performances. Within a year of the première, the Opéra had reduced the work to three acts, and then began the custom of giving just Act II as a curtain-raiser for the ballet. Rossini once met the director of the Opera in the street and was told, 'Maestro, we are playing the second act of your *Tell* tonight.' 'What,' said Rossini, '*all* of it?' The second may be the finest of the four acts, but it is a jewel the lustre of which is better appreciated in its proper setting. In the Italian première in 1831 the role of Arnold was sung by Gilbert-Louis Duprez, the inventor of the *ut de poitrine* or high C sung from the chest. In 1837 he sang the role in Paris in an important revival of *Tell*, and astounded the Parisians in the fourth act *stretta* in which the tenor must twice ascend from G by way of A, B flat, and B natural to a sustained high C. But the thrilling sound Duprez must have made in this passage was not to Rossini's taste, who said that 'Nourrit sang it in head voice and that's how it should be sung.' Head voice—the light, floated, but weak high notes that give a singer the sense of the voice functioning at the top of the head—has not disappeared, but since

Duprez the virile, open-throated, perhaps coarser sound has been the characteristic tenor sound.

As the Rossini revival which began in the 1940s continues, and scholars and performers reveal more about his operas, it seems that our estimation of his influence can only increase. In his middle years he was easily the most famous of living composers, and although he retired early from operatic composition his influence continued to be felt through his directorship of the Théâtre-Italien. In the 1860s, meeting the ageing Rossini at his famous social gatherings in Paris brought the rising generation of musicians into contact with a legend—Saint-Saëns in particular was a youthful admirer then, and he lived until 1921. The predominance of Rossini's comic works in the modern repertoire has distorted our image of the artist who laboured harder and longer over his serious operas. Doubtless in the realm of *opera buffa* we cannot place him—or anyone—above Mozart. But in terms of his impact upon the development of opera, Rossini was the most significant artist between Gluck and Wagner. Perhaps Wagner should have the last word. In March 1873 his wife Cosima wrote in her diary: 'R. comes to the subject of Rossini and the *Gazza Ladra* overture in particular. When our copyist admits with a smile that he does not know it, R. gets heated and says, "My dear man, only Beethoven stands above Rossini." '

DONIZETTI AND THE *ROSSINIANI*

Italian cities needing new operas could not always have Rossini, but they could approach a follower of his style, one of the so-called '*rossiniani*'. One such was Giovanni Pacini (1796–1867), who wrote in his autobiography,

> Everyone followed the same school, the same fashions, and as a result we were all followers of the Great Luminary. But, good heavens, what was one to do if there was no other way of making a living? If I was a follower of the great man of Pesaro, so was everyone else.

Pacini was very prolific as a young man, at one stage writing fourteen comic operas in four years. His *opera semiseria Adelaide e Comingio* (Milan, 1817) was his earliest success, and *Alessandro nell'Indie* (Naples, 1824) was played seventy times in a row at the San Carlo, where the following year Pacini became director. The new Romanticism of Bellini meant such a complete *rossiniano* had less appeal for a time, but he learned from younger rivals and produced his best work in *Saffo* (Naples, 1840), which shows a greater seriousness and more subtle harmony and orchestration than his earlier operas. He continued his success with *Medea* (Palermo, 1843) and *Maria, regina de'Inghilterra* (Palermo 1843). His gift for lively tunes earned Pacini the soubriquet '*il maestro della cabaletta*'.

Saverio Mercadante (1795–1870) was another *rossiniano* at first, but then developed a more original style. His seventh opera *Elisa e Claudio* (Milan, 1821) gained him a European reputation. This was a comedy, but his natural inclination towards serious subjects is clear from his use of Metastasio plots on four occasions, including *Didone abbandonata* (Turin, 1823). He was invited by Rossini to write for France, but *I briganti* (Paris, 1836) failed. Mercadante had begun to move away from the Rossinian style with *Caritea regina di Spagna* (Venice, 1826) and reached a new originality in the best-known of all his sixty operas, *Il giuramento* (*The Oath*, Milan, 1837). This represented a conscious reform, as a letter written soon after makes clear: 'I have continued the revolution I began with *Il giuramento*; forms varied, trivial cabalettas banished, crescendos out, vocal lines simplified, fewer repeats, more original cadences, emphasis on the drama, orchestra rich but not swamping the voices, no long solos in the ensembles—which force the other parts to stand coldly by to the detriment of the action, not much bass drum, and a lot less brass band.' This reads like an indictment of the worst excesses of Rossini's weaker followers, and Mercadante played an important part in the transition to a new style. In *Il giuramento*, despite a complex plot in which much has happened before the opera begins, we can hear why Verdi so honoured its composer.

Gaetano Donizetti (1797–1848) also began his career as a follower of Rossini. He studied at Bergamo under Mayr, and then at Bologna under Rossini's teacher Mattei. Mayr also gave Donizetti his first opportunity to write an opera and the resultant work, *Zoraida di Granata* (Rome, 1822) led to a commission from Barbaia. *La zingara* (*The Gypsy*, Naples, 1822) was so well liked that it was revived several times in the next fifteen years. Thus Donizetti established himself in Naples just as Rossini was leaving the city, and produced twenty-three operas, mostly for Naples, in the next eight years. He was at this stage a skilful purveyor of the genre the public had come to expect. But there are also many individual touches which look forward to his maturity, especially in the comic operas, *L'aio nell'imbarazzo* (*The Tutor in a Fix*) (Rome, 1824), *Olivo e Pasquale* (Rome, 1817), and *Il giovedi grasso* (*Shrove Thursday*, Naples, 1829). But it is the subject of the *opera seria Il castello di Kenilworth* (Naples, 1829), derived ultimately from Walter Scott's novel about Tudor England, which seems to us now the harbinger of his future tragic works, for Scott also provided the subject of *Lucia di Lammermoor* (Naples, 1835) while English Tudor history yielded the eponymous hero and heroines who lose their heads, *Roberto Devereux* (Naples, 1837), *Anna Bolena* (Milan, 1830) and *Maria Stuarda* (Milan, 1835).

Il castello di Kenilworth is too dependent on the Rossinian formulae that Donizetti never quite shook off completely to be a musical turning-point. The composer recognised the constraining effect of such conventions, and told his friend Marco Bonesi that once he was established he would develop his own style. Bonesi reported: 'He had many ideas how to reform the predictable situations, the sequences of introduction, *cavatina*, duet, trio, finale, always fashioned the same way. "But," he added sadly, "what to do with the blessed theatrical conventions? Impresarios, singers, and the public as well, would hurl me into the farthest pit at least, and—*addio per sempre*." ' Such was the strength of the Rossinian archetypes that it took Donizetti a long time to forge his own style. The process began in the late 1820s, when Rossini's French operas, *Le siège de Corinthe* and *Moïse*, with their vocal lines divested of much of the Neapolitan *fioritura*, made their way to Italy. More influential still was the vocal directness and the heightened passionate expression of Bellini's *Il pirata* (1827).

These influences, and Donizetti's full individuality, are first revealed in *Anna Bolena*. With a text by Romani and a strong cast headed by the soprano Giuditta Pasta, the tenor Giovanni Rubini, and the bass Filippo Galli, *Anna Bolena* finally established Donizetti, with Bellini, as the leading composer of Italian opera. The score contains several self-borrowings, including material from an early *opera semiseria*, *Enrico di Borgogna* (Venice, 1818), and sums up all the composer had yet achieved. The finest scene is the last, in which Anna, condemned to death, enters to a noble theme on the strings. Her attendants weep, but the Queen, whose mind has given way, imagines it is her wedding day and asks them why they are weeping ('*Piangete voi?*'). Then comes Anna's aria of longing for her birthplace '*Al dolce guidami*', which has great pathos, but the echo of 'Home, sweet home' at her *cantabile* '*Cielo, a' miei lunghi spasimi*' is disconcerting. The *cabaletta* '*Coppia iniqua*' with its chain of long rising trills brilliantly suggests a proud personality *in extremis*. Much other material is incorporated into this scene, but the whole is convincingly held together by Donizetti's skill in large-scale construction.

The vogue of the 1820s and 1830s for such mad scenes perhaps derives ultimately from *Hamlet*, Act IV Scene 5, the entrance of 'poor Ophelia / Divided from herself and her fair judgement'. Significantly enough, Shakespeare's Ophelia sings in her plight, and if we agree with Laertes' remark to her, 'Hadst thou thy wits . . . It could not move thus,' then we can see why the mad scene came into its own in operas of Romantic tragedy. Better known than the *Anna Bolena* passage, indeed probably the best known in Donizetti, is Lucia's mad scene in *Lucia di Lammermoor*. In his late *opera semiseria Linda di Chamounix* (1842), Linda believes that her beloved has married; she loses her reason, but her lover proposes to her and restores her sanity. There was nothing risible in all this for audiences, or for the singers they came to hear perform these operas. The mad scene was an opportunity for singers to display both vocal and histrionic gifts. Just as *Anna Bolena*'s scene was written for Pasta, *Lucia* was created for Fanny Persiani. Indeed on some occasions we might say *Lucia* was created *by* Persiani, for she liked to improvise different embellishments and cadenzas for each performance. It is surely no accident that the revival of these works since the 1950s has been led by virtuoso singers such as Joan Sutherland, Montserrat Caballé, and Maria Callas. In their performances, and perhaps those of Callas especially, we can appreciate how compelling the best mad scenes can be, and say with Laertes, 'Thought and affliction, passion, hell itself / She turns to favour and to prettiness.'

With the rise of Romanticism in Italy, the tragic ending to a serious opera—rare in Rossini's day—became the norm. Those of Donizetti's tragic works which have survived include *Lucrezia Borgia* (Milan, 1833), *Maria Stuarda*, *Lucia di Lammermoor* and *Roberto Devereux*. But his operas contain equally fine work in all genres. There are the French grand operas, *La Favorite* (Paris, 1840) and his last work *Dom Sébastien, roi de Portugal* (Paris, 1843), as well as the comedies for which he is perhaps still most valued, *L'elisir d'amore* (Milan, 1832), the *opéra comique La fille du régiment* (Paris, 1840), and above all *Don Pasquale* (Paris, 1843).

Probably the most striking of Donizetti's innovations was his casting of the hero as a baritone in *Maria Padilla* (Milan, 1841) and *Maria di Rohan* (Vienna, 1843). The tenor hero was common by this time, as in *Lucia di Lammermoor*, and baritones were still thought of as secondary or comic figures. But the prodigious acting talent of the baritone Giorgio Ronconi so impressed the composer that in these and other works he gave him some of the finest music. Another vocal convention which he challenged was the requirement for a prima donna to be given a showpiece scene to end the whole work. Thus Lucia's madness occurs in the penultimate scene, and it is the tenor Edgardo's death that brings down the curtain— though this did not prevent many nineteenth-century productions from cutting the last scene and ending with the mad scene anyway. This itself is distinctive in having a slow expressive *cabaletta* rather than a brilliant fast one, as in the *Anna Bolena* scene. Donizetti is by now deploying Rossinian structures with innovatory freedom, and may combine forms within a single aria: thus in *Maria Stuarda* Leicester's *cavatina* '*Ah rimiro il bel sembiante*' is partly a duet and partly an aria with *pertichini*, interjections from a second character.

Donizetti's innovations were not always immediately influential. The recitative in *Don Pasquale* is accompanied by string chords, and yet for thirty years after it was first played most recitative in *opera buffa* was still accompanied on a keyboard instrument. Donizetti would have liked the opera to be performed in modern dress, but gave in to the wish of the singers and the librettist Ruffini who did not share the composer's daring and wanted period costume. Among several unusual aspects of the work's structure there is the omission of the expected choral contribution to the finale of Act II. But it is not formal innovation but the vigour of the comedy and the high quality of the music that endears *Don Pasquale* to audiences. The characters and voices are exactly what we expect of the *opera buffa* genre—tenor and soprano young lovers, *basso buffo* for the ageing would-be suitor, and *basso cantante* to pull the strings of the plot. As such *Don Pasquale* is the last true *opera buffa* to remain in the repertory, as well as the best Italian comic opera between Rossini's *Il barbiere di Siviglia* and Verdi's *Falstaff*.

Donizetti is the most difficult of the major nineteenth-century opera composers to assess because scholars and audiences are still rediscovering his output of more than seventy operas. Although more assured and productive than his great contemporary, Bellini, he is ultimately less original and influential. There is no characteristic trait that one can point to in the work of other men and say it is 'Donizettian' in the way long melodies of a certain cast are called 'Bellinian' in the music of Chopin and others. But that matters little to the many people who love the half-dozen or so Donizetti operas that are indispensable to the repertory.

BELLINI, ROMANI AND ROMANTICISM

The career of Vincenzo Bellini (1801–35) lasted just ten years, in which he wrote ten operas which brought the Romantic feeling of a new age to Italian musical theatre. He studied in Naples under Zingarelli, and his first stage piece the *opera semiseria Adelson e Salvini* (Naples, 1825) was a student work. However, its quality earned a commission from Barbaia to write for the San Carlo in Naples and the result was *Bianca e Gernando* (1826), later revised as *Bianca e Fernando* (Genoa, 1828). Barbaia also commissioned *Il pirata* (Milan, 1827) which gave Bellini his first international success. This opera and *La straniera* (*The Stranger*, Milan,

1829) had libretti by Felice Romani (1788–1865), who provided texts for all the composer's subsequent operas except his last, *I puritani* (Paris, 1835). For *Zaira* (Parma, 1829) Bellini had to write more quickly than he liked and the work failed, although he used some of its music for his next opera, *I Capuleti e i Montecchi* (Venice, 1830). Romani's libretto for this work is based less on Shakespeare's *Romeo and Juliet* than on an earlier Italian source, and the score has a *travesti* Romeo, a part written for the mezzo-soprano Giuditta Grisi. *La sonnambula* (Milan, 1831) has a sleepwalking heroine, whose somnambulism provides the kind of pathos in this *opera semiseria* that madness does in the heroines of *Il pirata* and *I puritani*. *Norma* (Milan, 1831), a tragic tale of a Druid priestess who has broken her vow of chastity, is the highest achievement of the Bellini-Romani collaboration. Composer and poet fell out, however, over the latter's slowness in providing the text of *Beatrice di Tenda* (Venice, 1833) and *I puritani* has a libretto by Count Pepoli derived ultimately from Scott's novel *Old Mortality* (1816). Bellini and Romani were then reconciled and planned future operas, but Bellini's sudden death intervened.

'In my Eden, a man who dislikes Bellini has the good manners not to get born,' said the poet W. H. Auden, and Bellini is a composer who still often inspires devotion, as he did among his contemporaries. He wrote from Milan in 1829: 'My *Straniera* had its first performance on Saturday . . . and I can find no words to describe its reception, which cannot be called a furore, raising the roof, frenzy—no, none of these terms is sufficient to express the pleasure aroused by the entire music which made the whole audience shout as if they had gone mad.' The frequency with which Bellini's works were greeted in this way amounted to a new vogue for his frankly emotional style, which is encapsulated in his description of opera as 'the difficult art of drawing tears by means of song'. Bellini was the first to break with the hectic style of working life that Rossini and Donizetti had endured; his output of only one opera each year, his desire to work closely with one librettist, and to select his subjects with care, perhaps marks a change in the attitude of the artist to his art. He wrote no *opera buffa*, always preferring plots which placed his characters into what he called '*situazioni laceranti*', or harrowing predicaments. Several of his operas focus on the soprano heroine and end with a big final number for her, complete with virtuoso *cabaletta*. The one for Amina at the end of *La sonnambula* is perhaps the best related to the drama, since the slow, dreamy music of the first section depicts her recollection in sleep of her grief, and the final flourish captures her joy at awaking and discovering her love again. The powerful ending to *Norma* is quite different, the chorus calling the priestess 'accursed even in death' as she and her lover are led into her funeral pyre; there is no place for a showy *cabaletta* here.

Such scenes made great demands on the singers, whom Bellini expected to act. Giovanni Rubini, although the composer's favourite tenor, had trouble adapting to this new style. At a rehearsal for *Il pirata*, he could not satisfy the composer with his singing of Gualtiero. 'You are an animal,' the great tenor was informed. 'You are not putting half your spirit into it. Are you thinking more of Gualtiero or of Rubini?' The singer claimed that Bellini would permit none of the usual vocal decorations and expected all his notes to be sung just as written—although one wonders whether this ambition was ever realised in performance.

Yet Bellini greatly valued singers and liked to write for specific ones; and for all his desire for dramatic verisimilitude, his letters always refer to singers rather than characters. Reporting on Rossini's reaction to the score of *I puritani*, Bellini writes, 'He found Tamburini's *cavatina* graceful, the duet between Lablache and Mme. Grisi most beautiful, and the chorus just before Rubini's entrance orchestrated with great taste . . .' These singers—Rubini the tenor, Grisi the soprano, and the basses Antonio Tamburini and Luigi Lablache—became known as the 'Puritani quartet'. Bellini never went so far as to demote singers from their principal position in the operatic hierarchy.

If conventional in this, Bellini was less so in his devotion to a single librettist and in the closeness of his collaboration with him. When in 1828 a collaboration with another librettist was suggested Bellini wrote, 'However good the libretto Rossi might provide . . . he could never be a poet like Romani, especially as far as I am concerned, for whom good verses are so important; this you can see with *Il pirata* where it was the poetry and not the dramatic situations which filled me with inspiration, particularly in "*Come un angelo celeste*", and so for me, therefore, Romani is a necessity.' Gaetano Rossi was a distinguished librettist who had provided the text of Rossini's *Tancredi* and *Semiramide*, but Bellini's faith in Romani was total. He once wrote to the poet, 'It seemed impossible for me to exist without you.' In some ways it is a surprising partnership, for Romani, resident theatre poet at La Scala, was thirteen years older than Bellini, and his admiration for Metastasio equalled his caution towards the new Romantic movement. He was the librettist of Rossini's *Il turco in Italia* and of several Donizetti works, but seems to have held his Bellini operas in the highest regard of all. Yet Bellini was very demanding. Romani was asked ten times to rewrite the final *cabaletta* of *La sonnambula*, and eight times the lines of Norma's invocation to the moon, although the final form is worth it:

Casta Diva, che inargenti	Chaste Goddess, who silvers
Queste sacre antiche piante,	These sacred ancient trees,
A noi volgi il bel sembiante,	Turn upon us your fair face,
Senza nube e senza vel!	Cloudless and unveiled!

Romani was a master of the syllabic verse-forms which formed the basis of all Italian opera libretti, and no one listening to Bellini's exquisite setting of these words can doubt that he was inspired by them. Sometimes Romani's patience ran out; over *La straniera* he burst out, 'For goodness' sake, what do you want?' and Bellini explained, 'I want a delirium!' Delirium was not easy to provide in *ottonarii* (eight-syllable lines) but Romani once said, 'That boy does what he wants with me . . . it is impossible to resist.'

The music to which Bellini set Romani's lines amazed the public and the critics. The florid style or *canto fiorito* that had prevailed up to then was much less in evidence in *Il pirata* and Bellini's next work, *La straniera*, went still further in the direction of a syllabic style of vocal writing, with hardly any *melisma*, that is, writing with several notes to a syllable. The critics called this *canto declamato*, but the phrase was not coined entirely in a hostile spirit, for they recognised the importance it gave to the words. However, in both *Zaira* and *I Capuleti e i Montecchi* he reverted to the *Tancredi* tradition of a *travesti* hero with much *canto fiorito*. The last operas then allow the female roles some *fioritura*, but always with a musical or dramatic point, never just for the greater glory of the prima donna. Thus the coloratura in Elvira's mad scene in *I puritani* serves the same purpose as that in *Lucia*'s mad scene in Donizetti, namely to express the character's loss of her senses. The *melisma* of the opening bars of '*Casta Diva*' is part of the musical line, not superfluous decoration. And from the time of Bellini's Rubini roles onwards, *fioritura* gradually disappears from the music for male singers in Italian opera. '*A te o cara*' from *I puritani*—or in Bellini's terms 'Rubini's entrance'—is an example of a new lyrical and declamatory style of tenor writing. Rubini was a high tenor but did not follow the Duprez manner of using full chest resonance throughout his register. The line of '*A te o cara*' is moulded to display what the English critic Chorley called Rubini's 'honeyed elegance', and Rubini would have taken the high leaps in the line in head voice. The few moments of melismatic writing in the number are a composer's concession to Rubini's skill. Curiously, for some listeners of his time the characteristic Bellinian seamless legato—spare but sensuous—spelt the death of true singing.

Bellini's elegiac melodies have a similarity of mood that suggest he responded to the sound of the syllables rather than the sense of the words. There is little polyphonic interest, and the harmonies, though often daringly dissonant, are sometimes crude. But his range is not confined to a melancholy lyricism—no opera composer can hold the stage with a single mood. There is the bellicose sound of *'Suoni la tromba'* in the Act II finale of *I puritani*, and of the chorus *'Guerra! Guerra!'* in *Norma*. Norma herself has one of the great roles of the operatic stage, encompassing vengeful fury as well as tender solicitude. *Norma* and *I puritani* are remarkable also for the extensive role of the chorus. Verdi admired Bellini, though not uncritically, as we can see from a letter he wrote in 1898:

> Bellini is poor, it's true, in instrumentation and harmony, but rich in feeling and his own individual melancholy. Even in his lesser-known operas, such as *La straniera* and *Il pirata*, there are long, long, long melodies, like nothing that was ever written before him. And what truth and power in declamation there is, for example, in the duet of Pollione and Norma! And what nobility of thought in the first phrase in the introduction to *Norma*, followed a few bars later by another phrase, badly orchestrated, but no one has written anything more beautiful or celestial.

The effortless spaciousness of Bellini's melodies may have influenced two other artists noted for the same quality: Chopin and Berlioz. Wagner confessed to a Bellinian melodic inheritance. Referring to themes from *La straniera* and *Norma*, Wagner heard '. . . real passion and emotion; it only needs the right singer, and it carries you away. I learned from it something that Messrs. Brahms & Co. didn't learn and that I have in my melodies.' But perhaps we should not be surprised that Wagner admired the music of a man who felt that 'opera, through singing, must make you weep, shudder, die'.

By the middle of the century, Romanticism had fully flowered in France and Germany with the work of Berlioz and the first achievements of Wagner. In Italy, however, the pace of change was slower. Rossini, at heart a classicist whose musical god was Mozart, dominated the age. Romanticism was imported along with operatic subjects. The Italians had no native tradition of spoken drama to draw upon and turned to the plays and operas of Paris and to the literature of Great Britain. Rossini introduced Scott and Shakespeare to Italian opera, and Scott was the source of one of the central works of the *primo ottocento*, Donizetti's *Lucia di Lammermoor*. Yet in the 1840s Italy, unlike her neighbours, was still on the threshold of her Romantic apogee. Bellini's emotional style was a departure point which an early death prevented the composer himself from developing. Italian Romanticism was to reach its climax in the coming decades with the conjunction of the Risorgimento and Giuseppe Verdi.

10

WAGNER'S MUSIC DRAMAS

Wagner's theory of opera. 1849–64: from Switzerland to Munich—Schopenhauer and Tristan. *1864–76: from Munich to Bayreuth—The* Ring *and* Die Meistersinger. *1876–83:* Parsifal, Bayreuth *and Wagner's influence.*

Wagner's work up to *Lohengrin* belongs to the development of German Romantic opera (*see* Chapter 8). His later operas, for which he preferred the term 'music drama', were to be written in a revolutionary new style. They are, with their dates of completion rather than of their premières, *Tristan und Isolde* (1859), *Die Meistersinger von Nürnberg* (1867), the four operas which constitute the *Ring* cycle—*Das Rheingold* (*The Rhine Gold*, 1854), *Die Walküre* (*The Valkyrie*, 1856), *Siegfried* (1871), and *Götterdämmerung* (*Twilight of the Gods*, 1874)—and *Parsifal* (1882). The complex genesis and the great significance of these works is best discussed in the context of the composer's remarkable later career.

WAGNER'S THEORY OF OPERA

Wagner's involvement in the 1848 uprising in Dresden led to his exile from the German states for twelve years. He had finished *Lohengrin* in 1847, and in 1848 wrote the libretto of a work to be called *Siegfrieds Tod* (*The Death of Siegfried*). This was largely the text of *Götterdämmerung*, but it was not until 1851 that Wagner decided to proceed with *Der Ring des Nibelungen*, the whole text of which he finished in 1852. He considered other subjects at this time, and went to Paris to try to interest the French in a three-act opera called *Wieland der Schmied* (*Wieland the Smith*), of which he had written the scenario, but without success. In retrospect we can see that this was the crucial phase in Wagner's artistic development, that the artist in him was, in a sense, waiting—for a clearer vision of 'the music of the future', as he called it, and for the right moment to create that music. And while he waited, he wrote his theoretical works, clarifying for himself as well as his readers the essential elements of operas as yet unwritten.

These writings, *The Artwork of the Future* (1849), *Opera and Drama* (1850–1), and *A Communication to my Friends* (1851), have a reputation for being written in prose of impenetrable obscurity, and older English translations tended to support this view. But the main elements in Wagner's theory are clear. As he saw it, the contemporary theatre had degenerated from its Greek origins. In Greek tragedy as performed in the ancient world all the arts—poetry, music, dance and mime—were combined to present mythical subjects. The whole community took part and the performance was a kind of religious ritual. But by the nineteenth century the arts had gone their separate ways and the theatre had become merely a frivolous entertainment. Wagner called for a return to the integrity of the Greek ideal in a new *Gesamtkunstwerk* or 'work of unified art' in which words, spectacle and music would serve the drama. The subject of the drama would not be politics or society or even personal relationships, but rather the inner experience and psychology of the characters. Since Beethoven, music had become uniquely able to express a world of feeling, but the typical operatic plot had become—in Wagner's view—little more than a peg on which to hang the music. The inner world of men and women, which for him was the real world, was best revealed through myth, the symbols and archetypal situations of which had a universal communicative power.

Wagner did not stop with these historical observations and prescriptions, but also gave a detailed explanation of how words and music should be allied and organised in the new music drama. He recommended that the text should avoid strict verse and regular metre and employ *Stabreim*, a free verse form which linked words through alliteration. Alliterative consonants, he claimed, communicated meaning more readily than vowels, and linked consonants could link even quite different concepts in a way perceptible to the ear, as in the phrase *die Liebe bringt Lust und Leid* (love brings joy and sorrow). The music to which this would be set must also link and distinguish the three concepts it contains; thus 'love' and 'joy' are consonant ideas, and the key should be the same for both, but 'sorrow', though linked to the first two concepts by alliteration and the sense of the line, is conceptually dissonant, and so the music should change on '*Leid*' to a chord which expresses the pain without obliterating our sense of the joy. The power of Wagner's music derives partly from the fact that he possessed the skill to do precisely what he recommends. Nietzsche was not joking when he called Wagner a 'musical miniaturist' for despite the scale of his operas they are full of such telling detail. Another aspect of Wagner's theory was that the music should be continuous rather than separated into numbers such as arias, duets and choruses. Instead of such closed forms there would be *unendliche Melodie*, or 'endless melody'. The use of *leitmotifs* is also important, as discussed later in this chapter (*see* page 186). Finally, since the operatic chorus had outlived its artistic vitality, the orchestra must assume a role akin to that of a Greek chorus, commenting on the drama as it unfolds. Cosima, the composer's second wife, recorded in her diary on the 29th September 1871 that Wagner described the great funeral music following Siegfried's death in *Götterdämmerung* as a Greek chorus 'to be sung, as it were, by the orchestra'.

Wagner took more from other composers than he cared to admit openly, and we have already noted his admiration for Gluck and his comments on such unlikely predecessors as Halévy and Bellini. It is clear, too, that the best operas of any period are in a sense music dramas. But none of this detracts from Wagner's stature as an innovator. His mature operas are unusual in that they are mostly settings of myth, have a continuous orchestral texture that constantly varies to convey the sense of the text and the meaning of the drama, and concern the inner world of the characters more than the plot. Above all, these works have an integrity and seriousness which suggest that art might once again become central to life as he desired. His theoretical works contain some bogus history and special pleading; but there is much insight as well and theory is not inflexible—for example *Die Meistersinger* has some 'old-fashioned' set pieces—for the artist and man of the theatre always had priority over the theorist. But Wagner's theory of opera is an attempt not to prescribe a formula but to articulate a vision.

1849–64: FROM SWITZERLAND TO MUNICH—SCHOPENHAUER AND *TRISTAN*

Wagner's Swiss years are a complicated tale of amorous escapades and serious love affairs, a failing marriage and a growing reputation, debts and luxuries, friendships and betrayals, but through all this his unshakeable sense of mission enabled him to survive all setbacks. During this period he saw few of his works on stage, banned as he was from Germany throughout the very decade in which performances of *Tannhäuser* and *Lohengrin* were spreading his fame there. He gave concerts in Zurich in 1853 of extracts from his work, a new method of presenting his music to the public which he was to use often in later years. A series of London concerts in 1855 failed to clear his debts but enhanced his reputation with musicians as a gifted conductor. After Berlioz, he is in fact the most important figure in the development of the modern school of conducting. Characteristically he wrote an essay, *On Conducting* (1869), in which he put forth his doctrine of 'modification of tempo', which meant changing speed at certain points in order to make the significance of a passage clearer and to relate the different parts of a score to the whole.

His most important activity during the period was literary: the creation of the text of the *Ring*. He gave his friends several readings of the entire libretto, which exerted a great fascination at a time when most libretti could not stand apart from their music, and when Wagner was the only important composer who wrote his own texts. Many might quail at the prospect of sitting through such a reading (Berlioz attended one which he said he 'endured with admirable patience') but Wagner was a consummate actor, and most of his audience were enthralled, not least by the astounding scale and originality of the concept. The score of *Das Rheingold* was completed on 26 September 1854 and that for *Die Walküre* on 23 March 1856. *Siegfried*, however, was put aside in June 1857, only half complete. Wagner told Liszt he had conducted Siegfried into the solitude of the forest, left him under a lime tree and 'taken leave of him with heartfelt tears'. It was to be almost twelve years before he took up the *Ring* again.

In the meantime a new subject clamoured for treatment. Again Liszt was the first to know:

> As I have never in my life tasted the true joy of love, I will set up a monument to this most beautiful of all dreams in which from first to last this love shall for once be utterly satisfied. I have planned out in my mind a *Tristan und Isolde*, the simplest yet most full-blooded musical conception. With the black flag that flies over its close I shall enshroud myself and die.

This statement illuminates a key aspect of Wagner and his work. He refers to *Tristan* as a 'musical conception', and this suggests he did not follow a rigid sequence of selecting a topic, writing a text, then setting it to music. As early as 1844 he had written:

> Firstly I am attracted only to matter the poetic and musical significance of which strike me simultaneously. Before I go on to write a verse or plot or scene I am already intoxicated by the musical aroma of my subject. I have every note, every characteristic musical motif in my head, so that when the versification is complete and the schemes arranged the opera is practically finished for me; the detailed musical treatment is just a peaceful meditative after-labour.

We know from Cosima's diaries and Wagner's sketches that composition was often rather more than 'a peaceful meditative after-labour', but there is no doubt that the musical atmosphere of *Tristan* was present from the outset—he even wrote of the early stages of composition, 'Music without words for the present. There are some places where I will probably do the music before the words.' This does not mean that the text is in some way secondary, or that *Tristan* can be regarded as an enormous symphonic poem. *Tristan* is the work which most completely fulfilled Wagner's theory of music drama, because both text and music served the drama, the total theatrical experience which was greater than the sum of its constituent parts. He told Cosima in later years, 'As a pure musician I would not have been of great significance. It is the conjunction of the poet and composer in me that is important.'

Two other figures entered Wagner's life at this period and both stand behind the genesis of *Tristan*. The first was Mathilde, the wife of his wealthy friend, Otto Wesendonk, who admired his work and had given him an allowance since 1852. In 1857 he gave Wagner and his wife Minna lodging in a house called '*Asyl*', or 'Refuge', set in the grounds of Wesendonk's own villa near Zurich. Mathilde Wesendonk was young and highly sympathetic to Wagner's ideas. Women were often attracted both to Wagner himself and to his works—in which, from Senta in *The Flying Dutchman* to Brünnhilde in the *Ring*, they are usually cast as redeeming agents. It has often been debated whether Wagner turned to the *Tristan* subject because he was in love with Mathilde, or turned to Mathilde because he was in love with his latest project. Certainly a sensual atmosphere seemed to heighten his creative responses—hence his notorious need for silk clothing, luxurious furnishings and exotic scents—and whatever their relationship, Mathilde became one of those individuals who claimed immortality solely because they once knew Richard Wagner. The same cannot be said of the other figure who stands behind *Tristan*, the philosopher Arthur Schopenhauer (1788–1860).

'The world is my idea.' Wagner opened Schopenhauer's *The World as Will and Idea* (1818) and, like many others, was struck by its first sentence. Unlike many others, he read on, fascinated, to the end and re-read the book many times. It is, as the author tells us, really the exploration of the single philosophical thought contained in its first sentence and first stated by Plato, although he was more concerned with its later development by Immanuel Kant. The notion that the world as it presents itself to our senses is not the 'real' world was linked here to the Buddhist idea of 'maya', of the surface of things as an illusion. The other central idea is that of the 'will to live', which is focused most intensely in human sexuality but which for Schopenhauer was inevitably linked with suffering, so that he defined human happiness simply as the absence of desire and salvation as lying in asceticism and the renunciation of the will to live.

These ideas had immense appeal for Wagner, as did the importance

Schopenhauer attached to art in general and music in particular. Wagner recognised in his work much that he already believed but had never encountered in so systematic and articulate a form. He wrote to Liszt, in that same letter of 1854 in which he announced *Tristan*:

> Besides my—slow—progress with my music my sole preoccupation now is with a man who has come like a gift from heaven to me in my solitude—though only a literary one. This is Arthur Schopenhauer, the greatest philosopher since Kant whose ideas—as he himself tells us—he is the first to have thought out to a conclusion . . . Schopenhauer's main conception, the ultimate negation of the will to live, is terribly stern, but in it alone is salvation. Of course it was not new to me, and no one can conceive it at all except him in whom it is already inherent, but nevertheless this philosopher is the first to awaken me to fuller consciousness of it.

Tristan und Isolde shows the clear influence of Schopenhauer. Tristan's repeated attempts to die, the hatred the lovers have for day and the world daylight brings, their longing to escape into the night and death, above all the equating of the most profound love with the most intense suffering, leave the ethos of the medieval story far behind. In *Tristan*, as in all mature Wagner, the rambling manner of the medieval source is abandoned, and the plot concentrated on a very few key actions. The essential drama is thus revealed as an interior drama. The power of the score, whose chromatic harmony is so advanced it is still considered the beginning of modern music, was recognised on all sides as *Tristan* became known in the later nineteenth century:

> The work which always arouses my greatest admiration is *Tristan*. This gigantic structure fills me time and time again with astonishment and awe, and I still cannot quite comprehend that it was conceived and written by a human being. I consider the second act, in its wealth of musical invention, its tenderness and sensuality of musical expression and its inspired orchestration, to be one of the finest creations that has ever issued from a human mind. This second act is wonderful, wonderful. . . .

One might think this the delirium of a rabid Wagnerite, but the speaker is the eighty-six-year-old Verdi, in an interview for the *Berliner Tageblatt*.

In fact it was Act III which Wagner expected to have this kind of impact. Here, when the mortally wounded Tristan lies under a burning sun at his castle in Brittany, longing for death and for Isolde, sundered by the sea and the cursed day from all he holds dear, Wagner's capacity to overwhelm the spectator and overcome any resistance reaches its apogee. 'Child,' he wrote to Mathilde, 'this *Tristan* is turning into something dreadful! That last act!!! I'm afraid the opera will be banned … only mediocre performances can save me, completely good ones are sure to drive people mad.' Yet this was the work which Wagner at the outset had intended to be 'a simple piece', to be widely (and lucratively) performed in Germany. Until 1865 *Tristan* was to languish unperformed.

In 1861 Wagner was granted an amnesty and was free to return to all German states except Saxony, which remained closed to him for a further two years. He also revised *Tannhäuser* for a notorious Paris production which, although politically motivated riots forced him to withdraw the work, can in retrospect be seen as the birth of French Wagnerism. Baudelaire's essay 'Richard Wagner and *Tannhäuser* in Paris' and Mallarmé's sonnet *Hommage* show that the first impact was on the literary world — it was later in the century that French musicians succumbed. Wagner moved on to Vienna, where he was fêted at performances of *The Flying Dutchman* and *Lohengrin*, but was ultimately frustrated in his attempts to get *Tristan* premièred there, it proving beyond the capacity of the Court Opera. Already thinking of his next work, *Die Meistersinger*, Wagner spent 1862 and 1863 giving concerts in Germany, Vienna and Russia. He and his wife Minna separated in 1862. He set up another luxurious home near Vienna, as usual anticipating income that never arrived, and was forced to flee his creditors once again in early 1864. His fortunes seemed at their lowest ebb; he had no money, no wife, no settled home, no opportunity to hear his latest work, and small prospect of completing the *Ring*. Then, with perfect timing, the new King of Bavaria, Ludwig II, summoned him to Munich on 3 May 1864.

1864–76: FROM MUNICH TO BAYREUTH — THE *RING* AND *DIE MEISTERSINGER*

Ludwig settled Wagner's debts and gave him an allowance, but no specific duties were required of him — in effect this was the salary without a job that Wagner had sought for years. Ludwig's support of Wagner, which enabled him to finish the *Ring* and *Die Meistersinger*, create *Parsifal* and build the Bayreuth theatre and festival, makes the young monarch one of the most important patrons in the history of opera. Wagner's brief stay in Munich was the most notorious episode in his career, and the scandal surrounding his affair with Cosima von Bülow, his luxurious living at the King's expense, and his interference in court politics, forced him to move on once more at the end of 1865.

Although apparently another setback, the Munich interlude can be seen as the turning point in Wagner's personal circumstances. He obtained and retained the patronage he needed; it became clear that Cosima, daughter of his friend Liszt, was the sympathetic and able consort his genius required; and he learned from the first performance of *Tristan* (Munich, 1865) that his most taxing work was not only performable, but performable to the highest standards. Ludwig Schnorr's achievement in creating the *Heldentenor* role of Tristan so overwhelmed Wagner that he spoke of allowing no more performances, since they could never be as fine. The death of the tenor at the age of twenty-nine soon after, widely (and wrongly) blamed on the physical and emotional exertions of singing Wagner's music, was a severe loss, and Wagner's essay *Recollections of Ludwig Schnorr von Carolsfeld* (1868) is a moving tribute from creator to interpreter.

Living once more in Switzerland, Wagner completed *Die Meistersinger von Nürnberg* in October 1867, and the new work was given its first performance in Munich eight months later. This is a very Wagnerian kind of comedy, full of melancholy and pathos. Even Carl Dalhaus, the most perceptive of recent commentators on Wagner's work, calls it 'the child of an untrustworthy sense of humour'. The character of Beckmesser is a cruel caricature of Wagner's critical adversary Eduard Hanslick, and the role is commonly played as broad farce. But Beckmesser is nevertheless a mastersinger and the friend of Hans Sachs, and though he is a pedant he is not an unmusical buffoon. As with Rossini or Mozart, Wagner's best jokes are musical ones. Beckmesser's serenade in Act II is a witty parody where every fussy melodic device is sent up by Wagner. David's accidental recollection of this tune before Sachs in Act III is as funny as Mozart's recollection of *Figaro* in Don Giovanni's supper scene. A less certain touch is shown when Hans Sachs likens his situation to that of King Mark in *Tristan und Isolde*, and the music refers to Mark's lament. So individual is the sound world of each of Wagner's major works that for a moment this reference disorientates the listener, transporting him from sixteenth-century Nuremberg to the bleak dawn of the day of Tristan's disgrace.

Meistersinger deploys and triumphantly restores those archaic musical forms which in theory Wagner had banished. The emotional climax of the work lies in the glorious—and very Italian—quintet in Act III. Elsewhere such forms serve to evoke the historic setting of the work, especially in the use of the sixteenth-century mastersinger's own *Bar*-form. A *Bar* is a strophic structure in which two *Stollen* (verses) have the same music to two stanzas of text, followed by an *Abgesang* (aftersong) which is musically different. Thus it is broadly an AAB structure. But Wagner and his rebellious hero Walther von Stolzing (tenor) often confound formal proprieties while still creating satisfying forms, so *Bar*-form itself is used to underpin the artistic message of the opera. Thus in Act I, Walther's 'Trial Song' *'Fanget an!'* is an enormously extended *Bar*-form, in which the A sections are themselves in two parts, making an AB, AB, C structure 160 bars long. Beckmesser, in his role as 'marker' noting the offences against the rules, interrupts Walther after the first part of the second *Stollen* (the second A section), understandably assuming that he has completed an ABA piece. Beckmesser's criticism of the song is in an appropriately correct *Bar*-form, and only many bars later at the end of the act does Walther conclude his larger *Bar*, closing the form with his *cantilena* soaring above the confusion his innovations have caused. Thus the whole scene is framed by the 'Trial Song', the structure of which serves to illustrate Walther's artistic vision and provides the dramatic opportunity for Beckmesser to display his own lack of true formal mastery and imagination, for which, in Wagner's aesthetic, adherence to rules was no substitute. In this way, deploying a form he had never used before, Wagner brilliantly allies musical structure with dramatic meaning.

Die Meistersinger is also the work in which Wagner displays the widest range of relationships between the stage and the orchestra. The norm, as always in his mature work, is for the orchestra to reveal to us what the characters are feeling at each moment, as in the melancholy music associated with Hans Sachs in his philosophical moments, which reaches its fullest expression in the prelude to Act III. In the transition to the festive final scene of Act III, up to the entry of the mastersingers, it is a co-celebrant with the citizens of Nuremberg, and accompanies the little succession of choral scenes for each of the guilds, while in Act II it creates the atmosphere of the magical summer night. Wagner was a master of nature music and scenes such as the 'forest murmurs' from *Siegfried* or the glittering rainbow at the end of *Das Rheingold*, while owing something to Beethoven, are also forerunners of musical impressionism. Here as Sachs savours the nocturnal scent of the elder tree, the orchestra breathes with him and wafts a delicate perfume across to the audience. Most subtle of all these various stage-orchestra relationships also comes in Act II, where Beckmesser has stolen into Sachs's home and found the newly written manuscript of Walther's prize song. He peruses the text, and the orchestra gently reminisces on the tune which Walther has just sung to it. At this moment, the orchestra conspires with the audience against Beckmesser, telling us what he will never perceive, for he does not hear the melody as he reads, and when he sings the words soon after he is laughed out of the song contest. *Meistersinger* is a warning for all who would generalise about the role of Wagner's orchestra. As Nietzsche told would-be commentators on his writings, 'do not rest until you have also found the contradiction'.

In 1872 Wagner left Switzerland for the Bavarian town of Bayreuth, where a new theatre was to be built to his own design. He had also designed a house there which he called '*Wahnfried*' ('peace from illusion'), and which was the only home he ever owned. The wanderings were over at last. On 21 November 1874 Wagner finished the full score of *Götterdämmerung*, and completed the project he had begun in 1848 with the text of that same work. Since the *Ring* tetralogy was so long in the making, its unity of style is remarkable. That unity derives largely from the application of the system of *leitmotif*. The use of the *leitmotif* (leading motive) was outlined in *Opera and Drama*, where it is referred to as a recurrent melodic element permitting the construction of a unified artistic form. These motives in the *Ring* are often very brief and simple, sometimes a broken chord (the nature motif) or a single interval (Hagen's falling diminished fifth) being all that Wagner needs to conjure up the required association. There are well over a hundred in the whole *Ring*, but many are interrelated in a way that gives unity to the enormous structure, and provides a continuous symphonic texture. Yet their directness ensures that even in the most complex passages they can be recognised and their dramatic significance apprehended.

At the beginning of the *Ring* cycle, in *Das Rheingold*, the motifs are few in number and the texture straightforward, with few passages of contrapuntal combination of them. This is appropriate to the exposition of a narrative as well as reflecting Wagner's style at this stage of his career. By the time of *Götterdämmerung*, the climax of the cycle, there are many more motifs to deploy and many previous events in the drama to reminisce upon. Also Wagner's musical powers were then at their height. Even in this last instalment of the cycle Wagner introduces new motifs such as the one which occurs in the first act when Siegfried and Gunther sing an oath of blood-brotherhood. By Act II, Gunther has become ensnared in Hagen's plot to kill Siegfried, but at the moment of committing himself to this betrayal, Gunther has misgivings—the blood-brotherhood motif is brayed out high in the horns, and we know exactly what is going through Gunther's mind. This stirring moment of 'the orchestra as conscience' also reminds us of the essential tension which drives all the *Ring* operas— the conflict between love and power, between loyalty to people and principles and the pressures of expediency. This timeless theme and its mythical setting in a world of giants, dwarves, gods and humans together give the *Ring* its universal significance.

Yet within its musical and narrative unity the *Ring* offers variety also. *Das Rheingold*, founded on Wotan's well-meant machinations, is the most political opera, concerned with property and the keeping of promises. *Die Walküre* is the most satisfying heard out of the context of the whole cycle, and was once the most often performed of the individual *Ring* operas. Its progress from Siegmund and Sieglinde's sibling love, through marital strife to Wotan's chastisement and farewell to Brünnhilde is exquisitely supported by lyrical inspiration. *Siegfried* has been called 'the scherzo of the *Ring*' and is a fairy-tale opera of the forging of a sword, the slaying of a dragon, the winning of a treasure and of a woman, and the growth of a hero through the discovery of love. But as Siegfried awakens Brünnhilde with a kiss we recall Wagner's observation that 'the kiss of love is the first intimation of death, the cessation of individuality'. Siegfried and Brünnhilde close the opera defying '*lächender Tod*' (laughing death), and *Tod* is the last word of the score. *Götterdämmerung* sees the death of both Siegfried and Brünnhilde, but also the birth of new hope as the 'redemption through love' motif soars upwards in the strings to close the cycle with a benediction.

The *Ring*'s mythical setting and vast scope have always inspired commentators to offer interpretations of its meaning. For George Bernard Shaw in *The Perfect Wagnerite* (1898) this was a political allegory in which the capitalist Alberich exploits the enslaved Nibelung workers and creates a loveless and materialist world which the anarchist hero Siegfried is destined to overthrow. But any socialist message is abandoned in *Götterdämmerung*, which Shaw saw as a conventional grand opera with political thought suppressed by a 'love panacea'. There is some support for this view in Wagner's own revolutionary interests at the time of the *Ring*'s conception, and Patrice Chéreau's production at Bayreuth in 1976 demonstrated that it can be convincing. Shaw at least related Wagner's work to the age in which it was written, even if he emphasised the political dimension at the expense of other aspects.

But then any one view of the *Ring* has tended to be more single-minded than the tetralogy itself. In Robert Donington's *Wagner's Ring and its Symbols* (1963) all the facets of the work are interpreted in terms of Jung's psychology. The mythological elements are archetypal symbols; the gold at the bottom of the Rhine is 'libido lying unused in the unconscious'; the ring forged from the gold represents 'our individual experience of the self'; the dragon Fafner symbolises 'a terrible danger from our mother-image', and 'For Siegfried to thrust his sword into Fafner is . . . a veiled symbol for phallic penetration. Since the penetration is of his mother-image, this amounts to a psychic incest.' The characters and actions are aspects of the development of the psyche: ego, persona, shadow, and anima, with Wotan standing for the dominance of the ego which must be overcome in the wider interests of the whole personality. For Donington, the *Ring* tells of a struggle to overcome unconscious mother-longings and other obstacles to realising the self. Redemption is 'transformation in the psyche' and the end of *Götterdämmerung* is the 'shattering upheaval and creative pangs of rebirth'. Few readers have accepted all this view, but most feel that it enhances their understanding of Wagner's cycle. Its power seems constantly to call for explanation in print or a new illumination in a staged production. Otherwise we might simply agree with Shaw that 'Most of us are . . . so helplessly under the spell of the *Ring*'s greatness that we can do nothing but go raving about the theatre between the acts in ecstasies of deluded admiration.'

1876–1883: *PARSIFAL*, BAYREUTH AND WAGNER'S INFLUENCE

The first complete performance of *Der Ring des Nibelungen* (Bayreuth, 1876) did not satisfy the composer, and the financial failure of the festival meant that he could not revise the production. But he learned from it, and although *Parsifal*, like all his later works, had been first thought of as early as the summer of 1845, the finished work of 1882 shows the hand of a practical artist who knew his works in the theatre. The tenor role of Parsifal is less strenuous than that of Siegfried or Tristan, although it is still demanding in requiring the singer-actor to grow from uncomprehending naïvety in Act I to royal authority in Act III.

Parsifal is the work of an artist who, though no longer in the earliest vigour of inspiration, has reached the pinnacle of his dramaturgical and musical mastery. The score, begun in 1877, was finished on 13 January 1882, though Wagner had to score the last page a few weeks prematurely to hand to Cosima, as he had promised, on her birthday on Christmas Day. In contrast to the *Ring*, which constituted the first Bayreuth Festival, the sixteen *Parsifal* performances in 1882 at the second Festival, the last Wagner himself saw, showed a healthy profit. This was helped by the last of Ludwig's magnificent gestures, the placing of his entire Munich chorus and orchestra at Wagner's disposal. Wagner had intended to keep *Parsifal* solely for performance in the Bayreuth Festival theatre, though even before the copyright ran out in 1913 it had begun to appear elsewhere. He wrote the work with Bayreuth's beautiful acoustic in mind, and so it will always be most at home there.

Parsifal, which Thomas Mann described as 'majestic in its sclerotic languor', is Wagner's most perfect score. From first to last the spectator is drawn into a world of suffering and compassion, and the drama makes its impact with such force as to suspend all questioning of its precise meaning. T. S. Eliot, who like Joyce, Proust, Lawrence and Mann was influenced by Wagner, spoke of poetry which affected the reader long before its meaning became clear. Wagner went one further—the first dramatic impact *was* the meaning, and subsequent attempts to analyse that meaning were unnecessary. When asked why, in the *Ring*, Wotan and the gods must perish when the Rhinemaidens have regained the ring, Wagner could only refer to the emotional necessity of this conclusion, explaining 'we must become knowers through feeling'. Commentators have had a particularly difficult task in explaining the message of *Parsifal*, not least its closing words, 'Redemption to the redeemer', sung as the newly crowned ruler of the Knights of the Grail, Parsifal, raises the Grail as a dove hovers over his head and Kundry, the work's only female character, falls dead. This *Bühnenweihfestspiel* ('stage consecration festival play') as Wagner clumsily termed it, appropriates Christian symbols to a typically Wagnerian drama of renunciation and redemption which, like the *Ring*, has an ambiguous conclusion. In fact Wagner's sense of the poetic quality of the concept of redemption was always greater than his desire to explain what it meant.

Being Wagner's final work, *Parsifal* is especially rich in links with his previous operas. Parsifal is the father of Lohengrin, as Lohengrin himself tells us, and when in Act I Parsifal kills a swan, the creature dies to the strains of the swan motif from the earlier work. Wagner called Amfortas 'my Tristan of Act III raised to an incomparable pitch of intensity', and at one stage planned to have Parsifal walk into Act III of *Tristan* in search of the Grail. Like *Die Meistersinger*, the opera is partly about a community whose harmony is threatened from within, and the riot in Act II of *Meistersinger* is a precursor of the chorus in Act III of *Parsifal* in which the Knights of the Grail implore Amfortas to perform his office and reveal the Grail. Parsifal himself stands in the same relation to Amfortas as Siegfried to Wotan, Stolzing to Sachs, and Tristan to Mark—in each case the younger man in some sense usurps the role of the older one in an event which is central to the drama. Such echoes across the Wagner operas, and there are many others, add to our satisfaction with any single work, while a knowledge of them all illuminates individual dramas.

Of *Parsifal*'s many remarkable features, perhaps the most influential has been its orchestration. Debussy spoke of 'that orchestral colouring that seems to be lit from behind and of which there are so many wonderful effects in *Parsifal*'. He may have been thinking of the second statement of the opening theme of the prelude, when the first trumpet and three oboes pierce the swirling string texture in an anguished plea for compassion sounding through a formless mist. *Parsifal* employs quadruple woodwind, like the *Ring*, but does not require the enormous brass complement of the tetralogy. (*Tristan* has triple wind and *Meistersinger* only double wind.) The complex blending and overlapping of instrumental lines character-istic of *Tristan* here gives way to a more frequent use of block orchestra-tion, deploying the instruments in their family groups—again the prelude is an illustration of this. Block orchestration was often used in the early works, but in *Parsifal* the technique is much more refined, and used to dramatic purpose, representing the hierarchic and ritualistic elements in Acts I and III.

Wagner died in Venice on 13 February 1883, a few months after the triumphant first performances of *Parsifal* at Bayreuth. Verdi, on hearing the news, wrote to Ricordi, 'It is a great individual who has disappeared. A name that leaves a powerful imprint on the history of art.' But before sending it Verdi crossed out '*potenta*' (powerful) and wrote '*potentissima*' (most powerful). He has been proved right, for no musician, and perhaps even no artist, of the nineteenth century has had a greater impact on his contemporaries and his successors. Bryan Magee, in his *Aspects of Wagner* (1968), has shown how Wagner's influence went beyond music to the spoken drama and other literary forms, and to philosophy and psychology. With Wagner's career and subsequent reputation, opera reached the peak of its influence upon Western intellectual life.

One of the less happy effects of Wagner's dominance is the eclipse, outside Germany, of most of the operas of his German contemporaries. Hermann Götz (1840–76) took Mozart as his model in an age when musicians revered the greater dynamism of Beethoven, and Götz's opera on Shakespeare's *The Taming of the Shrew* (*Der widerspenstigen Zähmung*, 1874) is heard even less often than Nicolai's *Die lustigen Weiber von Windsor* (Berlin, 1849). Friedrich von Flotow (1812–83) was Wagner's exact contemporary, and perhaps regretted the fact. His light style, exemplified by his *Martha* (Vienna, 1847), had more appeal in Paris than in Germany. Peter Cornelius (1824–74) was a disciple of Liszt and Wagner, composed *Der Barbier von Baghdad* (Weimar, 1858) and *Der Cid* (Weimar, 1865), and achieved in these works something of the individu-ality he so feared his great mentors might stifle. The career of Karl Goldmark (1830–1915) centred on Vienna, and his fame rests on his first opera, *The Queen of Sheba* (Vienna, 1875), whose tuneful and colourful music gave it a wide currency throughout greater Germany. Eugen d'Albert (1864–1932) was a British-born pupil of Liszt, and his *Tiefland* (Prague, 1903), a blend of Wagner and *verismo*, keeps a tenuous hold on the repertoire. Only Richard Strauss among German composers was able to follow on from Wagner without being overwhelmed by his example. But the Wagner influence is perhaps too strong in Engelbert Humperdinck (1854–1921), who worked as an assistant on the first performances of *Parsifal*, even composing a few extra bars (now dropped) to cover a scene change. Such impeccable Wagnerian credentials were put to good use in his fairytale opera, *Hänsel und Gretel* (Weimar, 1893), which was declared a work of genius by Richard Strauss who conducted the première. The opera has remained a favourite in Germany, and is quite often played in Britain and North America. It began life as incidental music for a group of children to perform at home, but the full opera allies the folk and nursery elements to Wagnerian harmony and orchestration. This gives the score a unique flavour, a blend of naivety and sophistication which enables children and their parents to enjoy the work equally.

Curiously, Wagner's influence has been more fruitful in non-operatic music and, via Bayreuth, in styles of staging and performance. The symphonists Anton Bruckner (1824–96) and Gustav Mahler (1860–1911) acknowledged this influence. Bruckner dedicated his Third Symphony to Wagner, and Mahler once announced 'After Beethoven, there is only Richard'—meaning Wagner, not Strauss. (Strauss was called by the conductor Von Bülow 'Richard the Third' because after Wagner there could be no Richard the Second.) In France, César Franck and his circle were devoted Wagnerians, but Debussy's relationship to Wagner is more ambiguous, as a comparison between *Pelléas et Mélisande* and *Tristan* will show. The radically new music of the Second Viennese School of Schoenberg, Berg and Webern was a development out of Wagner's chromatic musical language—thus not for the first time the general history of music was shaped by opera. Even completely different aesthetics, such as that of Les Six in France, were so partly out of a reaction against Wagnerism as music to be heard 'head in hands'.

The Festival Theatre at Bayreuth is the Mecca for all Wagnerians. Its successful design is Wagner's compromise between a Greek amphitheatre and a nineteenth-century opera house; and it has clear sight lines from all seats, a beautiful acoustic and an orchestra pit which is screened from view. The theatre is used solely for Wagner's music, and several of the operas are played there each year at the Festival for which a special company of singers, instrumentalists, designers and directors is assembled. The Festival is run by Wagner's heirs, following the tradition he and subsequently Cosima established. There have been changes, the most radical being the revolutionary style of production developed in the

1950s by Wagner's grandson. Wieland Wagner's stripping away of the inessential and his replacement of realism with a more austere concentration on the symbolic essence of the dramas has been widely influential.

The centenary of the first Bayreuth Festival fell in 1976, and a new centenary production of the *Ring* cycle was entrusted to two Frenchmen, the conductor Pierre Boulez and the director Patrice Chéreau. It was at first highly controversial, but it was filmed and has since become much admired. Many who will never go to Bayreuth made their first acquaintance with this work by watching it on television. Gramophone recordings of various Bayreuth productions have been issued, and often with lasting success. But if there is still a Bayreuth performing tradition it is no longer the only way to perform Wagner, or even always the best way. It may no longer even represent the composer's way musically, since Wagner himself appears to have conducted his music much faster than we are now accustomed to, to judge from his complaints that other conductors took too long over his works. No doubt there will always be new insights from performances of these endlessly challenging music dramas. Wagner, the great artistic revolutionary, would have been the last to want a tradition to ossify. As he told performers at one Bayreuth rehearsal, 'Children, do something *different!*'

> My passion for the Wagnerian enchantment has accompanied my life ever since I first became aware of it, and began to make it my own and penetrate it with my understanding. All that I owe to him, of enjoyment and instruction, I can never forget; the hours of deep and single bliss in the midst of the theatre throngs, hours of nervous and intellectual transport and rapture, perceptions of great and moving import such as only this art offers.
>
> (Thomas Mann: *The Sufferings and Greatness of Richard Wagner*)

As we have seen, Thomas Mann was one among many people who have willingly submitted to Wagner's spell. What is it about Wagner's works that enables them not only to dominate the repertoire—all of the ten operas that Wagner admitted to the canon are in production somewhere in the world most of the time—but also to exert an influence, like no other operas, beyond the theatre?

In the last analysis we are forced back to Wagner's original vision of an all-embracing artwork with universal relevance that is celebrated in the theatre. To know Wagner only from scores, records or broadcasts is to miss the essence of him. Ultimately it is the great theatrical scenes in this art which, long after the performance is over, continue to resonate—Tristan expiring, as much from love as from his wound, at the moment of

Isolde's return, Hans Sachs pretending to examine the shoes Eva is wearing to hide his feelings at the moment he must relinquish her to the knight who has just entered, Wotan bidding farewell to Brünnhilde in a noble and tender access of paternal love, Siegfried's joyous nuptial procession bursting on the scene just as Hagen finishes plotting his death, Parsifal apprehending all the world's pain through Kundry's lustful kiss, and a dozen others besides. All these moments share a dramatic, musical, and consequently emotional directness, towards which all elements act in consort. But the spectator need not analyse what is happening to appreciate it — and indeed the Wagnerian aesthetic requires an emotional surrender. Wagner's great intellect was used to create works which operate on the audience in a non-intellectual way, and yet intellectuals have been among his greatest admirers. This is perhaps why Mann called his achievement 'one of the most splendidly questionable, ambivalent, and fascinating phenomena in all artistic creation'.

11

VERDI

Nationalism and 'years in the galley'. Maturity: Rigoletto, Trovatore, Traviata. *Grand operas and changing conditions. Shakespearean climax:* Otello *and* Falstaff.

NATIONALISM AND 'YEARS IN THE GALLEY'

The first opera of Giuseppe Verdi (1813–1901), *Oberto, Conte di San Bonifacio*, was given its first performance on 17 November 1839 at La Scala, Milan. With hindsight we recognise this as a key date in Italian operatic history, but few can have thought so at the time. Although Bellini had been dead for four years, Donizetti was in his early forties and had many fine works still ahead of him. Rossini had written no opera for ten years, but was still an influential figure in France and Italy. There is little in *Oberto* that would have surprised these three, who would have noticed its provenance in the work of Bellini and Mercadante. They might even have considered the composer to be making a late start at the age of twenty-six, but at least it was not a false start. *Oberto* was successful enough for the publisher Giovanni Ricordi to buy the rights in the score and for La Scala to give Verdi a contract to write three more operas.

Verdi's second opera was a comedy, *Un giorno di regno* (*King for a Day*, Milan, 1840), that failed resoundingly. But his third was successful. 'With *Nabucco*,' wrote Verdi, 'my career can be said to have begun.' Indeed *Nabucco* (Milan, 1842) had a remarkable triumph, and when it was revived in the next season it ran for fifty-seven performances, still a record in La Scala's history and amazing in an age that demanded novelty each season. The composer and his librettist, Temistocle Solera, were able to repeat their success with their next opera, *I lombardi alla prima crociata* (*The Lombards at the First Crusade*, Milan, 1843). The stirring patriotic chorus of the Hebrew slaves ('*Va, pensiero*') from *Nabucco*, with its potent cry of '*O mia patria, si bella e perduta*' ('Oh my country, so beautiful and so lost') had already become a rallying call for Italian nationalism, and now the Lombards' yearning for their native vineyards in Act IV of *I lombardi* was a successful attempt to stir the same emotion.

Verdi was born near, and brought up in, the town of Busseto in the

Duchy of Parma, which in 1813 belonged to France. After Napoleon's defeat in 1815 Northern Italy was assigned to the Austrians, and the Habsburgs were eager to discourage the growing sense of Italian patriotism which the French Revolution had brought to the peninsula. The Italian nationalist movement, the Risorgimento, did not create an independent nation state until the 1860s, so that Verdi's youth and maturity were spent in an era of foreign repression and of burgeoning hopes for self-determination. It was a cause to which he was personally committed and for which some of his friends and colleagues gave their lives; the Risorgimento formed him and he in turn gave the movement its popular voice and became its most celebrated symbol. In 1859 the letters of Verdi's name became a code for *V*ittorio *E*manuele, *Re D'I*talia and allowed a cry of '*Viva Verdi*' to be used as a covert Risorgimento slogan. In Verdi's *Attila* the line '*Avrai tu l'universo, Resti l'Italia a me*' ('You may have the universe, but leave Italy to me') galvanised anti-Austrian feeling. If the police banned the line, there was a demonstration in the theatre—for the opera house was the chief centre of recreation in an Italian town and the focus for the expression of communal feeling. Then as now, even unmusical people went regularly to the opera. Copies of the libretto were available at each performance, and the house lights stayed up throughout, so police anxiety about the text is understandable. In the 1840s each of Verdi's operas contained a scene, chorus or line that could provoke a patriotic response—even *Macbeth* has its chorus of Scottish exiles lamenting the fate of their oppressed country, '*O patria oppressa*'. In Venice, the audience threw bouquets of red and green—the Italian colours—and when the police banned red and green, they threw bouquets of yellow and black—the Austrian colours—in the sure knowledge that the singers would disdain to pick them up. Small wonder that Verdi, like Donizetti before him, received such close attention from the censorship; that he was asked by the great Italian statesman Cavour to stand as a parliamentary candidate in 1861 for the emerging nation state; and that at the very end of his life Italian patriotic feeling was transferred to the person of Verdi himself—at his funeral the mourners began to sing, spontaneously and inevitably, '*Va, pensiero*'.

A later Italian composer, Luigi Dallapiccola, once wrote, 'The phenomenon that is Verdi is unimaginable without the Risorgimento.' But although nationalist sentiment may explain the scale of the success of *Nabucco* in Milan in 1842, it does not explain why it should have been played in 1844 in other centres such as Barcelona, Berlin, Stuttgart, Malta, Oporto and Corfu. Within a decade *Nabucco* had been heard in cities as far afield as London, New York, Constantinople, St Petersburg and Buenos Aires. Such conquest of the operatic world was not unique in Verdi's career, for although it is true that many passages in his operas had a special meaning for the subject peoples of the Italian peninsula, their music also possessed a universal appeal.

Between *Nabucco* in 1842 and the work which announced Verdi's full maturity in 1851, *Rigoletto*, Verdi composed a dozen new works, and revised one more. These were what he called his 'years in the galley', and the operas were produced in conditions similar to those prevailing in Rossini's heyday. These conditions were to change, if only gradually, partly through Verdi's own force of will. At this stage the procedure was still to negotiate with the impresario, find a subject and librettist, prepare the score (Verdi insisted on holding back some decisions on orchestration until piano rehearsals had begun), and coach the singers. Meantime negotiations would be in train with the next city. In this way Venice obtained *Ernani* (1844) and *Attila* (1846), Rome *I due Foscari* (1844) and *La battaglia die Legnano* (1849), and Milan *Giovanna d'Arco* (1845). Florence gave *Macbeth* its première in 1847 and Trieste *Il corsaro* in 1848, while Naples commissioned *Alzira* in 1845 and *Luisa Miller* in 1849. There were foreign commissions from London (*I masnadieri*, *The Robbers*, 1847) and from the Paris Opéra, for which the composer reworked *I lombardi* into *Jérusalem* in the same year. All these earlier operas have been staged and recorded in the post-war Verdi renaissance, yet this has not resulted in any radical revaluation of their relative merits as it has in the case of Rossini. The few works from this period that have kept a real hold on the repertory remain the most worthwhile: *Nabucco* for its patriotic fervour and a choral splendour rivalling that of its model, Rossini's *Moïse*, *Ernani* for its wealth of vital melody, *Macbeth* for its truly Shakespearean power, especially in the 1865 revision, and *Luisa Miller* for its first sounding of a note of intimate, domestic tragedy in Verdi's work and, in Act III, introducing music of a quality that announced the composer's second period.

The roles of both Nabucco and Macbeth were written for leading baritone singers, following not only *Moïse* in its use of a low voice but also Donizetti's example. The operatic disposition of vocal types was determined by a convention requiring a '*prima donna soprano*', a '*primo tenore*', a '*basso comprimario*' (a *comprimario* role was a sub-principal one), a '*seconda donna soprano*', '*secondo tenore*' and so on. These designations indicated the relative rank of the artists and the size of their roles. The exact disposition for any production varied according to the singers engaged but there was usually a balance of types. When critics complained of the 'mournful colour' of the 1857 version of *Simon Boccanegra* they surely had in mind its unconventional casting—the four characters of the Prologue are Boccanegra (*primo baritono*), Fiesco (*primo basso profondo*, or deep bass), Paolo and Pietro (both *baritono comprimario* roles).

Nabucco's music was written for Giorgio Ronconi, Donizetti's favourite baritone, and we owe *Macbeth* partly to the availability of another baritone, Felice Varesi, for the title role. Verdi wrote to Varesi to secure his participation, and consulted him over the details of his music and even over the orchestration. The singer was nevertheless instructed to pay more attention to the words than the music, so that the text would come across to the audience: Verdi was never an admirer of purely beautiful voices and technically accomplished singers. He once wrote of the role of Lady Macbeth, 'Tadolini sings to perfection; and I would rather that Lady didn't sing at all. Tadolini has a marvellous voice, clear, limpid, and strong; and I would rather that Lady's voice were rough, hollow and stifled.' Verdi's encouragement of vocal acting, and the demands he made on singers especially with his high baritone *tessitura*, were often criticised, and von Bülow called Verdi 'the Attila of the throat'. But the difficulties with which his roles challenge singers are never perverse, and are always directed towards character and dramatic truth.

Macbeth (Florence, 1847) was the first of Verdi's three Shakespearean operas, and never popular in the composer's lifetime. He was especially incensed when one critic suggested after the première of the revised version (Paris, 1865) that he did not understand Shakespeare: 'It may be that I have not done justice to *Macbeth* but that I don't know or understand or feel Shakespeare—no, by God, no. He is one of my favourite poets; I've had him in my hands since my earliest youth and I read him over and over again.' But there are many moments when Verdi *has* done justice to *Macbeth*: Macbeth's dagger speech and most of his wife's music create the characters we recognise from the play. The F minor prelude sets the mood of grim foreboding and the witches' shrill and cackling opening chorus, far from being trivial as some have suggested, is the ideal representation of Shakespeare's 'unnatural hags'. The weird sisters adopt an appropriately sinister tone when they prophesy to Macbetto (as the protagonist, but not the opera, is called). The supernatural elements are frighteningly effective, both the appearances of Banquo's ghost and the 'shew of kings' on Macbeth's second visit to the witches conveying a genuine *frisson* of terror. Sometimes the conventions work against Verdi's aim of fidelity to the Bard—just as Shakespeare's three witches must here become three groups of six singers, so Banquo has little chance against a whole male chorus of murderers, and their rather jolly music would have alerted all but the deafest of hunted men to their approach.

Even in the 1865 revision certain of the cruder aspects of the first version remain, such as Verdi's habit of doubling the vocal line with a raucous solo trumpet, as in Lady Macbeth's *cavatina* in the first act. But some of the best music also survived unchanged from 1847, including the sleepwalking scene. Perhaps in homage to the composer of *La sonnambula*, Verdi introduces his '*Gran scena del sonnambulismo*' with a superb melody of Bellinian length and pathos, and the repeated accompanying pattern perfectly evokes the obsessive dwelling on blood and past crimes to which Macbeth's once powerful consort is now reduced. For all the inconsistencies that beset any substantially revised Verdi opera, it is such scenes as this which dominate in a good performance. No wonder the Teatro della Pergola in Florence carries a plaque to commemorate the opera which it commissioned.

MATURITY: *RIGOLETTO, TROVATORE, TRAVIATA*

Rigoletto (Venice, 1851) is based on Victor Hugo's play *Le roi s'amuse*, which Verdi considered 'perhaps the greatest drama of modern times'. It was a subject he was eager to set, and he wrote to the librettist, Francesco Maria Piave, 'The subject is grand, immense, and there's a character in it who is one of the greatest creations that the theatre of all countries and of all times can boast ... the character I'm speaking of is Triboulet.' Triboulet became Rigoletto and despite battles with the censors the opera had immediate success and its popularity has never abated. Yet it is an innovatory score: there are no big choral numbers, no grand finales, few conventional aria structures, and an astonishing gallery of characters. These include Rigoletto the hunchbacked court jester, his public wit cruelly barbed and his private love of his daughter tenderly overprotective; Gilda herself, who grows from innocent girl to a woman prepared to sacrifice her life for a worthless lover; and the Duke who while playing the conventional heartless seducer, must still convey something to suggest that her sacrifice is a plausible act. When Rossini assessed *Rigoletto* as the first opera in which Verdi displayed his full genius, he must also have seen that the musical structures he himself had created and which had served Italian opera for nearly forty years were here largely dismantled.

The character of Rigoletto (baritone) is one of the great roles of the operatic stage, and in delineating it Verdi demonstrates a Shakespearean range. We first meet him in his professional role of jester, which he hates but executes with skill and venom. In his great soliloquy in Act I, '*Pari siamo!*' ('We are the same') he likens his profession to that of the assassin

Sparafucile—'I with my tongue, he with his dagger'—and spews out his loathing of the courtiers who have made him a villain. 'Tears, the consolation of all men, are denied me,' he laments, anticipating that other tragic clown, Canio in *Pagliacci*. 'But here I am another man,' he sings as he goes into his house to greet his beloved daughter Gilda. In Act II, when the courtiers have kidnapped her, Piave and Verdi again give us two sides of Rigoletto's nature in a single number, as his anger with the courtiers gives way to pleas for mercy. The reiterated vowels conjure up Rigoletto's contempt for the vile race of courtiers in '*Cortigiani, vil razza dannata*', but the jester's anxiety for Gilda leads him to end on a different note, '*Pietà, signori, pietà*'. This juxtaposition in Rigoletto of rage and repentance, of the terrifying and the pathetic, has led some commentators to liken the opera to that other great drama of paternity, *King Lear*, which Verdi wanted to set but never found the occasion, the artists, and perhaps the courage to undertake. While *Rigoletto* does not attain the awesome sublimity of *Lear*, it is surely the one of Verdi's settings of a non-Shakespearean play which most justifies the epithet 'Shakespearean'.

In *Il trovatore* (*The Troubador*, Rome, 1853) Verdi did not continue with the formal innovations of *Rigoletto*, but largely deployed the aria, duet and finale forms of the day. For this reason it has been called a backward step in his development that is redeemed only by the excellence of the material poured into the decaying moulds. But such a view is tenable only if art is regarded, in the way that some have looked on society itself, as necessarily evolving and improving. There is little evidence that Verdi held such a view, and a letter to his *Trovatore* librettist Salvatore Cammarano suggests that he saw his different 'manners' as options to be selected from according to the subject and the commission. Certainly he hoped to reform Italian opera with his later works, but at this stage he was still 'in the galley' and even talking of retiring from a career he claimed to detest.

Among the other myths surrounding *Il trovatore* is the suggestion that the plot is unintelligible. Certainly some aspects are far-fetched, such as the gypsy Azucena's mistaken incineration of her own infant, but what matters is the effect upon Azucena's psychology and the relationships of the principal characters with which Verdi's set pieces are concerned. And implausibility is not unintelligibility, as the critic Spike Hughes admits: 'I have read an intelligible synopsis of the plot that is no more than 148 words long, though nothing will induce me to say where this miracle of non-copyright précis can be found.'

Nor are the musical structures of *Il trovatore* rigid. The heroine Leonora might seem to have a two-part aria in Act IV, but the *cantabile* first half ('*D'amor sull'ali rosee*'), is divided from its *cabaletta* '*Tu vedrai che amore in terra'* by the *Miserere* scene with the chorus and tenor, which is longer than either of Leonora's solo passages. Regrettably, sopranos who find the line of this fine *cabaletta* too taxing sometimes cut the piece. The final scene of the opera moves from a 'number' style to the more continuous manner of *Rigoletto*, and has a very abrupt ending. Verdi considered the supreme crime in an opera was to bore the audience — 'I dozed,' he reported on his first *Lohengrin*, 'but so did the Wagnerites' — and he liked the curtain to fall as soon as possible after the *dénouement. Il trovatore* never bores; and those who criticise Verdi's so-called 'rum-ti-rum' accompaniments have surely never examined the varied and vital instrumental figures with which he underlines his splendid vocal writing. Caruso's celebrated observation that all one needs to perform *Il trovatore* is the four best singers in the world rightly reflects the challenge of the four main roles, but perhaps the role of Manrico makes *Trovatore* Verdi's chief 'tenor opera'. Not all the notes Manrico sings were written by Verdi of course. The now normal top C's at the end of Manrico's *cabaletta 'Di quella pira'* were first added by the tenor Enrico Tamberlik, with Verdi's permission — though he insisted that 'The top notes had better be good.'

If *Il trovatore* is a tenor's opera, *La traviata* (Venice 1853) is dominated by the soprano role of Violetta, the 'fallen woman' of the title. Violetta is based on a real character, Marie Duplessis, a Parisian courtesan of celebrated beauty who died of consumption in 1847 aged twenty-three. Alexandre Dumas *fils*, a former lover, wrote a novel and then, in 1852, a play about her. Verdi saw the play, *La dame aux camélias*, in which Marie had become Marguerite Gauthier, and Marguerite became, on 6 March 1853 at the Fenice theatre, Violetta Valéry. Of the disastrous première Verdi wrote, '*Traviata* last night — a fiasco. Was it my fault or the singers'? Time will tell.' The subject was bold and contemporary, and had some relevance to Verdi's own personal situation at the time, since he was living with a woman to whom he was not married. He wanted *Traviata* played in modern dress; but the nineteenth century was as fond of putting settings back in time as the twentieth is of bringing them forward, and the artists performed in period dress and wigs. In our own time Verdi's period is the usual setting, but by now Violetta has achieved almost archetypal status as the 'fallen woman' who finds true love and then renounces it for her lover's sake. The theatrical situation of people divided by the power of social norms rather than by a villain is a strong one, and Verdi's opera is one of the best loved in the repertory.

La traviata makes use of the *banda*, or stage band, which dates back to Paisiello, and became commonplace after Rossini used one in *Ricciardo e Zoraide* (1818). Verdi usually wrote for *banda* where one was available, as in Venice (*Attila* excepted). Act II Scene 2 of *Traviata* also has gypsies and matadors superfluous to its setting in a grand Parisian *salon*. The traditional *cabaletta* fits rather uneasily into this essentially domestic drama. The end of Act I, however, does solve this problem. Violetta's dedication to a hedonistic existence has been shaken by Alfredo's ardour, and her '*Ah, fors'è lui*' touchingly conveys her uncertainty over whether this is true love and whether true love is for her. But she rejects this dream and launches a *cabaletta*, '*Sempre libera*', which celebrates her returning belief in emotional freedom. Her resolution weakens when she is interrupted by Alfredo singing offstage, but with dazzling coloratura flourishes she reaffirms her intention to remain 'forever free'. Form and dramatic content are here perfectly matched, as indeed they are in a quite different way in the great centrepiece of the drama, the duet between Germont, Alfredo's father, and Violetta in Act II. Violetta is gradually persuaded to relinquish her lover for the sake of bourgeois propriety. As Violetta bows to the force of Germont's arguments, Germont is impressed by Violetta's renunciation and so moved by her plight that he takes no pleasure in his victory. This is one of those scenes where Verdi's music expresses both the dramatic truth of the stage situation and his own great humanity.

GRAND OPERAS AND CHANGING CONDITIONS

By 1853 Verdi's years in the galley were over, and the pace of his operatic output slackened. His fame was now considerable and *Traviata* in fact closed the mainly Italian period of his career. He increasingly turned to Paris, the Opéra, and the genre of French grand opera. The rewards and resources available there were one reason, the artistic challenge of Meyerbeerian form another. At least he could now take more time, and living in Paris with Giuseppina Strepponi, still not yet his wife, raised fewer eyebrows than in his home town of Busseto.

Les vêpres siciliennes (Paris, 1855) was Verdi's first original score for the Opéra. Like Rossini before him, his first work for Paris had been an adaptation of an earlier piece: as we have seen, *I lombardi* had in 1847 acquired a French text, some extra music, and a new title, *Jérusalem*. But in 1852 he contracted to write a completely new work for France, with a libretto by the poet of Meyerbeer's grand operas, Eugène Scribe. Verdi seems to have wanted to rival *Les Huguenots* and *Le prophète* in grandeur and spectacle, and wrote to the librettist requesting 'a subject that is grandiose, impassioned, and original; a *mise-en-scène* that is imposing and overwhelming'. What he received was hardly original: *Les vêpres siciliennes* drew upon *Le duc d'Albe*, a libretto for Donizetti which that composer had left incomplete in 1839, and which Scribe and his collaborator Charles Duveyrier transferred to Sicily and to 1281, the time of the rebellion known as the Sicilian Vespers in which the French rulers were overthrown. Against this background Scribe added the usual love story and the well-worn device of a son in conflict with his father. The latter, the French governor Guy de Montfort (baritone), is one of Verdi's lonely authority figures, a study for Simon Boccanegra and Philip II in *Don Carlos*, and in his Act III aria '*Au sein de la puissance*' he laments the solitariness of power. The mood is that of King Herod regretting the '*misère des rois*' in Berlioz's oratorio *L'Enfance du Christ*, which Verdi may well have known since it was first performed in Paris while he was there working on his opera in 1854 and the two composers were acquainted.

Les vêpres siciliennes was liked well enough for it to be performed sixty-two times in the ten years after its première, yet it then fell out of the repertory. Grand opera set stereotyped characters against a colourful historical backdrop, and Verdi's ambition was to enlarge it by replacing these with flesh-and-blood characters. Except perhaps for Guy de Montfort, he failed here, but the failure is undeniably a magnificent one. Berlioz wrote: '... in *Les vêpres* the penetrating intensity of melodic expression, the sumptuous variety, the judicious sobriety of the orchestration, the amplitude, the poetic sonority of his ensembles, the warm colours glowing everywhere and that sense of power, impassioned but slow to deploy itself, that is one of the characteristics of Verdi's genius, stamp the whole work with a grandeur, a sovereign majesty more marked than in the composer's previous creations.'

Simon Boccanegra (Venice, 1857; revised Milan, 1881) has a more secure hold on the repertory than its predecessor but is usually regarded as a work for the connoisseur rather than a popular favourite. For this there are at least two reasons; it has no famous aria, and the change in Verdi's style between the original and revised versions was so radical that the 1881 score, which is always the one performed, can give the listener a jolt when earlier and later passages are juxtaposed. But the importance of this occasional stylistic discrepancy has been exaggerated. Few spectators in the theatre notice anything amiss once they are caught up in this fascinating drama of the fourteenth-century corsair, Boccanegra himself, who becomes Doge of Genoa, recovers a long-lost daughter, is poisoned, but dies reconciled to his old enemy, Fiesco.

We have already noted the dark vocal colouring of this work, and the composer's concentration on the enmity between Boccanegra and Fiesco, a baritone and a bass respectively, gives the score an unusually austere *tinta.* Boccanegra had no solo in the 1857 version, and the preponderance of declamation and syllabic writing in the part led Verdi to warn the singer who was to create the role that 'If there are no *melismata* there's no need to tear your hair out and throw a mad fit.' In 1881 the omission of a solo for Boccanegra was magnificently made good; the Council Chamber scene and especially the Doge's great call for unity, *'Plebe! Patrizi! Popolo!'* are among Verdi's finest inspirations. Inspired too is the orchestral writing, not least the exquisite prelude to Act I evoking dawn over the sea, an impressionist seascape to put alongside such later examples as Ravel's *Daphnis et Chloé* or the Dawn Interlude in Britten's *Peter Grimes.* Yet it is the very opening of the work that remains most memorable of all. The prologue is introduced by twenty-two bars of a richly scored melody of haunting beauty, which develops through the opening scene and binds the singers' exchanges into a musical unit. There is no chorus or *cavatina* here, just two characters talking politics as at the start of a Shakespeare play such as *Cymbeline* or *The Winter's Tale.* The text is unchanged from the 1857 libretto, but the great melody was composed for the 1881 revision, and no Verdi opera, not even *La traviata*, opens more beautifully.

Perhaps the opera of this period which most closely involves us in its characters' fates is *Un ballo in maschera* (*A Masked Ball*, Rome, 1859). The sensitive subject of the opera, regicide, led to one of Verdi's epic battles wth the censors, which turned the King into a Count and shifted the location of the drama from Sweden to Boston. For Igor Stravinsky *Ballo* was a work which 'like my own [*The Rake's Progress*], I love to the point where criticism ceases to make any difference', an entirely appropriate reaction to the Verdi work that is most completely concerned with love. The central love duet between Riccardo and Amelia is Verdi's most passionate, and has even led to the work being dubbed 'Verdi's *Tristan*'. Verdi praised the text his librettist Antonio Somma had provided for this scene by saying it had the 'disorder' of passion, and he responded with some of his most ecstatic music. The conspirators, Samuel and Tom, are handled with deliberate comedy at times, and the soprano *travesti* role of Oscar the page provides a brilliant ironic counterpoint to what is essentially a dark drama. *Un ballo in maschera*, although a title forced on the creators because the censors objected to the original *Gustavus III*, is nonetheless one of Verdi's most appropriate. For this is not only a drama in which the characters twice put on masks, but is also about human beings forced to mask their true feelings. For Renato, betrayed both by his friend and his wife, *Ballo* is a tragedy of the impossibility of ever knowing another person. *Un ballo in maschera* has another, perhaps curious, claim to distinction in the Verdi canon. It is one of only three Verdi operas that are usually given uncut—the other two are *Aida* and *Falstaff*.

In contrast with the tight-knit drama of *Ballo*, *La forza del destino* (St Petersburg, 1862; revised Milan, 1869) is a sprawling epic set in Spain and Italy in the eighteenth century, in which the force of destiny pursues the main characters with a series of accidents and coincidences. It is the tenor hero Don Alvaro who sets all this in motion at the start, when he is prevented from eloping with his beloved Leonora by the intervention of her father, who regards the Peruvian Alvaro as unacceptable not least because of his skin colour. In the struggle Alvaro's pistol goes off accidentally and wounds Leonora's father, who dies cursing his daughter. Thereafter the plot is concerned largely with the vengeful pursuit of the lovers, who become separated, by Leonora's brother Don Carlo. There is a wealth of crowd scenes and skilfully drawn secondary characters, such as the pedlar Trabuco, the gypsy Preziosilla and the comical cleric, Fra Melitone. Despite the retirement of both Alvaro and Leonora separately and coincidentally to the *same* monastery, Carlo tracks them down and forces a *dénouement* in which all three characters die.

At least they did in St Petersburg in 1862. But there is usually no more a definitive text of a Verdi opera than there is of a Bruckner symphony, and of the works from *Rigoletto* onwards only *Un ballo in maschera* has no extra or alternative music. In the case of *La forza del destino* there are two substantially different versions, that of the original Russian production and that of the Milan revision. The latter brought many changes including a magnificent new overture which is perhaps the composer's finest, and an ending to the whole work which replaced Alvaro's demonic curse and suicide with him living on in Christian resignation. It is the later score which we usually hear today. In either version Alvaro is a fated character, actively seeking death as much as Wagner's Tristan is. (Alvaro's Act III '*Lasciatemi morire*' is quite as significant as Tristan's Act II '*Lass mich sterben*'.) Having failed to leave the world through death in combat, he leaves it by entering a monastery, so that his flight to God is a negative one as is shown by the struggle he has to remember his vows when challenged by Carlo. The original ending was much more consistent with this— Alvaro declared himelf an emissary from Hell, cursed all mankind, threw himself off a precipice, and the opera closed with a very exciting and almost Satanic piece of choral writing. It remains the appropriate conclusion to the composer's most nihilistic piece, a work which places haunted individuals at the centre of a society caught in a dance of death. Verdi is here revealed as a pessimistic artist, a man who once wrote in response to a complaint about the number of deaths in *Il trovatore*, 'But after all, death is all there is in life. What else is there?'

After Russia, Verdi's next work took him once more to France. In *Don Carlos* (Paris, 1867) the Opéra received one of Verdi's richest scores, but also one of his longest. Much material was cut even before the first night and not recovered until over a century later. Verdi made further cuts for the 1884 Milan production, reducing the five acts to four by dropping most of Act I. In 1886 another version appeared restoring the opening act, and in 1970 the material cut before the Parisian opening night was found in the library at the Opéra. The work has become known in either the 1884 or 1886 versions as *Don Carlo* in Italian translation. But recently claims have been made for the original French, which was the only text Verdi ever used even for later revisions, and *Don Carlos* has been recorded in the original language and with the missing 1867 material restored. It remains to be seen whether *Don Carlos* or *Don Carlo* now becomes the norm outside France and Italy.

Don Carlos, in any version, contains some of Verdi's greatest music, and some of his subtlest musical portraiture. Based on Schiller's play about Philip II of Spain and the affair between his wife Elisabeth and his son Don Carlos, its events are far removed from historical fact but provide the kind of scenes at which the composer excelled, with complex characters whose personal lives are caught up by forces larger than themselves. Philip himself is the profoundest of Verdi's authority figures, a man who can command everything except love, and his tremendous scene with the Grand Inquisitor (Act IV, Scene 1 of the five-act version) places the struggle between Church and State before us in a conflict of two powerful wills. Rodrigue, Marquis de Posa, is Carlos's friend and their Act II duet, '*Dieu, tu semas dans nos âmes*', is one of the score's plums, its melody so stirring that one forgives the uncharacteristically sentimental little phrase that leads to its reprise. The women, Elisabeth and the Princess Eboli, are nicely contrasted and each is allotted a supreme Verdi aria, respectively '*Toi qui sus le néant*' (Act V) and '*O don fatal*' (Act IV). Most original of all these portraits is that of Carlos himself, complicated and unbalanced, and cast in an heroic role which he is ill-equipped to perform. He has only one solo, and his character is explored mainly in duets, including three with Elisabeth. The second of these comes in Act II, when Elisabeth has married Philip and becomes Carlos's Queen and stepmother. She wounds Carlos simply by addressing him as '*mon fils*', and this attempt to establish the proper basis for their new relationship provokes Carlos's cry, '*Pitié! Le ciel avare ne m'a donné qu'un jour, et si vite il a fui!*' ('Have pity! Jealous Heaven gave me but one day, and how quickly it fled!'). This is set to one of Verdi's arching, aching phrases, as noble and despairing as Carlos himself is. In

Don Carlos Verdi ranks with Mozart and Wagner in depth and detail of musical characterisation.

In this respect *Aida* (Cairo, 1871), for all its splendour and deserved popularity, is a lesser achievement. It is, however, Verdi's most successful combination of the spectacular elements of grand opera and the lyrical warmth and personal drama of his earlier works. The triumph scene (Act II, Scene 2) is the best of its kind because of the quality of the invention, with its obstinately memorable trumpet tune and the fine ballet music, and also because it involves all the principals and carries the drama forward. Some of Verdi's most subtle orchestral writing is found in *Aida*. The opening of Act III, the Nile scene, is a wonderfully effective piece of orchestral evocation, with the flute's meandering against a background of shimmering strings perfectly evoking the iridescent Egyptian night. Of the many passages of essential Verdi in the vocal writing, the final duet '*O terra addio*', in which the entombed lovers say farewell to the earth in a long fade-out, is one of Verdi's most memorable endings. Perhaps few are moved by the fate of the rather stereotyped characters, but the work's popularity means that opera house managers are moved to produce *Aida* at fairly regular intervals and always will be.

After 1859, Verdi never again dealt with an impresario directly—a sure sign of change from the operatic world of the *primo ottocento*. For now the impresario was to be replaced by a new alliance of composer and publisher. More scores were published, and in the middle of the century an effective copyright law, which Verdi himself helped to draft, was established giving composers more status and money. The hire of orchestral scores became a lucrative activity, and it increased because repertory opera had come to take the place of the former need for new works to be commissioned. Verdi's *Alzira* had been commissioned by the San Carlo in Naples in 1845, at a time when that theatre was still mounting two or three new works a year—new, that is, to Naples. But in the 1830s the San Carlo had been presenting five works new to the city in each year, three of them written for the theatre. Of *Alzira* Verdi wrote—wrongly as it transpired, but his expression is significant—'It will remain in the repertory . . . and go the rounds along with its sister operas.' It is difficult not to feel that the development of repertory opera is in many ways regrettable, when we consider the rarity today of a première at a major opera house and the consequent relative unimportance of opera in contemporary music. The great 'new' event in an opera season is now more likely to be the production of a lesser-known Verdi opera like *Alzira*.

For Verdi, there were artistic compensations: as fewer works were demanded, there was more time to write them. The care he lavished on his later scores is perhaps also only partly an artistic development—he perhaps would not have produced an *Aida* when he was writing two operas a year. The importance of orchestral and choral writing had grown, and the increasing need for co-ordination of the complex works brought the opera conductor into prominence, largely thanks to Angelo Mariani (1822–73), the composer's friend and frequent interpreter. Verdi was the first to be able to demand that his music was performed as written, without the cuts and transpositions that Bellini and Donizetti had railed against but could not prevent. He was sometimes willing to make alterations, but only when he specified or executed them himself. The audience, too, was changing. The opera house ceased to be the social club of the upper class, and became the place of entertainment for a wider public. The operas they saw were presented in a way controlled by the composer and his publisher, often through production books specifying the set and costume designs, a method copied from Paris.

Verdi had long sought the kind of complete artistic control represented by these production books, and like Bellini before him, and Puccini after him, he could be a cruel taskmaster for his librettists. Francesco Maria Piave (1810–76), librettist of several Verdi works including *Macbeth*, *Rigoletto*, *La traviata*, the 1857 *Simon Boccanegra*, and *La forza del destino*, suffered more than most. Over the last of these operas Piave received the following Verdian harangue:

> Dear Piave,
> I have received your verses and, if I may say so, I don't like them. You talk to me about 100 syllables!! And it's obvious that 100 syllables aren't enough when you take 25 to say the sun is setting!!! ... you don't say the Lord's Prayer at a death bed. You will say I put it in my scenario, but you know that I only intend these scenarios as a guide to you ... Now then, can't you do better, retaining as far as possible the words I sent you, but turning them into better rhymes?

But Verdi respected the contribution of his collaborators, and in his work on the new copyright law tried to ensure that the librettists' rights were protected as well as those of the composer. Another crucial change in the period concerned stage direction; in Italy this was commonly undertaken by the librettist who, as we have seen, was usually attached to the commissioning theatre. But Verdi increasingly felt the need for a central, controlling figure to supervise all the details of a production, and since the professional producer did not enter the theatre until the twentieth century, he often performed this role himself.

Verdi knew his worth as an artist, and asked theatres and publishers for increasingly high rewards. For *Nabucco* in 1842 he received 4,000 lire; for *Macbeth* in 1847 Florence paid 18,000. Later he could almost name his price—his fee of 20,000 roubles for *La forza del destino* outraged some Russian composers, to whom a similar commission brought only 500 roubles. To help us place a value on the latter figure we have Verdi's authority that it would have bought one hundred bottles of fine wine—he wrote of his Russian trip, 'The railway carriages that took us from Dunaberg to Kovno were unheated, and even the wine—a good one at five roubles a bottle—turned to ice!' This composer who knew the value of money even kept a watchful eye on the accounting practices of his publisher Ricordi. His keen sense of their relative importance, and his feeling that this was not reflected in their respective gains, are shown in a very outspoken letter of 1855 to Tito Ricordi, the son of Giovanni Ricordi who since his father's death in 1853 had directed the firm:

> I shall explain: if the (French) translation of *Il trovatore* is so successful that it is also performed in the provinces, in twenty years it will make a profit of 25 to 30 thousand francs (I may have over-estimated this amount). In compensation for all my labour, loss of time and the expenses I have to incur here, I shall earn in ten years from eight to ten thousand francs. And you earn the same amount while you are strolling around Lake Como. . . . I hoped that you would not behave like this to me. Many a time I have done things for you that I was not obliged to. I, after all, am the main source of your colossal fortune. Don't deny it. Examine your books and observe the profits you have gained from my operas.

Verdi could none the less be generous to friends and colleagues. When his librettist Piave was paralysed by a stroke and unable to move or speak for the last eight years of his life, the composer gave substantial financial assistance to the wife and daughter of his old friend. And he called 'my last and best work' the Casa di Riposo, the rest home in Milan for elderly musicians which he built and in which he is buried.

SHAKESPEAREAN CLIMAX: *OTELLO* AND *FALSTAFF*

Having helped to bring about the reforms he desired in the operatic life of his country, Verdi withdrew from that life. After *Aida* he intended to compose no more operas, but he was lured back, not once but twice, by three men: his publisher Ricordi, who first raised the possibility and nursed it along, his librettist Arrigo Boito, who in these last operas gave him two of his best texts, and Shakespeare, whom he had loved all his life. *Macbeth* had always been one of the composer's own favourites among his works, and *King Lear* had been the chief among his many unrealised projects. With *Otello* (Milan, 1887) and *Falstaff* (Milan, 1893) Verdi did more than justice to Shakespeare and surpassed even the finest of his earlier operas. No artist ever came out of 'retirement' to greater purpose.

In Arrigo Boito (1842–1918) Verdi found the ideal collaborator for Shakespearean opera. Boito was a literary, cultured man and a successful critic, composer, and librettist. His opera on the Faust legend, *Mefistofele* (Milan, 1868), was a success when revised in 1875, and his libretti included *La Gioconda* for Ponchielli (*see* Chapter 12). As a leading figure among the Italian group calling for artistic reform, the *Scapigliati*,* his journalism had offended Verdi. But after Boito's work on the 1881 revision of *Simon Boccanegra* Verdi was won over. The libretto for *Otello* is masterly; where he cut the play, it adds pace and focus—as witness his excision of all of Shakespeare's Act I, allowing the entire action to take place in Cyprus. Where he adds, for example the '*credo*' in which Iago expounds his nihilist philosophy, it is to provide a musical and dramatic opportunity. Verdi once wrote of Shakespeare, whom he called 'Papa', 'It is quite possible that he, Papa, might have come across a Falstaff of some kind; but it's most unlikely that he ever met a villain as villainous as Iago or women as angelic as Cordelia, Imogen, Desdemona . . . and yet they are so true.' In the same letter he speaks of the need for the dramatist to 'invent truth'. In *Otello* Verdi and Boito have invented truth.

Arguably *Otello* offers a more satisfying dramatic experience than Shakespeare's play of evil and destructive jealousy. The notorious difficulty of Iago's motivation is less worrying in opera than in spoken drama, not least because in the play he offers many implausible reasons for his villainy whereas in the opera Boito has reduced them to a convincing Coleridgean 'motiveless malignity' in Iago's Act II *credo*. 'I am evil because I am a man, I feel the primeval slime within me,' Iago tells us: it explains little, but explanation is for the rational man who could never understand Iago. The truth is provided by Verdi's setting of the *credo*, in particular by the orchestra which introduces it with an awesome figure on the whole orchestra, *ff tutta forza*, hurled down through five octaves like a descent into the abyss. Iago's creed is much like that of Wagner's Hagen and Britten's Claggart in *Billy Budd*, the only other operatic characters whose evil, like Iago's, is innate, essentially unmotivated.

The dramatic problem of Othello's credulity is similarly avoided in the

*Literally, 'dishevelled, disorderly ones'.

opera. It was Verdi himself who had the idea of establishing Otello's heroic stature with his entrance, the notoriously taxing '*Esultate*', and it was also the composer who suggested a love duet to end the first act, so that the beauty of Otello's relationship with his wife is established before it is destroyed by his jealous rage. But this love duet between Otello and Desdemona does more than this, for we are here shown the dangerous flaws in the great general's character. In its central section Otello describes how she was wooed and won by his tales of his military exploits. As he recalls their courtship ('*Pingea dell'armi fremito*'), the orchestra depicts the bold sorties and whistling arrows with frenetic flourishes of high woodwind, cornets and trumpets, while his own vocal line rears up and suddenly breaks off. When we consider that this is a man recalling his courtship of his wife in a tender moment with her, his sudden ferocity is significant. Thus arguably Verdi and Boito, even more than Shakespeare, give us an Othello whose later collapse is all too believable.

If *Otello* is Verdi's finest tragedy, *Falstaff* is perhaps his greatest opera of all. The subject had been the basis of several previous operas, not least *Die lustigen Weiber von Windsor* (Berlin, 1849) by the German Nicolai. But Boito's work draws not only on Shakespeare's *Merry Wives* but also on *Henry IV, Part I* which contains the essential Falstaff. Verdi's ability to set comedy had sometimes been doubted, and as we have seen, his *Un giorno di regno* (Milan, 1840) had been a failure, (though it was later successfully revived as *Il finto Stanislao* in Venice and Naples). But there had been no comic opera since then and, as Boito suggested, if there was a better way to end a career than with *Otello*, it was with *Falstaff*.

'You that are old consider not the capacities of us that are young,' says Shakespeare's Falstaff* and Verdi might well have echoed his ironic sentiment, for only so experienced a composer could have given us such an eternally youthful work as *Falstaff*. It has not always been popular, for it can seem to lack melody. But close acquaintance shows that there are a large number of melodies, motives, and lyrical phrases, though they succeed each other so rapidly at times that the ear has barely had a chance to grasp one attractive idea before another takes its place. Also the formal organisation of the score does not present these materials in a familiar pattern of arias and ensembles. There is hardly a closed form in the opera, and when there is, such as in Falstaff's description of himself as a slender young man '*Quand'ero paggio*' it is so fleeting that the flow of Verdi's quicksilver score is hardly interrupted. Indeed, formally *Falstaff* marks a considerable advance even on *Otello*, where in such places as the big

*Henry IV, Part 2; Act I, Sc. 2

concertato finale to Act III and elsewhere, the structures of middle-period Verdi are certainly not disowned. The fact that *Otello* and *Falstaff* were both written after Verdi's retirement from operatic composition following *Aida* has led to them being paired as 'late Verdi'. But stylistically the real leap is not between *Aida* and *Otello*, but between *Otello* and *Falstaff*, which is his most revolutionary score since *Rigoletto*. The Shakespearean credentials of this miraculous score are attested to in rather a striking way by the story of W. H. Auden's New York lecture on Shakespeare's *The Merry Wives of Windsor*, when the poet arrived armed only with a recording of Verdi's *Falstaff* which he proceeded to play in its entirety. The opera has also earned the admiration of many composers, including the young Richard Strauss who, having heard it in Berlin, sent Verdi the score of his own first opera *Guntram* and wrote that he was '. . . unable to find words to describe the extraordinary beauty of *Falstaff* or to express my gratitude for this rebirth of the intellect . . .' Strauss had no love of Italian opera, but all his life he made an exception for *Falstaff*.

12

VERISMO

Verdi's contemporaries. Mascagni and the birth of verismo, *Leoncavallo and other* veristi. *Puccini.*

VERDI'S CONTEMPORARIES

Composers liberated alike from the . . . censorship [and] the strait-jacket of the *primo ottocento* convention were at a loss as to what to do with their new freedom. Like prisoners released after a long confine-ment, they seemed to yearn for the safety of the cells they had left. Hence their readiness to lapse into the commonplaces of thirty years before. (Julian Budden: *The Operas of Verdi*)

After about 1850, the accepted Rossinian forms seemed increasingly irrelevant. Verdi himself, having shown in *Rigoletto* how the tradition might be renewed with formal innovations, partly reverted to his earlier style and partly looked to French grand opera for a new challenge. As for his contemporaries, his domination of Italian opera was such that they are now largely forgotten. But that cannot be ascribed merely to his genius, or their mediocrity. Italian opera was losing its way.

Nevertheless some useful work was done. Since Verdi had left comedy severely alone since the failure of *Il giorno di regno*, it was here that others were best able to succeed. The Neapolitan brothers Ricci—Federico (1804–77) and Luigi (1805–59)—wrote operas both singly and together, and of their joint compositions the most celebrated was a '*melodramma fantastico-giocoso*' called *Crispino e la comare* (Venice, 1850). But Federico Ricci went soon after this to work in St Petersburg and wrote no opera at all for sixteen years; he then spent the last years of his life in Paris and wrote successful French comic opera. Similarly, Lauro Rossi (1812–85), Enrico Petrella (1813–77), Carlo Pedrotti (1817–93) and Antonio Cagnoni (1828–96) all trod the well-worn path of *opera buffa* with more success than they had in serious subjects.

The situation seemed still worse during the period after *Aida* in 1871 when no new Verdi work appeared for some years. During that time only two new Italian operas were heard abroad, Ponchielli's *La Gioconda* (Milan, 1876), with a libretto by Arrigo Boito (1842–1918), and Boito's own *Mefistofele* in its second version (Bologna, 1875). The latter is a Faust opera, but unlike Gounod's version it incorporates both parts of Goethe's play. Its first production had failed crushingly in 1868 partly because of its great length: cast in a prologue and five acts, it lasted until well after midnight. The revised version has four acts. Although *Mefistofele* has many striking passages, they do not coalesce into a compelling drama: it seems certain that the subject and text—the libretto was Boito's own— were alike much too ambitious for a first opera. He made some further revisions, and then worked for nearly thirty years on a second opera, *Nerone*. This account of the notorious Roman emperor has a libretto of real distinction, which Verdi admired, and has been called 'a work of extraordinary originality, even perversity ... a unique and awesome monument to the spirit of decadence in art'. But it was left unfinished at his death and was completed by Vincenzo Tommasini and Arturo Toscanini (Milan, 1924).

Arguably, Boito's skill lay more in writing than in music. He wrote sharp critical articles in his youth and was associated with the *Scapigliatura* artistic movement that aimed at reform. In one poem he declared that the altars of Italian music were 'befouled like the walls of a brothel', and gave much offence to many—including Verdi, who thought these comments were directed at him. Later, as we know, they became close friends. In fact Boito's main contribution to opera was as a librettist, not only of *Otello* and *Falstaff* but also of another Shakespearean opera, the 'lyric tragedy' *Amleto* (Genoa, 1865) of his friend Franco Faccio (1840–91). The interest of this work lies not so much in the music, which has been summed up as 'what is good ... isn't new and what is new is a little boring', but rather in the text. Boito recognised that the metrical schemes underlying all Italian opera were too rigid, and here he used a great variety of verse forms, matching each to the dramatic needs of the moment. It was Faccio whom the young Boito saw as the artist born to reform Italian opera: but he was wrong, for after *Amleto* the composer decided that writing opera was not his destiny and he concentrated on a conducting career, giving several Verdi premières including that of *Otello*.

As we have seen, Boito also provided the libretto of Ponchielli's *La Gioconda*. Amilcare Ponchielli (1834–86) had had earlier success in Milan with an 1872 revision of his first opera, *I promessi sposi*, and again two years later with *I lituani*. *La Gioconda* was a popular and critical success, and has never fallen into the obscurity of most Italian operas of the time. The plot is supposed to be drawn from Hugo's play *Angelo* (1835), but a comparison of the two plots makes this almost incredible. Boito's concerns a street singer, La Gioconda, who loves Enzo Grimaldo: he does not return her love because of his attachment to Laura, and finally La Gioconda sacrifices herself to allow their escape from the vengeance of Laura's husband Alvise. In some ways this plot is conventional, but Boito has less conventionally kept four main characters at the centre of the drama rather than concentrating on just the tenor-soprano pair—Laura is a mezzo and the state spy, Barnaba, a baritone. The plot is driven along by Barnaba who desires La Gioconda (literally, 'the joyful girl'). It is by promising herself to him that she secures the lovers' escape, but when he comes to claim her she kills herself—'You desired my body, accursed demon? I give it to you!' Not since *Il trovatore*, perhaps, had four principals been swept along with such passion, and if Ponchielli's music is not on Verdi's level, its melodiousness is hard to resist. Enzo's '*Cielo e mar*' is only the best known of several plums in this rich score. The suicide scene is impressive too, and seems to have influenced Puccini in the '*Si, pazzo son*' in Act III of *Manon Lescaut*, while Barnaba provides something of a model for Iago in *Otello*. But its success was not matched by Ponchielli's two later works for La Scala. The singer Teresa Stolz remarked that *Il figliuol prodigo* (1880) was not very prodigal towards the theatre's coffers, though there is an impressive orchestral intermezzo preceding Act IV in this middle-oriental piece, and Ponchielli's last opera, *Marion Delorme* (1885), also failed.

Ponchielli worked mainly within the grand opera conventions of his day. So did Antonio Carlos Gomes (1836–96), a Brazilian who became acquainted as a young man with the music of the great Italians from Rossini to Verdi and came to Italy after winning a government grant with his opera *Joana de Flandres* (Rio de Janeiro, 1863)—the first opera from the 'New World' to be mentioned in this book, incidentally. After the success of *Il Guarany* (Milan, 1870)—which Verdi called the work of a 'truly musical genius'—came *Fosca* (Milan, 1873), which failed, and *Salvator Rosa* (Genoa, 1874), which triumphed and was seen in six major theatres. Gomes' music is bold, theatrical and strongly coloured. In this respect it contrasts with that of Alfredo Catalani (1854–93), whose typical mood is one of elegiac lyricism. This is heard at its most affecting in his last opera, *La Wally* (Milan, 1892), a work in which La Wally and her lover Hagenbach finally perish in an avalanche. Catalani's earlier operas *Elda* (Turin, 1880) and *Dejanice* (Milan, 1883) still depend on the grand opera style which was more than ever becoming stale. Of all the works in this particular genre dating from this period of 1870–85, only *Aida* and *La Gioconda* are still staged today. Of the rest, one Italian critic wrote, 'They drive out of the theatre in the second act all those who have not fallen comfortably asleep in the first.' It was time for something new.

Verismo, meaning 'realism', is a term applied to a type of opera which emerged in Italy in the 1890s and which is defined by its subject, literary style and music. The stories are personal ones with little of the political and historical element found in grand opera. High-born men and women caught between love and duty are here replaced by humble characters strong in passion and swift to vengeance. The plot usually culminates in a murder and/or suicide, often on stage, and a new realism means that no one sings after being stabbed, like Gilda in *Rigoletto*, or suffocated, like Desdemona in *Otello*. Musically there is a great directness, with often powerfully dissonant harmony, fervent and even lachrymose melody, and orchestration and vocal writing which combine to deliver an emotional body blow. This last element is especially potent in the self-pitying tenor aria in which a hero may vent his grief before the *dénouement* which often brings his death. The total effect of *verismo* style may be vulgar, but for most opera-lovers it is irresistibly cathartic.

The origins of *verismo* are literary, beginning with the French *naturaliste* writers led by Émile Zola in his twenty Rougon-Macquart novels (1871–93), exemplifying a theory derived from Taine's philosophy that human behaviour is determined by heredity and circumstances and thus often brutal. In Italy Giovanni Verga (1840–1922) wrote stories of the struggle for existence of the peasants of his native Sicily: his *Vita dei campi* (1880) contains one called *Cavalleria rusticana* that he dramatised three years later. It was to Verga above all that contemporaries applied the word *verismo*, possibly with an element of punning on his name, and it was transferred to opera when Mascagni's work with this title became famous. Of course there had already been some anticipation of the style: for example we find the *squarcio de vita* or 'slice of life' mentioned in *Pagliacci* in such a work as Verdi's *Rigoletto* with its display of strong passions, and even *La traviata* is a topical domestic tragedy. Among other influences on the developing *verismo* style were French operas, those of Massenet and—above all—Bizet's *Carmen* with its low-life *dramatis personae* and onstage murder.

Cavalleria rusticana (*Rustic Chivalry*, Rome, 1890), has one of the least likely success stories in operatic history. Its composer, Pietro Mascagni (1863–1945), was a provincial music teacher who submitted it in a competition for one-act operas and was one of three winners—in fact, according to his recollection long afterwards, it was his wife who sent in the score without his knowledge. It soon gained a place in the international repertory and spawned many imitations. Part of its success was due to the fresh straightforwardness of plot, character and motivation taken over from Verga's original. The action takes place in a Sicilian village on Easter Day and is firmly set in the late nineteenth century, although one feels that these people's lives have not really changed for generations. The young soldier Turiddu has seduced Santuzza, but still loves his former girlfriend Lola, the wife of the village drover Alfio. In her jealousy the pregnant Santuzza tells Alfio that he is being cuckolded. The peasant code of 'rustic chivalry' to which the title refers demands that the two men fight a duel, and Turiddu is killed.

The *Cavalleria* score sets this personal drama firmly in a social context. We hear the villagers singing as they gather for Mass at the start, and later when groups inside and outside the church combine for the 'Easter hymn'. Against this a series of numbers describe a steeply rising curve of excitement. In Santuzza's '*Voi lo sapete, o Mamma*' she confesses her betrayal with anguish, and the forceful descending string phrase which punctuates the aria is a characteristic *verismo* gesture. The harrowing scene between Santuzza and Turiddu depicts a degree of passion that threatens to burst across the footlights into the audience. The intensity is maintained through the famous orchestral intermezzo that divides the two scenes, with its relentlessly protesting repeated notes at the climax, and on to Turiddu's fatalistic farewell to his mother. The entire operatic 'brew' is as intoxicating as the *vino spumeggiante* of Turiddu's drinking song.

Mascagni wrote several more operas after *Cavalleria rusticana*, but none achieved the same fame, perhaps because he moved away from *verismo*, save in the unsuccessful *Silvano* (Milan, 1895). His comedy *L'amico Fritz* (Rome, 1891) is a story of a confirmed bachelor landowner (Fritz), a matchmaker and the tenant's daughter Suzel with whom he falls in love: with its attractive 'Cherry Duet', it is sometimes revived. *Guglielmo Ratcliff* (Milan, 1895) and *Parisina* (Milan, 1913) are romantic tragedies after Heine and Byron respectively. *Le maschere* (which had simultaneous premières in six Italian cities, 1901) is a *commedia dell'arte* work which failed except in Rome, where the composer conducted. *Iris* (Rome, 1898) anticipates Puccini's *Madama Butterfly* in its nineteenth-century Japanese setting, and has a librettist who later wrote for Puccini, Luigi Illica: its pure heroine is abducted by a brothel-keeper and when her father curses her, believing she went voluntarily, she drowns herself. Illica also provided the libretto for *Isabeau* (Buenos Aires, 1911), based on the legend of the eleventh-century Lady Godiva who rode naked through Coventry in Britain so that her husband the Earl of Mercia would remit an unjust tax. Mascagni's long life, like that of his German contemporary Richard Strauss, carried him through into the Fascist era, when he became perhaps willy-nilly a virtual court composer to the dictator Mussolini, a role for which he was disgraced on the Duce's fall, dying four months later. It was a sad end to a career which had begun so brilliantly long before. He once remarked: 'It was a pity I wrote *Cavalleria* first—I was crowned before I was king.'

LEONCAVALLO AND OTHER *VERISTI*

Ruggero Leoncavallo (1857–1919) was writing an Italian Renaissance trilogy called *Crepusculum* when *Cavalleria rusticana* had its première. The sudden success of a composer six years younger than himself made him interrupt these rather Wagnerian labours—he finished only *I Medici* (Milan, 1893)—and join the *veristi*. He wrote: '. . . after the success of Mascagni's *Cavalleria rusticana* I lost patience . . . and shut myself up in my house, desperate but determined to attempt a last battle, and in five months I wrote the libretto and music of that *Pagliacci* which was bought by the publisher Sonzogno on reading the libretto alone.'

The première of *Pagliacci* (Milan, 1892) was conducted by Toscanini and established it at once. The story is of a troupe of strolling players, the 'clowns' of the title, whose leader Canio discovers that his wife Nedda plans to run away with a lover. In the play now staged, he plays Pagliaccio and Nedda Columbine, who is supposed to be deceiving him with Arlecchino. This is too close to reality for Canio, who abandons his role and stabs first Nedda and then—as her lover Silvio rushes forward—him too. 'The play is over,' he tells the audience. Although in two acts, *Pagliacci* is of the same length as *Cavalleria*, about seventy minutes, and of course is also a tale of jealousy set among the ordinary people of the Italian south. Perhaps it was inevitable that 'Cav and Pag' would go around the world's opera houses in a double bill.

The character of the hunchback Tonio, who when repulsed by Nedda betrays her to Canio, was first sung by the composer's friend Victor Maurel. He was a baritone who had created Verdi's Iago in *Otello*, and suggested that he should have an aria to match those given to the tenor and soprano Canio and Nedda. Leoncavallo agreed and provided the striking prologue in which Tonio, reversing the usual *commedia* announcement to the audience, tells them that we are to see a real story about real people, a 'slice of life'. This anticipates Canio's '*Vesti la giubba*', in which the unhappy man grieves that he must go on stage to play Pagliaccio although racked by jealousy. At the climax of this aria, he cries '*Ridi, Pagliaccio, sul tuo amore infranto*'—'Laugh, Pagliaccio, though your love lies broken'—and tenors invariably add copious sobs. The idea of a play within a play in which reality and play-acting become mingled is taken further by the prologue, which almost suggests that the action is real. In this way *verismo* comes closer to ancient Greek theatre than anything from the seventeenth or eighteenth centuries. A great performance of *Pagliacci* should come beyond the proscenium arch so that we who sit in La Scala, the Met. or Covent Garden become the *pagliacci*, the clowns who must smile through heartbreak.

Pagliacci is the perfect *verismo* subject, and this work defined the genre even more than *Cavalleria rusticana*. There we find more theatrical decorum, for Turiddu is killed offstage. Here Canio slays Nedda and Silvio before our eyes and then turns to the crowd—to *us* – to announce that '*la commedia è finita*'. But these words, like the final words of *Cavalleria*, are spoken and not sung. There, doubtless, lies one reason why *verismo* was short-lived. A striving for realism can only culminate in an attempt to deny the essential nature of opera—an art form in which people sing, not speak.

Like Puccini, Leoncavallo wrote a *La bohème* (Venice, 1897). The public prefers Puccini's work, produced a year earlier, but of these two treatments of Henri Murger's novel and play *Scènes de la vie de Bohème* (1849) Leoncavallo's own libretto follows the original story more closely in his four acts. However, this results in a curious structure. The central characters are Marcello and Musetta, tenor and mezzo, while Rodolfo and Mimi (Puccini's leads) are secondary. But when the former couple separate at the end of Act III, Rodolfo and Mimi are suddenly thrust into prominence and the work closes, like Puccini's opera, with Mimi's death scene. Furthermore, where Puccini mixes the serious and the comic throughout, though with a gradually deepening pathos, Leoncavallo makes a sharp break: all the fun and charm are in Acts I and II, and then there is a switch to even darker emotions than in Puccini in the second half. However, this unusual shape seems to work in performance. The score has many felicities, and the role of Schaunard the musician provides much onstage music and pastiches including a delightfully Rossinian 'cantata', while the scene in which Marcello and Musetta meet has a waltz theme that Puccini might have envied. In recent times, this 'other' *Bohème* has been revived and recorded. Another Parisian subject provided the libretto for *Zazà* (Milan, 1900), a 'lyric comedy' about a music-hall singer loved by two men which is still perhaps Leoncavallo's best known opera after *Pagliacci*.

Other *verismo* operas have a more tenuous hold in the repertory. Francesco Cilea (1866–1950) gave Caruso early success in the self-pitying tenor aria for Federico in *L'Arlesiana* (Milan, 1897). *Adriana*

Lecouvreur (Milan, 1902), set in the early eighteenth century, is his most celebrated opera, based loosely on the life of the Comédie-Française actress of that name who dies—in the opera, at least—through inhaling the scent of poisoned violets sent by a rival in love. Cilea is more lyrical and less vigorous than Mascagni and Leoncavallo, and this score is suffused with the poignancy of Adriana's music.

Umberto Giordano (1867–1948) wrote ten operas, mostly in *verismo* style. *Fedora* (Milan, 1898) tells of the tragic love between a Russian nihilist, Count Ipanov, and the Romanov Princess Fedora. *Andrea Chénier* (Milan, 1896) is his one work still frequently performed. Luigi Illica provided the excellent libretto for this tale of a poet who is first an advocate and then a victim of the French Revolution, going to the guillotine with his lover Madeleine. This text is set with broad brush-strokes; but the lyricism does not wholly flower in Chénier's quasi-declamatory tenor solos. The story has parallels with *Tosca*, but Giordano cannot stand comparison with Puccini in melodic and instrumental invention.

Ermanno Wolf-Ferrari (1876–1948) was mainly a composer of comic opera. His one-act *Il segreto di Susanna* (Munich, 1909)—which was not that she had a lover, as her husband thinks on smelling tobacco in the house, but that she smoked—remains popular. Rather less well known is the composer's one *verismo* piece, *I gioielli della Madonna* (Berlin, 1911). To prove his love for Maliella, Raffaele (baritone) wants to steal the jewels from a statue of the Virgin, but his rival Gennaro steals the jewels and takes the girl also. Maliella confesses her sin to Raffaele and drowns herself, while Gennaro in remorse returns the jewels to the statue and stabs himself. Wolf-Ferrari was Venetian-born but half German, and studied in Munich: his melodic vein is strong, somewhere between Mahler and Puccini.

As we have seen, the output of all these composers cannot simply be subsumed under the label of *verismo*: even Mascagni, who began the fashion, moved away from it. His pupil Riccardo Zandonai (1883–1944) was taken up by the publisher Ricordi as a possible Puccini successor, but his best known opera, *Francesca da Rimini* (Turin, 1914), is based on the entirely 'unveristic' source of Dante's *Inferno*. It is possible to redefine *verismo* to some extent at this point: perhaps we may say that in essence it deals less with 'low-life' characters than with artists. The *pagliacci* are strolling players, Chénier a poet and Lecouvreur an actress, Tosca and Zazà are singers and Cavaradossi a painter. Puccini's and Leoncavallo's Bohemians are artists. This does not detract from the realism expected. Though the life of a *diva*, actor or poet is as unfamiliar to most people as that of a ruler or noble, we can respond to the presentation of the artist as someone like ourselves but with one skin less, who feels more deeply and perhaps acts more violently than the rest of us.

If Rossini marks the classical phase in nineteenth-century Italian opera and Verdi its romantic and nationalist climax, then *verismo* represents the decadence of a great tradition. Unlike those of their predecessors, the musical gestures of the *veristi* were incapable of development and could only be repeated. Canio's 'On with the motley', with its minor harmonies, wide melodic intervals, orchestral doubling of the vocal line and slow pace was a much imitated archetype. Even Puccini with Cavaradossi's '*E lucevan le stelle*' in *Tosca* could do nothing with it beyond providing a superior example. For Verdi, the term *verismo* was one of abuse, since he was a musical patriot who deplored what he saw as foreign influences in the style. When Massenet's *Le roi de Lahore* (Paris, 1877) reached Milan two years later, he called it '*verismo* opera without a shade of verity', a false realism.

Yet *verismo* made Italian opera flourish again internationally after a period when only Verdi had shone. Despite its artistic limitations, it influenced composers outside Italy who saw and appreciated the power of Mascagni, Leoncavallo and Puccini. Janáček's admiration for *verismo* is reflected in his operas, while Berg's *Wozzeck* and *Lulu* as well as Shostakovich's *Lady Macbeth of the Mtsensk District* and Britten's *Peter Grimes* all owe something to it. But among Italian composers only one could deploy the style in a wider and richer way than Mascagni and Leoncavallo, who were indeed virtually 'one-opera composers'. This was, of course, Puccini, whose work gave Italian opera its Indian summer.

PUCCINI

Giacomo Puccini (1858–1924) came from a line of musicians centred on his birthplace, Lucca in Tuscany. He studied with Ponchielli, had a success with his first opera, *Le villi* (Milan, 1894), and was then taken up by the publisher Giulio Ricordi, who became a friend and father-figure. His second opera, *Edgar* (Milan, 1889), took four years to compose and failed. Years later he sent a friend a copy of the score with adverse marginal comments—writing alongside the closing choral shouts of '*Orror*', 'How right they are!' but noting 'This is good' against Fidelia's '*Addio mio dolce amor!*' and '*Nel villaggio d'Edgar*'. Although he made revisions and cuts, *Edgar* remained what he called *una cantonata*, a blunder. The subject, resembling that of *Carmen*, had been imposed on him and did not suit him. After this he spent more time seeking good subjects for opera—and harassing librettists to put them into words—than writing music, which is why in a career of forty years he wrote just twelve operas, three of them one-acters.

Manon Lescaut (Turin, 1893) established Puccini, and when it reached London in 1894 George Bernard Shaw wrote that its composer seemed 'more like the heir of Verdi than any of his rivals'. This time Puccini rejected the efforts of three different writers before enlisting his publisher Ricordi's literary aid and—above all—engaging Giuseppe Giacosa and Luigi Illica. These two men were variously gifted. Illica provided dramatic shapes and Giacosa versification, the former using 'lots of imagination', as the composer put it, and the latter a special sensitivity to words. They were also to write the texts of Puccini's next three operas, *La bohème* (Turin, 1896), *Tosca* (Rome, 1900) and *Madama Butterfly* (Milan, 1904). But they always worked in active collaboration with the composer himself—Ricordi called them 'the Holy Trinity'—who had strong views about what suited him. He declared that 'the basis of an opera is its subject and its dramatic treatment', and like Wagner he thought in terms of a whole, taking an active interest not only in his music and the text but also staging, costumes, and even lighting—which he said should be organised 'with an attentive ear'. His stage directions are far more elaborate than Verdi's.

La bohème (*The Bohemians*, Turin, 1896) is one of the most often performed of all operas. Its scenes of youthful high spirits are brought off with considerable flair, each member of the quartet of friends—Rodolfo the poet, Marcello the painter, Schaunard the musician and Colline the philosopher—being drawn with deft strokes. Debussy wrote of this opera: 'If one didn't keep a grip on oneself one would be swept away by the sheer verve of the music. I know of no one who described the Paris of that time as well.' The love music has the special glow of young love itself, and countless music lovers have warmed to its tender eroticism. There is craft as well as inspiration, notably in the symphonic shape overall, with four acts falling into a sequence of allegro first movement, scherzo, slow movement and finale with much musical reminiscence. The first performance, under Toscanini, was not wholly successful, but today some consider the opera to be the composer's masterpiece. Certainly no anthology of tenor arias would be complete without Rodolfo's '*Che gelida manina*' to Mimi at their first meeting in Act I, to which she replies with the almost equally famous '*Mi chiamano Mimi*'. It should perhaps be added, though, that some musicians have disliked *Bohème*: thus Britten was to find 'cheapness and emptiness', but at times reveals his debt to the Italian master, while Shostakovich, interestingly, had reservations about Puccini's music but still saluted these works as 'great operas'.

Puccini's Manon and Mimi are the first in a series of doomed heroines, and Butterfly followed them. Tosca also dies, but in a magnificent and defiant gesture. This opera has been a target of anti-Puccini critics: disturbed perhaps by its heady mixture of the political, the erotic and the sadistic in a story in which the three principals all die, they seek to find fault with the score. One passage that has been criticised is the end of the work. Tosca has just seen her lover Cavaradossi shot by a firing squad. The execution was to have been a mock one, in return for her giving herself to Scarpia, the police chief. But both have cheated on the bargain: Tosca has stabbed Scarpia as he claims her, and he has arranged a genuine execution. As Tosca resorts to a suicidal leap from the castle battlements, the orchestra (sneers the musicologist Joseph Kerman) 'screams the first thing that comes into its head', the melody of Cavaradossi's '*E lucevan le stelle*'. This is, we must know, irredeemably un-Wagnerian: the Scarpia motif of three accented chords should instead have closed the opera. But the emotional effect is what Puccini valued. We may ask what is wrong, in opera, with doing the instinctive 'first thing' that comes to the artist's head, and above all his heart? This melody, which brings down the curtain, is superbly effective as theatre. May common sense spare us from critics' jargon about 'motivic integrity', for musicians and audiences sometimes know better about music.

Tosca's impact also derives from its dramatic shape. The middle act focuses on the confrontation between Scarpia and Tosca and contains some of Puccini's most impressive manipulation of rising tension as Scarpia's lust for her becomes more urgent, the screams of her lover under torture become more audible and her own situation more hopeless. After she kills Scarpia Puccini finds room for dramatic details such as Tosca's ritual with the candlesticks, cross and corpse as the act closes with a long stretch of quiet music that maintains the tension right up to the curtain. Acts I and III have a tenor aria near the start and a love duet in the middle, while ending with a *coup de théâtre*: in Act I the spectacular *Te Deum* with cannons, bells and Scarpia's blasphemous interjections, in Act III the melodramatic climax of Cavaradossi's execution and Tosca's congratulations on his 'performance', followed by her realisation of the truth and her suicide. Act I is the longest, alternating passages of action with more static and lyrical moments, and Act III the shortest, as Puccini skilfully tautens the drama as the climax is approached—literally the catastrophe of Greek drama. The author of the original Tosca story, Victorien Sardou, actually thought this opera more dramatic than his own play.

Madama Butterfly is the quintessential Puccini opera in that it again depicts the destruction of an innocent woman. Cio-Cio San, who marries an American naval officer and bears his child but is then abandoned by him. Set in Nagasaki, its exotic flavour is enhanced by the use of some authentic Japanese melodies and the fact that his own tunes tend to use the same five-note (pentatonic) scale as much oriental music: the score sounds both oriental and Puccinian in consequence. There is all the major-mode lyricism one expects—of all the set-pieces, only Butterfly's '*Tu? Tu? Piccolo Iddio*' is not in the major—and much atmosphere too. The love music in Act I is lingering yet rapturous, while Butterfly's '*Un bel dì*' in Act II is a magnificent though all too short soprano aria and the offstage 'humming chorus' later in that act is especially haunting, somehow as unreal as her dream of Pinkerton's return and the renewal of their old happiness. It was this scene that so moved Puccini when he saw David Belasco's play, based on a real incident, and convinced him it would make an opera. It has the directness that the composer called for when he demanded that opera should convey 'the evidence of a situation' musically and visually even where actual words were not understood.

After *Butterfly*, Puccini wrote no opera for six years, partly because of marital troubles and partly because he was seeking for a new kind of subject, harder and more virile. It was another Belasco play, *The Girl of the Golden West*, that provided him with the plot of *La fanciulla del West* (New York, 1910). This opera set in California at the time of the gold rush tells of the love of Minnie, a saloon owner, for Dick Johnson, an outlaw called Ramerrez. The sheriff Jack Rance, who also loves her, tells her who Dick is and she then rejects the bandit, only to pity him later: in the end Minnie and Dick ride off together to a new life. *Fanciulla* is a powerful work, but it has never achieved the success of the earlier operas. Its happy ending, the unusual Wild West setting with homesick goldminers weeping for their mothers, and the musical continuity which denied the audience the usual big lyrical set pieces were all in some respects advances, but they also militated against Minnie being as popular as his earlier heroines.

At present Magda, the 'swallow' of the title of *La rondine* (Monte Carlo, 1917), is heard still less often than Minnie. This opera began as a musical comedy for Vienna for which Puccini was to compose only some eight to ten numbers, the rest being spoken dialogue. But he found the commission difficult, and for the same generous terms he provided them with a whole opera. However, a resemblance to the plot of *Traviata* has done *La rondine* harm: here a Parisian courtesan called Magda renounces Ruggero in a final scene that is nearer tragedy than operetta. Yet there is much to praise in this relatively little-known Puccini opera. The vigorous syncopated opening tells us that we are in the city of *La bohème*, which is also recalled in the brilliant conversational flow of some scenes. Doubt-less the 'separate number' original form survives in that the opera has more set pieces than *Fanciulla*, and some of these are atmospheric and charming, such as the waltzes and the first aria, Prunier's '*Che il bel sogno*'. Though there are more *longueurs* than usual for Puccini, it is more the libretto that disappoints: the tenor lead Ruggero hardly appears until Act II, and the piece hovers awkwardly between comedy and sentimental pathos.

Puccini never wrote a full-scale comic opera. But his one excursion into comedy, *Gianni Schicchi*, comes as an effective third in his trilogy of one-act operas called *Il trittico* (New York, 1918). The sequence is that of Parisian Grand Guignol: a grim horror story, a tragic episode and a comedy. The first is *Il tabarro* (*The Cloak*), a *verismo* tale of adultery and murder among Seine bargees, its atmosphere evoked by the orchestra from the start. *Suor Angelica* tells of a young nun who has taken the veil to expiate her sin in having a love affair and a child; on learning that the child has died, she herself commits suicide but is forgiven by the Virgin in a vision. *Gianni Schicchi* is a Falstaffian work of comic vigour in which Schicchi impersonates a dead man at the request of the relatives to dictate a false new will in their favour, but outwits them by leaving property to himself. This comedy was at first more successful than the other parts of the *trittico* and has often been given without them, though the composer disapproved of this. However, the three one-acters do appear to best advantage when they are seen together as he intended.

For his next opera, which was to be his last, Puccini continued his search for a different kind of subject, aiming as he said to '*tentar vie non battute*', try new paths. He chose Carlo Gozzi's play *Turandotte*. Its story, set in China in legendary times, is of the cruel Princess Turandot who sets three riddles for any suitor: correct answers will win her hand but failure means death. Prince Calaf solves the riddles and then offers his life if she can discover his name by the next morning. She tortures the slave-girl Liù, who loves him, to know it, but fails as Liù dies silent. Now Turandot realises what love really is, is transformed in character and gladly accepts Calaf: for 'his name is love'.

None of Puccini's works was so long in the making or caused him such self-doubt as *Turandot*, and when he died it was left incomplete: the last two scenes were finished from his sketches by Franco Alfano. At the première the conductor Toscanini stopped at Liù's death, but dramatically this is wrong, and even though Alfano's completion is not up to the musical standard of the rest it is the best we have. The ending remains controversial, not least because Puccini made it clear that he intended the final duet between Calaf and Turandot to be the key to the whole work. Yet this opera remains his finest, allying the musical advances of *La fanciulla del West* to the lyrical expansiveness of *Tosca* and *Butterfly* in a final synthesis containing all that is best in his art. There is hardly a weak moment. His mastery of atmosphere is shown in the moonrise scene; his control of mounting tension is remarkable in the passage leading up to Calaf's striking the gong; a lighter vein is called on to good effect in the pacing and characterisation of the court officials Ping, Pang and Pong; and last but not least there is the soaring lyricism of Turandot's '*In questa reggia*' and Calaf's '*Nessun dorma*'. Like Rossini and Verdi before him, Puccini gave the world a rich score in his final opera.

It is not enough just to call Puccini a *verismo* composer. His first two operas predate the style: *Manon Lescaut* and *La bohème* have elements of earlier romantic opera as well as *verismo* ones; and the degree of *verismo* differs in *Tosca*, *Madama Butterfly* and *La fanciulla del West*. *Il tabarro* at least derives from the genre, but the other two operas of the *trittico* do not. In *La rondine* and *Turandot* he pursued different aims. The veristic elements are strongest in *Tosca*, with its unrestrained passion at moments of crisis, its juxtaposition of the violent and the lyrical, and more technically the orchestral doubling of melodies meant to carry a powerful emotional charge. The fastidious may find it all too strong for their sensibilities, and musicologists may regret the subordination of all to theatrical effect and deplore the composer's lack of thought for those for whom opera is chiefly a matter of study and analysis. Edward Greenfield, in his book *Puccini: Keeper of the Seal*, has neatly pricked such pomposity:

> Professor Dent drily remarks of Puccini's Grand Tunes that 'lest the humblest member of the audience should fail to catch them they are generally played by the bass of the supporting harmony as well as the treble'. If Puccini was reaching the emotions of the humblest member of the audience then he was succeeding in one of his primary aims. What matters [presumably, to Professor Dent] is whether in reaching the humblest member of the audience he has thereby alienated any of the more perceptive listeners at Professor Dent's end of the scale.

From *Manon Lescaut* on, Puccini lived his subjects. When composing the scene of Mimi's death in *La bohème*, he stood up and wept 'as if I had lost my own child'. But his attitude towards his most famous operas was perhaps curious. In later years he seems only to have enjoyed the last act of *Bohème*, and the only opera he cared to watch all through was *Butterfly*. His doomed heroines are striking: Manon, Mimi, Tosca, Cio-Cio-San,

Angelica and Liù all die through or for love—the last four driven to do so by their own hands. His *oeuvre* amounts in fact to a compulsive exploration of the relationship between sex and suffering. The most extreme case is that of Butterfly, where Cio-Cio-San, touchingly innocent and naive in her longing for Pinkerton's return, is systematically destroyed before our eyes to the most potent music. In even a poor performance of this opera the end is usually accompanied by members of the audience weeping. Cio-Cio-San has been compared by Rodney Milnes to Britten's Billy Budd, another innocent who goes 'like a lamb to the slaughter' for our artistic pleasure. Perhaps Puccini and Britten, both of whom took the keenest active interest in their libretti, can be charged with putting their psycho-sexual fantasies on the stage. But if so, what of the opera-lovers who fill the theatre when *Butterfly* or *Budd* is announced?

Puccini made life difficult for his librettists. The team of Giacosa and Illica nearly broke up several times in the face of the composer's demands, although they acknowledged his flair for knowing what would work in the theatre. By this time the elaborate system of syllabic verse which had served Italian opera for so long was breaking down under the pressure of the movement towards realism. The *decasillabi* and *endecasillabi* of classical practice gave way to freer lines that Giacosa dubbed '*illicasillabi*'. Puccini did not care for the stricter verse forms, and once said that the sight of a *romanza* in regular metre put him into a sort of seizure, doubtless feeling that such a thing was a contradiction in terms.

This composer's influence on a libretto was usually to tighten it so as to increase its pace. He liked the dénouement to be reached and drawn in bold strokes and then to bring down the curtain as soon as possible, while the impact was still strong. Thus the last act is usually the shortest. Similarly, he liked to launch into the action without too many preliminaries, hence the absence of an overture and a typically bustling first scene as in *Bohème* and even *Tosca*. But he also understood the need for variety and could take his time in painting an atmospheric scene, such as the chilly outdoor opening to Act III of *Bohème* with its bare fifths dropping from the flutes and its sharp shouts through the cold night air, or the beautiful Roman dawn of the last act of *Tosca*, when the bells peal and the shepherd boy sings. But even in such scenes there is tension as the drama unfolds: the Roman dawn is to be Cavaradossi's last, and it is a Puccinian turn of the screw to make it especially magical—now more than ever, a condemned man might wish to live. Butterfly's vigil, when she waits to the sound of the 'humming chorus' for Pinkerton's return, brings instead the unbearable truth that causes her suicide. Even the gloriously painted moonrise in *Turandot* precedes the execution of a failed suitor.

Every scene and even stanza contributes to the overall effect, even if some good devices are overworked—for example Mimi, Butterfly and Tosca are all heard offstage before making their entrance. When Puccini was happy with a libretto, he said so, and revealingly: '. . . It seems to me that we have really succeeded! The last act and the death of Mimi, especially, will call forth torrents of tears. I myself was much, much moved.'

Yet good theatre was achieved above all through his music. In our admiration for his melody and orchestration it is perhaps easy to overlook the technical mastery with which Puccini organised large stretches of music, although this drew comment from the start of his career. Verdi observed: 'I have heard the composer Puccini well spoken of . . . He follows modern trends, naturally, but he adheres to melody which is neither new nor old. The symphonic element, however, seems to be predominant in him. Nothing wrong with that—but one needs to tread cautiously here. Opera is opera and symphony is symphony . . .' This was in 1884, when only *Le villi* had been written! But if Verdi was too early to judge Puccini's mature style, we may quote also George Bernard Shaw on *Manon Lescaut*, admiring the 'genuine symphonic modification, development and occasionally combination of the thematic material . . . so that the act is really a single movement . . . in *Manon Lescaut* the domain of Italian opera is enlarged by the annexation of German Territory'.

Some younger Italian composers also wrote operas, though their names and works are barely known to the international public. Ildebrando Pizzetti (1880–1968) has a mainly rather serious style using archaic subjects throughout an exceptionally long career, from the unperformed *Sabina* (1897) and his first produced work, *Fedra* (Milan, 1915), to the Eliot-inspired *Assassinio nella cattedrale* (Milan, 1958) and *Clitennestra* (Milan, 1965). Pizzetti also wrote an *Ifigenia* for radio (RAI, 1950). Ottorino Respighi (1879–1936) was a master of glittering orchestration, a pupil of Rimsky-Korsakov, and this contributed to the success of such operas as his tale of love and witchcraft, *La fiamma* (*The Flame*, Rome, 1934).

There was also some reaction against Puccini and all that he stood for. The scholar Fausto Torrefranca attacked him in a book, *Giacomo Puccini e l'opera internazionale* (1912): but that was not surprising coming from a man who considered that 'a musician's creative activity is a pure expression of his intellect, by the intellect'—a case of chalk and cheese. Gian Francesco Malipiero (1882–1973), a scholar and composer alike, called for a return to a classical tradition as exemplified by Corelli and Vivaldi; this admirer of Monteverdi also wrote many operas including an Orpheus triptych called *L'orfeide* (Düsseldorf, 1925) and a Shakespearian *Giulio Cesare* (Genoa, 1936) and *Antonio e Cleopatra* (Florence, 1938). Such subjects were far from Puccini's world, as was the Orpheus treatment by Alfredo Casella (1883–1947), *La favola d'Orfeo* (Venice, 1932).

But at present *Turandot* is the last Italian opera to hold the stage. Thus with Puccini's death a great tradition stretching back over three hundred years to Monteverdi's *Orfeo* comes to an end. There are many reasons why this should be so, and Wystan Auden, who perhaps saw Puccini as the decadent phase of that tradition, has offered an observation if not an explanation in his *The Dyer's Hand and Other Essays* (1962):

> The golden age of opera, from Mozart to Verdi, coincided with the golden age of liberal humanism, of unquestioning belief in freedom and progress. If good operas are rarer today, this may be because not only have we learned that we are less free than nineteenth-century humanism imagined, but also have become less certain that freedom is an unequivocal blessing, that the free are necessarily the good. To say that operas are more difficult to write does not mean that they are impossible. That would only follow if we should cease to believe in free will and personality altogether. Every high C accurately struck demolishes the theory that we are the irresponsible puppets of fate or chance.

13

RUSSIA

Glinka and Dargomyzhsky. Mussorgsky, Borodin and Rimsky-Korsakov.
Tchaikovsky. Taneyev and Rachmaninov.

GLINKA AND DARGOMYZHSKY

When Peter the Great (1672–1725) opened Russia up to the West in the early eighteenth century, his new capital, St Petersburg, was designed by Western architects. In due course, the Russian aristocracy who gathered there developed a taste for European luxuries, among them Italian opera, and various Italian composers became resident at the court to present it. Among them were Francesco Araia in 1735–40, Galuppi in 1765–8, Paisiello in 1776–83, and Cimarosa in 1787–91. Araia's *Tsefal i Prokris* (*Cephalus and Procris*, St Petersburg, 1755) had the distinction of being the first opera to be sung in Russian, though in style and content this treatment of Greek myth remained an *opera seria*. Towards the end of the century several operas were composed by Russians, though none is produced today, even in Russia itself. The Empress Catherine the Great was so interested in the form that she wrote some libretti herself, including that for the fairy-tale opera *Fevey* (St Petersburg, 1789) by Vasiliy Pashkevich (ca 1742–97) which has some folk melodies in it. *The Miller-Magician, Cheat and Matchmaker* (Moscow, 1779) by Mikhail Sokolovsky (ca 1750–80) was more completely Russian, with many folk-tunes, a village setting and spoken dialogue rather than recitative. Though it reflected a reaction against Western styles, it also owed something to the influence of the German *Singspiel*.

Certainly, during the eighteenth century folksong and liturgical music were more recognisably Russian than native opera or concert music. However, the patriotic feeling inspired by the Napoleonic invasion of 1812 brought about a search for national identity to which opera would be central because it allowed the folk heritage to be explored through a combination of the arts. Russia had much to gain from creating an independent style, and when the gradual development of industries and transport systems brought the growth of towns and thus broadened the potential audience, the time was ripe for a cultural flowering. This was further stimulated by the emergence of two creative giants, the poet Pushkin and the composer Glinka.

Mikhail Glinka (1804–57) was a self-taught musical dilettante, though in time his talents earned him international stature. His main importance was to lie in the role of pioneer, and indeed Tchaikovsky once described him as 'the acorn from which the oak of Russian music sprang'. He studied in Italy for three years from 1830, meeting Bellini and Donizetti, and then moved on to Berlin for further studies on his way home. By now he was aware of a wide range of Western styles, and had become skilled in the techniques of composition.

Glinka admitted in his memoirs that the impulse to write a Russian nationalist opera came from the homesickness he experienced in Italy. *A Life for the Tsar* (St Petersburg, 1836) made him the effective founder of the Russian national school and led to his appointment as *Kapellmeister* to the Imperial Chapel. Yet this opera was not totally without predecessors: *Askold's Grave* (Moscow, 1835) by Alexis Verstovsky (1799–1862), had had elements of folk music and magic owing much to *Der Freischütz*, a clear vocal style and imposing choruses.

A Life for the Tsar was originally called *Ivan Susanin*, but before its première it was renamed by permission of Nicholas I, who had visited a rehearsal. The peasant Susanin is compelled by the Polish enemy to act as their guide as they hunt the Tsar in the war of 1612. However, he lays a false trail and so sacrifices his own life to ensure a Russian victory. The opera ends with general rejoicing and the sound of the Kremlin bells. This heroic and historical opera was the precursor of Mussorgsky's *Boris Godunov*, Borodin's *Prince Igor*, and even Prokofiev's *War and Peace*, but its music reveals Glinka's eclecticism: the vocal writing is still often frankly Italianate, and the big choral and ballet scenes owe much to French grand opera. While the dance music and the instrumentation have a distinctively Russian flavour, these foreign influences were to remain potent for many years in music by later Russian composers.

If Glinka's *A Life for the Tsar* is an historical epic, then his *Ruslan and Lyudmila* (St Petersburg, 1842) is a brilliant fairy-tale. Here the plot brings an oriental flavour and a reliance on folksong too, although the overture is a virtuoso piece that gives only the merest hint of what is to follow in the body of the opera. One of *Ruslan and Lyudmila*'s most striking features is its harmonic boldness: harsh bare fifths are frequent, together with chromatic Persian-sounding melodies. The whole-tone scale—say C, D, E, F sharp, G sharp, A sharp—is used as the motto of the evil dwarf Tchernomor (literally, 'black plague'), and in Act III appears on a solo trombone. There is a similar directness in vocal writing, rhythm and orchestration: the music is often abrupt in character rather than smooth and sophisticated.

Glinka made effective use of folk material, for he did not deny its essential simplicity. An example is the 'Chorus of Maidens' in *Ruslan and Lyudmila*: it has five verses, and the melody, already repetitious in character, is repeated for each of them, with only the accompaniment changed. There is no attempt to develop by extension or modulation, for the repetition is an essential ingredient in this style. It was one of the features that was to remain in Russian music, together with a certain 'oriental' richness of harmony and instrumentation.

Alexander Dargomyzhsky (1813–69) met Glinka in 1834, and resolved to undertake a thorough study of composition. His first opera, *Esmeralda* (Moscow, 1847), had a libretto based on Victor Hugo and was completed in 1840; but it had to wait seven years for its production, and then failed. His next opera, *Rusalka* (St Petersburg, 1856), was more successful; its libretto used a play by Alexander Pushkin (1799–1837), the greatest literary source of inspiration to Russian opera composers. Dargomyzhsky's last and most ambitious project was *The Stone Guest* (St Petersburg, 1872). In this opera on the *Don Giovanni* story he developed a style he described as 'half-recitative', in which short and often irregular phrases emphasised the words and the orchestra remained subordinate to the voices. He realised, however, that this approach to vocal writing might alienate him from his audience: 'The great majority of our public and press regard me as uninspired. I have no intention of debasing music to the level of mere amusement for their sake; I want the notes to express exactly the same things as the words: I want truth.'

Dargomyzhsky's music is at times written without key signatures in tonal schemes that shift rapidly to emphasise dramatic tension. *The Stone Guest* lacks even the occasional virtuoso set piece, since the whole work is in a kind of conversational style. There are *leitmotifs* — for instance a four-chord figure characterises Donna Anna — but these are not used systematically.

Dargomyzhsky worked on *The Stone Guest* during the failing health of his final years. The scene of Don Juan, the Monk and Leporello was sketched on his deathbed, and it was at his suggestion that his friend César Cui completed the vocal score and Rimsky-Korsakov the orchestration. When the opera was eventually produced it had a cool reception, but Cui remained faithful: 'If Mozart had lived in our time, it is probable that his opera would have resembled *The Stone Guest* more than the *Don Giovanni* of 1787.' And in general the younger generation of composers was enthralled by this work, which became an inspiration to Rimsky-

Korsakov in his *Mozart and Salieri* and even to Mussorgsky in *The Marriage* and *Boris Godunov*.

MUSSORGSKY, BORODIN, AND RIMSKY-KORSAKOV

Modest Mussorgsky (1839–81) joined the Russian army as a young man and was stationed in St Petersburg, where he met not only Dargomyzhsky and Cui but also Mily Balakirev (1837–1910) and the influential critic Vladimir Stasov. Balakirev was at the heart of the new developments in Russian music, as Tchaikovsky observed: 'He is the inventor of all the theories . . . in which are to be found so many undeveloped, incorrectly developed, or prematurely decayed talents.' It was Balakirev who induced Mussorgsky, Rimsky-Korsakov and Borodin to compose. He did not find composition easy himself, and wrote no complete opera, though he wrote fragments of one called *The Firebird*. From his first meeting with his idol Glinka at the age of eighteen, he had devoted his life to furthering the progress of Russian music, and when Glinka died Balakirev took over the mantle of leadership. He travelled to Prague in 1866 to supervise the first productions there of Glinka's two major operas. His outstanding gifts were recalled by Rimsky-Korsakov in his autobiography: 'Balakirev held us absolutely spellbound by his talents, and by his authority and personal magnetism.'

After leaving the army Mussorgsky earned his living as a minor civil servant and composed in his spare time. He abandoned three operatic projects, *Han of Iceland*, *Oedipus in Athens*, and *Salammbô*, before writing an opera which he based on Gogol's *The Marriage* (1868; performed St Petersburg, 1909). This owed much to Dargomyzhsky's methods and preserved the dialogue of the play to create what Mussorgsky called 'a conversational opera': 'I should like my characters to speak on stage just as real people speak, but at the same time, the nature and force of the characters' intonation should directly achieve its goal; that is, my music should be an artistic reproduction of human speech in all its subtle nuances.' All these operatic projects were essential to Mussorgsky's development, but their music and stagecraft were rather dry: it was by adding lyricism and folksong to this 'conversational' technique that Mussorgsky created *Boris Godunov*, arguably the greatest of all Russian operas.

Boris Godunov (St Petersburg, 1874), Mussorgsky's historical epic based upon Pushkin, was completed rapidly. He submitted the score in 1869 to the Imperial Opera, who found its realism baffling and rejected it. The composer accordingly revised it by including a greater proportion of set pieces, including arias and a love duet, but this version was rejected too. However, in 1874, when he was already at work on his next opera, *Khovanshchina* (St Petersburg, 1886), sections of *Boris Godunov* were successfully performed at a benefit concert and subsequently published. Already, during Mussorgsky's lifetime, the matter of 'versions' had become contentious. After his death from alcoholism at the age of forty-two, his friend Rimsky-Korsakov revised most of Mussorgsky's works. Rimsky believed that 'clumsiness and illiteracy' obscured the genius of *Boris Godunov* and he reworked the original, using his own sumptuous orchestral textures instead of Mussorgsky's leaner lines, and making the form more rounded and sophisticated. This was done with complete altruism and indeed achieved the desired result of establishing the opera with the public, but in many ways it contradicted the kind of operatic experience Mussorgsky had intended. Realism, rather than sophistication and colour, was always his priority, and during recent years many musicians, and, indeed, also audiences, have preferred the original, though the Rimsky-Korsakov version also remains popular, especially in Russia.

For all its originality, *Boris Godunov* still shows the influence of Glinka and Dargomyzhsky at every stage. The story could hardly be more Russian, and by its very nature the opera avoids an evolving flow of action: instead there is a series of tableaux welded together by their common theme relating to the tragic figure of Tsar Boris. There are epic scenes featuring the chorus as the Russian people, and others which are more lightweight, such as the girls' chorus in the Polish garden. An intensely personal expression is given to the main characters. Mussorgsky preferred to build his music from the repetition and accumulation of ideas, so that there is little attempt at thematic development. Thus at the start a simple folk tune is repeated four times against changing accompaniments and at once creates a Russian atmosphere. There is much use too of vivid national material, such as the *polonaise* to give a Polish flavour to the beginning of Act III and the boisterous Russian song for the drunken monk Varlaam in the tavern scene in Act I.

The whole of *Boris* is notable for its directness, forceful rhythms and orchestration, and often abrupt vocal lines, all of which are intended to convey the utmost realism. Perhaps the best example is the famous 'hallucination scene', in which the Tsar, who has had killed the legitimate heir to the throne, is so tortured by guilt that he imagines he sees the dead child approaching him in the figures of the clock as it strikes the hour. This powerful scene sounds remarkably modern with its dissonances against a sustained bass line and a vocal part that is disjointed and terror-stricken, building in intensity until the anguished Boris sinks to his knees, begging forgiveness for his crime.

In such music the contribution of the singer is so important that it took a great actor-singer, Fyodor Chaliapin (1873–1938), to bring the work to real success on the stage. He sang the magnificent bass role of Boris for the first time in an 1898 Moscow production, and he wrote of the experience: 'I suddenly felt in this strange music something astonishingly akin and familiar to me. It seemed that all my tangled, difficult life was expressed in it; it was everywhere in the world.'

In its content, balance, and pacing, *Boris Godunov* is by far Mussorgsky's most important contribution to the repertory. He did attempt two further operas: a second national epic, *Khovanshchina*, and another Gogol opera called *Sorochintsy Fair*, which was a comedy flavoured attractively with Ukrainian folksong. Neither was finished. *Khovanshchina* was to his own libretto, and it was mostly left in vocal score to be completed by Rimsky-Korsakov, whereas *Sorochintsy Fair* is remembered chiefly for its *gopak*, a vigorous dance, and the powerful orchestral interlude called *The Night on the Bare Mountain*. Mussorgsky wrote relatively little, but his influence on later composers has been enormous; much of the work of Janáček and Debussy would have been impossible without his innovations.

Like Mussorgsky, Alexander Borodin (1833–87) was a part-time composer who maintained a commitment to music after meeting Balakirev in 1862. His operatic masterpiece is *Prince Igor* (St Petersburg, 1890), on which he worked from 1870 till his death. Once again Rimsky-Korsakov prepared a performing edition, this time with the help of Alexander Glazunov. Based upon an epic of ancient Russia, its four acts comprise a series of imposing and colourful tableaux like those of *Boris Godunov*. The famous 'Polovtsian Dances' form the climax of Act II as slaves are brought to entertain the Prince. They culminate in the glorification of Khan Konchak, who is holding Igor prisoner, but who still treats him in part as a guest. While the bright and sophisticated orchestral colours may owe more to Rimsky than to Borodin himself, the vigorous melodic and rhythmic invention reflects middle-Asian influence as well as that of Russian folk music. Although Borodin seldom quoted folksongs directly, he assimilated their spirit so thoroughly that he effectively recreated them.

In 1880 the Mariinsky Theatre in St Petersburg commissioned a number of composers to participate in a special scheme to celebrate the twenty-fifth anniversary of the reign of Alexander II. *Mlada* was to be a series of grand allegorical tableaux featuring both opera and ballet; the composers were to be Rimsky-Korsakov, Cui, Mussorgsky and—for the ballet music—Leon Minkus. Although the project was eventually abandoned after the Tsar's assassination the following year, much of the music was already written, and Rimsky eventually wrote an opera-ballet of his own with the same title. That Nicolai Rimsky-Korsakov (1844–1908) should emerge as the central figure in this group is appropriate, for he provides the link between the earlier Russian nationalists and the masters of the twentieth century.

Having left a naval career, Rimsky taught composition at the St Petersburg Conservatoire. It was Balakirev who encouraged him to join the nationalist camp, and this unselfish artist was later to devote much time to the works of others, especially their operas. At about the time he completed Dargomyzhsky's *The Stone Guest*, he collaborated with César Cui (1835–1918) on his *William Ratcliff* (St Petersburg, 1869). This, the third of Cui's ten operas, was described by the critic Stasov as 'one of the most important compositions of our time', and used both 'musical realism' and 'melodic recitative' as well as lyrical melody. However, it did not secure a place in the repertory because, according to Rimsky, the orchestral writing showed 'neither inclination nor ability'. Cui's later operas included two Pushkin settings, *A Feast in Time of Plague* (St Petersburg, 1901) and *The Captain's Daughter* (St Petersburg, 1911), but he made his strongest contribution to Russian musical life through his lively writings.

With Balakirev, Rimsky produced performing editions of the two Glinka operas, and beyond this he edited *Boris Godunov* and *Khovanshchina* and completed *Prince Igor*. Meanwhile, he composed his own first opera, *The Maid of Pskov* (St Petersburg, 1873), which is sometimes called *Ivan the Terrible*, and thereafter he maintained a consistent interest in opera, writing no fewer than fifteen works in the form.

By the 1890s Rimsky was the most famous of Russian composers. Even so, he never saw his last opera, *The Golden Cockerel* (Moscow, 1909), which was banned because its plot lampooned bureaucracy, a sensitive subject with the Imperial government in the wake of the Russo-Japanese war. When his second opera, *May Night* (St Petersburg, 1880), was performed, Stasov was disappointed that it did not adopt the historical stance of *Boris Godunov* and *The Maid of Pskov*. Instead the composer had turned to the Russian folk tales which he found his most natural source of inspiration. The libretto derives from a fairy-tale by Gogol, in which young lovers are able to marry in spite of a disapproving father, thanks to the intervention of *rusalki* (water-nymphs). Colourful settings suited his virtuoso technique, and in *May Night* the orchestra admirably conveys the magical atmosphere. The dramatic realism of Mussorgsky is uncommon in the operas of Rimsky-Korsakov: the only one to adopt this approach is the short *Mozart and Salieri* (Moscow, 1898), of which he wrote:

> The melody of songs began to become for me a purely vocal line following the turns of the text, with harmony and modulation simply suggesting an accompaniment for them. The accompaniment did not result or take shape until after the composition of the melody, whereas previously, with few exceptions, the melody had been written simultaneously in an instrumental way and, consequently, only corresponded to its general content. I sketched a little scene from Pushkin's *Mozart and Salieri*, whereby the recitative for me was to be shaped freely and flowingly, and was to be placed in the foreground.

Despite his high opinion of the work, perhaps the failure of *Mozart and Salieri* with the public discouraged Rimsky from maintaining a realistic style in his later operas.

The Snow Maiden (St Petersburg, 1882), *The Tale of Tsar Saltan* (Moscow, 1900), and *The Invisible City of Kitezh* (St Petersburg, 1907) have typical Rimsky characteristics—nationalism, orientalism, and elements of magic and fairy-tale. After 1889, when a German company had brought the *Ring* to St Petersburg, he admitted that he tried to add Wagnerian touches to his music. But the works of Liszt, especially the symphonic poems, were a more important influence still, for Rimsky was no mere nationalist. His bright orchestral colours and tunefulness combined to support both diatonic, folk-inspired music and a more exotic, chromatic style. The latter idiom suited the fairy-tale world in which his operas were set, and the same approach is found in his pupil Stravinsky's ballet *The Firebird.*

A typical example of Rimsky-Korsakov's imagery is found in the music of the *rusalki* in Act III of *May Night*, where the orchestra conveys the atmosphere in a cello solo against woodwind *arpeggios* and a silken violin line. Similarly *Sadko* (Moscow, 1898) has a fine scene of an underwater fantasy-world, with that favourite Russian device, the whole-tone scale, providing an ambiguous harmonic flavour. The most enchanting of all his operas is *The Invisible City of Kitezh*: the lullaby of the forest maiden Fevronya, with its sensitive instrumentation and lyrical vocal line, is among Rimsky's finest creations. His operas are typical of his love of illusion: 'I am actually of the opinion that art is the most enchanting, intoxicating lie.' What could be further from the realism of Mussorgsky?

For all his eclecticism, Rimsky-Korsakov shows most of the characteristic features of the Russian school, such as melodic recitative, folksong, choral dance scenes, historical and magical stories, orientalism, lyrical vocal lines and vivid orchestration. Only two of his operas, *The Maid of Pskov* and *The Tsar's Bride*, rely on the common operatic tension of love versus duty. All of them contain fine music, and it seems a pity that at present they are popular only in Russia.

TCHAIKOVSKY

Pyotr Ilyich Tchaikovsky (1840–93) spent much of his life in the creation and preparation of works for the stage, writing ten operas and three full-length ballets. He said that it was attending a performance of Mozart's *Don Giovanni* as a boy which determined him upon a musical career, and throughout his life he adored Mozart, writing in a letter to his patroness, Nadezhda von Meck: 'You say that my worship of Mozart is quite contrary to my musical nature. But perhaps it is just because, being a child of my time, I feel broken and spiritually out of joint that I find consolation and rest in Mozart's music.' Tchaikovsky also shared Mozart's fundamental view that opera is most effective when dealing with characters who behave like real people instead of symbolic figures, legendary heroes or fairies.

Tchaikovsky's best operas are those in which he felt an identity or sympathy with his characters. However, he was well aware of what was happening in the musical world outside Russia, and his output covered a range of styles. The first opera he completed was *The Voyevode* (*The Polish Landowner*, Moscow, 1869), but he doubted its quality and became so disillusioned with it that he destroyed the music, incorporating some into later works. He also destroyed the manuscript of *Undine* when it was rejected by the Imperial Theatres in St Petersburg, and part of the love duet was reworked into the ballet *Swan Lake*. His first surviving opera is thus *The Oprichnik* (St Petersburg, 1874), which used some music from *The Voyevode*. The plot conveys conventional tensions and has a very Russian theme, for the '*oprichniki*' were the powerful secret police established by Ivan the Terrible.

Seeing Bizet's *Carmen* in Paris in 1875 was one of Tchaikovsky's greatest experiences. That opera's obsession with fate impressed him, as did its boldly realistic subject matter. Soon after, he attended the first production of Wagner's *Ring* at Bayreuth which moved him far less, though he admired Wagner's genius. He wrote, 'He lets music slip quite out of sight in his efforts to attain reality . . . Wotan, Brünnhilde, Fricka etc. are all so impossible, so little human.' Given Tchaikovsky's growing experience of opera outside Russia, it was likely that the music of his next opera, *Vakula the Smith* (St Petersburg, 1876), would be more expressively dramatic. Its passion is balanced by some delightfully tuneful dances, but the plot, which centres on Vakula selling his soul to the Devil, relies on that magic element that suited Tchaikovsky less well than Rimsky-Korsakov. Cui, who reviewed the opera, wrote:

> I know of no subject more lively, spicy and amusing than *Vakula*, unless it be the farces of Offenbach. And yet on this subject Mr Tchaikovsky has contrived to compose music that is melancholy, elegiac, and sentimental. Who, until he heard it, could have believed that minor keys and relatively slow tempos would be prevalent in this score? With the exception of the Devil and Solokha, all the characters spend their time in lamentation.

Despite these strictures, the music remains the work of a master, not least in its skilful use of folksong. Tchaikovsky clearly retained an affection for the opera, since he returned to it ten years later to revise it and divide its three acts into four, with a new title, *Cherevichki* (*The Slippers*).

Tchaikovsky was usually at work on the next opera well before the previous one had been performed, and of his sixth, *Eugene Onegin* (Moscow, 1879), he wrote: 'I worked quickly . . . *Onegin* was written in an incredibly short space of time. The chief thing is to love the work.' Here at last he found a subject to suit his talents; and here too the influence of *Carmen* had its fullest effect. This was a story of deep human interest into which he could wholeheartedly throw himself. He wrote to his brother Modest:

> Recently I was at Mme Lavrosky's. The conversation turned to opera libretti . . . Suddenly she remarked, 'What about *Eugene Onegin?*' The idea struck me as curious, and I made no reply. Afterwards, while dining alone at a restaurant, her words came back to me, and on reflection the idea did not seem at all absurd. I set off at once in search of Pushkin's works. I spent a sleepless night; the result—a sketch of a delicious opera based on Pushkin. You have no idea how excited I am about the subject. How delightful to avoid the commonplace Pharaohs, the Ethiopian Princesses, poisoned goblets, and all the other puppet tales. *Eugene Onegin* is filled with poetry.

The completion of the project was, however, delayed by his disastrous marriage to Antonina Milyukova, who had written him a love letter in circumstances strikingly similar to those of Tatyana and Onegin. Admitting that he was 'in love with the image of Tatyana', he was all too easily drawn into this unhappy relationship. Soon after the marriage he fled to Switzerland, where *Onegin* was completed.

The central character is Tatyana (soprano), who is both very young and impressionable, and falls in love with the more worldly Onegin (baritone). Tatyana writes him an impassioned letter expressing her feelings, but his response is cold. At her birthday ball, he quarrels with a friend, Lensky, and in the resulting duel, Onegin shoots Lensky and kills him. The final act is set some years later at a fashionable St Petersburg ball. Tatyana has by now married Prince Gremin. When Onegin arrives as a guest he realises that now he loves Tatyana. In the ardent final scene between them, she is emotionally torn but decides to stay with her husband, and Onegin leaves in despair.

Tchaikovsky's emotional approach to the story contrasts sharply with Pushkin's ironical tone. Tatyana's music is as passionate as any he wrote, and indeed Onegin is at times little more than a foil for her, instead of the leading character in the drama. Like *Carmen*, *Eugene Onegin* tends towards *verismo* by uncovering raw emotions, and central to the opera is the great 'Letter Scene', a soliloquy which was written first. The pacing, orchestration, characterisation and musical quality make it the composer's finest achievement in opera. The scene of the ball in honour of Tatyana's birthday in Act II is a notable example of opera placing the individual in a social context, represented musically through the relationship between solo and ensemble. *Eugene Onegin* is also an opera of synthesis, bringing together and balancing tragic fate and deeply felt personal emotion, the peace of the country and the sophistication of the town, big set pieces and simple folksong.

Tchaikovsky's next project was very different: a grand opera with which he aimed to conquer the Paris Opéra. *The Maid of Orleans* (St Petersburg, 1881), to a text after Schiller, uses the principles of grand opera with crowd scenes and processions, battles and courtly pomp. Again Tchaikovsky was drawn towards his heroine, Joan of Arc, but although much of the music is fine, the composer knew he was not at ease: 'Medieval dukes and knights and ladies captivate my imagination but not my heart, and where the heart is not touched there can't be any music.'

Mazeppa (Moscow, 1884) has a Russian setting again, and as usual Tchaikovsky began by composing the music for the central aspect of the opera in order to gain sympathy with the characters. But he did not find it easy, as he admitted:

I have reread the libretto and Pushkin's poem; I found many of the verses and situations moving. I am at work upon the scene between

Maria and Mazeppa, which in the libretto reproduces Pushkin's text word for word. So far I have found no such profound joy as I did, for instance, when composing *Onegin*. The score makes gradual progress, but I must say that I do not find the characters particularly attractive.

Nevertheless there is expressive music for the heroine Maria, whose poignant lullaby over the dead body of her lover Andrei is among Tchaikovsky's finest inspirations. The dances are excellent too, as they are in *The Enchantress* (St Petersburg, 1887), in which the composer returned to the Russian world of folk magic.

In Tchaikovsky's penultimate opera, *The Queen of Spades* (St Petersburg, 1890), the story is once again drawn from Pushkin and has fully developed characters. This time the person to whom Tchaikovsky felt closest was the young officer Herman (tenor), a man so obsessed with gambling that he loses everything and eventually kills himself. Typically, the composer made changes to mould the plot to his own ends, in particular to the fate of Herman, who in Pushkin's original is left alive, though insane in an asylum. The commission for the opera came from the Mariinsky Theatre, and he worked on the libretto with his brother Modest. The instruction 'to compose a grand opera in the French manner: a Russian *Carmen*, but more sumptuous', fired his enthusiasm:

> Yesterday morning I did the finale. When I came to Herman's death and the chorus of gamblers, such pity overcame me for my hero that I burst into tears. Never so far had any of my characters made me weep so passionately, and I wondered why this should be. I realised that Herman was not merely an excuse for composing music, but a man who had lived, and deserved sympathy.

The Queen of Spades has a considerable range: there is the charm of the children's chorus imitating soldiers on parade, the expressive music for Herman and his beloved Lisa, and the eerie atmosphere which surrounds the mysterious Countess, whose secret of how to win at cards obsesses Herman. The supernatural scene in the barracks, in which he is visited by her ghost, is chillingly effective, with subtle orchestration and an offstage chorus. When the Countess recalls her youth in Versailles, she sings a variant of an aria from Grétry's *Richard Coeur de Lion*, while during the ball scene there is a Greek pastoral pastiche of Daphnis and Chloë, which is pure eighteenth-century entertainment music. Yet, the main influence remained Bizet's *Carmen*: Herman's fate is to be betrayed by the cards, by the Queen of Spades on which he has staked everything. For once a masterwork received due recognition, and the première was a triumph.

Tchaikovsky's last opera was the one-act *Iolanta* (St Petersburg, 1892), to a libretto by his brother Modest in which a blind princess is cured by love. The sentimental story is given typically beguiling music with a number of memorable tunes, and the dramatic pacing is always sure, while its theme of love's power appealed to the composer, whose psychological make-up included a fatalist streak. The opera was planned to be a double bill with the ballet *The Nutcracker*, and after the production Tchaikovsky wrote that 'the opera was evidently very well liked, but not the ballet'. Time, it seems, has decided otherwise, although in its early days the opera did divide critical opinion. Rimsky-Korsakov, for instance, referred to *Iolanta* as 'one of Tchaikovsky's feeblest inspirations'; but, on the other hand, Gustav Mahler liked it well enough to programme it at Hamburg, where he was Opera Director, soon after the première and included it in his Vienna season of 1900.

Like many of Tchaikovsky's operas, *Iolanta* is weakened by its libretto. He was at his best in works which allowed his natural expressiveness to move from recitative through *arioso* style to full emotional statements, and this was only possible for him when he could identify with the characters. Yet his gift as a lyrical composer capable of powerful emotion made him a natural man of the theatre, and he brought to opera his own unique capacity for feeling and a sense of humanity.

TANEYEV AND RACHMANINOV

By the time of Tchaikovsky's death in 1893 at the early age of fifty-three, the next generation of Russian composers was emerging. In opera the most prominent of these were Sergey Taneyev (1856–1915), Sergey Rachmaninov (1873–1943), and Igor Stravinsky (1882–1971)—though whereas Taneyev and Rachmaninov created their operas for Russian audiences, Stravinsky's were only to be written after he had left his homeland, and represent a new kind of Russianness that made many breaks with the post-Glinka tradition. Taneyev's music was mainly instrumental, and most of his time was spent teaching at the Moscow Conservatoire, of which he was Director from 1885. His one opera, *The Oresteia* (St Petersburg, 1895), used a Greek subject which could hardly have been less nationalist. It therefore stands apart from the mainstream of nineteenth-century Russian opera, and although it was received enthusiastically it has not maintained its popularity. Perhaps Taneyev's lyrical style was too obviously at odds with the intense, often brutal, drama of the original story.

Sergey Rachmaninov's reputation as a composer in other fields has overshadowed his achievement in opera. This is unfortunate, for even when he was only twenty his one-act *Aleko* (Moscow, 1893) was performed at the Bolshoi. It made a considerable impression, with several arias encored, and Tchaikovsky expressed his admiration for the work, which had been written as a final graduation exercise at the Moscow Conservatoire. Throughout the 1890s Rachmaninov maintained his contact with opera as a conductor, including a collaboration and friendship with the bass Fyodor Chaliapin. His association with the Bolshoi led him to compose two further operas, *The Miserly Knight* and *Francesca da Rimini* (both Moscow, 1906), which were given as a double bill. *The Miserly Knight*, which like *Aleko* is based on Pushkin, employs a rich harmonic language and full orchestral textures; its most striking feature is that it requires an all-male cast. *Francesca da Rimini*, to a libretto after Dante by Modest Tchaikovsky, contains in the love scene for Francesca and Paolo, which was the first part of the opera to be written, some intensely lyrical and passionate music, culminating in an orchestral postlude to accompany (in the composer's words) 'an embrace that lasts for fifty-one bars!' The two tableaux are framed by a Prologue and an Epilogue, the whole taken from Canto V of *The Inferno*. There is an effective recurring feature in the shape of the theme sung as a unison chant by the lovers: 'There is no greater sorrow than to recall in misery former times of happiness.' At the end of the epilogue, Rachmaninov treats this theme even more directly as it is intoned by a chorus of the damned spirits in Hell.

The music of *Francesca da Rimini* is often impressive, but it lacks the narrative forward thrust of drama. The year after his prestigious double bill, Rachmaninov elected to abandon opera, and he never returned to the form. It seems probable that he wished to leave behind the hectic schedule imposed by life at the Bolshoi in order to concentrate on composition and on his career as a pianist. Even so, both as a composer and as a conductor he had maintained the Russian operatic tradition into the twentieth century.

If opera proved less attractive to the Russian composers of Rachmaninov's generation in the years before the Revolution, the strength of the repertory created by earlier masters more than compensated. In fact Rimsky-Korsakov continued to compose operas right up to his death in 1908, by which time a new school of Russian singers had created an important performing tradition. Russia had led the way in nationalist opera for other countries, and during the twentieth century this repertory would have a lasting influence in the general adoption of folk material by composers as different as Gershwin, Falla, and Vaughan Williams. Above all, through the dramatic realism of *Boris Godunov*, it would affect the work of Janáček and even Berg. This influence should in no way be underestimated, for it ranks equally with that of Wagner as the most significant legacy of nineteenth-century music drama.

14

EASTERN EUROPE

Hungary and Poland. Smetana and Czech Nationalism. From Dvořák to Weinberger. Janáček. Martinů.

HUNGARY AND POLAND

In the nineteenth century, other national operatic styles were emerging in Europe, though none of them were to have the far-reaching effects of the Russian one. Hungary and Poland, countries which were occupied by more powerful neighbours, Austria and Russia respectively, and were dominated by their cultures, were both affected. One recognisably Hungarian opera of this time was *Béla's Escape* (Pest, 1822) by Jószef Ruzitska (ca 1775–after 1823), which featured national dances such as the *verbunkos* but also borrowed from Italian and German styles. It was a composer of a later generation, Ferenc Erkel (1810–93), who became a leader in this field in 1835, when he became conductor of the Hungarian Theatre Company. As a composer he made his reputation with *Bátoria Mária* (Pest, 1840) which, though it used the structures and character-types of current French and Italian operas, also employed national dances, just as Ruzitska had done. This success encouraged Erkel to concentrate on music for the stage, and his second opera, *Hunyadi László* (Pest, 1844), achieved a lasting popularity and gained the admiration of Liszt. It has a subtle use of dance styles; the three-part form of the *verbunkos*, starting slowly and expressively and becoming faster with each section, is frequently used in arias.

Erkel had become skilled in setting Hungarian, including narrative. He continually searched for potential librettos, and developed a new genre, the *népszínmű* or 'people's theatre', a popular play with music akin to the English ballad opera. These works contained folksongs and popular songs, and the most widely performed has been *Two Pistols* (Pest, 1844). But his best known opera is the tragic *Bánk bán* (*The Palatine Bank*, Pest, 1861), with its nationalist historical subject, the thirteenth-century revolt against a ruling foreign court. The music is melodically rich and shows a development in his style which allows more attention to be given to characterisation in the ensembles. The instrumental writing emphasises chamber textures, and for the first time the Hungarian stringed instrument, the cimbalom, was used orchestrally, in a colourful folk idiom and atmosphere.

The demands of his work at the National Theatre meant that Erkel could never be prolific. Later in life he often collaborated with two of his sons, Gyula (1842–1909) and Sándor (1846–1900)—who had already helped with the instrumentation of *Bánk bán*—for example in *Brankovics György* (Budapest, 1874). This opera shows Serbian and Turkish musical influences as well as Hungarian, and has a mostly through-composed style and advanced harmony. However, his later music seems to have lacked the spontaneous excitement he had achieved previously in creating a native operatic style, and of his operas today, only *Hunyadi László* and *Bánk bán* have remained in the repertory of the Budapest Opera.

In Poland opera developed during the later eighteenth century. The first full-scale national opera using a libretto in Polish is *The Supposed Miracle or The Krakowians and the Highlanders* (Warsaw, 1794) by Jan Stefani (1746–1829), a skilful composer of *polonaises*, who gave it a traditional rural setting. But the works of József Elsner (1769–1854), such as *Leszek the White* (Warsaw, 1809) and *The Women of Wislica* (Warsaw, 1818), have more obviously historical themes. Polish opera was also written by Karol Kurpiński (1785–1857), who became Opera Director in Warsaw in 1810. His vivid *The Castle of Czorsztyn* (Warsaw, 1819) remained in the national repertory for about a century.

The most celebrated of all Polish composers, the half-French exile Chopin (1810–49), wrote no stage works although he had been urged to do so by his teacher Elsner, and in nineteenth-century Poland the leading opera composer became Stanislav Moniuszko (1819–72). His *Halka* (revised version Warsaw, 1858) was enormously successful, and brought him appointments as conductor of the Warsaw Opera and professor at the Conservatoire. The plot is a love story that has a partly social theme—a simple peasant girl, Halka, is seduced and abandoned by an aristocrat called Janusz and then drowns herself. This associated it with the peasants' revolt of 1846 and the further uprisings of 1848 and, together with its romantic theme and national dances, ensured its success with the public. Moniuszko's other well-known opera is *The Haunted Manor* (Warsaw, 1865), also in part a love story, whose setting emphasises the agreeably supernatural element so popular with the Romantics. Here the rhythms of Polish dances, such as the *polonaise*, *mazurka* and *krakowiak*, are fundamental to the musical style. There are fine arias and ensembles, and an unusual reliance on the chorus, for which the composer wrote splendidly, not least in the chorus of laughing huntsmen. A recent recording (1986) has reminded us of the comic and colourful elements in this work, which is still in the Polish repertory.

For all its Polish characteristics, Moniuszko's graceful yet vivid style was strongly influenced by Rossini and French composers of the time, particularly Auber, whose operas he not only conducted but also provided with interludes of his own, and his operas and operettas rely on the conventional structures of recitative, aria and ensemble. *Halka* remains his most popular stage work, and its historical significance lies in the fact that it inaugurated a prolific period of opera composition in Poland. In the ten years after 1858 some forty new operas were staged in Warsaw. However, it was not until Karol Szymanowski in the twentieth century that Poland again produced a composer to match the stature of Moniuszko.

SMETANA AND CZECH NATIONALISM

Czechoslovakia lies at the heart of Europe and has always been surrounded by larger neighbours. The Czech nation did not come into existence until after the First World War; before then its regions— Bohemia, Slovakia, and Moravia—were provinces of the Austro-Hungarian Empire. In 1780 schools in Bohemia and Moravia were forbidden to teach in Czech, and four years later the Austrian Empire decreed that German was to be the only official language. As a result, by the middle of the nineteenth century the Czech middle classes were German-speaking, while villagers still used their own dialects. This situation was a breeding ground for nationalism, and one of its first manifestations was the publication of a *History of Czech Literature* (1825) by the Director of the Prague Grammar School, Josef Jungmann. The next year brought the first opera written in Czech, *Dráteník* (*The Tinker*, Prague, 1826) by František Škroup (1801–62).

In the 1780s the English musicologist Dr Burney had called Bohemia 'Europe's conservatory', so impressed had he been by the quality of music-making in the region. Furthermore it was for Prague that Mozart had written his *Don Giovanni*, and that master had a high regard for the city's musical life and particularly admired the *Singspiele* composed by Jiří Antonín Benda (1722–95). With this background, it seems inevitable that the seeds of national opera would flower, as indeed they did through Bedřich Smetana (1824–84), a pupil of Jungmann in Prague. In 1848 he had composed a 'March for the Prague Students' Legion' during the revolution against the Austrians, for though he had been brought up as a German speaker, his commitment to the nationalist cause was firm. But it was not until he was thirty-two that he summoned sufficient confidence actually to write a letter in Czech, and throughout his life he had problems in coping with the language. A generation later the Swedish-speaking Sibelius was to have a similar experience in Finland.

Smetana lived in Sweden for the six years from 1856, working as a conductor, pianist and teacher, as well as composing symphonic poems modelled on those of Liszt. But he remained committed to Czech nationalism, and in 1861 he heard of a competition to encourage the creation of new Czech operas. Prizes were offered for the best scores, the regulations being that one opera should be based on the history of the Czech people, while the second 'should be of lighter content and taken from the national life of the people in Bohemia, Moravia, and Silesia'. Here, in a sentence, were the two approaches to national opera which would allow Smetana to develop his creative talents through eight works. Czech history was a natural subject for national opera; and as for village life, it was here that traditional ways and language had been best preserved.

Smetana set to work as soon as news of the competition reached him, starting the piano score of *The Brandenburgers in Bohemia* (Prague, 1866) early in 1862. Prague already had what was called the German Theatre for German or French works, but later in that same year the Provisional Theatre was opened, with an opera company as well as actors, to perform plays and operas in Czech, though not exclusively so. It was so called because the theatrical society responsible viewed it as a mere starting point, and the foundation stone for a new, larger, permanent and better equipped National Theatre was laid in 1868 by Smetana himself. In the meantime the repertory of Czech plays was far stronger than that of Czech operas, but the one existing opera, Škroup's *Dráteník*, was the second production there, the first having been Cherubini's *Les deux journées*, which although not nationalist, at least dealt with the concept of freedom. Initially, therefore, the Provisional Theatre's repertory broke little new ground, mainly producing popular Italian works. Nor were Czech operas necessarily successful with the public when they did appear, while German-speaking singers also found performing them difficult.

In 1863 Smetana submitted the full score of his opera *The Brandenburgers in Bohemia* to the competition judges. The epigraph on the title page revealed an awareness of the essential issue: 'Music, the language of feeling—words, the language of ideas.' He was awarded first prize, and in due course this patriotic opera received a triumphant première in the Provisional Theatre. Just a few months later, at the end of May 1866, it witnessed the first performance of his second opera, *The*

Bartered Bride, which did not immediately gain an enthusiastic reception. The gathering clouds of war may have contributed to its failure, for only a fortnight later the Austro-Prussian War broke out. After the Prussian victory at the Battle of Königgrätz in early July, Smetana felt compelled to flee Prague and live in rural seclusion, fearing that if they entered the city the Prussians might shoot him as the author of two nationalist operas.

But by the autumn Smetana was back in Prague, and he now became the conductor at the Provisional Theatre, where his wide experience enabled him to exert considerable influence on the development of Czech music. He had worked both as a composer and a performer, and during 1864–5 he was also music critic of the prominent newspaper *Narodni Lišty*. His reviews often reveal his views on opera, as when he wrote of *The Bohemian Girl* by the Irish composer Michael Balfe:

> Of all the weak operas which have been put on in our theatre from the very beginning this must be the weakest . . . It lacks well-defined situations and individual characters. The melodies have no connection with their contexts. They are suitable for quadrilles and ceremonial marches and are consequently much liked in dance halls and on parade grounds. The characters on stage simply divide up these melodies between them: all sing exactly the same despite their different personalities.

At the time Smetana wrote this he had been working with his librettist Karel Sabina on *The Bartered Bride*, which responded to the second of the two required categories in the national opera competition. The opera had an original design which was nearer a *Singspiel*, with spoken dialogue separating the musical numbers. However, the composer's four later revisions up to 1870 included the addition of material such as the polka, *skočna*, *furiant* and 'Beer Chorus' which did so much to make the opera popular, while two acts were expanded to three and dialogue was replaced by recitative.

The plot of *The Bartered Bride* tells of the love between Mařenka (soprano) and Jeník (tenor), which resists and finally overcomes her parents' scheme that she should marry a man she has never met. Since there is little reference in this opera to places, it could be set anywhere in rural Europe, and it is simply the music and the Czech language which give it its national flavour. The characters are general types too: impetuous lovers, older suitors and greedy parents. The part of Kečal, the pompous marriage-broker, was probably developed from that of Bett in Lortzing's comic opera *Zar und Zimmermann*, which had been in the Provisional Theatre's repertory during 1863. In 1875, when the opera had become enormously popular, Smetana wrote of it: 'I have already firmly decided to experiment whether I might be successful with a lighter style, in which I had not yet composed anything, so as to show my enemies that I could succeed perfectly well in small-scale musical forms.'

But what Smetana meant with this new approach was misunderstood by many critics; in fact he was bitterly upset when his opera was likened to the operettas of Offenbach, then all the rage in Prague: 'Did none of those gentlemen realise that my model was Mozart's comic opera?' Smetana much admired *The Marriage of Figaro*, and thought it 'an unsurpassable example of the most delightful moods and the most lively comic action without ever ceasing to be beautiful or descending into triviality'. Thus the bubbling *presto* of the overture, which Smetana wrote first, has the same exuberance as Mozart's. A cursory comparison reveals that *The Bartered Bride* indeed has many parallels with *The Marriage of Figaro* in character, plot, structure and basic themes: there are two pairs of lovers in each case, and both operas are resolved by the realisation that someone is a long-lost son and that there is cause for all-round reconciliation.

It is thus ironic that *The Bartered Bride* should have become the yardstick against which other Czech nationalist operas—whether by Smetana himself or by Dvořák, Fibich, even Janáček—are judged, since many of its set national pieces were late additions to the original concept. It is *The Bartered Bride*'s liveliness that has brought its international success; and that at least did stem from that most national of all the ingredients, the Czech prose of the original version's spoken dialogue, which remained when the sung recitatives were added.

Smetana's later operas have a more complex and serious approach, and none has matched the popularity of *The Bartered Bride*. Yet he felt his other projects to have been more ambitious, and when he spoke at the banquet celebrating the hundredth performance of *The Bartered Bride*, he described it as 'but a toy'. His next opera, *Dalibor* (Prague, 1868) returns to the heroic-historical stance. The ideas in it share the lofty nobility of Beethoven's *Fidelio*, and the two plots have a common theme in the wrongful imprisonment of the hero, but in *Dalibor* there is no happy ending. This hero's suffering was intended to reflect that of the Czech people, and sympathy for him is encouraged by the fact that he is a knight as well as a political hero. Dalibor (tenor) is rescued by his enemy's sister, Milada (soprano), who disguises herself as a boy, but the opera ends tragically, for she is fatally wounded and the remorseful Dalibor stabs himself. Smetana's adoption of the heroic style led to accusations of 'Wagnerism', and he was bitterly disappointed that this opera was relatively unsuccessful during his lifetime. In fact, dramatically the work seems closer to Verdi than to Wagner, and also uses Liszt's principle of 'thematic transformation', as in Dalibor's own theme, first played near the beginning and then used in various ways to bring cohesion and tension to the drama. The chorus often represent the Czech people, and their music has a feeling of peasant strength and stability. Like *Fidelio*, *Dalibor* has intense music and lighter contrasts: the hero's aria in Act I builds to a triumphant and logical climax with both chorus and orchestra, and there is a fine lyrical love duet in Act II. *Libuše* (Prague, 1881) was composed in 1872 but not performed until nine years later at the opening of the National Theatre. Shortly afterwards the building was gutted by fire, but public subscriptions soon raised enough money for another, which opened in 1883. In this, his fourth opera, Smetana at last felt that he had done justice to the Czech language. *Libuše*, perhaps the most ambitious and patriotic of all his operas, tells of the marriage of the foundress of the city of Prague to a wise peasant; and it is clearly an attempt to fuse his two previous styles, the historical and the national and rural. The solemnity of the pageant encourages declamatory vocal writing, although not at the expense of lyricism, and the composer's apt description of this work was 'a solemn festival tableau'.

By the time his next opera, *The Two Widows* (Prague, 1874), was completed, Smetana had begun to suffer from the deafness which plagued him for the rest of his life. Eventually he had to retire from conducting and the loss of fees brought financial hardship. However, *The Two Widows* is a lively and well characterised comedy. It was always a favourite of Richard Strauss, who may have used it as a model for his *Intermezzo*, and enjoyed it so much that he liked to make his visits to Prague coincide with performances.

Smetana's creativity was not halted by disability, however, and he completed two more operas, *The Kiss* (Prague, 1876) and *The Secret* (Prague, 1878), each of which had a Czech rural setting. The subtleties of characterisation and instrumentation are not, however, found in his last opera, *The Devil's Wall* (Prague, 1882), which suffers from a confused libretto. He called this 'a comic-romantic opera', a description which suggests that with each new opera he brought a fresh approach to the medium. Certainly he established a national identity and tradition for Czech opera, and his views about the nature of the form, expressed both as a composer and as a critic, influenced his successors strongly.

FROM DVOŘÁK TO WEINBERGER

During the nineteenth century only one other Czech composer emerged to rival Smetana in stature. This was Antonín Dvořák (1841–1904), whose reputation was achieved in forms other than opera, though his own view was unequivocal: 'I am seen as a composer of symphonies, but many years ago I proved that my main leaning was towards dramatic works.' This statement dates from his last year, and his career bears it out, for he always maintained his interest in the theatre and wrote eleven operas. He had come to know opera through playing the viola in the orchestra of the Provisional Theatre, and as a young man his first performed one, a comedy called *King and Charcoal Burner* (Prague, 1874), was rehearsed under Smetana but initially rejected because of its awkward vocal writing. He learned much from this salutary experience.

The international success of his *Moravian Duets* and *Slavonic Dances* only strengthened Dvořák's resolve to compose operas, and before 1880 he wrote three more. *The Cunning Peasant* (Prague, 1878) and *The Stubborn Lovers* (Prague, 1881), with its *buffo* bass, were comedies probably inspired by the example of Smetana, whom he greatly admired: '*The Bartered Bride* opened up the way for Czech light opera, indeed one may say that it created the genre.' On the other hand, *Wanda* (Prague, 1876) was a five-act grand opera on a Polish subject with an orchestral part that rather overshadows the singers. *Dimitrij* (Prague, 1882) is another grand opera that was initially successful; interestingly, its plot begins almost exactly in Russian history where that of *Boris Godunov* leaves off. *The Jacobin* (Prague, 1898) tells of a Czech 'prodigal son' who returns to his native Bohemia, and this setting was close to Dvořák's heart because it reminded him of his birthplace. Here he could indulge his lyrical gift, and the progression of scenes is highly successful; he preferred to make set pieces rather than Wagnerian through-composition the central feature of his style.

In 1892 Dvořák went to the United States, but while he was there opera remained a preoccupation. He contemplated setting Longfellow's *Hiawatha*, but decided instead on a thorough revision of *Dimitrij*. Discussions with his conductor friend Anton Seidl encouraged him to study the operas of many composers, including Meyerbeer, Verdi, Smetana and Wagner, to further his own operatic ends. When he returned from America in 1894 he seemed increasingly to be inspired by Czech folklore. *The Devil and Kate* (Prague, 1899) reveals also the close links existing for him between the two forms of opera and symphonic poem; there is, for instance, a splendid orchestral climax when the Devil describes his enormous red castle.

Fine though *The Devil and Kate* is, it is doubtless *Rusalka* (Prague, 1900) which is Dvořák's operatic masterpiece, for it brings together all his stylistic features. The libretto, by Jaroslav Kvapil, is a reworking of Hans Christian Andersen's *Little Mermaid*, and it allowed the composer to combine set pieces with an onward flow of drama. The music has much in common with his symphonic poem *The Water Sprite*, which is hardly surprising since *rusalki* were water creatures, and structurally this is Dvořák's most cohesive opera. There are several fine set pieces, of which the most famous is Rusalka's invocation to the moon. *Rusalka* was a triumph at the National Theatre; on the morning after the première Dvořák asked Kvapil for another libretto so that they could build on their success. When told there was none ready, he replied, 'Then write one quickly while I am in the mood!'

Dvořák's last opera, *Armida* (Prague, 1904), has tensions which arise from the love-duty conflict, and the scale is ambitious with some reliance on *leitmotif* technique and symphonic development. However, the heroic subject seems less suited to Dvořák's talents than the stories of magic or of the peasantry which he so spontaneously brought to life, though his commitment to opera remained wholehearted: 'In the last five years, I have composed nothing but opera; as long as God gives me strength, I would wish to devote all my powers to the composition of opera.' He declined all invitations to write other works during these years, devoting himself to the task which he believed to be 'the most important for the nation'.

Although Dvořák and Smetana have rightly become famous, other Czech composers made worthwhile contributions to opera. Dvořák's friend Zdeněk Fibich (1850–1900) wrote seven operas, the most famous being *Šárka* (Prague, 1897), a setting of the famous Czech legend in which the abandoned girl Šárka takes vengeance on the male sex, despite her love for one of them. Of the six operas of Josef Foerster (1859–1951), *Eva* (Prague, 1899) is perhaps strongest in conveying the emotions of the characters. Like Janáček's *Jenůfa*, *Eva* is based on a story by Gabriela Preissová, and the situation in both operas is similar—a closed village society, a central character humiliated in public, and a tragic ending, in this case suicide. Vitězslav Novák (1870–1949), with the comic *The Imp of Zvíkov* (Prague, 1915), the patriotic *Karlštejn* (Prague, 1916) and *The Lantern* (Prague, 1923), together with Otakar Ostrčil (1879–1935), whose *Johnny's Kingdom* (Brno, 1934) has been the most performed of his eight operas, also carried Czech opera into the twentieth century. Jaromir Weinberger (1896–1967) enjoyed a triumph with his *Schwanda the Bagpiper* (Prague, 1927), a lyrical work with fine dances which is firmly based, for all its modern date, on nineteenth-century principles. But Weinberger did not build upon his one success.

Leos Janáček (1854–1928) was only thirteen years younger than Dvořák, but his late recognition and development, and indeed his musical language, place him as a twentieth-century composer. His style emerged from those of his predecessors, and he maintained links with his native Moravia throughout his life. His earliest compositions reflected the lyricism of Dvořák: his first opera, *Šárka* (1888; performed Brno, 1925), on the familiar legend, preceded a short comic opera, *The Beginning of a Romance* (Brno, 1894).

It was not until he was fifty that the successful première of *Jenůfa* (Brno, 1904) effectively launched Janáček's career. Like Foerster's *Eva*, with which it is practically contemporary, it is based on a story by Gabriela Preissová dealing with the oppressive tensions in a village community resulting from the rejection by Steva (tenor) of Jenůfa (soprano), who carries his child. Her foster-mother, the *Kostelnička*, or sexton (contralto), takes the baby and drowns it in the hope of avoiding disgrace and securing a better future for Jenůfa. When the body is found she confesses her guilt. The composer's constant investigations into the nature of peasant speech and the sounds of rural life are here used so flexibly that the music can be both uncompromisingly forceful and supremely lyrical, so that great contrasts exist. An *ostinato* figuration in the orchestra, evoking the turning mill-wheel, pervades the opera as an obsessive fate-motif. This simple device is effective and typical of Janáček, who explained his theories in an article published in 1905:

> The melodic curves of speech are an expression of the complete organism and of all phases of its spiritual activity. They demonstrate whether a man is stupid or intelligent, sleepy or awake, tired or alert. They tell us whether he is a child or an old man, whether it is morning or evening, light or darkness, heat or frost, and disclose whether a person is alone or in company. The art of dramatic writing is to compose a melodic curve which will, as if by magic, immediately reveal a human being in one definitive phase of his existence.

But it is not for this reason alone that *Jenůfa* is an operatic masterpiece. All the aspects of the form are there: characterisation and feeling, the folk style of much of the music, and also the dramatic use of voices and orchestra.

Although *Jenůfa* was successful in Brno it was not produced in Prague. In the meantime Janáček completed his next opera, *Osud* (*Fate*, 1906; performed Brno, 1958), and his bitterness about his failure to gain wider recognition resulted in his discouraging another Brno première: the result was that *Fate* was never performed during his lifetime. When *Jenůfa* eventually received its Prague première in 1916, it was a triumph and his interest in opera revived.

The last twelve years of Janáček's life were to bring an astonishing creative achievement. Now in his sixties, he produced a stream of major works; the music covered a wide variety of genres, but the central one was opera. His later operas maintain the standards of *Jenůfa*, with masterly orchestral writing and a basic language relying on recurring rhythmic motifs. A theme of life-affirmation is common to them all, although the manner of delivery can change enormously: in the last three operas, it changes from a strip cartoon animal story (*The Cunning Little Vixen*) to a science-fiction time play (*The Makropoulos Affair*) to Dostoyevsky's biographical portrayal of Siberian prison life (*From the House of the Dead*).

The only Janáček opera to receive its first performance in the Czech capital was *The Excursions of Mr Brouček* (Prague, 1920), which was based on a pair of novels by Svatopluk Čech, hence the two halves of the opera, the first being an excursion to the moon and the second one back to the fifteenth century. It took some ten years to write overall; but of that time the second excursion took only a matter of months. The libretto had been the problem, for Janáček had collaborated with no fewer than nine librettists in part one of his opera: henceforth he did away with them altogether. The second excursion was set during the Hussite Wars, and therefore suited the feeling of nationalism that greeted the creation of the new Czech state after the First World War.

Káťa Kabanová (Brno, 1921) returned to the powerful social issues of *Jenůfa*. This opera is one of several works inspired by Kamila Stösslová, a young married woman with whom Janáček became infatuated (though there is no evidence of an actual love affair) and with whom he corresponded regularly. Based on Alexander Ostrovsky's play *The Storm*, it tells of a woman whose marriage is unhappy and who falls desperately in love with another man, with fatal consequences: she throws herself into the river when she can no longer abide the moral indignation of the local community. In a letter to Kamila, Janáček wrote revealingly: 'I know a most wonderful lady. I have her perpetually in my mind. My Káťa grows in her, in Kamila! This will be the most gentle and tender of my works . . . I never met greater love than in her. Through her may the opera be blessed.'

The opera also reflects his other great passion, which was Russia and Russian literature. He had contemplated an opera on Tolstoy's *Anna Karenina* several years before, and had only recently completed his orchestral rhapsody *Taras Bulba*, inspired by Gogol. He said too that his one brief visit to Moscow in 1896 had been the greatest experience of his life. *Káťa Kabanová* is a masterpiece of concise drama and psychological understanding where he achieved his ideal of setting speech musically without recourse to set numbers and forms.

Janáček's instinct and sympathy for rural life comes most clearly into focus with *The Cunning Little Vixen* (Brno, 1924), in which he transformed a newspaper cartoon strip into an affirmation of the cycle of life. The rustic characters and the animals afford splendid opportunities for designers, but the music is inspired too, especially the sunrise scene and the moving conclusion in which the young vixen appears and succeeds her dead mother, thus confirming the renewal of life. The natural order is found also in *The Makropoulos Affair* (Brno, 1926), but here the central character has taken a potion that has made her immortal and thus condemned her to misery. Emilia Marty dominates the opera, and her music has a rich flow of ideas, of which the composer said: 'This time everything flies about completely out of control. I don't know yet how to get the ideas into order.' The music, rather than the staging, is much more the focus of attention than it was in *The Vixen* because there is comparatively little action.

The same is probably true of the final opera, *From the House of the Dead* (Brno, 1930). Janáček's outlook was expressed in the quotation he placed at the head of the score: 'In every human being there is a spark of God', and his libretto is a free adaptation of Dostoyevsky's study of life in a Siberian prison camp. The mood is serious, but has moments of lighter relief. The complex rhythmic textures, often using unusual orchestration with an emphasis on percussion, give the music a quality unique even in Janáček, but it was typical of him to try to break new ground even at the age of seventy-four. Yet he remained true to his credo: 'The study I have made of the musical aspects of spoken language has led me to the conviction that all the melodic and rhythmic mysteries of music can be explained by reference to the melody and rhythm of spoken language.' For Janáček, folksong was linked to the rhythms of speech, an attitude which made him the heir of Mussorgsky. As a result, his music is seldom sophisticated, although the control of material over both long and short time-spans is absolute. In general, a key is chosen for a mood and then maintained until the plot brings the need for a change: love scenes tend to be in D flat major.

Janáček was a modernist who sought to extend the boundaries of the possible in order to achieve dramatic expression, but always with a total commitment to his beliefs, for he was never interested in technique for its own sake: 'I communicate because there is truth in my work; truth to its very limit. Truth does not exclude beauty. On the contrary, there should be more and more truth and beauty. Life is young. It is the spring. I am not afraid of living: I like it terribly.'

MARTINŮ

Bohuslav Martinů (1890–1959), though born in Bohemia, spent nearly all his career outside his homeland: in Paris, the United States, and Switzerland. Martinů was prolific, but though his output is uneven all fourteen of his operas are of interest. Although he had written music before he left Czechoslovakia, his creative life only really began when he went to Paris in the early 1920s to study with Roussel: he had felt drawn to the French capital ever since falling under the spell of French music, and especially Debussy's *Pelléas et Mélisande*, before the First World War. His first mature compositions date from after he was thirty, and reflect a range of musical styles which in his operas correspond to his eclectic literary taste.

Martinů's first opera, *The Soldier and the Dancer* (Brno, 1928), is a three-act comedy after Plautus's *Pseudolus* which owes much to Offenbach. Its most striking feature is a Black Bottom number whose refrain is sung through a megaphone, an effect which also recalls the Paris of the period. Even before it was complete, Martinů had begun his second opera. This was *The Tears of the Knife* (1928; performed Brno, 1968), a one-act jazz piece in seven scenes, timed to last a mere twenty minutes. It is predominantly surrealist, for a hanged corpse hovers above the stage over a wedding ceremony, and at the end the hanged man returns to life in the guise of Satan. This approach was continued in *The Three Wishes* (1929; performed Brno, 1971), a more substantial work whose complex orchestral textures are exemplified in the powerful symphonic interlude entitled 'The Departure', used to move the action from Paris to New York. But the most ambitious idea is the attempt to introduce film into the staging: a play within a play in a film studio, with actors identifying themselves with the characters. While each actor is on stage his imagination is portrayed simultaneously on the screen behind, and the mixture of reality and dreams was a world to which the composer would return. As in Stravinsky's *Oedipus Rex*, a chorus comments on the action, and the musical mixture of jazz, speech-song, and advanced harmonies owes a good deal to Krenek's *Jonny spielt auf* (*see* Chapter 18). Initially the opera was judged to be unstageable, and more than forty years passed before it was produced.

Martinů's fourth opera, *The Miracle of Our Lady, or The Plays of Mary* (Brno, 1935), comprises a cycle of four mystery plays. Such plays had been performed in twelfth-century Prague, but the immediate inspiration came from those the composer had seen outside Notre Dame in Paris. Furthermore, he must have been aware of Debussy's *Le Martyr de St Sébastien* and Honegger's *King David* and *Judith*. He unequivocally stated his own attitude with regard to religion:

> As far as faith goes, I think it does not play a big role here; I myself am not pursuing any religious aims, and I chose these subjects because they are well suited to my music, i.e. treating them in folk style, and then also they permit me, as fairy tales in fact, quite logically to throw away all the inessentials of contemporary opera. And anyway, this work is a return to the old theatre, and that is the theatre I was looking for. It has been conceived, not in a religious sense, but in a folk or popular way.

The first part of *The Miracle of our Lady*, called *The Wise and Foolish Virgins*, is based on a Provençal folk tale, and its reflective character is emphasised through an unaccompanied chorus and an orchestra without violins. This is followed by *Mariken de Nimèque*, in which the heroine eventually achieves salvation, but which uses dancing almost as much as singing; there is also a narrator and a full chorus. The third part, *The Nativity*, is a short folk cantata, whereas *Sister Pasqualina* is the longest of the four parts, with a story that allows for music of expressive power and sustained argument. Pasqualina is a young novice who leaves her convent to follow the knight with whom she has fallen in love. When he dies, she is accused of his murder, but she is proved innocent and returns to the convent where she finds her place has been taken by the Virgin Mary. The work thus occupies the world of dreams with which Martinů identified, and as in the original play there is a combination of song and dance, mime and narration. Acts I and III are designed as shorter introductions to Acts II and IV, and now that a recording has allowed *The Miracle of Our Lady* to be properly assessed, it emerges as one of Martinů's finest achievements.

Next Martinů wrote two radio operas, *The Voice of the Forest* and *The Comedy on the Bridge* (both Czech Radio, 1935). The former has a folk character with tuneful arias and vigorous dances, and is based on the tale of a hunter who is kidnapped and then rescued by his wife, whereas in the latter there is a timeless plot after an eighteenth-century play by Václav Klicpera. It deals with a bridge which links the towns on either side of a river, and during a war when friends want to visit one another the authorities allow exit permits but none for entry. Thus several become trapped on the bridge, only to be released with the signing of an armistice. Martinů here uses fanfares, clashing harmonies for the opposing factions, and broken recitatives for the guards, a mixture which allows this one-act comic opera to make a brilliant impression. In *The Suburban Theatre* (Brno, 1936) the composer chose a folk theme, the entertainment provided by travelling players at a fair, and this brought a simpler harmonic language and swiftly moving scenes. Martinů wrote: 'I'm still following the idea of my own theatre . . . and have now found myself in the sphere of the *commedia dell'arte*. I should like to do it rather as a fair or a circus—in brief, as a folk spectacle.'

The single-act *opera buffa Alexander bis* (1937; performed Mannheim, 1964) preceded the work commonly held as Martinů's operatic masterpiece. *Julietta* (Prague, 1938) provided him with his first triumph in opera. It is based on a play by Georges Neveux dealing with the relationship between reality, dreams and memory. The orchestral textures are inventive and impressive, for the composer had found a subject which captured his imagination: 'Through the network of unforeseen situations and illogical conclusions runs the scarlet thread of the human mind, of memory, on which the history of our actions and of our life depends. Here, however, we are faced with a world in which the thread of memory is cut . . . It is basically a psychological and philosophical problem: What is man? What am I? What are you? What is truth?'

The central character is the tenor Michel, the only person with a memory, and Julietta is his ideal woman. But is she real? This dilemma involves the music in moods of expressive intensity, and accordingly it is passionate and richly textured, with surges of sound in the style of Janáček, whose influence is also to be found in the declamatory vocal line. The opera is haunted by Julietta's music, and there is little distinction between aria and recitative. *Julietta* meant a great deal to Martinů, and both chronologically and musically it is the central work in his output.

During the 1940s, his years in America, Martinů devoted little time to opera, and it was not until 1952 that he returned to the form. *What Men Live By* (New York, 1953), a chamber piece for seven characters, has a rather static quality because it was intended for television and not the stage: this setting of one of Tolstoy's *Tales for the People* was among the first such ventures. *The Marriage* (New York, 1953), after Gogol, employs the classical forms of recitative, aria and ensemble, with some attractive dances to provide contrast. But these operas were eclipsed by *Mirandolina* (1954; performed Prague, 1959), a comedy which Martinů described as a 'light, uncomplicated thing, with something of Goldoni'. The plot concerns the efforts of a hostess to seduce one of her guests, a confirmed hater of women; but having succeeded, she rejects him on the grounds that her purpose was really to test the fidelity of Fabrizio, the humble waiter. *Mirandolina* seems Martinů's most effective comedy; the characterisation is skilful, while the Italian atmosphere is captured in the interludes, and in the exciting coloratura of the soprano title role.

Martinů remained interested in opera until the end of his life. *Ariadne* (1958; performed Gelsenkirchen, 1961) is based like *Julietta* on a play by Neveux, but its genesis was unusual. So impressed was the composer by the broadcast performances of Maria Callas that he determined to write a chamber opera for her, including a virtuoso role with a wide *tessitura* (vocal range), but basically lyrical. She never sang the role, however.

A series of short scenes also provides the basis of Martinů's last opera, *The Greek Passion* (composed 1956–9; performed Zurich, 1961). In fact this is his only tragic opera: it was based upon Nikos Kazantzakis's novel *Christ Recrucified.* Martinů cut the four hundred pages of the book to just forty typed sheets, omitting some characters. Again there is a play within a play, in which the characters in the village Passion Play take on the nature of their roles when a group of refugees arrive. The curtain falls with nothing resolved but with the tragic issues having been effectively presented, as the refugees go off, still homeless. Martinů researched the hymns and chants of Greek Orthodox music in a search for authenticity, and his music has both range and power. The problem is the producer's: there are many short scenes and if there is to be a cumulative effect, they must not stop the flow of the music.

Martinů's fourteen operas cover a very wide range, and now that more of them have been staged and recorded, it is possible to rank him among the twentieth century's great composers. The following passage, written in 1934, shows how he complements the methods of Janáček without necessarily contradicting them:

Action is not the same in spoken drama as in opera, where it is sometimes delayed by the singing and replaced by a musical extension—a lyric or dramatic passage inserted into the work, during which action partly or altogether ceases. And though by obeying the laws of spoken drama, we may occasionally preserve a purely musical expression, it is not always in the interests of the work.

15

LATER FRENCH OPERA

New trends in French opera. Massenet and Charpentier. Messager to Roussel. Ravel. Ibert and Les six.

After the French defeat in the Franco-Prussian War of 1870–1, Parisian operatic life resumed its course in a somewhat changed form. A reaction against foreign influence was symbolised by the foundation in 1871 of the Société Nationale de Musique with its motto *Ars gallica* and its function as a forum for new French concert music. Bizet's untimely death twelve weeks after the first performance of *Carmen* in 1875 marked a milestone in French musical history, in that opera now came to lose its paramount place and musicians gave more attention to oratorio and instrumental music.

The Belgian-born composer César Franck (1822–90) composed two four-act operas in his last decade, *Hulda* and *Ghiselle*, but neither was left quite complete or received performance during his lifetime. His pupil Vincent d'Indy, who helped to realise the score of *Ghiselle* for its première (Monte Carlo, 1896), declared later that 'Franck's genius did not tend to the theatrical . . . his operas are, to tell the truth, less dramatic than his oratorios'. D'Indy (1851–1931) himself composed a handful of operas, mostly to his own libretti, of which the best remembered are *Fervaal* (Brussels, 1897) and *L'étranger* (Brussels, 1903). Fervaal himself, a heroic tenor role, is a Celtic chieftain engaged in battle with Saracen invaders of France who is wounded and restored to health by a Saracen enchantress, and the story is of a love-and-duty conflict, ending with a fine chorus on the Gregorian melody '*Pange lingua*'. If the large orchestra and use of *leitmotif* in *Fervaal* suggest Wagner, *L'étranger* is simpler and includes some folksong melodies, though its tale of the expiation of illicit love through death still relates to *Tristan und Isolde*. D'Indy's later 'sacred history' called *La légende de Saint Christophe* (Paris, 1920) is less the story of the saint than an attack on freethinkers and 'false artists' who express their 'hate for ideal art . . . we make and follow fashion . . . no more rules, no more studies': but this doctrinaire attack by an elderly composer on younger artists hardly made for successful opera.

Wagner had encouraged French composers to use their own national legends, and his musical language and concept of music drama became so influential that he dominated the whole French intellectual climate. The scholar Romain Rolland was later to write (1908) that 'Writers not only discussed musical subjects, but judged painting, literature and philosophy from a Wagnerian point of view ... The whole universe was seen and judged by the thought of Bayreuth.' A *Revue Wagnérienne*, founded in 1885 by literary figures rather than musicians, promoted 'the study of Wagner as poet, thinker and creator of a new art form'. It laid out its creed in its third issue, berating musicians who in its view were still essentially conservative:

They simply continue the tradition of Meyerbeer's melodrama or Adam's operetta which they learned at the Conservatoire, and adjust them to modern taste. These gentlemen have now discovered the scores of Wagner and as musicians are struck by the ingenious nature of the orchestral development, the powerful instrumentation, the harmonic richness, the brilliant use of the whole *technical* apparatus which is all that they can see. So they borrow his principle of thematic development, his instrumentation and his harmonic idiom, which they imitate as best they can. The milder spirits among them attenuate, the bolder exaggerate these 'Wagnerian' traits: all equally fail to understand them ... So they use *leitmotifs* and we get the 'letter theme' or the 'bishop theme'. They have found that Wagner gave the orchestra an important role, so they load their scores with noisy instrumental combinations and accompany a sentimental romance with the most erudite dissonances ...

Be that as it may, many composers went to Bayreuth and returned in varying degrees touched by Wagner's spell, among them d'Indy, Chabrier, Chausson, Saint-Saëns, Messager, Fauré and Debussy. The scholar Martin Cooper has called *Gwendoline* (Brussels, 1886), by Emmanuel Chabrier (1841–94), 'perhaps the most notable monument of French Wagnerism'. Here, in another conflict of love and duty in the accepted manner, the Viking King Harald loves the daughter of his Saxon prisoner: refusing to kill Harald on her father's command, Gwendoline kills herself. *Leitmotifs* and chromatic harmony abound, as well as a sword song for Harald and a spinning song in Act I, Scene 4 ('*Blonde aux yeux de pervenche*') based on an Irish tune, while the orchestral prelude to Act II has been seen as a link between Wagner and Debussy. Yet there is an individual idiom at work also, and one that is recognisably Chabrier's own, vital and colourful. The same composer's vivid *Le roi malgré lui* (*The*

King in Spite of Himself, Paris, 1887) is an *opéra comique* about the future French King Henri III and a plot against him which he foils by disguising himself and joining the conspirators. Another composer, Ernest Chausson (1855–99), was recognisably Wagnerian in his unfinished *Le roi Arthus* (Brussels, 1903), a 'lyric drama' to his own libretto, rich in *leitmotifs*, in which an old king fixes 'upon all things a gaze free from anger' and embraces a faith in pure, lofty ideals.

Even where no attempt was made to imitate Wagner's musical style, these operas owe something to him in their search for a new kind of naturalism and expressive force. As a Frenchman caught up in this new aesthetic movement which originated in Germany but which could have universal validity, Chabrier wrote:

> I want my work to be beautiful throughout, and there are thirty-six forms of beauty. Never the same colour, and everywhere variety, shape and above all vitality. Naivety too if possible, but that is the hardest of all.

This composer also wrote operettas and *opéra bouffe* in a more consciously French tradition, and indeed made his name with the *bouffe* piece *L'étoile* (*The Star*, Paris, 1877). The composer Reynaldo Hahn referred to it as 'that rare jewel of French operetta in which the buffoonery and poetic verve of this other Offenbach are presented with all the musical charm, elegance and richness he possessed without knowing it or seeking for it'. *Une éducation manquée* (*A Missed Education*, Paris, 1879) had less of an instant success but is also a delightfully Gallic work.

Camille Saint-Saëns (1835–1921) knew Wagner personally and visited Bayreuth. But he stands a little aside from some of his contemporaries in being more classically French in his standpoint, and perhaps looking back with nostalgia to the more rhetorical kind of grand opera. His *Samson et Dalila* (Weimar, 1877, conducted by Liszt) has a Biblical subject and was first conceived as an oratorio. Perhaps because of this it did not reach the French stage until 1890 at Rouen, being given at the Paris Opéra two years later. The two principal characters dominate the work, but not at the expense of the atmosphere and pace. Delilah (mezzo) has a fine aria known in English as 'Softly awakes my heart' ('*Mon coeur s'ouvre à ta voix*') which is actually in part a duet since Samson (tenor) joins in. But the composer's special skill lies in his effective writing for the chorus. His other serious operas, including a *Henry VIII* (Paris, 1883), featuring an English tune he found in the Buckingham Palace library, are virtually forgotten today: it seems that for all their solid workmanship they are not very theatrical. However, his early *opéra comique La princesse jaune* (*The*

Yellow Princess, Paris, 1872) has an attractive orientalism: Fauré called this Japanese piece 'witty, tender and splendidly coloured: an exquisite *divertissement*'.

Edouard Lalo (1823–92) was another relatively conservative composer who, like Saint-Saëns, is remembered chiefly for a single very successful opera. *Le roi d'Ys* (Paris, 1888) is a story of jealousy in which two sisters love Mylio (tenor): the rejected sister Margared (mezzo) lets in the sea to flood the Breton coastal town of Ys on the wedding night but then in remorse kills herself so that the patron saint of Ys will intervene to save the town. The score has vigorous melodic and rhythmic invention and effective orchestral writing, with a fresh and elegant wedding scene in Act III and another featuring an offstage organ and supernatural voices, while Saint Corentin himself has churchlike music and the rival sisters, Rozenn (soprano) and Margared, are well contrasted.

Léo Delibes (1836–91) produced several operettas in the *bouffe* tradition before his three operas *Le roi l'a dit* (*The King has Spoken*, Paris, 1873), *Jean de Nivelle* (Paris, 1880) and *Lakmé* (Paris, 1883). He was in turn a chorister, church organist and opera coach at the Théâtre-Lyrique and Opéra, and *Lakmé* in particular shows his stage flair and musical charm and skill. The opera tells of the doomed love of a British officer in India, Gérald (tenor), for a Brahmin priest's daughter called Lakmé, who in the end commits suicide. But despite this serious story the music is sparkling and lyrical in a mildly exotic way, and includes the heroine's 'Bell Song' (*Où va la jeune hindoue?*), one of the most famous of *coloratura* arias. At the same time, her father Nilakantha (bass) and Gérald are also well drawn, so that the opera is more than just a vehicle for a star soprano. Delibes's last opera, *Kassya* (Paris, 1893), was set in Spain: this '*drame lyrique*' was still in vocal score at his death and was orchestrated by Massenet.

MASSENET AND CHARPENTIER

Jules Massenet (1842–1912) was the son of a music teacher who studied at the Paris Conservatoire with Ambroise Thomas and won the Prix de Rome in 1863, gaining valuable experience also as a percussionist in the Opéra orchestra. His first opera to be produced was an *opéra comique* called *La grand'tante* (*The Great-aunt*, Paris, 1867), but his position as a leading opera composer was only established with *Le roi de Lahore* (Paris, 1877). This was an oriental tale in which King Alim (tenor) and his minister Scindia (baritone) alike love Sita (soprano), and after Alim's murder by Scindia he returns from death to Sita who then kills herself to be united with him in heaven. *Hérodiade* (Brussels, 1881) tells the Salome story with a difference: here the prophet John the Baptist admits his love for her and is executed by a jealous Herod, after which she stabs herself. If some Wagnerian influence is evident here in the use of *leitmotif* and heavy brass writing, Massenet still remained himself in his portrayal of a sweetly sensuous woman. Such soprano roles were to be a feature of his work, and the reformed courtesans Thaïs and Manon and even his early portrait of the not dissimilar Mary Magdalene in a *drame sacré* of 1873 are musically depicted with what d'Indy called a 'discreet and pseudo-religious eroticism'. Massenet himself said with wry humour: 'I don't believe in all this creeping Jesus stuff—but the public likes it and we must always agree with the public.'

With *Manon* (Paris, 1884), Massenet achieved his greatest success. This opera is based on the Abbé Prévost's novel used later also by Puccini in *Manon Lescaut*, and tells of a courtesan and her idealistic younger lover the Chevalier des Grieux (tenor); eventually she is condemned to transportation and dies in his arms. The original novel was set in 1731, and the music evokes the period in dances which provide a foil to the dramatic tensions. Although des Grieux is more involved than the self-absorbed Manon there is an effective love duet in Act III after he has despairingly decided to become a priest and she then persuades him to go away with her instead—here the full orchestra is effectively kept in reserve until the resolution of the climax. The scholar Martin Cooper has suggested that every scene in this opera is 'no more than the *décor* for Manon's amorous escapades'. This is too harsh a judgement, but like most Massenet heroes, des Grieux is not a very strong character in his own right but rather a boy 'in love with love', as Cooper puts it. The success of *Manon* was such that the composer was persuaded to provide it with a one-act sequel, *Le portrait de Manon* (Paris, 1894).

The protagonist in *Werther* (Vienna, 1892) is made of only slightly sterner stuff than des Grieux. When this commission from the Austrian capital came after *Manon* had been performed there, Massenet already had his opera ready, for on a trip to Germany he had been inspired by Goethe's novel *Die Leiden des jungen Werthers*, a tale of a young intellectual who suffers and finally dies for love. He wrote: 'Such rapturous and ecstatic passion brought tears to my eyes. What moving scenes and thrilling moments it would bring about! *Werther* it was!'

This opera is unusual for Massenet in that the central character is a man. Werther (tenor) is twenty-three and falls in love with Charlotte (mezzo), who returns his affection although engaged to Albert (baritone). Werther leaves, but cannot stay away, and returning to find her married he asks for Albert's pistols and shoots himself, knowing that only thus can he free her and himself from the bonds of their passion. A recurring *leitmotif* is associated with hopeless love and there is a near-hysterical tension in the final Act IV music of Werther's death. Such a story alone can hardly spread over a full-length opera, however, and it has many dramatic tributaries such as Werther's arrival at Charlotte's father's house in Act I, where he sings of his joy in this family home, and his later flowing and lyrical outburst in A flat major as he sees Charlotte with her younger brothers and sisters, '*O spectacle idéal d'amour et d'innocence, où mes yeux et mon coeur sont ravis à la fois!*' Albert is less fully drawn dramatically and musically, though he has a quietly domestic exchange with Charlotte in Act II after their marriage, '*Voici trois mois que nous sommes unis*', and he is effective when he coldly hands the pistols to Charlotte at the end of Act III to be passed on to Werther and then leaves the room 'with an angry gesture'. Her indecisiveness, a feature throughout, is symbolised in the actions that follow: she hands them to the maid to give to Werther but almost at once regrets doing so and rushes to the dying man to join him in a final exchange that occupies no less than twenty pages of the vocal score and thus stretches even an opera-goer's credulity rather too far. An effective irony is provided in this scene by the offstage children's voices singing a joyful Christmas carol.

Massenet's other operas include *Le Cid* (Paris, 1885), a treatment of the heroic Spanish story that can hardly have suited him and which failed, as did the spectacular *opéra romanesque* called *Esclarmonde* (Paris, 1889), a work in which some have seen Wagner's influence, for example in the semi-recitative of the vocal writing. *Thaïs* (Paris, 1894) is set in fourth-century Egypt and tells of a courtesan converted but then also loved by the monk Athanaël (baritone): its famous 'Meditation' featuring a solo violin is an orchestral intermezzo in Act II. Some element of *verismo* plays a part in *La navarraise* (London, 1894), with its story of love and war set in the Pyrénées and, for Massenet, quite vehement in style. *Cendrillon* (Paris, 1899) is a 'fairy opera' on the Cinderella story. In *Sapho* (Paris, 1897) we return to the world of a *femme fatale*, the artist's model Fanny Legrand who is loved by the country boy Jean Gaussin. Massenet was to create further woman-centred operas in his *Ariane* (Paris, 1906), *Thérèse* (Monte Carlo, 1907) and *Cléopâtre* (Monte Carlo, 1914), but these later works remain almost unknown.

However, in *Le jongleur de Notre-Dame* (Monte Carlo, 1902), based on a story by Anatole France, Massenet broke new ground in that, save for two angels, there are only men's voices. The story is of a wandering entertainer in medieval times who becomes a monk: ashamed of his lack of education, he uses his existing talents to dance and sing before a statue of the Virgin. The composer called this a miracle play and 'my faith'. But the opera is far from solemn and has vivid crowd scenes, a drinking song ('*Alléluia du vin*'), and a cloister rehearsal of a motet. In fact the monks' comic cook Boniface is drawn as strikingly as the *jongleur* Jean (tenor). *Chérubin* (Monte Carlo, 1903) is a comedy after Mozart's *Figaro* which invents further amorous adventures for the lively boy Cherubino. Though not Massenet's last opera, *Don Quichotte* (Monte Carlo, 1910) was his last success. Described as a 'heroic comedy', it is a reworking of the famous story of eccentric knightly deeds by Cervantes, and was composed as a vehicle for the Russian bass Chaliapin, who created the title role. Perhaps the best epitaph for Massenet is the one provided by Debussy, himself more than a little influenced by the older man:

> For Massenet, music was never the cosmic voice heard by Bach and Beethoven: to him it was rather a delightful avocation ... The harmonies are like enlacing arms, the melodies are the necks we kiss: we gaze into women's eyes to learn at any cost what lies behind ... Fortune, being a woman, certainly ought to treat Massenet kindly and even on occasions be unfaithful to him ... Massenet was the most truly loved of all contemporary musicians. His brethren could not easily forgive this power of pleasing which is strictly speaking a gift ... a delightful kind of fame, the secret envy of many of those great purists who can only enjoy the rather laboured respect of the cognoscenti.

Gustave Charpentier (1860–1956) was Massenet's pupil, and his fame really rests on a single work, the opera *Louise* (Paris, 1900). This is a *verismo* piece in that it is set in the lower levels of Parisian society, and the composer knew them well, having been born into a poor provincial family—his father was a baker—and then becoming a Bohemian student in Montmartre with 'an active distaste for authority' who then surprised everyone by winning the Prix de Rome in 1887.

Louise was Charpentier's first stage work. He wrote his own libretto as early as 1890 and read it to a group of friends, who suggested that he reduced what they saw as crude realism in favour of a more lyrical style. Taking their advice at least in part, he completed the score in 1896, and it was accepted by Albert Carré, the newly-appointed Director of the Opéra-Comique, two years later. His reputation had grown in the meantime, and although he nearly starved during 1899, the première in the following February was a triumph not only at the box office but also artistically. Paul Dukas expressed the feelings of many when he wrote,

'The first and last acts are the work of a master; the other two are those of an artist; the whole is the work of a man.' At one performance four hundred seats were given away to the dressmakers, the *midinettes*, of Paris, and Charpentier went on to found the Conservatoire Populaire Marie Pinson in 1892, an institution that gave free musical tuition to working girls. However, after *Louise*, Charpentier was curiously slow to continue his creative career. Eventually he went on to write a 'lyric poem' called *Julien* (Paris, 1913), but although this succeeded at first it has proved unable to stand in the repertory beside its illustrious predecessor.

Some of the praise of *Louise* was earned on social grounds. It was a drama of women's liberation and hailed as such by the cultural and political left wing: scenes included a family supper and workshop life, while many characters including ragmen and pea-sellers use a broad Parisian *argot*, being much more genuinely working-class than Puccini's Bohemians. 'Free love', parent–child relations and sheer poverty are other issues raised in this opera, and the imagination is stirred also by a mysterious figure who has been called a personification of Parisian pleasures, the Noctambulist or nightwalker. The composer said, '*Louise* represents a period of my life . . . that's why I need ten years to write a work—I need to live first.' He said he wrote it instinctively, but it is clear that this admirer of the passionate and impulsive Berlioz also knew his Gounod and, to judge from the use of *leitmotif,* Wagner. For all its *verismo* nature, *Louise* was conceived at much the same time as the Italian works usually thought of as inaugurating that movement, Mascagni's *Cavalleria rusticana* and Leoncavallo's *Pagliacci.* Charpentier wrote:

> I wished to give the stage . . . the lyric impression of the sensations that I reap in our beautiful, fairy-like modern life. Perhaps I see this as in a fever, but that's my right, for the street intoxicates me. The essential point of the drama is the coming together, the clashing, of two feelings in Louise's heart: love which binds her to her family, to her father, to her fear of leaving suffering behind her; and on the other hand, the irresistible longing for liberty, pleasure, happiness, love, the cry of her being which demands to live as she wishes. Passion will conquer because it is served by a mysterious helper which has little by little breathed its dream into her young soul— Paris, the voluptuous city, great city of light, pleasure and joy which calls her towards an undaunted future . . .

So the seamstress Louise (soprano) leaves her parents for her lover, the poet Julien (tenor), after their refusal to her marriage. Act III shows them romantically happy together, and she sings her famous aria '*Depuis le jour*', with its abundantly flowering lyricism. A festive party takes place in which she is crowned as the Muse of Montmartre, but during this her nagging mother appears to beg her to return to nurse her sick and anxious father, a kindly man, and in Act IV she is once again with her parents. But the call of love and Paris is too strong, and she finally leaves her parents once more at the end of the opera.

However, not all musicians were as enthusiastic about *Louise* as the public. We have already quoted Debussy on Massenet. Here he is on Charpentier's opera:

> It seems to me that this work had to be. It supplies only too well the need for that cheap beauty and idiotic art that has such appeal. You see what this Charpentier has done: he has taken the cries of Paris which are so delightfully human and, like a rotten Prix de Rome, turned them into sickly cantilenas . . . The sly dog!

But perhaps this was simply a restatement of Debussy's general view of *verismo*, 'a triumph of beer-hall music in the opera house' for which he had nothing but scorn, writing in 1913 of Italian *verismo* operas that 'the characters throw themselves at each other . . . in these one-act operas very little music need be written'. On the other hand, Richard Strauss adored *Louise*, and told Romain Rolland firmly: 'My dear friend, that's Montmartre. The French are like that . . . This is the picture we have of you in Germany, and very good and true it is. Every people has its faults. These are yours. You seem not to like the work?'

MESSAGER TO ROUSSEL

André Messager (1853–1929) studied with Saint-Saëns and Fauré and became a versatile musician: composer, pianist, critic, opera administrator, and the first conductor of Debussy's *Pelléas et Mélisande* – which is dedicated to him—and Charpentier's *Louise*. He was thirty when he began his career as a composer of operettas, and this continued until his death. He made his name with *La basoche* (Paris, 1890), with its title satirically meaning *The Lawmen*, and thereafter followed a number of Parisian successes including *Madame Chrysanthème* (1893), with a similar story to *Madama Butterfly* except that the heroine is deserted by a French naval officer, *Les p'tites Michu* (1897) and above all *Véronique* (1898). His success with *La basoche* in London led also to the composition of operettas for England such as *Mirette* (London, 1894) and *Monsieur Beaucaire* (Birmingham, 1919)—a work which despite its title had an English libretto based on Booth Tarkington's novel and which starred the English soprano Maggie Teyte, whose real name was Tate. The language should have given him little trouble, since he had married an Irish wife—herself a musician—in 1895. In one of his last operettas, *L'amour masqué* (Paris, 1923) his libretto was provided by Sacha Guitry (1885–1957), a playwright, producer and actor who was a leading figure in the lighter theatre, and Guitry and the celebrated singer Yvonne Printemps took the principal roles.

As musical director of the Opéra-Comique and later the Opéra, Messager conducted many Wagner performances and revived operas by Gluck and Rameau. He was also an occasional visitor to London's Covent Garden who conducted *Don Giovanni*, *Carmen* and *Faust* there. He wrote influential criticism for the French daily *Le Figaro*, and was a respectable pianist who liked to join Fauré in their jointly composed quadrille duet on themes from Wagner's *Ring* with the tongue-in-cheek title *Souvenirs de Bayreuth* (ca 1895). Fauré said of him that he was 'one of the first pilgrims to Bayreuth and [able] to play Wagner by heart at a time when he was still unknown in Paris'. As for his general taste, he was 'familiar with everything, knowing it all, fascinated by anything new'.

Reynaldo Hahn (1875–1947), born in Venezuela, came to Paris at the age of three and in time became a Massenet pupil at the Conservatoire; he also admired Messager for the 'neatness in all he did'. His *L'île du rêve* (Paris, 1898) is dedicated to Massenet 'in affectionate gratitude' and its mild exoticism is marked by its designation as 'a Polynesian idyll in three acts'. Hahn knew Proust and wrote piano pieces for the author's anthology *Les plaisirs et les jours* (1896), and he may have served as a partial model (Debussy was another) for the composer Vinteuil in *A la recherche du temps perdu*. A careful craftsman with a gift for melodic charm and neat instrumentation, Hahn profoundly admired Mozart and actually composed a light opera called *Mozart* (Paris, 1925) to a Sacha Guitry libretto dealing with the boy composer's visits to Paris. His most successful operetta was *Ciboulette* (Paris, 1923), which had in its principal male role the baritone Jean Périer who created the roles of Pelléas (though this is usually a tenor role), Ravel's muleteer Ramiro in *L'heure espagnole* and, in France, the consul Sharpless in *Madama Butterfly* – a fact reminding us of the fruitful interchange existing between the serious and lighter stage in France. As for the title of this operetta, meaning *Chives*, it is perhaps one that could only have been chosen in a country famous for its use of herbs in cooking. Hahn's talents were not confined to the lighter field, however, and later in life he composed two substantial Shakespearean operas, *Le marchand de Venise* and *Beaucoup de bruit pour rien* (both Paris, 1935 and 1936). But for its time *The Merchant* was a conservative work, a number opera with recitatives and arias and an orchestra playing only a subordinate role. At first it was very well received, but it has been neglected since. If not a genius, Hahn was a good craftsman who was proud of his skill. He once said:

> I have been composing music since the age of eight. I've lived in it all my life like a fish in water. I'm not keen on pedants . . . The day you construct, without anyone's advice or help, a four-act opera and it is criticised, you'll realise the disproportion existing between the work you have done and the remarks of those who talk about it.

Paul Dukas (1865–1935) is a major figure in French music: a composer, scholar and teacher who was on friendly terms with all his important contemporaries. Yet his surviving works are few in number — only the brilliant orchestral scherzo *L'apprenti sorcier* (1897) is popular — and include one opera only. This is *Ariane et Barbe-bleue* (Paris, 1907), based on a play by Maeterlinck that was specially written, according to the author: 'to provide musicians . . . with a theme suitable for musical development. It was not designed as anything more ambitious and my intentions are entirely mistaken by those who try to find some additional moral or philosophical message.'

The theme of this often noble three-act opera is the liberation of Bluebeard's captive wives by the latest one, Ariane. But they do not want to leave their husband. Whatever the playwright may have said, the opera's message seems to be, as Martin Cooper puts it, 'that women in general prefer marriage and security, even on the most degrading terms, to freedom'; and thus Maeterlinck's comment may have been his reply to those who saw in the work an ultra-conservative attack on feminism. Dukas's music is indebted to Wagner in its use of *leitmotif* and even more so to Debussy in its solemn atmosphere. It is less fluid than Debussy's opera although successful in such set pieces as the finding of the jewels in Act I; the work has been likened by Donald Grout to a 'huge symphony with the addition of choruses . . . and solo voices'. An excessive use of the 'vague-sounding' whole-tone scale weakens the momentum, however — a mistake never made by Debussy in *Pelléas* despite his liking for this scale and its associated harmonies; similarly Dukas's use of quasi-recitative is less flexible than in that earlier masterpiece also based on Maeterlinck. Perhaps the most positive and striking feature of the opera is its powerful orchestration. Of the vocal numbers, the folksong-like 'Song of the five daughters of Orlamonde' in the unusual key of D sharp minor has been singled out for praise, but one effective unison song for five voices does not make a major vocal-dramatic work.

Such serious stories allowed atmospheric music and psychological exploration, but were at odds with a general public taste that preferred operetta and the straightforward tunes and charm of Messager or Hahn. It was difficult to bring off such a work, and to explain its aims. Half apologetically and half defiantly, Albéric Magnard (1865–1914) wrote in the preface to his *tragédie en musique Bérénice* (Paris, 1911) that: 'My score is written in the Wagnerian style. Not having the genius necessary to create a new lyric form, I have chosen from among existing styles that which suits my wholly classical tastes and completely traditional culture.'

Such a declaration in the year of Stravinsky's *Petrushka*, as well as the designation *tragédie en musique*, sounds like a recipe for dull conservatism. Yet Magnard's idea of Wagner as a classic shows that the reality was not quite so simple. True, this opera, based on Racine's famous play set in the first century AD, has a sombre Act II mediation for the Roman Emperor Titus in the form of a fugue, and love scenes between Titus and Berenice featuring the academic device of canon at the octave; but at least this Jewish heroine, exiled from Rome in the final act because the populace will not tolerate a foreign empress, dedicates a lock of her hair to the goddess of love, Venus. Nevertheless it seems that in Magnard's opera the composer's preoccupation with technique detracts from drama.

Gabriel Fauré (1845–1924) enjoyed a long career in which his gifts were widely recognised. He was also a teacher whose pupils included Ravel and who eventually came to direct the Paris Conservatoire, retiring from this post only at the age of seventy-five. His first opera was *Prométhée* (Béziers, 1900), a three-act *tragédie lyrique* on the story of Prometheus stealing fire from the gods. The commission came through his friend Saint-Saëns, who thought Fauré should write more large-scale works than he had so far done, and *Prométhée* was written for outdoor performance in an amphitheatre. For that reason it is scored for no less than two hundred singers and an orchestra of twice that number including twelve harps (eighteen, according to another account) and a hundred strings. This opera of ultra-Wagnerian magnitude had spoken dialogue as well as singing: in fact Prometheus is a spoken role, though allied to an orchestral *leitmotif* of heavy striding octaves in C major. There are also *leitmotifs* for 'the gods', 'the fire' and even 'the hope of humanity' in true Wagnerian style. Given before ten thousand people, this ambitious work proved very successful, but it was less so in revivals with reduced forces in indoor venues such as the Paris Opéra.

Prométhée redresses the balance of a generally held view of Fauré as a rather small-scale, restrained and even ascetic artist. Nevertheless his *drame lyrique Pénélope* (Monte Carlo, 1913) is more characteristic of the musician known mainly from his serene Requiem (1890), songs and piano pieces. *Pénélope* was written slowly over some five years and is the story of Ulysses' wife in Homer who faithfully awaited her husband's return from the Trojan War. There were some troubles over René Fauchois's libretto—Fauré complained that he did not realise 'that what takes only two minutes to read takes at least three times as long to sing'—but in the end the work was well shaped, although its lack of vivid narrative and of actual arias deprives it of the kind of dramatic and musical vigour that has wide public appeal. It opened at the Théâtre des Champs-Elysées in Paris two months after the Monte Carlo first performance, but was then overshadowed by the sensational première of Stravinsky's *Rite of Spring* in the same theatre twenty days later. Between that time and 1980, the opera had only about a hundred performances in Paris. However, Martin Cooper is probably right in praising it for the 'grandeur and gravity . . . dignity and tenderness' of Penelope herself (a soprano role), and the Hellenistic atmosphere to which Fauré was well attuned: '. . . the hot noon of Act I, the evening falling on the cliff above the sea in Act II, and the early morning of Act III, all have that dry luminous quality which we associate with the Greek mind as well as the Greek climate; and Fauré's suggestion of this quality by musical means is wonderfully vivid.'

Albert Roussel (1869–1937) stands a little apart from his fellow French composers. He began his career as a naval officer and only took up music seriously in his mid-twenties, enrolling as a student at the Paris institution called the Schola Cantorum, founded in 1894 by d'Indy and others in his thirtieth year. Memories of his naval travels to the Far East remained, however, and in 1908 he took his wife on a tour to India and South-East Asia which inspired first an orchestral suite called *Evocations* (1911) and then his *opéra-ballet Padmâvatî* (Paris, 1923), a work begun before the outbreak of war in 1914. It is a spectacular piece about a Mogul chieftain, Alauddin (baritone) who demands Padmâvatî (contralto), the wife of King Ratan-sen (tenor) in exchange for signing an important treaty of alliance. In the end she stabs her husband and must die on his funeral pyre in suttee tradition. The most striking feature of the opera, suitably for one with a balletic element, is its rhythmic vitality, perhaps influenced by Stravinsky after the production in Paris in 1910–13 of his three ballets for Diaghilev's Russian Ballet. There is also a use of Indian-sounding scale patterns. Roussel himself said of *Padmâvatî*: 'I was drawn to the idea of writing for a large theatre a brilliant work which was neither old-fashioned opera nor contemporary operatic drama, and which would allow me to use all the resources of a large chorus, dances, crowd movements . . .'

Roussel went on to write more ballet music and was successful in this field. But his other venture into opera, the *bouffe* piece with small orchestra called *Le testament de la tante Caroline* (*Aunt Caroline's Will*, Olomouc, Czechoslovakia, 1936), was much less so, and indeed found no French producer: too much of its development, perhaps, relies on spoken dialogue.

RAVEL

Maurice Ravel (1875–1937) described his *L'heure espagnole* (Paris, 1911) as:

> . . . a musical comedy. There are no changes in the play of Franc-Nohain apart from a few cuts. Only in the final quintet, because of its form and florid vocal writing, is there a suggestion of normal operatic ensembles. Apart from this quintet I have written simple, straightforward declamation rather than florid song. The French language has its stresses and musical inflections like any other, and I don't see why one shouldn't use these correctly in musical prosody.

Stravinsky once likened Ravel to a Swiss watchmaker because of the perfect precision of his scores, and in this one-act opera the French composer creates a special atmosphere at the start by using the sound of ticking clocks. Characters meet in a clockmaker's shop, presenting the mechanical element in people as in artefacts; and since the vocal writing is largely conversational, the orchestra tends to bear the main musical argument. This instrumental writing is a miracle of delicacy and ingenuity as well as Spanish colour (the opera is set in Toledo) but at the end the five characters break the mould in the musical and dramatic sense by turning to the audience and addressing them with Boccaccio's moral, in *habañera* rhythm: 'In the pursuit of love, there comes a moment when the muleteer has his turn.' Ravel was amused, as are we, that in this story of a flirtatious wife with two pompous suitors it is the unsophisticated Ramiro (baritone) who gets the girl, the clockmaker's wife Concepción (soprano) whose custom it is to receive lovers during her husband's weekly absence of one hour in which he regulates the city's clocks.

Ravel's other opera has a moral too, but of a more conventional kind: the naughty child of *L'enfant et les sortilèges* (Monte Carlo, 1925) is redeemed by one spontaneous kind action. The *enfant* in this *fantaisie lyrique* to a brilliant text by Colette is a boy of about twelve whose ill-treatment of the creatures around him and even inanimate objects, from a dragonfly to an armchair as well as a storybook and textbook, is rewarded by their taking on life and voices to reproach him. When their anger becomes violent and a squirrel is injured, the child binds up its wounded paw and the *sortilège* or spell is broken, and all becomes well again as the repentant child calls for his mother. This opera in two scenes—the first in the nursery and the second in the garden—perhaps marks the composer's preoccupation with a world of childhood, of familiar objects, and above all of the eternally forgiving mother to whom a child can always turn; but at the same time it breathes a tenderness that is here as powerful an emotion as many more obviously operatic ones. This is a work that is difficult to stage and the child's part must normally be taken by a soprano of slight build. The orchestra is large, but hardly sounds so since its instrumental range is mostly used for colour rather than weight. For all its modernity of harmony and even jazz elements (there is a foxtrot in the first scene for a Wedgwood teapot speaking English and a *tasse chinoise* talking pseudo-Chinese), this is a number opera, one of these numbers being a love duet of varied miaows for two cats and another the child's simple and touching lament for the fairy princess lost to him since his destruction of his storybook, '*Toi, le coeur de la rose*'.

Ravel wrote of *L'enfant* with characteristic reticence:

> The emphasis is on melody, allied to a subject which I chose to treat in the spirit of an American musical comedy. Mme Colette's libretto allowed this liberty in treating this magical story. The vocal line is the important thing. Even though the orchestra does not reject virtuosity it is nevertheless of secondary importance.

But his friend and biographer Roland-Manuel has been more eloquent about this parable of love triumphing over the destructive instinct, and in particular about its calm choral finale:

> This ode to kindness gives the work profound significance. It ennobles it; it so enhances it that the last page of the score is one of the composer's most beautiful and harmonious. Music of the spirit and sensibility, filled with tenderness . . . which dies with a sob on the threshold of the house of man.

IBERT AND LES SIX

The 1920s, during which Ravel wrote *L'enfant et les sortilèges*, was an era of 'Bright Young Things' in France quite as much as in the United States and England. Jacques Ibert (1890–1962) studied drama before settling firmly on music, becoming a pupil of Fauré and winning the Prix de

Rome. His one-act farce *Angélique* (Paris, 1927) is a story of a husband called Boniface who tries to put his wife Angélique up for sale, and has cheerful melodies dressed with a sauce of dissonance, dance rhythms and a general *insouciant* sparkle. *Le roi d'Yvetot* (Paris, 1930) is on a bigger scale as an *opéra comique* in four acts and has been described by the scholar David Cox as 'beautifully conceived . . . with skilfully constructed airs, duos, trios and choruses — a pastiche with a fresh and vigorous approach'. A more serious work is *L'aiglon* (Monte Carlo, 1937): in this *drame musical* based on Rostand's story of the captive son of Napoleon with his dreams of glory Ibert collaborated with another composer, Honegger. His artistic ideals were eclectic, and he declared that 'All systems are valid provided one derives music from them . . . [music is] the expression of an interior adventure.'

Arthur Honegger (1892–1955) was a musician born in France of Swiss parents and is one of the group called Les Six who owed much of their youthful beliefs to the bright and somewhat iconoclastic aesthetic of Jean Cocteau (1889–1963), a many-sided artist whose skills included writing, painting and latterly film-making. Cocteau was the librettist of Stravinsky's *Oedipus rex*, Honegger's opera *Antigone* (Brussels, 1927) and Milhaud's *Le pauvre matelot* (Paris, 1927), while his 1930 play *La voix humaine* was set some thirty years later as a monodrama by Poulenc. Stravinsky himself, in his neo-classic and anti-romantic aspect — for example, the ballet *Pulcinella* (1920) — was one of the musical models for the new Les Six style, which aimed at a clean, athletic simplicity and wit, an artistic '*force discrète . . . grâce utile*' (Cocteau) that shunned effects of Teutonic heaviness and flimsy impressionism alike. Another was Eric Satie (1866–1925) — an eccentric but sensitive composer who collaborated with Cocteau in the ballet *Parade* (1917) but who did not write an opera as such, just one puppet piece called *Génevière de Brabant* (1899) and the 'symphonic drama' *Socrate* (1918).

But the composers of Les Six soon went their own ways. Honegger's penchant for big, serious themes is exemplified by his 'dramatic psalm' *Le roi David* (Mézières, 1921), on the Biblical story, *Antigone*, from the Sophocles play, and the 'stage oratorio' *Jeanne d'Arc au bûcher* (Basle, 1938) with its libretto by Paul Claudel. These are powerful if sometimes sprawling stage works, often using the text unconventionally in accentuation and letting voices speak, whisper, hum or even shout.

Darius Milhaud (1892–1974) was Jewish by religion and achieved his greatest operatic success late in life with *David*. This was written for the three-thousandth anniversary of the foundation of Jerusalem, taking its text from the Book of Samuel, and was given in a Hebrew concert version there (1954) before its first staging (Milan, 1955). Two other very large-scale operas by Milhaud are his *Christophe Colomb* (Berlin, 1930), a collaboration with Claudel with forty-five solo singers and major choruses as well as film inserts, and *Bolívar* (Paris, 1950), on a similarly epic subject, the patriot after whom Bolivia is named. On the other hand, his *La mère coupable* (*The Guilty Mother*, Geneva, 1965) is based on the third of the Beaumarchais Figaro plays and, though the opera seems virtually unknown since, must have had a lighter touch.

Three of Les Six—Auric, Durey and Tailleferre—contributed little or nothing to opera. But Francis Poulenc (1899–1963) is a major figure, and the one composer of the group who retained much of its aesthetic into his maturity, although two of his three operas are serious in theme. *Les mamelles de Tirésias* (*The Breasts of Tiresias*, Paris, 1947) is a *bouffe* piece based on a '*drame surréaliste*' of 1918 by Guillaume Apollinaire in which the message of a need for a higher French birthrate is treated with frivolity and absurdity: a husband and wife change sex and he produces forty thousand children, advising his audience to do the same, before reverting to his former state. The composer said of this work: 'I am a sad man . . . who likes to laugh, as do all sad men . . . I think I prefer this work to everything else I have written.'

The *Dialogues des Carmélites* (Milan, 1957) is very different, a story set during the time of the French Revolution in which an entire convent of nuns goes to the guillotine rather than deny their faith. The central characters are Blanche (soprano), showing human weakness and terror but finally going bravely to her death, and Mother Marie, the prioress (mezzo) whose calm resolve inspires the other nuns. One British critic, Paul Griffiths, has acidly complained about the need for 'a rather special taste to enjoy nuns exchanging sweet platitudes for nearly three hours before one by one they have their heads chopped off'; but another, Rodney Milnes, has pointed out that 'those who cannot stomach the score are of course musically illiterate, and those who think it is a devotional opera about nuns being guillotined are just plain obtuse'. *Chacun à son goût*. Certainly Poulenc's musical idiom is rich in its subtle exploration of shades of feeling as the situation develops in the community, but it is not epic or sublime in the way that some might expect in this work lasting some two and a half hours.

A subject that seemed tailor-made for Poulenc was Cocteau's *La voix humaine* (Paris, 1959). He called it a *tragédie lyrique*, but there is little of the classical French operatic style in this monodrama for a woman bidding a final agonising farewell on the telephone to the unseen and unheard lover who is leaving her for another. She is not even named: '*Elle*' was a role memorably created by the soprano Denise Duval, who had already been the first Thérèse, the wife in *Les mamelles de Tirésias*, and Blanche in the *Carmélites*: a French critic once wrote of her that 'with her slim figure and irresistible Parisian charm she was among the most gifted singing actresses of her time'. For Poulenc, the composer's task of sustaining the dramatic tension in these forty minutes must have been difficult, but his refined and wide-ranging melodic and harmonic idiom, with certain poignantly recurring motifs and a sharply searching instrumentation, proved equal to the task. There are also touches of black humour arising out of the state of the Parisian telephone system in the period, which is 1930: a constant fear of being cut off or interrupted, as at times happens ('please hang up, Madame . . . no, this is not Dr Schmidt'). After the first performance Cocteau wrote to Poulenc and paid the best tribute to this one-act masterpiece of middle-class anguish, ageing and loneliness, in a phrase that would please any opera composer: '. . . My dear Francis, you have found the only way to say my text.'

16

YOUNGER NATIONAL TRADITIONS

Viennese operetta. Spain. Scandinavia. The rebirth of British opera. The Americas.

VIENNESE OPERETTA

Of all the developments in nineteenth-century opera, none has been more popular than the Viennese operetta, of which Johann Strauss the Younger (1825–99) and Franz Lehár (1870–1948) are the two most celebrated masters. Their works still hold the world's stages as the most potent evocation of the seductive charm of the Emperor Franz Josef's Vienna. Strauss's *Die Fledermaus* conjures up the gay, frivolous Vienna of the heyday of the Waltz King; and Lehár's *The Merry Widow* evokes the more reflective mood of the imperial capital's last decade.

Operetta developed from comic opera, and has songs, choruses, dance music and spoken dialogue to carry along the often slender plot. Offenbach had established the genre, and it was probably this German-born composer of French *opérettes* and *opéras bouffes* who first persuaded Strauss to follow his example. Strauss was already established as the leading composer and conductor of Viennese dance music, with an international reputation, and he might well have been content to work solely in the field of which he was, by 1870, the undisputed master. But in the 1860s the Parisian operetta was becoming known internationally, and Offenbach's works were often performed in Vienna. In 1863 Offenbach came to the city to supervise several productions, including his *Orpheus in the Underworld*, and while he was there won a competition to write a waltz for the annual ball of the Vienna Press Association, although Strauss had also submitted an entry. Understandably mortified by losing on his home ground, both geographically and musically, Strauss decided in turn to try his hand at music for the stage.

However, it was not until 1871 that *Indigo und die vierzig Räuber* (*Indigo and the Forty Thieves*), the first Strauss operetta, was heard at the Theater an der Wien, and it was only a moderate success, as was his next, *Der Carneval in Rom* (Vienna, 1873), possibly because of weak libretti. But with *Die Fledermaus* (*The Bat*, Vienna, 1874) he had better help, including that of the poet, composer and conductor Richard Genée as librettist. The plot, adapted from a French play, tells how Alfred (tenor), the lover of Rosalinde (soprano), is arrested by mistake instead of her husband Eisenstein (tenor), who has insulted a tax inspector. The confusions which result at the party given by Prince Orlofsky (mezzo, now often tenor) produce a series of lively misunderstandings and ravishing music.

In *Die Fledermaus* Strauss produced what is perhaps the central work of the operetta repertory. Among its highlights is the sparkling trio '*O je, o je, wie rührt mich dies!*' in Act I and earlier in this act, Rosalinde's mock lament '*So muss allein ich bleiben*' has an elegant nostalgia and irony. The soubrette song for the maid Adele at the ball in Act II, '*Mein Herr Marquis*', is another memorable waltz, as is the '*Brüderlein*' chorus which ends the act, demonstrating the composer's expressive range within this one dance form. The '*O Fledermaus*' ensemble of perplexity in the final act reveals the deft touch which marks a master craftsman's skill.

Only one subsequent Strauss operetta approaches its quality and popularity, and that is *Der Zigeunerbaron* (*The Gypsy Baron*, Vienna, 1885), where he infused the genre with exotic harmony, gypsy songs and choruses and an intoxicating pseudo-Hungarian romanticism. The story is of a returning nobleman, Sandor Barinkay (tenor), who finds his ancestral lands have been occupied by gypsies during his years abroad. He falls in love with one of them, the beautiful Saffi (soprano), who proves to be really a princess.

The Gypsy Baron ran for eighty-seven consecutive performances, and the critic Hanslick praised the composer's skill 'in mastering greater forms and in the finer and more characteristic handling of the drama'. Strauss's last operetta, *Wiener Blut* (*The Viennese Spirit*, Vienna, 1899), with its plot set at the time of the Congress of Vienna in 1815, has more serious overtones and at first did not succeed with the public. However, from the time of its second staging in 1905 it has maintained its popularity, in Vienna at least.

In his operettas, Strauss captured an idealised Austro-Hungarian world, which appealed to the Viennese bourgeoisie of his day, gay, cosmopolitan and luxurious. For that same public, the authorities were undertaking projects like the building of the State Opera House, whose grandeur reflected the current prosperity of the capital rather than the long-term political and economic realities facing the declining Habsburg Empire. Such escapism was symbolised by the Viennese middle classes' use of French champagne to celebrate their financial or social successes.

A similar sparkle and lightweight charm is found in the operettas by the

Dalmatian-born Franz von Suppé (1819–95), whose two best-known operettas are *Die schöne Galatea* (*Beautiful Galatea*, Berlin, 1865) and *Die leichte Kavallerie* (*Light Cavalry*, Vienna, 1866). In two more operettas composed for Vienna, *Fatinitza* (1876) and *Boccaccio* (1879), Suppé's style had developed and was rather closer to lyric opera, but by that time he had been overtaken by Strauss. His works remain known mainly for their virtuoso and tuneful overtures, each of which has an imposing introduction leading to an allegro, then a lyrical waltz-song and a final galop. Some of Suppé's melodies reveal him as a master of his craft.

It is just one operetta, together with some individual dances and arias, that maintains the popularity of Franz Lehár (1870–1948). The son of a musician, his mother tongue was Hungarian, and after working in theatres and then as an army bandmaster, he eventually left the army in 1902 and made his career wholly in stage music as a conductor and composer in Vienna. He found two opera librettos in quick succession, and set both to music, *Wiener Frauen* (*Viennese Ladies*) and *Der Rastelbinder* (*The Tinker*). In fact they were premiered at two rival theatres—the Theater an der Wien and the Carl—within a month of each other in November–December 1902. Both were successful, especially *The Tinker*, and Lehár's career in operetta was launched.

The two librettists Victor Léon and Leo Stein found the plot for *The Merry Widow* in a French play called *The Attaché* by Henri Meilhac, and at once realised its suitability as an operetta. Transferring the setting to a Balkan principality, they wrote a libretto entitled *Die lustige Witwe*, intending it for another composer, Richard Heuberger. However, they did not care for his music for the first act when they heard it, and withdrew their libretto from him. Their choice of composer fell upon Lehár after they had heard his setting of a single number.

Die lustige Witwe (Vienna, 1905) had four hundred performances within two years, and went on from Vienna to conquer London, New York, Stockholm and other centres. It even won over the Viennese intellectuals—Hugo von Hofmansthal was heard to say that he wished Lehár had set some of his libretti, while Mahler too succumbed, as his wife Alma wrote in her memoirs:

> We went to *The Merry Widow* and enjoyed it. We danced when we got home and played Lehár's waltz from memory; but the exact run of one passage defied our utmost efforts. We were both too highbrow to face buying the music. So we went to Doblinger's music shop and while Mahler asked about the sale of his compositions I casually turned the pages of the various piano editions of *The Merry Widow*

and found the passage I wanted. I sang it as soon as we were in the street in case it slipped my memory again.

The success of *The Merry Widow* revitalised operetta, which was by now inclined to rely on stock formulae and gestures. There are none of these in Lehár's score, with its irresistible but never predictable melodies, its flesh-and-blood characters, and the seductiveness which led to occasional attempts to have it banned. Lehár was an artist of integrity who was aware, or in time became so, of the new musical horizons being opened up by Mahler, Strauss and possibly even Debussy. Later he became a friend of Puccini, whose *La rondine* owes something to him. The success of *The Merry Widow* was difficult to follow. But in 1909–10 Lehár gave Viennese audiences three more masterpieces within three months. These were *Das Fürstenkind* (*The Prince's Child*, 1909), *Der Graf von Luxemburg* (1909) and *Zigeunerliebe* (*Gypsy Love*, 1910). The composer's biographer, Bernard Grun, has called these 'among the best not only of his own works but among all operettas'.

With the coming of the Great War, the end of the Habsburg Empire, and the arrival of new forms of popular music from the USA, it seemed that Lehár had become a figure of the past. Yet he enjoyed a revival in the 1920s, largely through his collaboration with the tenor Richard Tauber (1892–1948), whose voice suited perfectly such lyrical songs as 'Girls Were Made to Love and Kiss' from *Paganini* (Vienna, 1925) and 'You Are My Heart's Delight' from *Das Land des Lächelns* (*The Land of Smiles*, Berlin, 1929). Tauber's recordings of these songs were immensely popular. Lehár's late works, including his last, *Giudetta* (Vienna, 1934), were somewhat more ambitious in scale than his early ones, and in fact *Giudetta* was first given at the Staatsoper rather than at an operetta theatre.

During the height of operetta's popularity, many other composers contributed to the form. Oskar Straus (1870–1954) enjoyed a triumph with his *Ein Walzertraum* (*A Waltz-Dream*, Vienna, 1907), and followed it with *Der tapfere Soldat* (*The Chocolate Soldier*, Vienna, 1908) which he based on Shaw's *Arms and the Man*. Leo Fall (1873–1945) also wrote operettas, of which *The Eternal Waltz* (London, 1911) is the best known. The Hungarian Emmerich Kálmán (1882–1953) settled in Vienna and wrote lively and tuneful works like *Die Czárdásfürstin* (*The Gypsy Princess*, Vienna, 1915) and *Gräfin Mariza* (Vienna, 1924). The last major exponent of the Viennese operetta, Robert Stolz, who composed *Frühling im Prater* (*Spring in the Prater*, Vienna, 1949), died in 1975 at the age of ninety-four.

SPAIN

Spanish opera had its origins in the seventeenth century but did not flourish until two hundred years later. In 1634 King Philip IV had rebuilt an old hunting lodge near Madrid named after a country inn called La Zarzuela—perhaps because it was in a wild forest glade since the word *zarzal* means a patch of brambles. There pastoral plays with music were given, with words by such literary figures as Calderón, and this dramatist is said to have helped to bring about the operatic style that came to be known as *zarzuela*. However, the music of these pieces is mostly lost, as are the names of the composers, though the *madrileño* Juan Hidalgo (ca 1614–85) was one. The style of the music that exists is mainly Italianate, with solos, duets and choruses, though there was some use of folksongs and dances. But the advent of the Bourbon kings in 1700 halted development, and for a long time native Spanish opera was virtually stifled by imported Italian works, although there were a few examples of music theatre using national dances like the *jota* and *seguidilla*, and a brief fashion for *tonadillas escénicas* (literally 'staged songs') in the first two decades of the nineteenth century also helped to keep some kind of national tradition alive.

In 1839 the poet Manuel Bretón de los Herreros, who had already written a satire attacking Italian opera, collaborated with a musician called Basilio Basili (1803–95)—actually himself Italian—in a one-act opera called *El novio y el concierto* (*The Lover and the Music*) which was described by its authors as a *zarzuela-comedia*. The old name for music theatre had survived and was to prove a rallying cry for a new national voice in Spanish music. Soon the *zarzuela*, full of humour and about ordinary people, was a popular form of opera that was partly spoken and partly sung but always lively and topical, often set in the capital city rather than the country, and with a plentiful use of folksongs and dances. It was the Spanish equivalent, broadly speaking, of the German *Singspiel*, the French *vaudeville* and the English and American ballad opera. Its chief individual figure is Francisco Barbieri (1823–94), who composed over sixty *zarzuelas*, some of which are still performed today, beginning with his *Gloria y peluca* (*Gloria and the Wig*, Madrid, 1850). It was he who also brought about the division of the style into the more serious genre called *zarzuela grande* and the lighter *género chico* or 'little kind' of *zarzuela*, inaugurating the *zarzuela grande* with his three-act *Jugar con fuego* (*Playing with Fire*, Madrid, 1851). Such was the success of *zarzuela* opera that a Teatro de la Zarzuela opened in the Spanish capital in 1857. Other names in this field are those of the composers Cristóbal Oudrid y Segura,

Pascual Arriete y Corera, Federico Chueca and Joaquín Valverde—these last two collaborating in the popular *La gran via* (*The Highway*, Madrid, 1886) which reached France and England—as well as Ruperto Chapí, Manuel Fernández Caballero, Jerónimo Giménez and Tomás Bretón, whose farcical *La verbena de la paloma* (*The Festival of the Dove*, Madrid, 1894) paints the Madrid street atmosphere in lively colours and may be the finest of *género chico* pieces.

In the final decade of the nineteenth century, 1500 *zarzuelas* were presented at Madrid's eleven theatres. Perhaps such an output could only lead to a loss of quality, and after this the *zarzuela* started to decline into a simpler and cruder kind of revue-sketch called *género infimo* – although good *zarzuelas* were still written, such as José Serrano's *La reina mora* (*The Moorish Queen*, 1905), José Maria Usandizaga's *Las golondrinas* (*The Swallows*, 1914), and Federico Torroba's *grande* piece in three acts, *Luisa Fernanda* (1932). Subsequently the flow of good new works has slowed, but the tradition of performance remains healthy. The parents of the celebrated present-day operatic tenor Placido Domingo were both *zarzuela* singers, and he made his début (singing baritone) in one, Caballero's *Gigantes y cabezudos*, which dealt with traditional carnival figures.

With the lively *zarzuela* tradition established, it was inevitable that Spanish librettists and composers would turn their attention to more ambitious operatic forms. Felipe Pedrell (1841–1922), Isaac Albéniz (1860–1909), Enrique Granados (1867–1916) and Manuel de Falla (1876–1946) all composed *zarzuelas*, but in their different ways they then went on to other things. Pedrell was the acknowledged creator of Spanish musicology, but his fervent artistic aim was the realisation and recognition of his *Los Pirineos* (Barcelona, 1902): this opera in a prologue and three acts was conceived as the first opera in a Wagnerian trilogy, uses *leitmotif* and has a Love Court scene in the first act and a Funeral March in the second. Yet the title *The Pyrenees* symbolises the national element, and the subject, on a story from Pedrell's native Catalonia, is epic. Strangely, its première in the Catalan capital was given in Italian. As a scholar Pedrell made skilful use of troubadour vocal forms, plainsong and older Spanish church music in this work, and the choral writing too has been praised: but *Los Pirineos* has not held the stage, perhaps because of a lack of melodic, rhythmic and narrative vitality. Pedrell's *La Celestina* (1904) has been called 'the Spanish *Tristan*', but has not yet been performed at all; this was intended as the second opera of his great trilogy, while the third, *Raymond Lully*, was never even finished. Later in life Pedrell destroyed much of his unperformed music, either 'recognising that his major talents lay elsewhere' according to the musicologist José López-Calo, or more probably in some bitterness that his gifts as a scholar were widely honoured at the expense of his artistic achievement.

Pedrell was the teacher of many Spanish composers of the next generation, including all of those mentioned below in this chapter. Albéniz was a child prodigy pianist who had an extraordinary early career, running away from home at the age of ten and travelling to places as varied as Cuba, Liverpool and Leipzig before he was fourteen. He lived in London from 1890–3 and wrote a comic opera to an English libretto called *The Magic Opal* (London, 1893). But his chief operatic success was *Pepita Jiménez* (Barcelona, 1896). This was in fact written to a libretto by an English banker by the name of Money-Coutts who paid Albéniz a large retainer to set his libretto texts to music, this one being a 'lyric comedy' based on a novel by Juan Valera. Later these collaborators planned a very ambitious *King Arthur* with operas to be called *Merlin*, *Lancelot* and *Guinevere*, but only the first was sketched out in full, while the second was left incomplete and the third not even composed at the composer's early death from Bright's disease.

Granados composed his opera in three scenes called *Goyescas* (New York, 1916) on the unusual basis of already written piano pieces which in their turn had been inspired by Goya's paintings. In consequence the story had to be fabricated, but this was done quite successfully: it is a *verismo* tale in which Fernando (tenor) attends a ball to which his beloved has been invited but which is being given by a toreador who is his rival in her affections. He and the other man fight and he dies in her arms. The work is musically rich, but had no successor, for within eight weeks the composer had drowned in the English Channel, a victim of the German submarine which torpedoed his ship. He had written after the première: 'I have a whole world of ideas . . . I am only now starting my work.'

Falla is the best-known name among Spanish composers outside Spain, and his operas are similarly more familiar internationally. His 'lyric drama' in two acts called *La vida breve* (*The Brief Life*, Nice, 1913) had been completed some time before this première: it had won a Spanish opera competition, but then did not receive a performance and was subsequently revised and reorchestrated after Falla's fruitful contacts with French musicians such as Dukas and Debussy during a stay in Paris from 1907–14. The story is basic: Salud (soprano) curses Paco (tenor), the lover who jilts her, and dies of a broken heart. (One feels that an Italian composer and librettist would have had at least one *crime passionnel* in this situation!) A more personal and vital work is *El retablo de maese Pedro* (Paris, 1923), a puppet opera with small orchestra to the composer's own libretto, based on an incident in *Don Quixote* and first staged at the home of Princess Edmond de Polignac, who commissioned it. The central role in *Master Peter's Puppet Show* is the boy treble who acts as the narrator, his music being a high-pitched evocation of Andalusian street cries, and it is he who, in an attractive mixture of reality and fiction, tells the audience the story of Don Gayferos rescuing Melisendra from the Moors with interruptions from Don Quixote and the puppet-master Maese Pedro (tenor). Falla's last opera (or '*cantata escénica*', as he called it) was *Atlántida*. This was an enormous project, a kind of miracle play in three parts that occupied the composer intermittently from 1926 to his death twenty years later. He wrote, 'I am working on it day by day, but how little time there seems to be,' but one cannot help suspecting a decline of his creative power and energy. The theme was the legend of lost Atlantis and the work was dedicated to the composer's native Cádiz. Closer to oratorio than to opera, *Atlántida* was completed by Ernesto Halffter and finally reached a staged performance (Milan, 1962), although it has not as yet been revived.

SCANDINAVIA

In Sweden, the Stockholm Royal Opera was inaugurated in 1773 and a number of composers worked there, of whom the best known was the German Johann Gottlieb Naumann (1741–1801). For a long time his *Gustaf Wasa* (Stockholm, 1786), on the subject of the sixteenth-century king who freed Sweden from union with Denmark, was regarded as the national opera. But native composers failed to develop a tradition, though Franz Adolf Berwald (1796–1868) wrote both operettas and operas—*I Enter the Monastery* (1842) is an example of the former, while the three-act *Estrella de Soria* (1862) is more ambitious. Parts of this work were to be used to open the new opera house in 1898, while the first opera specially written for the new building was the rather Wagnerian *Waldemarsskatten* (*Waldemar's Treasure*) by Andreas Hallén (1846–1925). A more characteristically Swedish style, though still showing Wagner's influence, was that of Ivar Hallström (1826–1901): his *The Bewitched One* (Stockholm, 1874) has some folk elements. Among contemporary composers, Lars Johan Werle (1926) wrote the opera *Tintimara* (1973), a lyrical mystery play commissioned to mark the two-hundredth anniversary of the Royal Opera. However, Sweden has as yet no major operatic repertory of her own, though she has produced many fine singers. The first was the

'Swedish Nightingale' Jenny Lind (1820–87), and other names are those of Jussi Björling, Set Svanholm and Birgit Nilsson.

Until the twentieth century, Finland was dominated culturally by Sweden. The first opera to a Finnish text was based on a folk tale: *The Maid of the North* (1899, produced Viipuri 1908) by Oskar Merikanto (1868–1924). This musician's son Aarre Merikanto (1893–1958) also composed an opera, *Juha* (1922, first staged 1963), which is a strongly national and forceful work that has been compared with the operas of Janáček. The most celebrated among Finnish composers, Jean Sibelius (1865–1957), completed only one opera, *The Maiden in the Tower* (Helsinki, 1896), and its text was in Swedish, the language at that time of the Finnish middle classes. He had earlier contemplated an opera on a Finnish libretto and based on an episode in the national epic, the *Kalevala*, which was to be called *The Building of the Boat*, but this came to nothing. The development of Finnish opera was to come much later after the achievement of independence in 1917 and the establishment of regular companies. *The East Bothnians* (1923) by Leevi Madetoja (1887–1947) represents a national school that stylistically followed Sibelius. The work of the principal figure of a later generation, Sallinen (1935), is discussed in Chapter 19.

Similarly, in Norway opera has developed slowly. The composer Waldemar Thrane (1790–1828) was a pioneer figure, whose folk comedy with spoken dialogue *A Mountain Adventure* (Christiania/Oslo, 1825) was an immediate success: Jenny Lind liked to include its 'Aagot's Mountain Song' in her recitals. Thrane actually incorporated folk style into his music, both in melody and rhythm, and set something of a national model for his successors, although Martin Andreas Udbye (1820–89), with his Weberian romantic opera *The Peacemaker* (1858), seems to have been little influenced by folk music. The chief among nationalist figures, and in Norwegian music generally, was Edvard Grieg (1843–1907). Grieg never completed an opera, although his *Olav Trygvason* (1873) was intended as the first part of one: an estrangement between him and his librettist intervened and the work survives only as a cantata. The only other names of note here are those of Ole Olsen (1850–1927), who wrote four operas between 1876–1910 in a style that was both Wagnerian and nationalist, and Christian Sinding (1856–1941)—best known for his piano mood piece *Rustle of Spring* but also the composer of the opera *The Holy Mountain* (Dessau, 1914), again a work owing something to Wagner's style. The Norwegian National Theatre has included opera in its performances since its foundation in 1899. The national company, called Den Norske Opera, which had its first season in 1959, has the government and the Oslo City Council as its backers.

Denmark's greater proximity to other European traditions made Copenhagen a lively centre for opera, and some comic operas to Danish texts were performed in the eighteenth century. The best known Danish composer of the nineteenth century, Niels Gade (1817–90), completed only one opera, however, the Mendelssohnian *Mariotta* (Copenhagen, 1850), and there were other composers who contributed Romantic or Verdian works. From 1883–1908, the Swedish musician Johan Svendsen was Director of the Royal Opera, and his successor was Carl Nielsen (1865–1931), the greatest of Danish composers, who actually began his career among the second violins of this theatre orchestra.

Both of Nielsen's operas, *Saul and David* (Copenhagen, 1902) and *Maskarade* (Copenhagen, 1906), ought by now to be in the international repertory, though sadly this is not yet the case. *Saul and David* is in four acts and treats a tragic Biblical theme. Its thrust stems from the contrast and conflict between the older man and the younger one destined for kingship: in the words of the scholar Robert Simpson, it 'depicts not so much a clash of personalities as a combination of circumstances in which Saul goes down and David goes up: the circumstances are not simply created by the differences of temperament between the two men, but by a larger human current that carries them, in which respectively they are so constituted as to sink or swim'. The choral writing for the Israelites in the opera fits easily into its dramatic context, and the plot is developed purposefully, with the final act cast in two scenes linked by a thrilling orchestral interlude depicting a battle. Indeed the orchestral writing is fine throughout, the most striking example being the Prelude to Act II, in which the final climax subsides to leave the voice of David soaring ecstatically alone, a moment of genius which adds to the character's stature. Nielsen said of this opera, 'This great and strange subject stirred and haunted me, so that for long periods I could not free myself of it, no matter where I was, even when I was sitting in the orchestra with my second violin, busy with ballets and vaudevilles.'

Nielsen's *Maskarade* is based on a comedy written by Ludvig Holberg and has a nationalist theme. It takes Mozart as its model, sharing the bubbling vivacity of *Figaro*. There is both wit and dramatic tension in this *buffo* piece which is also the love story of Leander (tenor) and Leonora (soprano), building to the scene of the unmasking at the ball near the end. These two fine operas could hardly be more complementary in temperament, subject matter, or musical style, and each is a masterpiece. Sadly, no Danish opera of proven distinction has followed them, despite the work of Knudåge Riisager (1897–1974), the composer of *Susanna* (Copenhagen, 1950), and Vagn Holmboe (1909–), whose *The Devil and the Mayor* (1940) attracted some notice. Among the younger generation, Holmboe's pupil Per Nørgård (1932–) has made an impression with his epic *Gilgamesh* (1973).

THE REBIRTH OF BRITISH OPERA

In the nineteenth century opera in Britain remained under foreign domination. Several theatres in London mounted opera, but the principal one at Covent Garden was known (from 1847) as the Royal Italian Opera House, and even French and German operas were often performed in Italian. At the end of the century the Moody-Manners and Carl Rosa companies were to tour the provinces with English operas and operas performed in English, but in the capital foreign works remained the staple diet. Even so, visitors were rarely impressed, and when Weber came to London in 1826, he complained about the omission of the music in the most important moments, in other words that there was merely a succession of songs interspersed with spoken dialogue. Henry Bishop (1786–1855), the Music Director of Covent Garden from 1810–24, showed a typically piecemeal approach by his adaptations of major operas such as *Don Giovanni*, *Figaro*, and *Fidelio* which actually incorporated some of his own music, while his own romantic fairy opera *Aladdin* (1826) is really a play with songs.

Before Bishop, a leading figure had been William Shield (1748–1829), the composer of *Rosina* (1782) and *The Travellers in Switzerland* (1794) as well as many other sung stage pieces. Shield learned his craft largely from playing in opera orchestras, as did Vincent Wallace (1812–65) who played the violin at the Theatre Royal in Dublin before travelling widely abroad. Wallace made his mark with the popular opera *Maritana* (London, 1845), which reflected the dual influence of Meyerbeer and of Spanish gypsy music. *Maritana* enjoyed success internationally, but Wallace's later operas in a grander style had a mixed reception.

The Irishman Michael Balfe (1808–70) studied in Italy and in Paris before settling in England, where he made his reputation with *The Siege of Rochelle* (London, 1835), followed by *The Maid of Artois* (London, 1836). Balfe's knowledge of vocal writing was based on practical experience, for he was a singer who played Papageno in the first British performance of *The Magic Flute* in 1841. He continued to travel, trying to establish British opera both at home and abroad, and made two trips to Russia. Of his twenty-nine operas, the most celebrated was *The Bohemian Girl* (London, 1843). The chief strength lies in his lyrical ballads; its main limitation is a lack of dramatic characterisation.

Arthur Sullivan (1842–1900) was the son of a bandmaster and soon acquired a skilful technique, a penchant for melody, and above all a light touch. His first comic opera, *Cox and Box* (London, 1867), was prompted by the success of Offenbach in London, but with the collaboration as librettist of W. S. Gilbert, whom he met in 1870, he developed a more English idiom. Gilbert was an equal partner in their series of operettas, works which are remarkable for their fertile melodious invention, bounding humour and keen sense of timing. Although their first collaboration, *Thespis* (London, 1871), was a failure, *Trial by Jury* (London, 1875) encouraged the impresario Richard D'Oyly Carte to stage more of their works. *The Sorcerer* (1877) and *HMS Pinafore* (1878) were even more successful, and were soon followed by *The Pirates of Penzance* (Paignton, 1879) and *Patience* (London, 1881). In 1881 D'Oyly Carte opened his new Savoy Theatre in London's Strand, and the operettas which were given there, *Iolanthe* (1882), *Princess Ida* (1884), *The Mikado* (1885), *Ruddigore* (1887), *The Yeomen of the Guard* (1888), and *The Gondoliers* (1889), are often called the Savoy Operas. But in spite of their huge success, Sullivan's heart was elsewhere, and eventually he broke with Gilbert and turned to grand opera. *Ivanhoe* (London, 1891) was initially successful, but public interest did not last and indeed the ambitiously named Royal English Opera House, where it was staged, was later turned into a music hall. A further *King Arthur* project remained unrealised, and Sullivan returned to comic opera. Reconciled with Gilbert, the two created *Utopia Limited* (London, 1893) and *The Grand Duke* (London, 1896), and Sullivan also collaborated with other librettists: his last work, *The Emerald Isle* (London, 1901), was left unfinished at his death, and was completed by Edward German (1862–1936).

Sullivan was an eclectic musician who frequently resorted to affectionate parody. He stands as the nearest British equivalent to Offenbach and Johann Strauss, but has an occasional depth and individuality of his own: thus the sad jester Jack Point's final song in *The Yeomen of the Guard* conveys genuine pathos. But though his word setting is neat, there is little vocal display save in certain comic patter arias such as the 'Nightmare Song' in *Iolanthe*, and while his orchestral accompaniments may be subtle, as in the woodwind decorations for the 'Three Little Maids' in *The Mikado*, his harmony and form break no new ground here and indeed are unadventurous. But the vivacity of his music and of Gilbert's texts keep the Savoy Operas popular with British audiences.

Charles Villiers Stanford (1852–1914) wrote ten operas, of which *Shamus O'Brien* (London, 1896) and *Much Ado About Nothing* (London, 1901) made some impression. Ethel Smyth (1858–1944) trained in Germany and composed six operas in all: the first two of them, *Fantasio* (Weimar, 1898) and *Der Wald* (Berlin, 1902) were well received and the latter even reached New York. The European influence in these works is also present in Smyth's more obviously English works *The Wreckers* (Leipzig, 1906) and *The Boatswain's Mate* (London, 1916). *The Wreckers* is a tragic love story set in Cornwall and tells of coastal folk who live by wrecking ships and plundering them. *The Boatswain's Mate* is a comic opera with folk songs that give a national flavour and effective choral work.

Nevertheless, opera remained relatively unimportant in British musical life. Performance standards were low—for example, the conductor Eugene Goossens admitted that he usually had to do without orchestral rehearsals—and a Master of the King's Music, Walford Davies (1869–1941), could speak contemptuously about the 'astonishing and phenomenal enormity of opera'. Perhaps because of this hostile climate, Edward Elgar (1857–1934) never completed an opera, though he did leave some fragments of one, *The Spanish Lady*, based on Ben Jonson's *The Devil is an Ass*.

However, not all musicians were deterred by the prevailing atmosphere and conditions. Frederick Delius (1862–1934) wrote his first opera, *Irmelin*, in 1890–2, and though it remained unpublished, Thomas Beecham staged it sixty years later (Oxford, 1953). But only the beautiful and lyrical prelude is performed today, while *The Magic Fountain* (composed 1893) was not heard until a BBC performance in 1977. *Koanga* (Elberfeld, 1897) is the closest of the Delius operas to the romantic tradition, with lyrical arias and Verdian dramatic choruses. It tells of a proud African prince, Koanga (baritone), who is brought as a slave to a Mississippi plantation, and has a rival in love for the mulatto girl Palmyra in the slave overseer Perez. In the end all three are killed. *Koanga* evokes the sounds and images Delius had learned to love when he worked on an orange plantation in Florida.

In 1900–2 Delius completed two more operas: *Margot la Rouge* remained unperformed, having been composed for a competition it did not win, but *A Village Romeo and Juliet* (Berlin, 1907) is a major work which uses chromatic harmony to convey a nostalgia which perhaps makes a stronger impression than the drama itself. Indeed the critic Cecil Gray described it as 'a symphonic poem with an implicit programme made explicit on the stage'. It offers a series of atmospheric scenes, and the orchestral interlude *'The Walk to the Paradise Garden'*, is at once ecstatic and poignant. Delius revealed his attitude to opera when he wrote of this work: 'Every gesture of the actors in my work must be controlled and ordered by the conductor, for my music is conceived in that spirit . . . An old actor–stage manager will be no good whatever for he will make the singers act from the stage and not from the music.'

The doomed lovers of *A Village Romeo and Juliet* may in some ways recall those of *Tristan und Isolde*, and it was hard for Delius to dispel Wagner's influence on his work, which remains in his opera *Fennimore and Gerda* (1910, staged Frankfurt, 1919), adapted from a Danish novel by Jens Peter Jacobsen. But Delius took the harmonies and fluid form of the post-Wagnerian era and moulded them to his own ends:

> I don't believe in learning harmony and counterpoint. Learning kills instinct. Never believe the saying that one must hear music many times in order to understand it. It is utter nonsense, the last refuge of the incompetent. For me music is very simple. It is the expression of a poetic and emotional nature.

This may have some wisdom, yet Delius could never be termed a natural opera composer. His vocal lines seldom develop the potential of the words, tending instead to float above the orchestral texture, and only in *Koanga* is there much dramatic thrust. Since opera must portray people and events rather than a response to nature, these often beautiful works seem likely to remain confined to recordings and rare revivals.

Gustav Holst (1874–1934) came to know the regular operatic repertory as a trombonist with the Carl Rosa Opera Company. He composed five youthful operas, none of which was produced, and later referred to the fifth, *Sita* (composed 1906), as merely 'good old Wagnerian bawling'. His first significant opera was *Sāvitri* (London, 1916), based on an episode in the Hindu *Mahabharata*. Its theme is the triumph of hope over death, and the atmosphere is powerful even though the forces employed are only three solo voices, a wordless female chorus and an ensemble of two flutes, cor anglais, string octet and double bass. The vocal writing is mostly fluid *arioso*, and the harmony sometimes boldly bitonal: an Eastern flavour pervades everything. *Sāvitri* is important in its own right, and in its psychological depth it is both the successor to Purcell's *Dido and Aeneas* and the precursor of Britten's chamber operas.

None of the remaining Holst operas is wholly successful. *The Perfect Fool* (London, 1923) failed, although its lively ballet music is deservedly popular. *At the Boar's Head* (Manchester, 1925) is based on the Falstaff tavern scenes in Shakespeare's plays and uses folk tunes. Neither this nor its light-hearted and witty successor, *The Wandering Scholar* (Liverpool, 1934), which is also in one act, has established itself.

A popular British opera when it first appeared was *The Immortal Hour* (Glastonbury, 1914) by Rutland Boughton (1878–1960), in which King Eochaidh (baritone), searching for 'The Immortal Hour, the Beauty of all Beauty', is led to Etain (soprano), Princess of the faery Land of Youth, but dies when she is lured back to her own country by her rightful lord, Midir (tenor). Boughton intended the word 'faery' to indicate something terrible and fundamental, the 'hidden people of Celtic legend'. A more tuneful work than this synopsis suggests, *The Immortal Hour* has been recorded, but a stage revival seems unlikely at present. Boughton sought in vain to establish an English equivalent of the Wagnerian music drama at Bayreuth, centred on the small west-country town of Glastonbury. Boughton's contemporary Joseph Holbrooke (1878–1958) completed an epic trilogy with a similarly Celtic flavour, *The Cauldron of Annwyn*, comprising *The Children of Don* (London, 1912), *Dylan* (London, 1914), and *Bronwen* (London, 1929). For a time Holbrooke's reputation was international—during 1923 *The Children of Don* was produced in Venice and Salzburg—but this success quickly and rather cruelly evaporated. As the scholar Michael Trend has written, Boughton and Holbrooke 'spent much energy and effort trying to develop a national form of opera . . . [but] it became more and more obvious that they were both going down the same cul-de-sac, and new young men of the post-war world were to do better by travelling in different directions'.

Thus it was Ralph Vaughan Williams (1872–1958) who was to become the most important of British opera composers before Britten. His training was eclectic, including tuition with Bruch in Berlin and Ravel in Paris, yet he was a staunch musical nationalist who declared that

> Art, like charity, should begin at home . . . Have we not about us forms of musical expression which we can take and purify and raise to the level of great art? . . . The art of music above all other arts is the expression of the soul of a nation.

These ideas are clearly reflected in *Hugh the Drover* (London, 1924), on which Vaughan Williams worked for ten years, writing of his 'idea for an opera written to REAL English words, with a certain amount of REAL English music, and also a REAL English subject'. Yet he also admitted, 'I see hardly any chance of an opera by an English composer ever being produced, at all events in our lifetime.' *Hugh the Drover* fulfils Vaughan Williams's intention of writing an opera 'full of good tunes and lively, and with one tune that will really COME OFF'. The opening scene of what he called 'my Ballad Opera' is set at a country fair with its spontaneous cries and folksongs, and it immediately captures the atmosphere of a nineteenth-century English market town, while the Showman's aria 'Cold blows the wind on Cotsall' is an excellent example of a composer creating a folk-like theme for a song. There is fine characterisation, especially of the heroine Mary, whose aria 'Here, Queen uncrowned' soars above a chattering ensemble. This work was central to the development of a British operatic style that was free from epic pretensions and post-Wagnerian yearnings.

Like his friend Holst, Vaughan Williams was attracted to Shakespeare, and he wrote a Falstaff opera called *Sir John in Love* (London, 1929). He knew of course that it would be compared with Verdi's *Falstaff*, but felt that his own music was so different that there would be no duplication, especially since *Sir John in Love* gave more emphasis to the romantic aspects of the plot. As in Holst's *At the Boar's Head*, a folk element is present, but the range of music is greater, and the characterisation is perhaps even more subtle than in *Hugh the Drover*.

Vaughan Williams's next two operas present a marked contrast. *Riders to the Sea* (London, 1937) sets almost all of the play by J. M. Synge, and the title page simply reads '*Riders to the Sea*, set to music'. The work is a portrait of an Irish village community and the vocal writing follows the lilt and rhythmic shape of their speech, while the orchestral part, which is generally chordal with simple woodwind phrases, becomes more expressive in reference to such major forces as God and the sea. There is a striking economy about *Riders to the Sea*, an opera in which much of the music derives from motifs heard in the prelude and first scene, and although it is not an immediately imposing work its final effect is powerful. By contrast *The Poisoned Kiss* (Cambridge, 1936) is merely a tuneful operetta, complete with spoken dialogue. The libretto is unsatisfactory, possibly because the composer had to make substantial cuts to satisfy the managers of the Cambridge Arts Theatre, who, as he explained, '. . . sent an ultimatum that the evening's entertainment must not start before 8.30 pm so that the dons may digest their dinner, and must finish by 11pm, in order that the undergraduates may be in bed by 11.30: that is to say 2 hours and 25 minutes including intervals. This will mean cutting to the bone . . .'

The Pilgrim's Progress (London, 1951) is Vaughan Williams's last and greatest opera. In some respects this 'mortality after John Bunyan' is the most central of all his compositions, for it occupied him for more than forty years. Already in 1904, when he was music editor of the *New English*

Hymnal, he had written a tune for Percy Dearmer's version of Christian's hymn, 'He who would valiant be', and his one-act pastoral episode 'after Bunyan', *The Shepherds of the Delectable Mountains* (London, 1922), was a further source of material. His Fifth Symphony (1938–43) has musical links with the opera, and the slow movement actually quotes the opening of the scene in the 'House Beautiful' in Act I. A prologue and epilogue frame the four acts, and in both gentle and powerful passages the composer shows a fine level and range of invention. Thus the scene in Act IV when Pilgrim meets Mr By-Ends has an appropriately easy-going flavour, which contrasts with the spiritual radiance of the 'Shepherds' sequence that leads Pilgrim to the Celestial City and the end of his journey, where the deployment of vocal forces both off and on the stage builds to a glorious choral climax. Incidentally, this self-proclaimed agnostic composer preferred the name 'Pilgrim' to Bunyan's 'Christian': nevertheless in this work he seems to make a major spiritual statement. Inevitably, perhaps, it hovers close to oratorio, and doubtless it is a difficult work to stage convincingly. Yet it shows a visionary genius, and it seems likely that a fine revival could give it a repertory place.

THE AMERICAS

As far as is known, the first complete opera given in the American continent was *La Partenope* (Mexico City, 1711), composed by Manuel de Zumaya (ca 1678–1756) for the pleasure of the opera-loving Duke of Linares, the Spanish viceroy in Spain's rich colony of Mexico. But there is no tradition of opera in the New World until over a century later, after Mexico had gained her independence in 1821. Italian opera reached Mexico in 1830 with a visiting company, and after this a number of native operas were produced, such as *Catalina de Guisa* (Mexico City, 1859) by Cenobio Paniagua y Vasques (1821–82) and *Ildegonda* (Mexico City, 1865) by Melesio Morales (1838–1908), a pupil of Paniagua who spent three years in Europe and had *Ildegonda* produced successfully in Florence. A more national note was struck in *Guatimotzin* (Mexico City, 1871), by Aniceto Ortega del Villar (1825–75): this was an opera in nine scenes telling of a defence of Mexico by an Aztec ruler and having a national flavour in the music that caused Ortega to be hailed as a Mexican Glinka. At this time also imported *zarzuelas* gave rise to native ones.

Venezuela and Colombia also had locally composed *zarzuelas* after the middle of the nineteenth century and other Latin American operas were created after the beginning of the twentieth century in Argentina, Peru, Chile and Cuba. Argentina had the strongest tradition: the *gaucho* drama

Pampa (1897) by Arturo Berutti (1862–1938) and the mythological *Huemac* (1916) by Pascual de Rogatis (1881–) alike have some degree of local colour. The Teatro Colón in Buenos Aires, the chief operatic centre, was opened in 1857 and replaced by a new building in 1908. Among more recent Argentinian operas, only *Bomarzo* (Washington, 1967) by Alberto Ginastera (1916–) has made some international impression. It is a strong and sensuous treatment, cast in two acts and fifteen scenes in an Italian sixteenth-century setting, of the adventures and neurotic frustrations of the hunchback Duke of Bomarzo (tenor), and was at first banned from performance in the composer's native Buenos Aires on the grounds of its overt sexuality, though it appeared there eventually in 1972. Its musical language is powerfully dissonant and occasionally violent, but the American scholar Gilbert Chase reminds us that though 'the idioms are contemporary . . . the tradition of grand opera is upheld . . . the spirit of Verdi watches in the wings'.

In Brazil, opera took root similarly after 1850. The first important name is that of Carlos Gomes (1836–96), although after his successes with *A noite do castelo* and *Joana de Flandres* (Rio de Janeiro, 1861 and 1863) he left to make his career mainly in Europe. The best known of later Brazilian composers, Heitor Villa-Lobos (1887–1959), composed two four-act operas forty years apart: *Izath* (1914, staged Rio de Janeiro, 1958) and, after Lorca, *Yerma* (1956, staged Santa Fé, 1971). However, the fact remains that not one of the Latin American operas mentioned here has as yet found a secure place in the international repertory.

The history of opera in the United States is at first mainly that of European companies playing to local audiences. In colonial times some ballad operas reached North America just as the Spanish *zarzuelas* came to the south, and *The Beggar's Opera* was seen in New York in 1750. In New Orleans there was European opera from about 1805, such as Rossini's *Barber of Seville* in 1823, sung in French, and a French opera house opened there in 1859. *The Barber*, in a production by the Spanish singer-impresario Manuel Garcia, was presented in New York in 1825, where the mezzo Maria Malibran, Garcia's daughter, caused a sensation in the role of Rosina. The Metropolitan Opera House in New York opened in 1883 with Gounod's *Faust*, and though its first season lost heavily, it flourished under the successive German directorships of the father and son Leopold and Walter Damrosch and gave German-language performances that included many Wagner premières in America. The Chicago Opera opened in 1865 and, like some other houses, raised its funds by subscription: opera was socially fashionable and wealthy industrialist families sought to enhance their prestige and that of their cities by supporting it.

Native talent surfaced only slowly and patchily. In Philadelphia William Henry Fry (1813–64) heard Bellini's *Norma* and was thus inspired to compose, to his own libretto, the first grand opera by an American-born composer to be publicly performed: this was *Leonora* (Philadelphia, 1845), based on a story called *The Lady of Lyons* by Bulwer-Lytton. An ambitious man, Fry then tried to have his opera staged in Paris, where his profession as a journalist had taken him, and although he failed, he did compose another opera called *Notre Dame of Paris* (Philadelphia, 1864). Both works relied obviously on European models such as Donizetti and Meyerbeer, but this pioneer also urged American composers, in public lectures and in print, to seek their own New World voice and to break free from European cultural domination, calling indeed for a second 'Declaration of Independence' that would apply to the arts.

Some composers followed Fry's example. One was the New Yorker George Frederick Bristow (1825–98), the composer of *Rip Van Winkle* (New York, 1855), a relatively lightweight work with spoken dialogue; and other names are those of Dudley Buck, John Knowles Paine and Silas Gamaliel Pratt. Unfortunately, however, important American composers of the time like Edward MacDowell and the French-born Charles Martin Loeffler neglected opera, and it was not until the early twentieth century that any kind of tradition began to be established. Possibly the three-act *Mona* (New York, 1912) by Horatio Parker (1863–1919) marks one milestone in the process; this was a romantic work set in ancient Britain — according to Donald Grout 'a slightly modernised *Tristan*' complete with *leitmotif* and rich chromatic harmony — which won a $10,000 prize, as did Parker's later opera *Fairyland* (Los Angeles, 1915). *Shanewis or The Robin Woman* (New York, 1918), by Charles Wakefield Cadman (1881–1946), used some Indian melodies and was based on an Indian story, the life of Princess Redfeather, and thus has a similarly backward-looking subject. So has *Merry Mount* (New York, 1933) by Howard Hanson (1896–), which is set in Puritan New England.

There were, of course, other American musical traditions too. In 1908 the *New York Age* reported: 'Music circles have been stirred recently by the announcement that Scott Joplin, known as the apostle of ragtime, is composing the score for a grand opera.' The black composer Joplin (1868–1917) did indeed work on an opera called *Treemonisha*, but although there was some kind of a performance with the composer at the piano in Harlem in 1915, it was unorchestrated and unstaged until 1972. It tells of a girl who has been given this name because she was found as a baby under a tree, and of her later life as a teacher and community leader. Black style melody and rhythms are treated here with a more European spaciousness, but though the music is agreeable the characterisation is limited.

It was inevitable that more modern-seeming operas would be written, and that a new generation should provide them. A distinguished example is another opera set in a black community, but written by a white Jewish-American musician, *Porgy and Bess* (Boston, 1935) by George Gershwin (1898–1937). Gershwin came from a poor family but soon developed a strong musical gift and went at sixteen to work in Tin Pan Alley, the New York popular music industry. With his brother Ira as lyricist he created a number of successful Broadway shows such as *Lady, be Good* (New York, 1924) and *Strike up the Band* (Philadelphia, 1927), and the enormous success of his *Rhapsody in Blue* for piano and orchestra in 1924 had also encouraged him to work as a 'serious' composer. The idea of writing a full-scale opera on Du Bose Heyward's play *Porgy* had occurred to him in 1926, but it took some time to realise his ideas musically, even after Hayward had dramatised his story for this purpose and they had corresponded about it. He started work seriously in 1934 and completed the three-act opera in October of the following year. The first performance was in Boston, but the main première was to a New York audience just after. At first the work puzzled people and was not entirely successful: perhaps the audience attended with the wrong kind of expectations from the 'commercial' composer, while 'serious' musicians stayed away for the same reason. But in the fullness of time the opera has become recognised as Gershwin's masterpiece, a kind of *verismo* piece set among the blacks of South Carolina in which the hero Porgy (bass-baritone) is a cripple who kills his rival for Bess's love, the stevedore Crown (baritone), before following Bess (soprano) to New York and the hope of a new life.

Gershwin actually went to Charleston, South Carolina, to study Gullah Negro music and ritual before composing this opera, and in it he united popular and serious styles with a sure hand. Like Bizet's *Carmen*, a work that it perhaps resembles more than any other repertory opera, it is full of feeling, colour and power, as well as a sense of danger. Romantic lyrical melodies are there — like the lullaby 'Summertime' sung by Clara — and so is the sharp humour of the drug-dealing Sportin' Life, a role associated with the black singer Cab Calloway. There are songs like show tunes or black folk ballads, recitatives moulded to speech patterns, folk-like hymns, choruses and ensembles, as well as deft and vivid orchestration. *Porgy and Bess* is not a musical comedy or a jazz drama but a great opera.

A more consciously European opera of this period was *Four Saints in Three Acts* (Hartford, Connecticut, 1934) by Virgil Thomson (1896–) —yet it was first performed by an all-black cast. The explanation doubtless lies in the degree of deliberate surrealism in the Gertrude Stein text, which for a start is in *four* acts, plus a prologue, and makes little attempt to characterise the saints concerned, who include Teresa of Avila and Ignatius Loyola. The setting is Spain, as these names suggest, but there is little plot as such: instead we find a sequence of tableaux and processions. The text incorporates word games and riddles, and rather provocative echoes of Anglican and even Protestant church music as well as popular dances like the tango and waltz. The opera made a considerable mark at the time and had New York and Chicago productions, but it has not held the stage: perhaps it was too much a work of its time, a period of stylistic self-consciousness in which American composers perhaps more than most felt under pressure to be 'new'. Thomson himself had had Harvard teachers who introduced him to French music including that of Satie. He had then studied in Paris with the distinguished teacher Nadia Boulanger and lived in the French capital for many years until the outbreak of war took him back to the United States.

Another Boulanger pupil was Aaron Copland (1900–), whose Jewish Brooklyn background was similar to that of Gershwin and who even had the same teacher, Rubin Goldmark. Yet Copland has been the most convincingly American among the composers of his generation. He wrote only two operas, and for some his main achievement perhaps lies in instrumental music, though his popular ballets *Billy the Kid*, *Rodeo* and *Appalachian Spring* remind us of his skill as a man of the theatre. His first opera was *The Second Hurricane* (New York, 1937), a 'school play-opera' written for children: imaginatively, it also includes a chorus of parents and an adult narrator. Copland played the opera to the young Benjamin Britten when he visited him in his Suffolk home in 1938, and it seems certain that this music of the great outdoors, with its innocent simplicity and fresh vigour, influenced Britten's own operatic development, not least his writing for children, something which was unusual at the time. *The Tender Land* (New York, 1954) is another country piece. The composer said: 'The action calls for a cast of five principal singers and takes place in a lower middle class farm in the middle west. Time is the present. The subject concerns the coming to maturity of a young girl.' The plot is the common operatic conflict between love and duty, here between the farmer's daughter's family ties and her love for an itinerant worker, a harvester. When he fails to elope with her as promised, she sets off to find her way in the world alone. Here, as in *Appalachian Spring*,

Copland relied on folk melodies, but his skill is such that they become very much his own.

Samuel Barber (1910–81) was a singer—unusually for a composer in the twentieth century, though not in the past—but wrote no opera until *Vanessa* (New York, 1958). This is a substantial work in four acts, in no way avant-garde in style, with a libretto by the composer's friend Gian Carlo Menotti. It has a tragic heroine (soprano) who has waited twenty years for the return of a lover, Anatol, who in fact has died. Instead his son (tenor) returns, confusingly also called Anatol, seduces Vanessa's niece Erika who becomes pregnant, and then marries Vanessa. According to Wilfred Mellers, in this curious tale 'Barber makes a tragic heroine out of a girl who is forced through circumstances to deny life . . . he gloats over the woman's self-imprisonment, both physical and mental.' Another Barber opera is *Antony and Cleopatra* (New York, 1966): here Shakespeare's play was turned into a libretto by the distinguished Italian director Franco Zeffirelli. But although spectacular and ambitious, the work has won little favour: indeed the British critic Desmond Shawe-Taylor considered that 'Barber's music, rich in substance and sometimes very engaging, was being submerged beneath the glitter and complexity of the spectacle.' The composer's disappointment at the reception of this opera seems to have led to his decision to leave the United States for Italy.

Leonard Bernstein (1918–) is a widely gifted musician, as well known for his conducting as for his work as a composer. He is the heir of Gershwin in that he has successfully bridged the unhealthy gap between popular and serious idioms in a kind of 'crossover music' that needs make no quality concessions. He wrote for the stage as early as 1944 but did not produce an opera until *Trouble in Tahiti* (Waltham, Massachusetts, 1952) when he wrote his own libretto for this story of the breakdown of a marriage. The musical *West Side Story* (New York, 1957) is of course by far his best known work of music theatre: approaching opera in its seriousness of purpose, it raised the Broadway musical to new heights of imagination, passion and scope. The Romeo and Juliet story is here transformed by the librettist Stephen Sondheim into one of low-life urban gang warfare, with Puerto Ricans set against tough New Yorkers, and Maria and Tony representing the lovers from the different factions. Interestingly, Bernstein's 1985 recording uses two non-American operatic singers, Kiri Te Kanawa and José Carreras, in these roles, though not for the spoken dialogue which requires authentic accents. The music mixes Latin American dance rhythms and big band jazz idioms with deeply felt love songs, the virtuoso writing for both vocal and instrumental forces producing a wide range of expression.

Like other fine operas equally set in their own time and place, *West Side Story* has a timeless quality. One can only regret that Bernstein has given it no substantial companion, though his *Candide* (New York, 1956) is a 'comic operetta' after Voltaire's 'philosophical tale' of 1759 and *A Quiet Place* (Houston, 1983) is a three-act augmentation of *Trouble in Tahiti*. Bernstein's achievement, like that of Gershwin and perhaps also Copland, has been to revivify opera by fusing it with new idioms and also to bring a distinctively American voice to the repertory, no small success in view of the multiplicity of cultures and ethnic differences that exist in the United States. Here too a national style has emerged, just as it did in the various European countries, and we can see how what began as a single operatic stream in Italy has now developed many tributaries, each of which adds to the international repertory of opera.

17

THE EARLY TWENTIETH CENTURY: SYMBOL AND EXPRESSION

Pelléas et Mélisande. *Women of power: Salome and Elektra. The knowledge seekers: Moses, Bluebeard, Oedipus, Faust. Berg's expressionism.*

PELLÉAS ET MÉLISANDE

Claude Debussy's opera *Pelléas et Mélisande*, an undisputed French masterpiece, was first performed at the Paris Opéra-Comique on 30 April 1902, an occasion described by the critic Romain Rolland as 'one of the three or four red-letter days' in the history of the French lyric stage. Yet *Pelléas* is his only opera, while no later full-length French opera has joined it in the international repertory. It might seem to follow that the work somehow closed a door rather than opening one and is thus a period piece valid only for its time. Yet *Pelléas* is more highly regarded today than ever before. We may wonder as to the reasons for the lasting power of this still elusive opera, based on an enigmatic play (1892) by Maurice Maeterlinck (1862–1949) and containing no star vocal roles, vivid ensembles or big choruses.

Doubtless the strength of *Pelléas et Mélisande* lies partly in its force as myth and symbol, in other words its power over the unconscious. Maeterlinck believed that a dramatist could go beyond ordinary dialogue to voice 'the more solemn and uninterrupted exchanges between a being and his destiny', and this search for a language higher than language quickly found a place for music. The poet Verlaine conceived of verse as 'music above all . . . where the blurred (*l'Indécis*) and the exact are made one' and declared, 'Take rhetoric and wring its neck — music, again and always!' Mallarmé said that 'Music joins verse to create poetry'. It was in part through the influence of the American writer Edgar Allan Poe that such ideas became especially fruitful at this time. Maeterlinck wrote: 'I owe to him the birth in my work of a sense of mystery and the passion for the beyond', and Debussy too admitted an obsession with this artist who declared that through music 'the soul most nearly attains the great end for which, when inspired by the poetic sentiment, it struggles — the creation of supernal beauty'. Poe wrote elsewhere that music should seek 'the mysterious correspondences which link Nature with Imagination'.

Thus, to quote Debussy's biographer Edward Lockspeiser: 'In *Pelléas*, the old castle in the imaginary kingdom of Allemonde, lugubrious and haunting its inhabitants with painful memories, is a counterpart of the crumbling House of Usher [in Poe]. The character of Pelléas himself . . . is a reflection of Usher, the quintessential man of an over-refined civilisation. Mélisande too has an affinity with Poe's characters . . . [women] destined to die of some unknown and unfathomable illness.' We may think too of Shakespeare's Hamlet and Ophelia, equally unable to endure reality, but in *Pelléas* the protagonists are less sophisticated and self-questioning—and here we may remember Golaud's puzzled and irritated reproach to them in Act III of the opera, '*Vous êtes des enfants . . . Quels enfants!*'

How real are these characters to us? Certainly we feel with and for them, and the opera has a plot which can be briefly told. Prince Golaud finds Mélisande in a forest weeping, but discovers almost nothing of her past; he then brings her to his castle and they marry. But when she and his younger half-brother Pelléas fall in love, Golaud kills him and Mélisande dies in childbirth. So much for the facts of the story. But as Poe once said, 'All that we see or seem is but a dream within a dream,' and in Maeterlinck Debussy deliberately chose a dramatist who in 'saying things by halves would allow me to graft my dream on to his, who could conceive characters whose story and background belonged to no time or place . . .' He thus in turn coopted the active imagination of us, the audience invited to yield itself to his artistic vision.

But the dream is hard to define, and the French writer Marguerite Yourcenar has written that 'we feel half assured that somewhere the white spring of sleep flows into the dark spring of death'. Is *Pelléas et Mélisande* perhaps not just a tragic love story but also a parable of death and fundamentally pessimistic? Certainly there were models: the love of Tristan and Isolde is consummated perhaps only in death, and the castle of Allemonde is like Bluebeard's in that no one leaves save by death's liberation. Golaud is the only character who really takes action, and that is in part destructive. It has been said that Mélisande 'innocently brings the hope of freedom and love' to this place, but both are extinguished and perhaps her child is born into a prison. 'Now it's the turn of the poor little one,' says the old King Arkel in the last line of the opera. The question has even been asked, by Nicholas John: 'Does Pelléas throw himself on Golaud's sword?' This would at least explain Mélisande's cry at this point, 'I haven't the courage!' The same writer adds perceptively that 'so much about Europe in the first years of this century suggests a world not quite blind to its imminent, inevitable destruction, and ready, when the moment came, to commit suicide.' We shall be reminded further, as this chapter proceeds, of the human death-wish that was defined at this time by Sigmund Freud.

According to Pierre Boulez, Debussy 'held the operatic world of his contemporaries in open contempt: idolatry of Wagner enraged him, Italian productions struck no chord of sympathy within him and French ones got on his nerves. The pompous posturing of most singers aroused his deepest scorn, and he was scarcely interested in their vocal accomplishments if they were not serving the cause of musical truth and necessity . . . In short, he had no confidence in striking attitudes on the stage . . . [thus performances of *Pelléas* must renounce] useless heroic gestures and grandiloquent posturing, without falling back on timid dull restraint as an alternative.'

Boulez puts this too simply. As a young man Debussy admired Wagner and adored *Tristan und Isolde*, and he surely saw the resemblances between that opera and his, both stories of forbidden love set by the sea in medieval northern Europe. In a letter written while he was composing it, already quoted in Chapter 10, he admitted the presence of 'the ghost of old Klingsor, alias R. Wagner'. But in the end the differences between *Tristan* and *Pelléas* are more striking than the parallels—compare the lovers' greetings in Debussy's Act IV and Mélisande's death scene with the corresponding Wagner passages. But Debussy's relative understatement does not rob his music drama of its power. As he said, he wanted 'to hold pathetic accents in reserve. There should be differences in the energy of expression. In places it is necessary to paint in monochrome,' adding that in Mélisande's death scene 'one leaves discreetly, like one who has had enough of this planet Earth and departs for where the flowers of tranquillity blossom'. Yet there is no lack of impressionistic atmosphere, as he wrote elsewhere: 'And the scene in the underground caverns was done [Act III, Scene 2], filled with subtle terror and mysterious enough to give vertigo to the best inured souls! And also the scene on leaving those same caverns, filled with sunlight, but with sunlight bathed by our good mother the sea . . .'

The vocal writing in *Pelléas et Mélisande* is highly personal, using quasi-recitative that can expand into lyricism or become still more reticent; there are no arias as such (though Mélisande's '*Mes longs cheveux descendent*' at the beginning of Act III is near one), nor ensembles. Yet a constant thread and musical logic unifies all, and there are themes and ideas associated with characters and situations in the Wagnerian *leitmotif* tradition. One such is the rippling fountain music when Golaud questions

Mélisande about the loss of her ring: she lies to him, but the orchestra clearly tells us the thought that is in her mind. The composer Vincent d'Indy said these themes sent out 'harmonic rays . . . that serve to present the musical speech in the atmosphere suited to it . . . intended to create a peculiarly exquisite atmosphere around the declaimed text'.

Much has been written about the restraint and subtlety of Debussy's opera. There are few orchestral *tuttis* and only some four *fortissimo* markings in the score. Yet for that reason they are all the more effective. There is a terrifying naked violence in Act IV Scene 1, where Golaud seizes his wife's hair and drags her about on her knees, while the orchestral interlude that follows is an outpouring of anguish and compassion that in sheer directness yields nothing to Wagner or Verdi. No one who hears this music could call *Pelléas et Mélisande* over-refined, but even in its quiet passages there is often a smouldering tension. Nothing is really understated; but the ungrandiloquent use of the voice makes this opera different from almost every predecessor. The subject was ideal for the composer, and perhaps it is not surprising that in spite of many efforts to do so he never completed another—though fragments of his projected opera based on Poe's *The Fall of the House of Usher* have been performed. *Pelléas* remains unique, both in his *oeuvre* and in opera as a whole.

WOMEN OF POWER: SALOME AND ELEKTRA

Although at the centre of the work bearing her name, Debussy's Mélisande is essentially weak and pliable, a woman whose actions are childlike and unconsidered. It is through simple human frailty that she deceives her husband, at least over the loss of her ring if not in the actual infidelity he suspects. Even on her deathbed she seems indifferent to the fate of the two men who have loved her, that of her newly born child and indeed finally her own. She seems without motivation. How different are the protagonists of Richard Strauss's operas *Salome* and *Elektra*!

Symbolism, as in Debussy, stirs the imagination in terms that are the stronger for their lack of realism. Expressionism, as in the Strauss works, intensifies the imaginative process into a super-real or 'surreal' experience in which human motivation is mercilessly explored and exposed. The areas of the psyche most apt for such treatment are those of strong and often suppressed impulses such as aggression and sexuality. It has been said by Paul Griffiths that these Strauss operas 'exemplify the display of exultant, turbulent or obsessive emotion . . . of a post-Wagnerian decadence'.

Strauss (1864–1949) was the son of a professional horn-player whose disapproval of Wagner could not stop the boy from discovering this exciting music. As he said, 'It was not until, against my father's orders, I studied the score of *Tristan*, that I entered into this magic work, and later into *Der Ring des Nibelungen*; and I can well remember how at the age of seventeen I devoured the *Tristan* score as if in a trance.' He also attended the first performances of *Parsifal* in 1882 while his father played in the orchestra. At twenty-one he became an assistant conductor at Meiningen and gained further experience at Munich and Bayreuth. By now he was a successful composer with his symphonic poems *Don Juan* and *Tod und Verklärung* already before the public. In January 1892, with his future wife Pauline singing Isolde, he conducted *Tristan* at Bayreuth—and this was 'the most beautiful day of my life', as he told Wagner's widow Cosima.

It was inevitable that Strauss should turn to opera, with his *Guntram* (Weimar, 1894). The libretto was his own and on a distinctly Wagnerian subject, the conflict between the hero's devotion to a holy fellowship and his love for Duke Robert's daughter Freihild. After completing the score, he wrote on it 'Thanks be to God—and holy Wagner.' A poor performance in Munich, where it was not to the company's taste, led him to take revenge on his native city in *Feuersnot* (*Need for Fire*, Dresden, 1901). Here he depicted Munich as a philistine community regarding Wagner as a sorcerer and Strauss as his apprentice. But though his model was doubtless *Meistersinger*, neither the music nor the libretto of *Feuersnot* could parallel Wagner's genial mature warmth and the work has not yet earned much affection. In the meantime, it gave Strauss a reputation as a musical scandaliser. He wrote with some bitterness: 'It's incredible what enemies *Guntram* has made ... I shall shortly be put on trial as a dangerous criminal.'

This reputation was consolidated by his next opera. For *Salome* (Dresden, 1905) Strauss turned to a play by another scandalous artist, Oscar Wilde. In one lengthy act, the opera tells of the young girl Salome's obsessive desire for John the Baptist, held as a prisoner in King Herod's dungeons. Rejected by the austere prophet, she dances for Herod, who desires her, in return for the granting of a wish, and then triumphantly claims the Baptist's head. Though appalled and fearful of the consequences, Herod gives the order, but on seeing her lascivious kissing and fondling of the head he is seized with revulsion and has her killed by his guards, who crush her with their shields.

Salome has a strangely unrelenting intensity. The writing for the relatively small number of voices is eloquent, avoiding the breaks and seams of conventional arias and ensembles. The instrumentation is remarkably resourceful, and the still young but confident composer used his skill to paint the sultry Palestinian night and convey the claustrophobic mood of a decadent, guilt-ridden court haunted by the warning voice of the Baptist offstage. Furthermore Strauss was able to enter most convincingly into the mind of the sixteen-year-old Salome herself, a girl both spoiled and ruthless who knows exactly how to use her young sexuality to advantage. Her dance itself is redolent of a deliberate, perverse sinfulness, with heavy but not clumsy instrumentation. As for the vocal writing, the opera has passionate soprano outpourings from Salome herself as well as the darkly simple and minatory language of the prophet Jochanaan, a baritone role.

Clearly *Salome* offers no conventional operatic love interest. But we are equally far from the gods and heroes of Wagner, and further still from Mozart, Beethoven and the homely *Singspiel* tradition. The decadent atmosphere here is heightened, not diminished, by the Biblical setting. It is worth noting too that the central character is a woman. The composer's marriage to a soprano singer helped sustain his lifelong preoccupation with that voice; and as we shall see, this gave his future operas a character and aspect of their own. In the meantime *Salome* ran into censorship problems following upon its première, but was nonetheless played at fifty different opera houses within two years. Though his fellow-artist Mahler found it a masterpiece, there was also some general sense of scandal, and in the United States in particular, after a performance at the New York Metropolitan Opera, press comments did not mince their words: 'The libretto is a compound of lust, stifling perfumes and blood, and cannot be read by any woman... I say after deliberation that *Salome* is a detailed and explicit exposition of the most horrible, disgusting, revolting and unmentionable features of degeneracy that I have ever heard of, read of, or imagined ... Richard's Strauss's music is aesthetically criminal.' Even the Kaiser remarked that he 'really liked this fellow Strauss, but *Salome* will do him serious harm'. In his turn the composer drily added that this 'harm' had still brought him the royalties that built his fine villa at Garmisch.

Strauss now forged a lasting alliance with the Viennese poet and dramatist Hugo von Hofmannsthal (1874–1929), an aesthete and idealist who believed that an alliance of poetry, drama and music could help to cure society's ills and who called his first stage works 'fantastic little operas and *Singspiele* without music'. In 1900 Hofmannsthal approached Strauss with a scenario for a proposed masque called *The Triumph of Time*, and though the composer rejected this he then asked Hofmannsthal in 1906 if he would collaborate in an opera to be based on the poet's own adaptation of Sophocles' *Elektra*. Their partnership was to continue fruitfully until the writer's death, and though their tastes often diverged, the two men realised early that the mix of their minds was more than the sum of its parts. As Strauss wrote, 'We were born for each other and are certain to do fine things together.'

Like *Salome*, *Elektra* (Dresden, 1909) is in one act. The drama is one of family vengeance: Elektra seeks to avenge the death of her father Agamemnon, and when her brother Orestes returns after a long absence he kills those responsible, namely their mother Clytemnestra and her lover Aegisthus. With her lust for vengeance sated, Elektra dances in insane triumph and falls dead at the final curtain. Again as in *Salome*, the protagonist is obsessed with a single desire, the fulfilment of which perhaps deprives her of her reason for living, and dances to express an emotion beyond words. But in neither opera does Strauss make the mistake of giving the best music only to the central character. In *Salome*, Herod and his wife Herodias are real people whose motives interest us, and similarly here the tormented Clytemnestra has a big solo scene (which the composer three times revised) that seems actually to portray the corruption of this guilty woman, 'sallow and bloated, covered with gems and talismans'.

In *Elektra* Strauss used a more advanced musical language than in *Salome*. Starting from an unusual 'motto chord', a kind of vertical (that is chordal, not melodic) motif whose flavour affects the generally dissonant harmony of the opera, he devised harmonies, colours and textures that together match the drama in obsessional intensity, conveying passions that go beyond the normal and have an inevitably fatal outcome, though at the same time there are other milder passages that serve to emphasise the most dissonant and disorientating ones.

Such an expressionistic portrayal of emotion and consequent action shows the human psyche in an alarming light. Sophocles and the other Greek dramatists had worked in a rather different context: that of drama seen in part as a religious tribute to dangerous gods, an act of ritual and catharsis. Certainly Greek plays were relevant to the lives of their audience, and the extreme actions of Clytemnestra and Elektra stirred people deeply because they touched on feelings such as illicit sexual passion, lust for power, aggression and hatred which could as well exist in the humblest peasant's hut as in kings' houses. But in the ancient world such a tale was supposed to enlighten and purge. Perhaps Hofmannsthal thought along similar lines, with his faith in drama's ability to fulfil a social and humanising role; indeed otherwise his choice of story seems strange for an intellectual who stated his dislike for the 'intolerable erotic screamings' of *Tristan und Isolde*. But whether Strauss agreed with him may be doubted. This intensely gifted artist was also a bourgeois and a practical man. Scandal and success seemed to go hand in hand. Certainly *Elektra* shows no stepping back from the boldness of his operatic subject-matter and musical language.

Strauss believed in directness. Indeed his response to Debussy's *Pelléas et Mélisande* was to ask despairingly, 'Is it *all* like this?' Inevitably he found it too muted. In his turn, Debussy thought *Elektra* contrived and cold-blooded: some harmonies, like the simultaneous sounding of A major and E flat minor triads, simply offended his ear. Though both owed much to Wagner, these two artists could hardly have been more different. Already in 1905 Debussy had sent a score of *Salome* to his publisher Durand as a New Year present with the question: 'Would you like to start the year with "*Salome* or the lack of cordiality between chords"?' When the two composers actually met at Strauss's suggestion over a lunch at the same publisher's house, the German talked mainly about the collection of his French royalties and little was said about music.

Elektra called forth conflicting responses when it was heard in London's Covent Garden Opera under Thomas Beecham in 1910. The critic Ernest Newman called it abominably ugly, but the dramatist Bernard Shaw was bowled over, and wrote: 'There are moments when our feeling is so deep and our ecstasy so exalted that the primeval monsters from whom we are evolved wake within us and utter the strange tormented cries of their ancient struggles with the Life Force. All this is in *Elektra* . . . not even Beethoven in his last great Mass comprehended so much.' In the United States the *New York Sun* critic found 'a counterpoint no longer required to be the composition of two or more melodies which shall harmonise with one another but of melodies which shall spit and scratch and claw at each other, like enraged panthers', while the same city's *Post* declared that 'If the reader who has not heard *Elektra* desires to witness something that looks as its orchestral score sounds, let him, next summer, poke a stick into an ant hill and watch the black insects darting, angry and bewildered, biting and clawing, in a thousand directions at once.' The naked face of expressionism was not to every taste.

THE KNOWLEDGE SEEKERS: MOSES, BLUEBEARD, OEDIPUS, FAUST

Both symbolism and expressionism explored areas of the human psyche, but these explorations were restricted not only by the nature and scope of the artistic imagination but also by their public acceptability. However, some operatic events avoided positive offence because of their setting and handling. Thus Golaud's jealous murder of his half-brother was acceptable because it was set in a remote and unidentifiable place where, as he himself says, 'it is the custom' in such circumstances. Similarly in King Herod's court Salome can demand the Baptist's head with reasonable plausibility, and Elektra's obsession and vengeance seem possible in the different culture of ancient Greece. Some suspension of belief was usually necessary—who believes Elektra could actually dance herself to death?—and that too made the events less disturbing and close to home. Yet for a staged story to be effective the audience had to identify to some extent with its persons and passions.

But too close an identification was dangerous. A jealous husband could not be encouraged to emulate Golaud; potential Strauss protagonists could not be permitted to turn their destructive dreams into action. The artist might aim to arouse emotion as strongly as possible, but as Aristotle stated in his *Poetics*, a 'purification of emotions by vicarious experience' or catharsis was then to take place. A convention of placing dangerous passions at a safe distance was at work, though it was probably used unconsciously. When it was broken, as later in Shostakovich's opera *Lady Macbeth of the Mtsensk District* (Leningrad, 1934), the opera was sharply denounced as 'neurotic and coarse' by the journal *Pravda*: it seems certain that this was chiefly because the drama was set among ordinary Soviet people. Thus while an artist's social role and freedom are limited, an unconscious acknowledgement is made of his power, of the strength of his dream and its potential effect. This remains true today, and there are arguments as to the effect of rock music—which with its theatrical and video aspects might be thought of as a form of popular opera—and its influence upon the impressionable young.

Dream, unconscious, neurosis . . . the use of Freudian terms in this last paragraph has been deliberate. The decade of the three principal operas discussed so far in this chapter was also that in which the psychoanalyst Sigmund Freud (1856–1939) defined his theories. To his central view that the libido or sexual drive was the strongest factor of human behaviour, there was a corollary that such ills as anxiety and neurosis were due to repression and that a permissive society could only be a better one. Essentially a materialist and pessimist, Freud believed that we all suffer from an inner strife between a drive (*Trieb*) towards life and another towards destruction and death. Death viewed as a refuge is a concept familiar in opera, from *Dido and Aeneas* to *Tristan* and beyond—we may think for example of Benjamin Britten's *Peter Grimes* and his final monologue before suicide, 'What harbour shelters peace?' The destruction aspect of Freud's theory is still more alarming, but this too finds its place: in a sense Mozart's Don Giovanni is a conscious destroyer of innocence, while in Bartók's *Bluebeard's Castle* another male destroyer-seeker is at the centre of a story in which each new wife is doomed. The death of Berg's protagonist Lulu at the hands of Jack the Ripper is the climax of a drama in which 'love', as prostitution, and death are dangerously identified. Significantly, the play on which *Lulu* is based is another work of the Freudian decade, Wedekind's *Pandora's Box* – a symbol, if ever there was one, of the deadly unknown of the unconscious into which opera now dared to delve.

Curiosity killed the cat, as the proverb tells us. We recall the terrible proud cry of the Sophocles-Stravinsky King Oedipus, '*Sciam*'—'I shall know'—as he drives himself into the trap prepared by the gods and the unbearable knowledge that will destroy him. In Britten's *Death in Venice*, based on Thomas Mann's novella, the intellectual Aschenbach awakens from a Dionysiac, lustful dream with the words: 'I can fall no further. / O the taste of knowledge./ Let the gods do what they will with me.' Should we simply read 'the forces of the psyche' for 'the gods'? We know that Mann was influenced by Freud—as, indeed, was Hugo von Hofmannsthal. But a quest for self-knowledge could take many forms. There was also 'the wisdom poets crave': and this other line from *Death in Venice* reminds us of the distinction between mere knowing (which is not necessarily a gain) and wisdom, which is always defined as positive and enhancing. This distinction was of course an ancient one. While an understanding of the mind and its relation to the external world was Freud's goal, the philosophers and the religious had been engaged on the same quest long before him, though they may have preferred to talk of the soul. One opera which in part takes such a quest as its theme is Schoenberg's unfinished but still performable *Moses und Aron* (1932, first concert performance of Acts I and II Hamburg, 1954).

For Arnold Schoenberg (1874–1951) the Jewish religion and his musical vocation became indissolubly linked. He considered that music at its best expressed man's longing for God and that therefore musicians 'must be truly priests of art, approaching art in the same spirit of consecration as the priest approaches God's altar . . . it is the task of Israeli musicians to set the world an example of the old kind that can make our souls function again as they must if mankind is to evolve any higher.' He said that the role of the 'chosen one' in his unfinished oratorio *Der Jacobsleiter* was based on himself as one divinely inspired; and his explanation for the bitter opposition which his music often met was that a public lacking in spiritual leadership and awareness 'must inevitably persecute the good and promote the bad'. Such an attitude may be called presumptuous, but we need not doubt the courage with which this artist followed the stern demands of his conscience.

However, the first of Schoenberg's four operas belongs to an earlier phase in his development. *Erwartung* (completed 1909, produced Prague, 1924) epitomises musical expressionism and belongs to a period in which the composer was associated with the *Blaue Reiter* painting group led by Kandinsky—who praised his 'refusal to employ the habitual forms of the beautiful [in favour of] procedures permitting the artist to manifest his own personality'. Schoenberg himself declared that the artist had the duty to create 'what his innermost urges compel'. But he had to pay a price for his extreme musical style—hence, for example, the long wait before the première of this opera.

In fact *Erwartung* is a monodrama: in this work for one singer there can be no interaction between characters. Yet we have dramatic tension as she wanders through a forest at night in search of her lover—the title means *Expectation*—only to come upon his murdered body. The event actually occurs fairly early in the opera, which is in a single scene lasting some thirty minutes, and we then go on to explore her emotions and recollections. But in any case this work which the composer thought of as a kind of dream hardly takes place in a realistic time scale or a real place. As for its form, here we have simply a 'stream of consciousness' with nothing in the way of set numbers, unified only in the broadest sense by motivic figures and with little in the way of tunes or accepted harmonic vocabulary.

Schoenberg's two other one-act operas are *Die glückliche Hand* (1913, produced Vienna, 1924) and *Von heute auf morgen* (Frankfurt, 1930). In the first of these the action is again psychological and explores the mind of a single character, this time a man, though there is also a commenting chorus and some mimed roles including that of the woman he loves. His vocation as an artist is symbolised by a trinket; as for the title, this means something like *The Knack*. *Von heute auf morgen* is a comedy in which a wife regains her husband's wandering attentions by engaging in flirtation herself. Such a story, with echoes of, say, *The Marriage of Figaro*, hardly sounds Schoenbergian, but the libretto of *From Day to Day* by the composer's wife Gertrud allowed him to show himself in a rather more homely and approachable light than usual, and to use some classical procedures such as set pieces and recitatives.

Moses und Aron, as has already been suggested, differs profoundly from these three preceding works and indeed is a kind of Schoenbergian profession of faith. It begins with God's assignment of prophetic leadership to Moses, who, however, feels that he lacks eloquence and appoints his brother Aaron as his spokesman. Strangely indeed for an operatic protagonist, Moses is a speaker and not a singer; Aaron on the other hand is a lyrical tenor. This allocation of vocal roles already seems to symbolise a weakening and softening of the divine message and Aaron's actions are similarly corrupted by expediency. Thus while Moses simply tells the doubting and fearful Israelites that God demands their faith and trust, Aaron performs miracles to reassure them, and in Act II he breaks God's law in his brother's absence by creating the golden calf around which a dance and orgy take place, ending only with the return of Moses and his destruction of the forbidden image. In the unwritten Act III Aaron was to have died and the Israelites to have achieved peace and oneness with God.

Even towards the end of his life, twenty years after his main work on *Moses und Aron*, Schoenberg still talked of completing the opera. As it is, it seems apt that it ends with Moses's cry, 'O word, word that I lack!' It has even been said that the composer could never have expressed the actual fulfilment of God's purpose, and that this was his reason for abandoning the work, even if he could never admit this to himself: as Oliver Neighbour puts it, 'it was his duty to continue to strive towards the expression of the inexpressible'. Be that as it may, the work we have is probably his operatic masterpiece. His musical and dramatic language allowed him here to portray a spiritual leader and also the weaker Aaron who is so much more fallible like ourselves—as are the Israelites with their fickle mass emotions of joy, uncertainty, mockery and yet fear of spiritual things, and aggression.

Schoenberg's Moses seeks knowledge only in the sense of wishing to know the divine will so that he may execute it. Bartók's protagonist in *Bluebeard's Castle* (1912, produced Budapest 1918) is driven on by a more egocentric search into his own lonely soul in the course of which each of his successive wives dies, or at least loses her identity, as she enters his mysterious castle. The 'quest motif' of twentieth-century opera is illustrated here too in the fatal curiosity of the latest wife, Judith. It is her insistence on opening a series of doors in the castle that brings about her own end, as she joins the other 'lost' wives. Perhaps the different rooms to which they lead represent areas of Bluebeard's own psyche—the Hungarian poet Endre Ady, whose poetry the composer admired, had used the phrase 'my soul is an ancient spellbound castle', while a parallel with Golaud's castle and Poe's House of Usher is also possible. Indeed this Bartók opera is based, like Debussy's *Pelléas*, on a play by Maeterlinck which had already been used by Dukas in his *Ariane et Barbe-bleue*. The Hungarian scholar Jószef Ujfalussy has suggested that the drama here 'personifies the tragedy of man's impenetrable solitariness'. Bluebeard's baritone voice, like that of Golaud, seems to symbolise a passing of the years beyond the hope of youth and beyond the hope of fulfilment through love—though that solution is still sought for. Perhaps we are meant to feel that every man is a Bluebeard unable to escape his isolating 'castle', and that the self-sacrificing love of another can only result in that other being trapped and losing her own identity.

Bartók admired Debussy. But his debt to the French composer in *Bluebeard's Castle* is only partial. The rich orchestration owes more to Strauss, and as we open in turn the doors leading to gardens, lakes of tears and a torture chamber we are aware too of the composer's personal style of harmony. Much of the tension in the music arises from a conflict of keys, for example at the tritone interval between C and F sharp, and the use of harsh minor seconds, in other words the simultaneous sounding of adjacent notes such as C and D flat. But there is also a rich melodic vein, often folklike, and some Hungarian critics have argued that this symbolises Bluebeard's relationship with the nature from which he springs and to which he must return.

'To the splendid art of the Greeks we look, to learn from an intimate understanding of it how the artwork of the future must be constituted!' Thus, as we have seen, Richard Wagner. The ancient Greek theatre and Freudian psychoanalytical theory may seem far apart in their approach to the human condition, but Freud's coining of the term 'Oedipus complex' reminds us that for him too the ancient dramatists had their relevance. In *Oedipus rex* (first staged Vienna, 1928), based on the Sophocles tragedy, Igor Stravinsky (1882–1971) treated the powerful tale of the Theban king whose obsessive desire to know the truth of his birth finally uncovers the reality that he has murdered his father and married his mother.

Before *Oedipus rex* Stravinsky had written an operatic 'fairy tale' based on Hans Andersen, *Le rossignol* (Paris, 1914). Act I had been composed by 1909, and the work then laid aside: it was only with reluctance that the composer took it up again, though he then enjoyed the task, writing that it was 'devilish good fun to compose such *chinoiserie*'. Even so, this three-act work, based on a fairly slender tale, fails to engage the heart for all its colour and ingenuity. This cannot be said of *Oedipus rex*. The composer's biographer Robert Craft called it 'a huge surprise, its sheer size and emotional force being utterly unlike anything its forty-five-year-old composer had done before'. The composer gave it an additional classic quality by calling it an opera-oratorio and setting the French text provided for him by Jean Cocteau in a Latin translation—'because I had no notion of how to treat Greek musically'. Although costumed, the principals do not act, but stand and address the audience: as the composer put it, they are 'vocally, though not physically, galvanised statues . . . the portrait of the individual as a victim of circumstances is made far more starkly effective by this static presentation'. A chorus representing the people of Thebes comments on the action, and a narrator in modern dress informs the audience in its own language of the progress of events. If this suggests the Greek theatre, it also relates to the Bach Passions; and the composer said that the work dates from his 'strictest and most earnest period of Christian orthodoxy'. The Christian message plays no real part in the other operas so far discussed in this chapter, and it seems significant that it enters here with a Russian composer of Orthodox faith rather than an artist from the more world-weary Germanic and Western European tradition. The final chorus sung as the self-blinded Oedipus leaves Thebes—'Farewell, Oedipus, we loved you'—is, although austere, compassionate in the Christian sense. True, Stravinsky said later that 'the geometry of tragedy . . . is what concerned me' and came to regard the final '*on t'aimait*' of Cocteau's narrator as sentimental. But he never repudiated the gentle and profound emotion which it expressed.

Schoenberg found *Oedipus rex* 'all negative' when he saw it in Berlin. But its composer understood that this Jewish-Austrian from a different tradition should feel as he did, hearing only 'empty *ostinato* patterns and primitive harmonies'. However, Ravel liked it and declared that 'Stravinsky . . . is seeking', while the young Britten wrote in his 1936 diary that this was one of the 'peaks of Stravinsky's output' and praised 'Jocasta's great and beautiful aria in Act II'. Arias and *arioso*, big choruses, the thrilling duet for King and Queen as Jocasta senses the danger of his drive for the truth—all these seemed to Schoenberg and many others anachronistic in the 1920s. But dogma about 'historical necessity' is as dangerous and foolish in art as it is in politics. Stravinsky himself once said that it was sometimes useful to work at an angle to the mainstream, and the angle could be surprising. An interesting light on *Oedipus* was shed by Leonard Bernstein when he found in it Verdian elements, and particularly echoes of *Aida*—but as Stravinsky admitted, 'If another composer is suggested in my score, it is Verdi.'

In a later opera, *The Rake's Progress*, Stravinsky was to create a likeable but foolish young man who mortgages his soul to the Devil in return for pleasure and riches. The story here, as also in the case of his *Soldier's Tale* of 1918, is a lighter variant of the Faust legend that has fascinated writers and musicians for some four hundred years. But the original Faust's motive was arguably more than a mere lust for pleasure and power, and may symbolise man's desire for knowledge and his will to be something beyond the mortal. The treatment of this story by the Italian composer Ferruccio Busoni (1866–1924) in his opera *Doktor Faust* (unfinished 1924, completed by Philipp Jarnach, first production Dresden, 1925) is a noble one, drawing principally on Marlowe's English play on the same theme, whose very title suggests an intellectual protagonist. Here Faust invokes the help of the Devil's emissary Mephistopheles to regain his youth and elopes with the married Duchess of Parma, who then dies. Meeting a beggar woman who proves to be his restored beloved, he chooses to sacrifice his own life in order to bring back life to the dead child she carries. From the child's body now arises a young man. Busoni wrote five operas, of which this elusive parable of sacrifice and rebirth is the best known, but none has achieved a place in the repertory, not even in Germany, where his style and authority are admired more than elsewhere. Yet he has persuasive advocates: the English scholar Edward Dent claimed that *Doktor Faust* moves on a plane of spiritual experience 'far beyond that of even the greatest works for the stage'. Elsewhere its theatrical effectiveness has been questioned. Nevertheless this Faust opera, with its theme of man's quest for himself outside the parameters of formal religion, takes its place in any history of the spiritual and humanistic seeking of the twentieth century, the intellectual fruit of the Renaissance and subsequent revolutionary thought.

BERG'S EXPRESSIONISM

The two operas of Alban Berg (1885–1935), with their lurid subject-matter, are far indeed from those of Schoenberg. Yet Berg was a fellow-Viennese and Schoenberg's pupil, and his second opera, *Lulu*, is dedicated to the older man. *Wozzeck* (Berlin, 1925), based on Georg Büchner's play *Woyzeck* (1837), portrays a simple soldier who is despised by his officer and experimented upon by an eccentric doctor; a drum major seduces his mistress Marie and beats him up; finally Wozzeck kills Marie and drowns himself. In *Lulu* (left unfinished, produced Zurich, 1937; a completed version London, 1979), Lulu is in turn the mistress, wife and murderess of Dr Schön and is also amorously involved with his son Alwa. After the murder she escapes with Alwa to a Paris gambling den, but must move again when threatened with exposure. Finally she ends her life as a London prostitute who is herself murdered by her last client, the notorious knifeman Jack the Ripper.

In these operas the exploration of the darker and less controllable side of human personality is carried still further than in the two Strauss operas discussed or even *Erwartung*. Berg made this explicit when he praised 'the emphasis on the sensual in modern works!! . . . at last we have come to realise that sensuality is not a weakness, does not mean a surrender to one's own will. Rather is it an immense strength that lies in us—the pivot of all being and thinking'. Though he adduced no real argument to support such a view of art, he was far from carelessly impulsive or undisciplined in his work, so that the musical construction of his operas is thoughtful and ingenious. In *Wozzeck* he used Wagnerian *leitmotif* technique and wrote orchestral interludes that break an act into scenes as in *Rheingold* and *Pelléas*. There are also procedures which he might have avoided as too classical, as he himself pointed out—'song forms, variations ... the various fugues, inventions, suites, sonata movements, variations and passacaglias'. But he added that the audience should not notice such things, but rather 'the social problems of this opera which by far transcend Wozzeck's own fate'.

The music of *Wozzeck* is dissonant and predominantly non-tonal in style, and by the time of *Lulu* Berg was using Schoenberg's twelve-note or serial system of composition. But tonality was not wholly excluded: thus the basic series (or fundamental musical motif) here consists of six notes in C major and six more in F sharp major. The management of this 'row' of notes is personal and so subtle that some scholars think the composer may have camouflaged his methods even from himself—if that means anything in terms of the complex conscious-unconscious process of musical creation. Still, he called attention in the score to his use of such classical structures as recitative, *arioso, arietta, canzonetta, Lied,* duet, *cavatina,* interlude and so on. Each of these numbers relates to the overall form of an act, and to the drama itself: for example a sonata-allegro movement in Act I represents Dr Schön's attempt to break with Lulu and the rondo in Act II portrays Alwa's attachment to her.

Berg placed all this musical sophistication at the service of a story plumbing the depths and dregs of human experience. Just as he had drawn upon his own 'humiliating and horrible' experience of military service when composing *Wozzeck,* here he showed his awareness of the sexual underworld in which respectable people sometimes moved. He had a sister who loved a prostitute and had tried to gas herself when things went wrong—'She's in complete despair, poor soul,' he wrote—and interestingly, the nearest thing to real love for Lulu is felt by the lesbian Countess Geschwitz. The victims of Lulu's charm in the earlier part of the opera—the Medical Specialist, the Painter, Dr Schön—return later as the same performers to take vengeance and are now in turn three clients: the Professor, the Negro, and Jack the Ripper.

In *Lulu,* love is denied and degraded, certainly: but is its theme wholly new? For example, is *Don Giovanni* so different, with its sex-conquering protagonist who finally pays for his sins, unrepentant to the last? Yet Berg's treatment of this story makes it possible to see expressionism as a morbid artistic movement in which the warm humanity of operas such as *Figaro* or *Meistersinger* is notably lacking. However, if Ruskin was right in believing that art reflects its time, we cannot reproach Berg. This was a period of disarray and despair in Europe. Indeed Berg wrote in a letter dated 29 June 1933 to his fellow-composer Webern of his 'utter depression over these times'.

Berg lived long enough to see the rise of Nazism in Germany, although he died before the Anschluss of 1938 that annexed his native Austria. It is tempting to see in the events of the 1930s the Freudian death- and destruction-wish emerging to threaten society at large in the form of trends hostile to the culture that had produced Mozart and Goethe. The exponents of expressionism in the arts had opened the Pandora's Box of human motivation, daringly stripping away much that was perhaps necessary for the continuance of civilised society. Now the contents of that dreadful box were abroad, and the scene was no longer a theatre but the real world.

18

THE LATER STRAUSS AND THE
MID-TWENTIETH CENTURY

The later Strauss. German opera. Russia and Poland. Opera in English.

THE LATER STRAUSS

After *Elektra*, Strauss and Hofmannsthal moved quickly on into a further collaboration. But now they chose a storyline, setting and atmosphere quite different from those of the earlier work. *Der Rosenkavalier* (Dresden, 1911) is a sophisticated love story set in eighteenth-century Vienna. One feature of the two preceding operas remains, however. The principal character is a woman, the mature Marschallin who realises that she must give up her teenage lover Oktavian to the much younger Sophie. Oktavian himself follows Mozart's Cherubino in being a breeches role sung by a soprano or mezzo. The chief male-voice character is a bass, the coarse and comic Baron Ochs von Lerchenau.

This retreat from expressionism doubtless occurred because the collaborators felt that they had drawn enough on that vein of inspiration. Indeed Strauss declared his intention to 'write a Mozart opera'. Seeking a *Nozze di Figaro* paradoxical blend of subtlety and simplicity, Hofmannsthal found his story in a French novel called *Les amours du Chevalier de Faublas* and outlined a scenario in which the setting was changed to Vienna. Strauss was at once enthusiastic: 'We'll go ahead with this one . . . go straight home and send Act I as soon as possible.' The new story allowed a certain elegant eroticism that was to his taste, while the setting in the Austrian capital of the Empress Maria Theresa—with an anachronistic use of the waltz—appealed to a nostalgia for a prettier and more stylish age. *Der Rosenkavalier* was immensely successful: following upon its Dresden première it quickly spread to other opera houses and it reached its hundredth Dresden performance within six years.

The instrumentation of *Der Rosenkavalier* is as opulent as the décor of the Marschallin's boudoir in which it opens. The score is rich too in melody—though there are no set numbers save for the tenor's in Act I, and he is an entertainer who regales the company with an Italian song—and the violins are nearly as songful as the voices. Nevertheless Strauss was anxious that this opera should not be vulgarised, and that it should have lightness and naturally flowing tempi—'Mozart, not Lehár', he said. The scene of the formal presentation of the silver rose to Sophie von Faninal by Oktavian in his formal role as Knight of the Rose on behalf of the Baron who courts her, the moment at which these two charming young people fall in love, is a dramatic high point touched in with celesta-tinted instrumentation that falls just the right side of sentimentality, while the Marschallin's eventual graceful renunciation of her young beau is equally touching. Fine women singers have devoted their skills to this opera, sometimes, like Lotte Lehmann and Sena Jurinac, graduating with the years from the innocent Sophie to Oktavian and finally the Marschallin. The ultimate musical celebration of these three voices comes at the end of the opera, when the crudities of Ochs have been amusingly dealt with and the Marschallin and the lovers express their feelings in a trio of renunciation and fulfilment that provides some of the most memorable pages of twentieth-century opera as well as some of its most affectionate writing for the soprano voice.

Strauss and Hofmannsthal next created *Ariadne auf Naxos* (Stuttgart, 1912)—of which the librettist was to write, 'Of all our joint works, this is the one I never cease to love best, every time I hear it.' Yet the opera as we have it today had a difficult and lengthy genesis. Hofmannsthal's original idea was to present a version of Molière's play *Le bourgeois gentilhomme* with incidental music by Strauss and then to follow this with a one-act opera called *Ariadne auf Naxos* which would tell the Greek story of the daughter of King Minos who was abandoned on an island by Theseus. But the first production showed that the economics of using both actors and musicians on the same evening were unrealistic; and as the composer also realised, 'the playgoing public didn't wish to listen to opera, while the opera lovers didn't want to see a play: the proper cultural soil for this pretty hybrid was lacking.' So the collaborators made a skilful revision (Vienna, 1916). In a prologue, Molière's *bourgeois gentilhomme* sends for an opera company and a group of *commedia dell'arte* players and tells them that the two entertainments devised for his pleasure must take place simultaneously so as to end in time for a fireworks display. We are taken behind the scenes to meet the Composer (a soprano *travesti* role), who is understandably incensed by the assault on his work but in part consoled by the comedians' leader, the vivacious Zerbinetta (coloratura soprano). In the commingling of stories and styles that follows, the comedians comment wittily on Ariadne's plight: when the god Bacchus appears, the distraught Princess at first greets him as liberating death but then proceeds to flirt with him instead and finally ascends as his happy bride to heaven. There is a curious alliance here between broad comic aspects and a rather mannered literary concept, but Strauss's vocal and instrumental technique, using a smallish orchestra of thirty-seven players, is confident and masterful. One of today's finest dramatic sopranos, the American Jessye Norman, describes the role of Ariadne as especially rewarding.

This partially Greek subject was eventually to lead Strauss and Hofmannsthal to yet another Greek opera, though this time set in Egypt. *Die ägyptische Helena* (Dresden, 1928) is a comic extravaganza complete with a sheikh, a sorceress, a magic potion and a talking omniscient sea-shell that the composer described as 'rather like a gramophone'. The original aim of this Helen of Troy story was something akin to musical comedy, a kind of modern equivalent to Offenbach's *La belle Hélène* that was intended to be 'operetta-like, in a much lighter style than *Ariadne*'. Yet the orchestra used here is larger than that of *Rosenkavalier* and glows richly. There is shapely *bel canto* melody for Helen herself (soprano), while her husband Menelaus (a *Heldentenor*) also has fine music to sing. Yet somehow one feels that the collaborators were unable to achieve the simplicity they sought. As Strauss's biographer Ernst Krause puts it, this is 'an opera whose action remains incomprehensible', and all its early productions failed. Perhaps half in defiance and half in apology, Strauss declared: 'My tragic vein is more or less exhausted . . . I feel downright called upon to become the Offenbach of the twentieth century . . . I'm the only composer today with some real humour and sense of fun.' At the same time he toyed with higher ideals: 'My music aspires to a noble Grecian character . . . melodious, sounding well . . . posing no problems whatever to ears that have got beyond the nineteenth century . . . Wagnerian, you think? Yes, but this is a Grecian Wagner . . .'

In the meantime Strauss and Hofmannsthal had produced a more important work, *Die Frau ohne Schatten* (Vienna, 1919). Michael Kennedy has called it the writer's 'most symbolic and intellectual creation, a mixture of fairy tale, magic and Freudian psychology'; and at first Strauss thought the characters less than full-bloodedly human and so had doubts as to its suitability. The woman without a shadow is an Empress (soprano) who is not wholly mortal and therefore cannot bear a child. Unless she finds the shadow which is here a fertility symbol, her husband the Eastern Emperor (tenor) will be turned to stone. Her nurse takes her to the house of Barak the Dyer (baritone), whose wife will sell her shadow. But the Empress cannot bring herself to cause the childlessness of another and her compassion is rewarded from the spirit world with the shadow she seeks. Although this complex parable of the mystery of parenthood, in which fertility is given ethical significance, is too intellectual for some tastes, the music is some of the composer's finest. And as he himself said in an interview in 1935, 'At the point where understanding fails, music starts to come into its own, being always the expression of the infinite.' For certain connoisseurs *Die Frau* is the most satisfying of all the Strauss-Hofmannsthal operas. The songs of Barak, his Act III duet with his wife and the Emperor's hymn of love have all been called inspired, and the illustrative music for the thunderstorm and the Emperor's petrification is vivid indeed. The very large orchestra of one hundred and seven players including eight horns, four Chinese gongs and two celestas is used imaginatively, not least in eight symphonic interludes. Some of the staging demands are challenging, however, with unborn children pleading to be given life and fishes materialising from the air—but so are those of many other operas, not least Wagner's.

Intermezzo (Dresden, 1924), for which Strauss wrote his own libretto, is based on an incident early in his marriage when a case of mistaken identity caused his wife Pauline to accuse him of adultery and brought them to the brink of divorce. He made no attempt to hide the autobiographical element in the story, and indeed at the première the singers in the roles of Storch and Christine were masked with likenesses of the composer and his wife; besides this, the German words *Strauß* and *Storch* are both bird names, ostrich and stork. The domestic scenes here include a cradle song for their child, quarrels with the cook, and a card game of the composer's favourite skat, and in this way the opera is a companion piece for the much earlier autobiographical symphonic poems *Ein Heldenleben* and *Symphonia domestica*. Such egotism may be accepted if we concede that an artist can be at his most universal when most personal, and Strauss was proud of his 'little marriage opera', especially when the producer Max Reinhardt declared the libretto good enough for a straight play.

'All passages of pure dialogue . . . resembling *recitativo secco* should be presented *mezza voce* throughout,' said Strauss, and perhaps the strong emphasis placed on the text in *Intermezzo* adversely affects the music so that a proper balance is not achieved. There is a cinematic succession of short scenes that makes the opera innovative in terms of form. The composer was of course aware of this and declared:

> In none of my works is the significance of the dialogue greater than in this bourgeois comedy, which offers very few opportunities for the development of *cantilena* [lyrical style]. By constant and careful refinement, the symphonic element has been reduced often to no more than a suggestion: even with inexact dynamics it can no longer be an obstacle to the vocal part, so that wholly natural speech . . . can

be clearly understood ... The lyrical element, representing the emotional experiences of the characters, reaches full expression mainly in the longer orchestral interludes. The singers have no chances for extended *cantilena* until the closing scenes of the first and second acts.

It remains only to add that there are but two acts to this domestic opera set in 1907, and that the dedication is 'to my dear son Franz', thus keeping *Intermezzo* firmly in the family.

The last of the Strauss-Hofmannsthal collaborations was *Arabella* (Dresden, 1933). In their eyes this was something of an attempt at 'a second *Rosenkavalier* ... the comedy might turn out better than *Rosenkavalier*', and its setting is also Vienna, although a century later (1860). Its somewhat Mozartian story of cultivated intrigue introduces us to Arabella (soprano), who in Hofmannsthal's words was 'the queen of the big ball and of the whole piece and, as in a fairy tale, she marries the rich stranger in the end'. He is the landowner Mandryka (baritone), 'the most remarkable character in the piece, from a semi-alien world (Croatia), half *buffo* and yet a grand fellow capable of deep feelings, wild and gentle, almost daemonic'. A subsidiary affair marries off Arabella's admirer Matteo (tenor) to her sister Zdenka (soprano). This was an opera which the composer wished to endow richly with arias. 'Could a little more lyricism be fitted into Arabella?' he asked his librettist: 'The aria, after all, is the soul of opera ... separate numbers with intervening recitatives; that's what opera was, is and remains.' Hofmannsthal responded with a fine aria text for the heroine to close Act I and Strauss sent his thanks. But now a tragedy occurred. The poet's son shot himself, and the grief-stricken Hofmannsthal suffered a stroke as he dressed for the funeral and died within minutes. Strauss was devastated, and wrote to his widow, 'No musician ever found such a helper and supporter: no one will ever replace him.' Four years later *Arabella* reached the stage. Its colourful but often delicate music has various erotic and Slavonic nuances as befits the story, though its three acts stretch the material rather far: doubtless it suffers to some extent from the lack of the collaborators' habitual thorough revisions. There are Viennese waltzes, a fine love duet in Act II, a 'polka song' and music to accompany the consumption of Moët et Chandon champagne at Mandryka's insistence—though the final curtain falls when Arabella offers him a glass of water, a chaste symbol of her acceptance of his proposal.

Strauss's five other operas are *Die schweigsame Frau* (*The Silent Woman*, Dresden, 1935), *Friedenstag* (Munich 1938), *Daphne* (Dresden, 1938),

Die Liebe der Danae (*The Love of Danae*, completed 1940, dress rehearsal Salzburg, 1944) and *Capriccio* (Munich, 1942). *The Silent Woman* marked the start of his association with Stefan Zweig, a partly Jewish writer who was to find Hitler's Europe intolerable and left it in 1938 for England and eventually Brazil, where he committed suicide. In the meantime the artistic partnership between the composer and this tortured intellectual pessimist bore fruit. *Die schweigsame Frau* is an effective *buffo* comedy with an eighteenth-century English setting drawn from Ben Jonson and a comic knight, the noise-hating old sea-dog Sir Morosus (bass), who is to be tricked into a mock marriage. Tributes to the past are evident and frequent: there is a Rossinian overture and a Figaro-style barber called Schneidebart (Cutbeard), busy ensembles, and an atmosphere owing something to Verdi's *Falstaff*. Possibly some of the material is over-extended, though, and cuts are sometimes made in performance.

Although the two following Strauss operas had libretti by another writer called Josef Gregor, Stefan Zweig had recommended him and still collaborated in their creation. Both are in a single act. *Friedenstag* (*Peace Day*), as its name suggests, celebrates peace (*Friede*) and is a relatively austere work set in the early seventeenth century during the Thirty Years War. The Commandant of a fortress under siege resolves to die rather than surrender, but then news of peace arrives and he and his former enemy embrace with vows to work for a better world. Strauss complained that this kind of text did not really suit his gift and gave him a 'tiring assignment': certainly it is unusual among his operas, with its male-voice predominance and the importance of the chorus, but its solemn choral writing and the lengthy and dignified aria for the Commandant's wife give it a special place in his work. Intended as a companion piece, the 'bucolic tragedy' *Daphne* is based on the Apollo and Daphne legend of antiquity. The critic Michael Kennedy has called it a 'celebration of pastoral love and Hellenism . . . [with a] flow of pellucid vocal melody set against an orchestral background of delicacy, strength and kaleidoscopic detail'. The nymph Daphne herself is designated as a 'youthful dramatic soprano', the god Apollo and her other suitor Leukippos are differing tenors (the first youthful-heroic, the second high and lyrical) and Daphne's father Peneios is a bass. Set pieces include a Dionysiac feast, a big love duet for Apollo and Daphne and the nymph's final transformation into a laurel tree.

The tense wartime atmosphere surrounding the preparation of *Die Liebe der Danae* is symbolised by the circumstances of its proposed première, cancelled after the July 1944 bomb attempt against Hitler. But once again the opera's Greek theme—described as a 'bright mythology' and drawing upon a hitherto unused Hofmannsthal storyline—seems the opposite of contemporary, being again the story of a god, Jupiter (high baritone), attempting to win a mortal woman, Danae (soprano). Strauss liked this opera and called it 'my last acknowledgement to Greece, and the final meeting of German music with the Grecian spirit'. He once pointed to heaven and said that when he arrived there he hoped he would be forgiven for taking the score along. Perhaps the most striking instrumental passage is the one with two harps, piano, flutes and muted strings which depicts the golden rain in which the god disguises himself.

It is quite hard to believe that *Daphne*, *Die Liebe der Danae* and *Capriccio* were all written in Nazi Germany. Perhaps it is not unjust to see Strauss as the kind of artist who preferred to avoid distasteful realities in favour of the world which he could create and control through his art. But if this seems a weakness in the man, arguably that kind of judgement is more moral than artistic. On a personal level he took a stand more than once in favour of oppressed minorities and stated himself to be indebted to Jewish friends and against the Nazis' anti-Jewish and pro-Aryan policy. In 1935 he asked scornfully, 'Do you suppose that Mozart was consciously "Aryan" when composing?' Yet in the escapism of the subject-matter in *Capriccio* he was true to himself once again. It is set in pre-Revolutionary France around 1775—the libretto actually says 'at the time of Gluck's reforms'!—in the château near Paris of the beautiful Countess Madeleine (soprano), who is loved by both the poet Olivier (character baritone) and the musician Flamand (lyrical tenor). Certainly this one-act libretto by Clemens Krauss—the conductor who also directed the première—helped the elderly composer in his long search to achieve a 'second *Rosenkavalier* without the *longueurs*'. The many felicities of *Capriccio*, with its central soprano role and its discussions of love and art, suggest his joy in setting it and it provides a fine summing-up of his operatic practice as well a conscious tribute to the treasured past. One character has the words: 'I guard the old, patiently awaiting the fruitful new, expecting contemporary works of genius—but where are they?' Doubtless the Countess's final soliloquy in this opera, in which she finds she cannot succeed in separating words from music, epitomises Strauss's achievement—as one writer has put it, 'none of his opera scores . . . ends so magically'. The composer himself once said, 'It is at the ending that the musician can achieve his best and supreme effects,' a remark that could perhaps also be applied to his operatic life-work.

The story of German opera during this period cannot, of course, be told only through Strauss. A country with such a tradition and so many opera houses had its other creators, even if these were of lesser stature. One was Franz Schreker (1878–1934), an artist who was influenced initially by Debussy more than Wagner and who came to be respected by both Schoenberg and Berg. But Schreker's Jewish faith together with his fulsome treatment of rather lurid stories brought about a suppression of his work in Nazi Germany and his operas have not yet been rehabilitated, though *Der Schatzgräber* (Frankfurt, 1920) may deserve staging—its title means *The Treasure Hunter*. Hans Pfitzner (1869–1949) composed five operas but is currently remembered only for his 'musical legend' *Palestrina* (Munich, 1917), based on the life of the Italian composer and a work of intellectual and spiritual force. It is also a treatment of an artist's vocation and his place in society, and as such it belongs in a German tradition exemplified by works as different as Wagner's *Meistersinger*, Schoenberg's *Moses und Aron*, Krenek's *Jonny spielt auf* and Hindemith's *Mathis der Maler*.

Max Brand (1892–1980) and Ernst Krenek were both pupils of Schreker. Brand's *Maschinist Hopkins* (Duisburg, 1929) is a parable of murder and revenge in an industrial setting with a mainly dissonant idiom and two effective jazz numbers, a tango and Black Bottom, which are nevertheless overlong and too close to plain imitation to fit in with the rest. Ernst Krenek (1900-) also associated jazz with a flexible harmonic style in his lively and spectacular *Jonny spielt auf* (Leipzig, 1927), composed to his own libretto. *Johnny Strikes Up* is a story of a black jazz bandleader who teachers the world to dance the Charleston, and it had a quick success. The composer said that one influence on the work was that of Puccini, while all was seasoned 'with the condiments of jazz', though the American scholar Donald Grout found the opera 'about as genuinely American in flavour as a French ice cream soda'. Krenek did in fact have an affinity with America and made his home there from 1938 after the Nazis had condemned him as a 'cultural Bolshevik', becoming a distinguished teacher as well as continuing to compose throughout his long career.

Paul Hindemith (1895–1963) had a relatively conservative training and then broke away towards expressionism and shocked the public with such pieces as his one-act opera *Sancta Susanna* (Frankfurt, 1922), which for all its innocent-sounding title is a fairly explicit presentation of a young nun's sexual fantasies. However, the comedy *Neues vom Tage* (Berlin, 1929), though satirising the crueller aspects of tabloid journalism, already took something of a moral line. Hindemith was moving towards a more consciously serious social-artistic purpose. Thus the opera *Cardillac* (Dresden, 1926) tells of a master goldsmith who murders in order to repossess himself of his creations, but it also considers an artist's relationship with society. This theme was treated again in a much more lofty way in this composer's best-known opera, *Mathis der Maler* (Zurich, 1938). The central character here is the sixteenth-century painter Mathias Grünewald (baritone), who first leads a peasant revolt against the authority of the Church and then questions the value of his artistic vocation in times of general distress and unrest, but finally recognises humanity's need for art. Thus yet again the view of the artist as leader-prophet surfaces in twentieth-century opera. It disturbed authority: the planned Berlin première of the opera was cancelled on Nazi orders. Hindemith's last opera, *Die Harmonie der Welt* (Munich, 1957), which like *Mathis* was to his own libretto, takes the matter of heavenly-earthly order a stage further in its treatment of the life and work of the Renaissance astronomer and visionary Johann Kepler, whose studies of planetary motion influenced Newton. As we see, in the face of totalitarianism both Schoenberg and Hindemith came to adopt a moral stance, reacting against their early self-exploratory expressionism in order to exhort and enlighten an uneasy public.

Kurt Weill (1900–50) resembles Krenek rather than Hindemith and such savagely witty and jazzy operas as his updating of *The Beggar's Opera* as *The Threepenny Opera* (Berlin, 1928) and *The Rise and Fall of the City of Mahagonny* (Leipzig, 1930) exemplify his evident intention to reach a wide audience by directness of utterance. Yet a seriousness remains, as with his literary collaborator in these works, Bertolt Brecht. *Mahagonny* is an anti-capitalist satire in three acts set in America: the newly founded city itself is a kind of pleasure centre devoted to sex, drink and sport, but its purposelessness soon discourages its citizens. Finally the hero, Jim Mahoney (tenor), is condemned to death for crimes including running out of money and the stated moral is that the proverbial bed made must be lain on, and that no help for anyone is at hand. The orchestra is small and features saxophone, banjo, bass guitar, piano, zither and accordion. *Die Bürgschaft* (*The Citizenry*, Berlin, 1932) again sounds a 'note of warning against evil social conditions' with its Greek-style commenting chorus criticising the prevailing order and a stage chorus representing an oppressed people. Like both Krenek and Hindemith, Weill left Hitler's Europe and settled in America, where he was to make a successful living in the lighter theatre with a series of Broadway shows between 1938 and 1943 including *Knickerbocker Holiday*, *Lady in the Dark* and *One Touch of*

Venus. Because of this, some consider his quite striking gifts to have been unfulfilled or squandered; but perhaps this part of his career may be seen more positively as the natural fruition of his commitment to artistic communication. Though latterly he apparently lost interest in the activities of his 'serious' contemporaries, he did not opt out of his responsibilities. To the end his musical shows had artistic substance without pretentiousness.

An apparently unconscious tradition of adherence to the oldest of operatic practices, namely the use of Greek drama and myth, survived in German-language opera well into the twentieth century. Besides Strauss's operas, there were such pieces as the *Leben des Orest* (Leipzig, 1930) by Krenek and two operas by the Viennese Egon Wellesz called *Alkestis* (Mannheim, 1924) and *Die Bakchantinnen* (Vienna, 1931). Carl Orff (1895–1982) composed an *Antigonae* (Salzburg, 1949) and *Oedipus der Tyrann* (Stuttgart, 1959). Orff has had a bad critical press, doubtless in part because he seems alone among German-Austrian composers of substance to have lived and worked with ease (which Strauss did not) under Nazism. But the infectious, fresh exuberance and sheer impact of his semi-dramatic cantata *Carmina burana* (Frankfurt, 1937) deserve respect as qualities that are all too rare in music of the period, and this work has earned wide public affection. For many people the *Carmina* are the beginning and end of Orff, whose important influence as an educationist is outside the scope of this book, but his operas should perhaps be better known. Certainly his aesthetic concept of a 'total theatre' drawing upon both Greek and Baroque traditions belongs in a historical line that has been drawn with surprising firmness.

RUSSIA AND POLAND

Sergey Prokofiev (1891–1953) was born in the Ukraine and had composed a three-act opera called *The Giant* before his tenth birthday, and he was to write thirteen more. Yet he was never really successful as an opera composer. The earliest of his operas to be staged was *The Gambler*, completed in 1917 for the Mariinsky Theatre in Petrograd but having its first production delayed because of the opposition of director and performers alike to its bold and violent idiom; the Revolution in the same year stopped the performance altogether, and it had to wait twelve years for its première (Brussels, 1929). This Dostoyevsky story was in part a study in obsession, though the treatment had elements of comedy also. The composer's penchant for biting irony and fantasy was also reflected in *The Love for Three Oranges* (Chicago, 1921). This abounds in musical energy and wit: yet apart from an attractively strutting little march its music is not very memorable and the fairytale plot lacks human interest. *The Fiery Angel*, completed in 1923 but not staged until after the composer's death (Paris, 1954), has a story set in medieval times that has magical elements and even an appearance by Faust and Mephistopheles, who eats and then resurrects a serving-boy; at the end of the opera its heroine Renata is sentenced to death for sorcery. Here again, the more grotesque aspects of Prokofiev's imaginative language seem often to submerge those human emotions with which an audience can identify. Perhaps some lack of broad humanity has been the chief reason for this composer's failure to have some of his operas staged immediately, or at all. Even the epic national opera based on Tolstoy which occupied him in 1941–3, *War and Peace*, was never given in his lifetime, although it conformed with Soviet artistic policy, as did the opera *Semyon Kotko* (Moscow, 1940), based on a book by Valentin Katayev called *Son of the Working People*. Similarly *The Story of a Real Man*, though telling the story of a Soviet air ace called Aleksei (bass) who loses his legs but flies again, was disliked at a concert performance in 1948 and its stage première (Moscow, 1960) had to wait until the cultural thaw which came after Stalin's death—an event which by an odd coincidence took place on the same day (5 March 1953) as the composer's own.

As a major composer who clearly possessed a lifelong drive towards opera, Prokofiev has been unfortunate. Even today, when at least two of his ballets and much other non-theatrical music are firmly in the repertory, attempts to establish, say, *War and Peace* still meet with only partial success. Perhaps his operas do not offer sufficiently rich and satisfying vocal roles. And probably the glorification of heroic deeds was not this sophisticated composer's forte—though no one denies the dramatic force of some of this music, or for that matter the celebrated *Alexander Nevsky* film score he wrote for Eisenstein in 1938. A new London production of *The Fiery Angel* is currently planned, however, and this may bring about some reassessment of the opera's viability.

Prokofiev suffered official adverse criticism and discouragement in the 1940s, at a time when he could have expected fame and favour as the Soviet Union's leading composer. For 'Stalin preferred things with tunes', as we know from Maxim Shostakovich, the conductor son of Prokofiev's younger colleague Dmitri Shostakovich (1906–75). Shostakovich's first opera, *The Nose* (Leningrad, 1930), was a biting satire on petty officialdom based on a play by Gogol. Its title was originally *The Dream*, the Russian word for which (*son*) the author then reversed to give '*nos*' or 'nose'. Major Kovalyov (baritone) loses his nose, which takes on a life of its own (as a tenor!) and treats the Major with scant respect until it is arrested and restored to its owner. Apart from the play on words mentioned above, Gogol seems to have had some kind of nose complex and once wrote that he was 'seized by a frenzied desire to change myself into one big nose' to imbibe nature's fragrances. But Freud has showed that dreams and jokes alike link to the unconscious, and there is perhaps a castration symbol also in the nose-loss in Shostakovich's opera which is reinforced by the casting of the Police Inspector as an all-but-impossibly-high *haute-contre* tenor: are we supposed to feel that establishment-serving emasculates? This story is unmistakably Russian in its knockabout humour, but even in the relatively free period of socialism when it was written it gave offence. To quote Maxim Shostakovich again, 'Everything about it was a bit modern; it was hard to perform; at that time more traditional things were preferred.'

A far greater scandal was caused by Shostakovich's second opera, *Lady Macbeth of the Mtsensk District* (Leningrad, 1934). After an initial success and nearly two hundred performances, this tense and dissonant drama of passion and murder among Russian country folk deeply offended Stalin, who saw it in 1936, and a bitter attack followed a few days later in the official newspaper *Pravda*. This journal declared that *Lady Macbeth* represented 'chaos instead of music' and was neurotic and vulgar in a way such as to titillate bourgeois audiences. It had its admirers abroad — for example, the young Benjamin Britten in 1936 called it 'a most moving and exciting work of a real inspired genius', and its layout in numbers with orchestral interludes linking scenes and big choruses may well have influenced *Peter Grimes*, another opera featuring a misfit provincial protagonist. Many years later the work was at last reinstated in the Soviet Union, having been revised and retitled as *Katerina Izmailova* (Moscow, 1963). But in the meantime its disgrace turned Shostakovich right away from opera. His only later ventures in this field were minor: another piece based on Gogol called *The Gamblers*, begun in 1941 but left unfinished, and a musical comedy called *Moskva, Cheremushki* (Moscow, 1959).

It is sad to reflect on the relative operatic failure of such major Russian composers as Prokofiev and Shostakovich, though the reasons relating to the older composer lie principally in his artistic personality and those concerning the younger are largely external. But arguably the period itself was unpropitious, with its rapid social change and often violent political and military activity. However, one outstanding individual figure to mention here is that of the Pole Karol Szymanowski (1882–1937). In a letter of 1912 he wrote: 'The thought of composing an opera fills my mind with great intensity ... I am looking for a new and effective libretto.'

Szymanowski's one-act opera *Hagith* dates from the following year, though it had to wait until 1922 for its première in Warsaw. Owing much to Strauss's *Salome*, *Hagith* has as its central figure the Biblical King David. Hagith is ordered to give herself to the aged monarch to restore his failing powers, but avoids doing so as she loves his son Solomon. David dies and Solomon arrives too late to prevent Hagith's punishment of death by stoning for her refusal. Despite the powerful story, the opera had only a cool reception.

Nevertheless Szymanowski went on to devote six years to the slow perfecting of his operatic masterpiece, *King Roger* (Warsaw, 1926). Admitting eroticism as a fundamental part of his artistic creed, he took a story that borrowed its theme from Euripides' *Bacchae* and tells of a handsome, mysterious young shepherd-prophet, in fact the disguised god Dionysus, who comes from India to a Sicilian court in the twelfth century. The Christian King Roger (baritone) at first resists his message, but the queen and citizens are captivated and led away by the stranger. But whereas in Euripides' original play the king is destroyed, here he is finally converted and yields to the ancient pagan religion. A Polish scholar has written that the essential thesis of this opera is that 'only through physical love can the mysteries of divine love be approached or creative work accomplished'—D. H. Lawrence, an exact contemporary, might have approved—and it can be argued that such a glorification of impulse and sexuality is more life-affirming than the self-torture of the expressionists who created in the context of a corrupted Jewish-Christian tradition. Perhaps because of this, *King Roger* is more harmonious and sensually seductive than most twentieth-century operas, and the vocal writing for the Shepherd (tenor) and Queen Roxane (soprano) has a joyous opulence.

The German critic H. H. Stuckenschmidt called *King Roger* 'the most important musical work ever produced by Poland' and even admirers of Chopin who cavil at that opinion would agree that it is Poland's most significant opera. It has been linked with Wagner's *Parsifal*, also a metaphysical statement, while its richly chromatic idiom also owes much to Strauss. The less obvious influence of Schreker has also been suggested; but Szymanowski was a well-travelled composer who also drew on his knowledge of Greek and Arab-Persian music to create an atmosphere owing nothing to simple imitation. Today no one blames it for expressing 'the sensuous ecstasy of a Byzantine imagination', and it has enjoyed successful post-war productions and gained a place on the edge of the repertory, though performances in the original Polish will surely remain rare outside Poland.

In the first edition of his book *Opera* (1940), Edward Dent wrote: 'If a young English composer could succeed in making an immediate and sensational success at Sadler's Wells, where else can that opera be performed?' In the second edition (1949) the same author was able to write that 'Five years later the unexpected actually happened.' Within three years of its première Benjamin Britten's *Peter Grimes* (London, 1945) had been translated into seven languages and produced in sixteen opera houses in Europe and America. 'Here at last,' wrote Imogen Holst, 'was a real English opera that was going to live side by side with any of the great operas of the world . . . In the fog of the terrible manhunt, the poor demented fisherman seemed to grow in stature until he was no longer a separate individual . . . he was bearing the burden of all those other outcasts who are rejected by their law-abiding neighbours because they are different from other people.' Is this opera then a universal utterance, with all the mythic and symbolic force implied by that? Not for John Drummond in his book *Opera in Perspective* (1980): here *Peter Grimes* 'probably does not succeed as a work with a message' and Peter and his friend Ellen Orford fail to 'become symbols of us all'.

Can both these opposing views be right, in the complex sense of truth which commonly applies where art is concerned? Perhaps so, if we consider together Drummond's characterisation of Peter Grimes as an 'outsider-hero', and Holst's word 'outcast'. By definition an outsider-outcast cannot symbolise the majority. Yet he can stand for those whose alienation from society is symbolised in Albert Camus's title *L'étranger* for a novel published in 1942, the year in which Britten (1913–76) began work on his opera. For Drummond, the nature of the alienation here is clear: 'Though this never surfaces as an open accusation, it is because Grimes is a homosexual that he is driven out of the community.' Yet there is nothing in the libretto that gives this statement explicit justification and much that says the opposite, namely Grimes's intention to marry Ellen and have children. It will, however, readily be admitted that Britten's own homosexuality as well as his wartime pacifism must have been in his mind when he said of himself and the singer Peter Pears, his lifelong friend who created the role of Grimes, that 'a central feeling for us was that of the individual against the crowd'.

For Leonard Bernstein, Britten was 'a man at odds with the world'. But he did not share Peter Grimes's helpless pessimism, since he had found early in life that even when (as Grimes cries) 'the horoscope's bewildering' he could as a brilliant and hardworking artist do much to relieve and redeem a difficult psychological makeup and in this process of self-healing give fully of his art for the general good—do we know that matters were much different for that other uneasy personality Beethoven? Opera was for Britten 'the most exciting of musical forms', and in 1951 he said in the town of his birth: 'As an artist, I want to serve the community.'

The skill that Britten demonstrated in *Peter Grimes* was the fruit of a long apprenticeship writing for film, theatre and radio; and he had also composed the music for the operetta *Paul Bunyan* (New York, 1941). His first vocal compositions dated from childhood and his interest in drama was documented as early as the age of seven, when he penned a tiny play with music about the British royal family. *Peter Grimes* was a work in the *verismo* tradition and doubtless none the worse for that: in 1945, in a weary Europe needing relief and reconstruction, no opera company would have accepted a radically avant-garde work even if a composer such as Britten could have written one. And as Peter Pears has said, this opera actually has 'plenty of tunes'.

As one might expect from an admirer of Verdi, *Peter Grimes* is a number opera with sections that range easily from brisk recitative, as in the courtroom prologue, via *arioso*, aria and ensemble to big choruses. Examples of a sort of half-number are Hobson's 'The carter goes from pub to pub' and Mrs Sedley's 'Murder most foul it is', the routine tread of the one and the Verdian melodramatic chromaticism of the other being at once characteristic and memorable. Among more extended solo songs, Grimes's 'Now the Great Bear and Pleiades' is nearer aria style with its agitated middle section and return; while still more fully-fledged arias are his 'In dreams I've built myself some kindlier home', a rare gentle moment for this tormented protagonist, and Ellen's 'Embroidery in childhood was a luxury of idleness'. The women's ensemble 'Do we smile or do we weep?', a trio for the pub landlady Auntie, her two nieces singing in unison and Ellen, is another moment of calm after the powerful confrontation scene between her and Peter skilfully placed against the background of a church service of Matins in which the liturgical words perfectly match the developing personal drama. Among the many unashamedly vivid choruses are the *fugato* of 'Look, the storm-cone' and the round 'Old Joe has gone fishing', both in Act I, and the 'Him who despises us we'll destroy' that follows upon the pub dance scene in Act III. The last orchestral interlude preceding Peter's lonely final appearance at night, with the offstage townsfolk seeking him to avenge the death of his apprentice, recalls the expressionistic language of *Wozzeck*, but the mad scene that follows is more Italian in tradition. So too is the suicide urged on Grimes by the sympathetic but realistic Captain Balstrode, and acquiesced in by Ellen, the woman Peter has hoped to love.

Commentators who view this opera chiefly as a parable of a misfit both persecuted and guilt-ridden, and thus threatened both from without and within, must presumably see this suicide as an act akin to Oedipus' self-blinding and self-exiling: 'Peter must accept the way he is,' writes Drummond, and that is not to be borne. It is true that in the apparently varied canon of Britten's operas from *Peter Grimes* to *Death in Venice* (Aldeburgh, 1973), certain dramatic features do recur. The theme of the outsider is to be found again, however changed, in the comedy *Albert Herring* (Glyndebourne, 1947), telling of the boy who is ridiculed while he fails to break from his mother's apron-strings and lose his virginity. It is there again in *Owen Wingrave* (BBC Television, 1971), where Owen as a pacifist is angrily rejected by his military family, and more subtly in *Death in Venice*, where the writer Aschenbach helplessly observes the progress of his own agonising alienation from acceptable behaviour as he becomes obsessed with a young Polish boy to whom he never speaks.

The failure of communication, trust and love between adults and children is another theme that preoccupied Britten, who arguably remained emotionally fixed at a psychological phase of passionate boyhood friendships. Thus an early draft of the *Grimes* libretto had Peter telling his apprentice to 'love me, damn you!', and an early comment on the opera by the composer's friend Edward Sackville-West mentions 'the helpless pathos which binds his soul, in a confusion of cruelty and tenderness, to that of the boy'. The apprentice John never once speaks, and it cannot be coincidence that the same is true of the boy Tadzio in *Death in Venice* – an exchange is impossible. Similarly the attempts of Peter Quint and Miss Jessel, the evil and tormented ghosts in *The Turn of the Screw* (Venice, 1954), to reach and possess the children Miles and Flora are constantly frustrated and the caring governess who seeks to protect them herself brings about the boy's death when she finally forces him to utter Quint's name.

Another central theme in Britten's operas is that of the persecution, corruption and loss of innocence. Peter Grimes may not be a wholly innocent victim of society; but in *The Rape of Lucretia* (Glyndebourne, 1946) Lucretia's famed chastity is violated by the Roman Prince Tarquinius—though, interestingly, he declares that her lips are 'red with wanting', while she admits dreaming of him and, as she kills herself, cries that 'wanton blood washes my shame away', so that it seems she has been tempted. In *Billy Budd* (London, 1951), Herman Melville's story is of a handsome and simply virtuous young sailor with a stutter that robs him of the power to reply when he is falsely accused by the Iago-like master-at-arms Claggart of mutiny, so that in frustration he strikes out and kills his accuser. Captain Vere recognises his essential innocence but must acquiesce in his hanging, to be forgiven and in some way redeemed by Billy's death. Even Sammy in *The Little Sweep* (Aldeburgh, 1949) is a child victim of an uncaring society who is rescued by children and their young governess: the implication is that these rescuers touched by pity have not yet been spoiled by the 'shades of the prison-house' and compromised morality surrounding most adults. Later, Britten's vision became darker, so that the Cabin-boy in the children's 'vaudeville' called *The Golden Vanity* (Snape, 1967) is allowed to drown as a sacrifice to expediency made by his captain and shipmates. Even Tadzio is attacked by an older boy and then walks alone 'far out to sea' in a complex symbol of childhood's end and lost innocence as *Death in Venice* ends.

Certain musical features also recur in Britten's operas. A *passacaglia* – in other words, variations above a repeated bass line—occurs in each of them. Variation form provides the basis for *The Turn of the Screw*, in which a twelve-note theme is used for much of the thematic-harmonic material without the style ever suggesting Schoenberg. But it would be wrong to give an impression that Britten stood still in stylistic and dramatic terms. He created a Verdian historical costume drama in his opera on the first Queen Elizabeth, *Gloriana* (London, 1953), written to celebrate the coronation of Elizabeth II, and again asserted his English roots when he set Shakespeare in *A Midsummer Night's Dream* (Aldeburgh, 1960), using a *fait accompli* story in a way that was unusual for him—he once said, 'I have to be in on it from the beginning'—and rather far from his usual area of dramatic material. Yet even here the theme of non-communication between the mortals and the fairies, notably between the down-to-earth rustics including Nick Bottom and Queen Tytania with her attendants, is clearly reflected in the contrasting sonorities and styles given to these groups. A musical enrichment following upon the composer's visit in 1955–56 to the Far East, especially Bali and Japan, was shown here and also in the new sonorities of the children's opera *Noye's Fludde* (Orford Church, Suffolk, 1958) and even more clearly so in the instrumentation and heterophony—semi-unison melodic writing—of the three church parables *Curlew River*, *The Burning Fiery Furnace* and *The Prodigal Son* (Orford, 1964, 1966, 1968) and *Death in Venice*.

Britten is the most important among twentieth-century composers writing opera in English, in terms of musical-dramatic quality and sustained achievement in a wide range of approaches to the form. These include big spectacular opera (*Peter Grimes*, *Billy Budd*), historical drama (*Gloriana*), comic opera (*Albert Herring*) and Shakespearean comedy (*A*

Midsummer Night's Dream). There is also chamber opera (*The Rape of Lucretia* and *The Turn of the Screw*), children's opera (*The Little Sweep* and *Noye's Fludde*) and the three 'parables for church performance' which like *Noye's Fludde* make Christian statements in a way already adumbrated twenty years earlier by the Male and Female Chorus who comment in *Lucretia*. Though this composer's persona seems to have been sometimes shy and awkward, he learned early how to communicate with his fellow-human beings through a practice of his art that allowed him, in a phrase of the art historian Bernard Berenson that he once quoted, to 'enhance their lives'.

Britten's first opera, *Paul Bunyan*, and Stravinsky's last, *The Rake's Progress* (Venice, 1951), had the same librettist in the person of Wystan Auden. Stravinsky and Auden had actually done what Britten nearly did, namely drawn up European roots to settle in the United States early in World War II, and despite the generation between them the two men became friends and artistic partners. In the composer's words:

> Hogarth's 'Rake's Progress' paintings, which I saw in 1947 on a chance visit to the Chicago Art Institute, immediately suggested a series of operatic scenes to me. I was, however, readily susceptible to such a suggestion for I had wanted to compose an opera in English ever since my arrival in the United States. I chose Auden on the recommendation of my good friend and neighbour Aldous Huxley ... Starting with a hero, a heroine and a villain, and deciding that these people should be a tenor, a soprano and a bass, we proceeded to invent a series of scenes leading up to the final scene in Bedlam that was already fixed in our minds. We followed Hogarth closely at first until our own story began to assume a different significance ... the plot and the scheme of action were worked out by the two of us together, step by step. We also tried to co-ordinate the plan of action with a provisional plan of musical pieces, arias, ensembles, and choruses.

Stravinsky later wrote in more detail: '*The Rake's Progress* is cast in the mould of an eighteenth-century number opera; the dramatic progress depends on the succession of recitatives and arias, duets and trios, choruses and instrumental interludes.' He rejected 'Wagnerian continuous melody, which consists, in effect, of orchestral commentary enveloping continuous recitative' in favour of a story 'told and enacted almost entirely in song', in other words in structured melody. We may compare him here with Britten, who wrote in 1945 of *Peter Grimes* that he 'decided to reject the Wagnerian theory of "permanent melody" for the classical practice of separate numbers that crystallise and hold the emotion of a dramatic situation at chosen moments'. It seems that both these major composers consciously drew on a non-Germanic operatic tradition, and in fact Stravinsky said that 'the *Rake* is deeply involved in *Così.*' He also wrote:

> Whether a composer can make use of the past as I did, and at the same time move in a forward direction is a question for Public Relations that concerned me not at all during the writing. Nor do I care about it now ... May I ask the listener to suspend these questions, as *I* did while composing, and instead to discover the opera's own qualities? I did not compose it to fuel debates on the historical validity of the approach, or 'the use of pastiche'—though I will gladly allow that that is what I did if it will release people from these silly arguments and bring them to the music.

Admirers of the early Stravinsky ballets may be disappointed to find in *The Rake's Progress* an eighteenth-century facility in the melodic writing and little trace of orchestral virtuosity. There is nothing exotic about this morality opera, and little that is identifiably Russian either—for those features we must go back to such pieces as *Le rossignol* or the two shorter theatrical ones, *Renard* and *Mavra* (both Paris, 1922). Still, the sinister graveyard scene, in which Tom must gamble with Nick Shadow (eventually a baritone role) for his soul but despite winning still loses his reason, has its parallels in the composer's *Soldier's Tale* (Lausanne, 1918)—while, as we have seen, gambling itself is much in the Russian tradition. Yet if we think of *The Rake's Progress* as a work outside the mainstream—whether that be Stravinskian, Russian or general—we risk not merely the composer's irritation but also a fall into a typical historian's error of misunderstanding the mainstream altogether: artists of Stravinsky's stature do not ride upon it but more often create it. Let the last word on this lighter-style Faustian opera rest with the composer's wife Vera:

> Igor used to claim no more for the music than that it was conventional. But what beautiful inventions are in it too: the chord progressions at the end of the first half of the *cavatina*, for instance; and the modulation to 'O wilful powers'; and the transformation of the Ballad Tune in the final scenes; and the style-embalmed representations of Tom's fear in the graveyard (the double *appoggiaturas*), and their reappearance during his madness. It seemed, however, that Igor saved his finest inspirations for the last scene: in

'Venus, mount thy throne', in the duet, 'In a foolish dream', and in 'Where art thou, Venus?' which to me is the most touching music he ever wrote.

Though much less important as a musician than Stravinsky, another European-American, Gian Carlo Menotti (1911–), has composed nearly twenty operas. *The Medium* and *The Telephone* (New York, 1946 and 1947) are shorter pieces, the one a tale of a fraudulent spiritualist dignified by the composer-librettist as a 'tragedy', and the other a light comedy with the subtitle *L'amour à trois*. A more serious vein is evident in the sub-Kafkaesque *The Consul* (Philadelphia, 1950), in which Magda Sorel, the wife of a political activist in a nameless European state, vainly endeavours to obtain an exit visa that will release her and her husband, and finally kills herself; but the evident sincerity of the text is not always matched by comparable musical substance. Nevertheless this opera has had considerable success. Menotti's talents, verging on the sentimental, are perhaps better represented in *Amahl and the Night Visitors*, the first opera written especially for television (NBC-TV, 1951): this story of a young crippled boy who for one winter night plays host to the Magi travelling towards Bethlehem and the cradle of the Infant Christ, is designed to touch the heart and has earned itself a regular place in American Christmas television schedules. *The Saint of Bleecker Street* (New York, 1954) is a *verismo* piece with a moral and *Maria Golovin* (Brussels, 1958) an exploration of a blind man's obsessive jealousy. Another television opera, *Labyrinth* (NBC-TV, 1963), was followed by a three-act *opéra-bouffe* for Paris (1963) called *Le dernier sauvage*: here this composer with a relatively unsophisticated musical language used passages of twelve-note music to satirise contemporary society and culture. His most recent operas are *The Boy who Grew too Fast* and *Goya*, the latter with a title role created for the tenor Placido Domingo. It has been said that Menotti's musical language is often a kind of facile borrowing from Puccini; but it is more positive to quote here the judgement of the American scholar H. Wiley Hitchcock, for whom this composer combines 'the theatrical sense of a popular playwright and a Pucciniesque musical vocabulary with an Italianate love of liquid language and a humane interest in characters as real human beings; the result was opera more accessible than anyone else's at the time'. Certainly that is no bad thing in a period in which many composers show little concern at their failure to achieve contact with the musical public.

However, we may salute the British composer Michael Tippett (1905–) for his achievement in making a considerable impact on the opera-going public in a challenging and often uncompromising musical language. He came to opera late, and possibly would never have done so had it not been for the success of his younger friend Britten, whose *Peter Grimes* in effect brought about a British renaissance of interest and opportunity. Others of Tippett's generation who now found themselves in a similar position included William Walton (1902–84), the composer of a Chaucerian *Troilus and Cressida* (London, 1954) and a comedy based on Chekhov called *The Bear* (Aldeburgh, 1967), and Lennox Berkeley (1903–), whose *Nelson* (London, 1953) was followed by the shorter operas *A Dinner Engagement*, *Ruth*, and *Castaway*. Similarly, Arthur Bliss (1891–1975) was late in composing his first opera, *The Olympians* (London, 1949); while, as we have seen, the doyen of British composers, Vaughan Williams, did not produce his *The Pilgrim's Progress* until 1951, when he was nearly eighty.

But among these latecomers it was Tippett who showed himself most powerfully as an opera composer. He had written a ballad opera called *Robin Hood* in 1934, but his first major opera was *The Midsummer Marriage* (London, 1955). As always in his case, this was to his own libretto and is a kind of reworking of the *Magic Flute* story of two pairs of young lovers who must undergo spiritual trials before union. The music is both visionary and ecstatic, rhythmically and harmonically flexible, and rich in soaring vocal *melisma*. Like much of Tippett's artistic utterance, it represents a statement of a profound personal belief and philosophy that is based largely on Jungian thought. In every human being, Tippett tells us, there is both darkness and light that must be recognised and accepted for wholeness to come about. In a statement about this opera which perhaps applies to all his work, he wrote, 'It is the only truth I shall ever say.' Though not everyone finds the libretto of *The Midsummer Marriage* easy going—the writing is awkward and the obvious class difference between the couples, paradoxically acceptable in Mozart, seems embarrassing here—the majority opinion as to its effectiveness is on Tippett's side.

Tippett's next opera, *King Priam* (Coventry, 1962), is tougher, starker and more declamatory as perhaps befits a work concerned with a Homeric world of war and heroes: even its Prelude with its dissonant brass and drums seems to speak of fighting and pain. There is relatively little tenderness here, despite the presence of Helen of Troy (mezzo) and the devoted friends Achilles (tenor) and Patroclus (baritone), and indeed this opera seems to turn its back on the rich life-acceptance of *The Midsummer Marriage* and, in the words of one commentator, emphasises 'the futility of attempting to create a present paradise'. However, in *The Knot Garden* (London, 1970)—where the title refers to a symbolic maze—we return to a contemporary world and a grappling with problems of the day. Thus upon an English domestic scene we find a psychoanalyst Mangus (baritone) as a kind of Prospero figure who deals in turn with a marriage on the rocks (Faber and Thea), a mixed-up teenager (Flora), a homosexual couple (the black writer Mel and the white musician Dov), and Thea's sister Denise, a 'dedicated freedom fighter' who has been tortured and for whom 'the rest of the world stands accused or condemned'. After a number of short scenes often linked by a *arpeggio* motif labelled 'Dissolve', the marriage is straightened out, Flora grows up, Denise and Mel go off together and Dov sets out to travel alone. Such a synopsis sounds novelettish, but broadly speaking, opera-goers have never been primarily concerned with the literary quality of libretti. As for the music in this rich score, the tenor Robert Tear, who created the role of Dov, has said: 'Michael's music is like an amazing trip that releases you from ordinariness, and that's a great gift. But he writes so many notes that they take your brain by storm. Michael's a Beethoven. He writes what he has to write and if you can sing it—fine.'

The Knot Garden has an effective blues with boogie-woogie at the end of Act I, and in his most recent opera, *The Ice Break* (London, 1977), Tippett's all-embracing humanity convincingly brings in many elements of black music—spirituals, blues, jazz including boogie-woogie and scat singing, and instruments such as electric guitar and electronic organ. It is as if he feels that only by getting into touch with really popular music can he speak with the universality of utterance he seeks. The libretto of *The Ice Break* rather defies intelligible summary—it is set in what seems to be America and includes a black hero-champion called Olympion (tenor) and his girlfriend Hannah (mezzo), a probably Russian ex-political prisoner Lev (bass) and his wife Nadia and son Yuri, whose girlfriend is Gayle, and finally in Act III an extraterrestrial messenger called Astron (sung by two offstage voices, mezzo and counter-tenor), who appears and is initially mistaken for God by a chorus of 'flower children' who have taken drugs. There are powerful scenes of racial tension and, in Act II, a riot in which Olympion and Gayle are killed. Yuri is seriously injured but recovers to be reunited with his father, his mother in the meantime having died peacefully. The title of the opera refers in part to the beginning of the Russian spring and in part to the release of human beings from stereotypes.

Tippett is eighty-two at the time of writing and already engaged on a fifth opera. This tireless composer has said of *The Ice Break* that although he had come 'out of the garden and into the street . . . I don't think it came off. It didn't do what I wanted . . . but there are some good things in it.' Elsewhere he has spoken of his social and artistic creed:

Shelley said poets are the moral legislators of mankind—I can't be that. It isn't possible today. But there is a strong moral sense about my work—a commitment in the tradition of Tolstoy, as opposed to the Chekhovian school of 'the art by itself'. That's what Stravinsky believed, and it's why I say that for him Belsen didn't happen. For me, it did, and it's something I have to know about.

OPERA TODAY

Orpheus in new guises. New paths in Europe. The death of Orpheus? Directions and directors. Epilogue.

ORPHEUS IN NEW GUISES

No other composer, wrote the Earl of Harewood, managing director of the English National Opera, in 1977, did as much as Britten 'to restore confidence in opera as a medium'. Yet a decade later we may feel less optimistic, at least as regards new operas. For Britten's work arguably ended an era, and no composer of his stature working today has devoted a major part of his creative life to writing operas. Historians' predictions are usually wrong, but at present it is hard to imagine the appearance of another music-dramatist comparable to the great figures of the past. However, as Debussy said in 1913, each generation of composers must rejuvenate old forms or find 'a wholly new approach to lyrical art'. Opera is still with us. The public since World War II has become increasingly interested in opera performance—admittedly mainly of the established repertory with international star singers—and composers, even among those whose aesthetics are of a radical kind, have turned at least intermittently to the form, even if only at times to interrogate and humiliate it with an intensity that seems at times to extract only the kind of answers given under torture.

Perhaps the nearest figure to Britten among the composers who came to prominence soon after the war is the German Hans Werner Henze (1926–). Childhood experience of music in a neighbour's partly Jewish household, given the political climate of the time, implanted in his mind an association between music and an anti-authority viewpoint that has remained in his maturity, when he has vigorously espoused Leftist causes which are reflected alike in the subject-matter and the stylistic directness of his music. Another stimulus came from a singer friend who had sung the anti-establishment role of Mack the Knife in Weill's *Dreigroschenoper* (*The Threepenny Opera*). Henze's association with opera began in 1945, when he became a répétiteur at the Bielefeld opera. Prolific by contemporary standards, he had written five operas by the age of thirty, among which were *Boulevard Solitude* (Hanover, 1952), a modern version of the Manon Lescaut story in which Des Grieux becomes a drug addict and is finally shot by Manon, and the radio opera *Das Ende einer Welt* (*The End of a World*, Hamburg, 1953), dealing with the artist's role in a society of false values.

Uneasy in post-war Germany, Henze moved in 1953 to the Mediterranean island of Ischia. There he completed his opera *König Hirsch* (Berlin, 1956), a curious fable of transformation and self-realisation in which a young king, abandoned in the wild and raised by animals, returns to his land but is at first unable to face the falsity of the kingdom that is rightfully his. He instead becomes a stag, yielding his throne to a corrupt worldly Governor, but driven by natural desires he finally resumes human form while the usurper is killed by his own forces. This three-act opera is rich instrumentally, with harpsichord, piano, accordion and guitar all contributing to a subtle sonority; vocally, too, it is rewarding if challenging. Henze next developed his existing interest in nineteenth-century Italian opera and brought new skills and emphases to *Der Prinz von Homburg* (Hamburg, 1960), in which he turned to Kleist's drama on the subject of an intellectual and independent-minded officer who is condemned, but later pardoned, for his insubordinate actions in battle; in the process perhaps the composer also showed his personal dislike of German military tradition. *Elegy for Young Lovers* (Schwetzingen, 1961), with a libretto by Auden and Kallman, tells of an egotistic poet called Gregor Mittenhofer who seeks his inspiration from the emotional stresses of others in a retreat in the Austrian Alps; finally he sacrifices his stepson and the boy's girlfriend so as to find the inspiration for his poetic *magnum opus*, whose title is also that of the opera. The theme of the artist's relationship with society and other individuals, here an uneasy and morbid one, thus recurs yet again in twentieth-century opera.

In *The Bassarids* (Salzburg, 1966) Henze used the same librettists to tell the story of Euripides' *Bacchae* in a one-act *opera seria*, composing it in a mood of 'ecstatic pessimism'. One may feel that in all these works, and also in the social comedy *Der junge Lord* (*The Young Lord*, Berlin, 1965), the composer presents us with an Apollo-Dionysus conflict between law and impulse, society and the individual, that has continued more starkly in later Marxist works such as the 'show for 17' called *Der langwierige Weg in die Wohnung der Natascha Ungeheuer* (Rome, 1971), with its extreme and disturbing vocal and instrumental techniques and language: the title means literally *The Tedious Way to the Dwelling of Natasha Monster*. However his 'actions for music' *We Come to the River* (London, 1976) treats a radical theme—again that of the 'fundamental antagonisms between personal liberty and established power'—in a more measured way, as appropriate for a work premièred in the conventional surroundings of the Royal Opera House, Covent Garden. Even so, its aesthetic creed as stated by the composer and his librettist Edward Bond was dogmatic and limiting. 'In our age,' they wrote, 'the artist must help to create the image and consciousness of the working class. There *is* nothing else art can do now, that *is* the definition of art in our time.' A recurring difficulty in resolving political and perhaps also personal challenges may have caused the comparative silence of Henze during the next few years.

His next opera, however, has proved an agreeable surprise. The two-act *The English Cat* (Schwetzingen, 1983) is a work of vitality and humour. Given the composer-librettist partnership, unchanged since the previous opera, political statement is surprisingly absent in favour of a comedy of manners set in the animal world in which the ageing bachelor cat Lord Puff (tenor) marries the pretty country cat Minette. Her sister Babette and the 'sexy play-cat' called—how else?—Tom (baritone) are other characters. The text is often elegantly polite: 'Good day, Miss Minette— I trust your journey was not too tiring?' is Puff's greeting to his future bride. Much of the musical language too is surprisingly mild, Minette's *spinto* first aria 'The world is wide' being firmly in C major and Tom's E major 'Last night I dreamed I was in bed' a bouncy number that would hardly be out of place in a Broadway show. The comedy, and its musical dress as a stylised number opera, is singularly reminiscent of Stravinsky's *The Rake's Progress* and pays a similarly open tribute to the more distant past of *buffo* style. Elsewhere, and not least in the instrumental writing with its chamber organ, recorder and percussion, the influence of Britten seems clear. Where *The English Cat* is leading Henze's development is impossible to say, and possibly this is a 'one off' work. But it is attractive, witty and cultured in a way that will please many people unable to respond to some earlier works of his.

At the time of writing, an interesting hope for the continued viability of the 'grander' kind of opera may lie with the Finnish composer Aulis Sallinen (1935–). His opera *The Horseman* (1974) is an allegory which despite loose dramatic construction shows a musical personality and purpose over a large canvas. *The Red Line* (1978) paints the life of the Finnish poor in the early twentieth century in a strong and vivid vocal-instrumental language: even the deep cold of northern Finland is imaginatively conveyed in its sonorities. Sallinen's third and most recent opera is *The King Goes Forth to France* (Savonlinna, 1984), commissioned jointly by the Savonlinna Opera in Finland and the BBC and Royal Opera House in Britain. The libretto, by the Finnish poet Paavo Haavikko from his radio play, tells a story of military campaigning and international intrigue set in England and France in the future and the fourteenth century, in which the English King Edward III and the chronicler Froissart feature, and is at the same time surreal—for example, an Ice Age permits the English to cross the Channel on foot, and the Prime Minister decides the outcome of the battle of Crécy by firing a cannon called Parliament. A 'theatre of cruelty' element is also present—twice the English King orders a flaying, the second time as the French King's punishment for the war crime of attacking in rain when English bowstrings were slack. At the end, the King orders Froissart to forget the royal part in events, 'for he had not made himself. He had been made by Time.' The Finnish commentator Irmeli Niemi has suggested that this story attracted Sallinen since 'The evil of the world has always given his music its gloomy strength and its counterforce the deepest hope . . . the music becomes the libretto's King . . . central in both music and action is the journey, the shaking up of geography and history. During the journey the image of being, separation and unity is transformed, repeated, broken up . . .' The Japanese appearance of the costumes in the first production may reflect the ritualistic aspect of Sallinen's music theatre; furthermore, in the relationship between the fantasising prince (later King) and his Prime Minister 'the emptiness of the concepts called "old" and "new" is revealed'. For Niemi, this is 'an opera about the "operalikeness" of an opera'.

A senior figure who has come late to opera is the French composer Olivier Messaien (1908–). His *St Francis of Assisi* (Paris, 1985) is monumental in its scope and religious-dramatic purpose, but borders on oratorio in its avoidance of action as such in favour of a kind of staged contemplation of the saint's sufferings and ecstasies. The opera has won respect, and perhaps more than that, from those among the composer's admirers who see in it something beyond a master's fervent testimony of personal faith. But doubts have yet to be resolved as to the theatrical staying power and viability of *St Francis*, just as in the case of Vaughan Williams's *A Pilgrim's Progress*, another spiritual and artistic credo produced as its composer approached eighty.

'The best British opera since *Billy Budd*.' This is the view of Peter Maxwell Davies's *Taverner* expressed by Edward Downes, the conductor of its première (London, 1972) and also of its London revival eleven years later. Maxwell Davies (1934–) studied in Manchester and Rome and soon established a reputation as a gifted member of a British avant-garde movement. However, work as a teacher kept him in touch with the realities of the composer-performer-listener relationship, and alongside advanced compositional techniques and an occasional willingness to distort and shock, his work shows a stylistic range that includes simple melodies and popular idioms. Indeed he has expressed a dread of being 'pigeon-holed' within a predictable language. Since 1970 he has made his home in Orkney and in 1977 he established a music festival in that remote part of the British Isles.

The composer's highly literate libretto of *Taverner* tells the story of the sixteenth-century English composer John Taverner, who was (according to available history at the time of writing) a Catholic, first accused of Lutheran heresy and then again becoming orthodox until a change in the English religious climate under Henry VIII caused him to repent 'that he had made songs to popish ditties in the time of his blindness' and to become a paid agent of Thomas Cromwell, the destroyer of monasteries and persecutor of Catholics. In fact most of this story is now disproved, but the opera remains a parable of the artist's role in society, and Maxwell Davies has said that the position of the Soviet composer Shostakovich was in his mind when he wrote it. As the critic Paul Griffiths has written, Taverner is not always 'his best self, the composer. Instead he is swayed by the nihilist, destructive anti-self that, long before Freud, Christianity taught us to recognise in ourselves. He is swayed by the great joker of the opera: Death.' In the final scene of Act I this Jester tricks Taverner of his soul, and early in Act II of this two-act work he spins a terrible Wheel of Fortune while holding up a chalice containing the black ape-head of the Antichrist Pope whom Taverner now repudiates as the 'Whore of Rome'. This is powerful material, and the music here makes no concessions — as one critic put it, 'The chorus roar out a savage unison against whirling violin scales, shrieking piccolos and thunderous brass.'

Not every feature of *Taverner* has been admired. Some have complained that this intellectual opera loses force because the words are inaudible under heavy scoring or weakened by awkward writing for the voices. Another criticism is that the pacing of the drama is so wrong that the first part seems excessive in length. But many readily acknowledge its intense feeling, together with music that keeps 'the ears and the mind tingling . . . the spark of genius glows in it'. For Edward Downes, there was from the start 'an atmosphere about it that touched me . . . Now that seems to me the function of a composer . . . It's the fact that you need music and you need drama and the conjunction of all those parts which adds up to something even greater: that is almost the *raison d'être* for opera.' We might agree to omit the 'almost' in that last sentence.

Taverner is the most substantial among several works that Maxwell Davies lists as dramatic. Working with the group called the Pierrot

Players (later the Fires of London), the composer has produced a series of quasi-theatrical pieces with histrionic and parodistic elements, like *Revelation and Fall* (London, 1968) with its 'blood-red nun shrieking through a loudhailer' and *Vesalii icones* (London, 1969), a non-vocal work in which a naked male dancer circles a white-clad female cellist or sits at a honky-tonk piano to play a Victorian hymn. But the strong expressionism of these pieces, whose forerunners are Schoenberg's *Pierrot lunaire* and Stravinsky's *Histoire du soldat*, has given way to a more moderate utterance in his recent works. Though in *The Lighthouse* (Edinburgh, 1980), with six characters played by three singers, a claustrophobic tension is the chief mood, another 'northern' piece, the chamber opera called *The Martyrdom of St Magnus* (St Magnus Cathedral, Kirkwall, Orkney, 1977), preaches peace in relatively direct and clear music. In it, for the critic Stephen Walsh, 'are resolved many of the psychological conflicts expressed in the music of a decade earlier'. A new Maxwell Davies opera is currently (1987) being written for performance at the Darmstadt Festival in Germany.

NEW PATHS IN EUROPE

France, once a major operatic country, today presents a sad picture. The recent Messaien opera *St Francis of Assisi* seems unlikely to have a successor, and the major figure in the next generation of composers, Pierre Boulez (1925–), has written no opera—indeed, though active in the opera house as a conductor, he has stated that such buildings 'should all be blown up'. 'Our age,' Boulez declares, 'is one of persistent, relentless, almost unbearable inquiry. In its exaltation it cuts off all retreats and bans all sanctuaries ... Despite the skilful ruses we have cultivated in our desperate attempt to make the world of the past serve our present needs, we can no longer elude the essential trial: that of becoming an absolute part of the present, of forsaking all memory to forge a perception without precedent, of renouncing the legacies of the past, to discover yet undreamed-of territories.' This very Gallic rodomontade inspires little confidence. Leaving aside the fact that Boulez in his sixties is hardly a pioneer leading the way to a promised land, having himself evidently slowed as a creator, no recognisable art can emerge from a total renunciation of tradition, which would involve the destruction both of existing instruments and the known musical language.

But such radicalism at least poses a challenge, and perhaps Boulez himself will yet respond to it, since reports in 1985 suggested that he is contemplating an opera on Jean Genet's erotic prison novel *Notre Dame des Fleurs*. Few agree with him that 'Berg knew he was bringing a tradition to its close,' and operas are still being written, even if some probe painfully into its nature. Besides being a public entertainment, music drama is a form of individual statement which many artists seem to need to make, and we have already seen how Henze has used opera to state a political viewpoint, just as Messaien has preached religion and Britten pacifism.

'Italian opera has remained vigorous, and continues to draw composers, from Puccini's successors such as Zandonai, Malipiero and many others, to the younger generation.' One wishes one could agree with the authors of *The Concise Oxford Dictionary of Opera* (2nd edition, 1979). But no Italian opera since Puccini is known to the public, unless we include those of Menotti, now an American writing in English. Yet operas of a somewhat political and intellectual kind are being composed. *Il prigionero* (broadcast RAI, 1949), by the Italian composer Luigi Dallapiccola (1904–75) was intended as 'protest music' against the deliberate mental cruelty inflicted upon a prisoner who is allowed to 'escape' into the hands of the Inquisition's torturers, and his *Ulisse* (Berlin, 1968) is a large-scale meditation on man's Odyssean search for life's meaning. Luigi Nono (1924–) is another Italian of the intellectual left, whose 'scenic action' *Intolleranza 1960* (Venice, 1961) portrays an immigrant caught up in the police bureaucracy of a capitalist state and makes him a symbol of all who suffer oppression; the presence of a commenting chorus emphasises the message. Nono moved away in this work from serial technique towards a simpler language in order to fulfil his need to communicate. A later 'scenic action' in two acts called *Al gran sole carico d'amore* (*To the Great Sun Charged with Love*, Milan, 1975) has a libretto by the composer consisting of quotations ranging from Marxist classics to the sayings of ordinary workers. In the words of the critic Claudio Annibaldi, who sees here a Brechtian approach, a plot as such is 'abandoned in favour of self-sufficient scenes, whose impassioned commemoration of the victims of an age-long class war should provide the spectator with many-sided materials for meditation'. Nono's most recent quasi-opera is *Prometeo* (Venice, 1984).

Nevertheless, to work as art, opera cannot descend to mere pamphleteering, however worthy the message. Probing into the form itself is also risky: most audiences want to see an opera and not an investigation into operatic form and *mores*. In the very title of *Opera* (Santa Fe, 1970), the Italian composer Luciano Berio (1925–) challenges existing views, and this work, loosely based on the story of the sinking of the *Titanic*, takes Monteverdi's *Orfeo* as a starting point for an examination of the similarly doomed structures of opera itself and of Western society.

Thus the work intends a 'celebration of the end of a sick society bound for shipwreck, descent into Hell and final judgement'. The eclectic nature of *Opera* allows Berio to denounce war (in Act II Scene 6) as well as quote from earlier music, including his own, and write parodies such as salon-like piano pieces (Act III). Perhaps we can find here a stimulating overall view, stated in operatic terms, of the theatrical 'pathetic commentary and alienating frame'. But a full perception of such a work must involve intelligence and emotion in a mix that is hardly easy for an audience. However, Berio had by no means said his last word in *Opera*, and there are other stage pieces by him including one which is currently in preparation for London.

It was Berio who said of *Votre Faust* (Milan, 1969) by the Belgian composer Henri Pousseur (1929–) that 'the main personage ... is the history of music, not out of the old Faustian urge to use the past but out of the desire and the need to deal with realities wherever they may be'. The quasi-autobiographical central character of this modern-dress opera is also called Henri, a contemporary composer who (like Taverner, perhaps) can earn his living but only at the cost of his soul. This '*fantaisie variable genre opéra*' (Milan, 1969) abounds in musical quotations from Monteverdi onwards, including Liszt's 'Faust' Symphony. The musical language is fundamentally serial and at times strictly organised, but it also incorporates tonal elements, necessarily so in the musical quotations, as well as electronic sounds on tape. There is also a degree of indeterminacy: the audience may be called upon to decide on the action.

If Pousseur's procedure here seems capricious, what are we to make of such pieces of music theatre as *Sur scène*, *Pas de cinq* and *Unter Strom* (*On Stream*) by the Argentine composer Mauricio Kagel (1931–)—the first of which is for bass voice, mime and instruments and 'shows musical life ... and sadly demonstrates its futility', the second for five walkers with walking sticks whose paces and stick-tappings are notated to make the music, and the third having three players making music on household gadgets? Kagel's musical aesthetic is based on expressionism and surrealism with the exaggerations implied by these trends, and he has also used drugs such as mescalin and LSD to open up new artistic vistas. No one should thus be surprised that in his opera or 'scenic composition' *Staatstheater* (Hamburg, 1971) we are presented with a kind of provocative revue or burlesque including a scene called 'ensemble' in which sixteen voices together take a satirical and disrespectful look at the whole previous history of opera. Here, said Kagel, was a work intending 'not just the negation of opera, but of the whole tradition of music theatre'.

Le Grand Macabre (Stockholm, 1978), by the Hungarian György Ligeti

(1923–), is another opera intended to provoke. 'A grotesque black farce' was the heading of a review of the 1982 London production, in which the critic saluted 'a triumphant and historic occasion . . . perhaps for the first time, an entirely successful operatic treatment of the theatre of the absurd'. Elsewhere this remarkable work with its elements of exaggeration and obscenity has been dubbed 'Pornopera', 'Sex'n'death' n'farce'n'fun', and 'an erotic comedy', while the English National Opera billed it circumspectly as 'perhaps not suitable for children'. The story is a parable: Nekrotzar, who is Death, or perhaps just a strange charlatan, comes to put an end to the world, forcing the drunken Piet the Pot to help him. In the kingdom of Breughelland, characters such as Prince Go-Go, Astradamors and his wife Mescalina, the goddess Venus and a coloratura-soprano (*sic*) Chief of Police are pursuing their daily business of lovemaking, exchanging often obscene insults ('Black!' 'White!' 'Quack!' 'Shite!' . . . 'You arsehole!') and what passes for the exercise of government until crisis occurs in the form of mysterious celestial portents, public disturbances and finally Nekrotzar's decree, 'I now smite the world to pieces!' But the cosmic event simply doesn't happen: in the next scene Piet the Pot and Astradamors find themselves still alive though floating above the ground, Prince Go-Go and others appear unharmed, Nekrotzar disappears in shame at his failure, and finally the pair of lovers whom we met at the start, Miranda and Armando (originally named Clitoria and Spermando and, oddly enough, a soprano and a mezzo in possible reference to Strauss's Sophie and Oktavian), emerge from lovemaking entirely untouched by events. Was it really Death? Astradamors asks. Piet's answer is, 'Well, who can say? Let's keep on boozing, come what may.' As for the lovers, they declare, 'When it comes, then let it be . . . Farewell, till then—live merrily!'

The Elijah Moshinsky London production of *Le Grand Macabre* was meant to represent 'civilisation grinding to a halt', and had a British motorway setting and multiple television screens, one of which showed Fred Astaire and Ginger Rogers dancing. What was the significance of all this? some asked: but as one critic wrote, 'pointlessness was perhaps the point'. Ligeti himself was articulate about his aims in this work, which took him thirteen years to bring to the stage following the original 1965 commission.

> Out of my 'anti-opera' there gradually arose an 'anti-anti-opera', which, though on a different level, is 'opera' again . . . I still retained my idea of a very colourful, comic-strip-like musical and dramatic action. The cartoons of Saul Steinberg were my ideal: characters

and situations should be direct, terse, non-psychological and start-ling—the very opposite of 'literary opera' . . . the music should be riskily bizarre, totally exaggerated, totally crazy . . . owing nothing to any tradition, not even that of avantgardism.

Le Grand Macabre begins with a prelude for twelve motor horns—Act II starts with electric bells—and it ends with a serene *passacaglia* to accompany the lovers' message of hope. Musical quotations are a feature, and these include themes from Rameau, Schubert, Offenbach (the famous can-can) and Beethoven (the 'Eroica' variation theme); and in this the composer says he 'was working quite deliberately in the sense of Pop Art . . . [they] become elements of an overall form and cease to look like quotations'. He has also said, however, that 'all these absurdities are in fact tragic at a deeper level . . . the music has a bitter flavour . . . Life utterly devoid of fear, life devoted entirely to pleasure, is in fact pro-foundly sad.' Thus at the end of it all we find a moral: Ligeti is too intelligent and responsible an artist to waste his time on real nonsense. A new opera from him is spoken of at the time of writing (1987), to be written for the English National Opera in London.

A fellow-Hungarian, who unlike Ligeti has remained working in his native country, is Sándor Szokolay (1931–). He is much more overtly a moralist, and not surprisingly a socialist one, but his operatic forte is a strong sense of atmosphere. His three operas to date are an intense treatment of Lorca's powerful play *Blood Wedding*, a *Hamlet*, in which the protagonist's introversion and indecision draw from him a more subtle language, and a Biblical *Sámson*. There is also a radio opera called *Deluded Peter*. All these were first produced in Budapest between 1964–78; since then *Blood Wedding* has found its way to several other opera houses, and *Hamlet* has been seen (1970) in Cologne.

Also in Eastern Europe, the Pole Krzysztof Penderecki (1933–) has shown a penchant for big religious and social themes. His St Luke Passion (1965) is one of several religious, and specifically Catholic, works for large vocal and orchestral forces, and at times his chief interest has seemed to lie in this area, particularly since a recent simplification of his style related partly to the establishment of the Solidarity social-political movement in his country. But he has also composed two operas using English libretto sources: *The Devils of Loudun* (Hamburg, 1969), based on John Whiting's play, and *Paradise Lost* (Chicago, 1978), which he calls a '*rappresentazione*', with Milton's text reworked by Christopher Fry. His most recent opera is *The Black Mask* (Salzburg, 1986), based on the short German play *Die schwarze Maske* (1929) by Gerhart Hauptmann and set in that writer's native Silesia, afflicted by plague after the Thirty Years War. Here a mayor's wife, Benigna (soprano), is haunted by her past in the shape of a voodoo figure which proves to be her former black lover: the murderer, with her connivance, of her first husband. In the final general destruction set to dissonant and expressionist music, the Amsterdam merchant Perl (baritone), presented as a sort of Wandering Jew, looks on as the sole survivor of a plague that also perhaps symbolises human corruption.

German and Austrian opera houses have flourished financially in the post-war period. Yet for all their enterprise regarding new works, relatively few of these have originated with native composers. Apart from Henze, German opera in these decades offers few international names. Boris Blacher (1903–75) composed a number of stage works including operas and some others oddly characterised (such as a 'dramatic notturno' and a 'ballet-opera'); among these the chamber opera *Romeo und Julia* (Berlin, 1947) is the best known and the one-act *Abstrakte Oper No 1* (Hesse Radio, 1953) the most advanced and provocative—here, 'instead of a narrative, the work presents basic patterns of human behaviour: love, fear, pain, panic'. Blacher's Austrian pupil Gottfried von Einem (1918–) has composed several operas of which *Dantons Tod* (Salzburg, 1947) has been most widely performed and is perhaps the strongest. Another Blacher pupil Giselher Klebe (1925–) has sometimes been thought conservative for his time—thus even his first opera, a version of Schiller's *Die Räuber* (*The Thieves*, Düsseldorf, 1957) 'is technically dependent on the Second Viennese School but its model is Verdi'. A more striking figure is Bernd Alois Zimmermann (1918–70), whose reputation rests on a single four-act opera called *Die Soldaten* (Cologne, 1965), which reached the wider public after his suicide. The subject area perhaps owes something to *Wozzeck*, and tells of a girl called Marie (soprano) who is seduced by the high-ranking officer Baron Desportes (tenor) and then becomes the soldiers' whore. A feature of the music is the use of collage and quotation arising from the composer's Augustinian concept of the unity of time past, present and future: the complexity of its application extends in the intermezzo in Act II to the simultaneous playing of two Bach chorale melodies, two marches at different speeds and the *Dies irae* plainchant. A younger man, Aribert Reimann (1936–), has written three operas of which the last is the powerful *Lear* (Munich, 1978).

A major music-dramatic event of the 1980s has been the opera by Karlheinz Stockhausen (1928–) called *Donnerstag aus Licht* (first staging Milan, 1981), together with its successor *Samstag* (outdoor performance, Milan, 1984). The composer calls *Donnerstag* an 'opera in three acts, a greeting and a farewell for fifteen musical performers (four solo voices, eight solo instrumentalists, three solo dancers), choir, orchestra and magnetic tapes' and has so far personally directed performances of its 'music libretto, dance, actions and gestures'. *Donnerstag* is literally 'out of' *Licht* in that it is one part of a gigantic operatic cycle called *Light* designed to be performed on and named after seven consecutive evenings. Its chief character is 'Thursday's Child', Michael—a singer-trumpeter-dancer who is the Creator-Angel engaged on the great experiment of Man despite the opposition of the intellectual Lucifer. Eve is represented first by Michael's earthly mother as he takes human form and then by his lover and muse Moon-Eve, 'half bird, half woman playing a basset-horn'. Lucifer also takes the role of Michael's earthly father. Both characters are also acted by a dancer/mime, while Lucifer's instrument is a trombone.

Already in such works as *Inori* (*Adorations*, 1974) for mime/dancer(s) and orchestra, Stockhausen had given clear evidence of the general direction in which his art was moving, namely towards a kind of ritual synthesis of dance, vocalising and instrumental or electronic sounds that could create a form of opera. The Wagnerian *Gesamtkunstwerk* readily comes to mind, and beyond this an element of German gigantism; but Stockhausen's energies are formidable and, though no longer the *enfant terrible* of thirty years ago, he is today perhaps in his artistic prime. How far the sheer economics of new productions as ambitious as *Donnerstag* will permit the realisation of his vision is debatable, but its bold invention may win the day, just as Wagner's did more than a century ago in still more difficult circumstances. In the meantime part of another of his operatic 'days', *Dienstag*, was heard as long ago as 1977 in the ritual 'temptations' piece called *The Course of Years* – which may be given as an instrumental work with 'tape and sound projection', as a ballet, or operatically with two male singers added.

Stockhausen's self-confidence is a strength, but so much more is needed for the creation of lasting music theatre. Though he realises that voices need tunes, his melodic invention is rather basic and not necessarily such as to yield the musically self-justifying range and substance of an opera lasting a week. And will the drama itself be sufficiently strong? Some have found his overall narrative childlike; and we may wonder if his whole grand metaphysical concept is becoming egocentric when Michael is portrayed in performances by his son Markus as a brilliant musician and his other children have also performed—his daughter Majella playing the piano for Michael's music examination in Act I and his younger son Simon playing the soprano saxophone as one of two angelic youths in Act III.

The three acts of *Donnerstag* are preceded by a 'Thursday Greeting' and followed by a 'Thursday Farewell', which at London's Royal Opera House in 1985 took place respectively in the foyer and crush bar and (with five trumpeters) on rooftops and balconies outside the opera house. The acts themselves are called 'Michael's Youth—Childhood, Moon-Eve, Examination'; 'Michael's Journey Round the Earth' and Michael's Return Home—Festival, Vision'. Visually the most ambitious is Act II when in a kind of virtuoso trumpet concerto Michael travels in an earth-globe to Germany, New York, Japan (with sumo wrestlers), Bali (with a dancer), India, Africa (with Masai warriors) and Jerusalem. Two swallow-clowns—'a cross between swallow and penguin'—playing clarinets and basset-horn accompany much of this pilgrimage, which includes a fight between them and some 'Lucifer' trombones. In the final act Michael returns to heaven. His last words are: 'Man have I become, to see myself and GOD the Father as a human VISION, to bring celestial music to humans and human music to the celestial beings, so that man may listen to GOD and GOD may hear his children . . . And I know that many of you will ridicule me when I sing to you: I have fallen in love eternally with Mankind, with this Earth and her children—in spite of LUCIFER—in spite of Satan—in spite of everything . . .'

Critical reaction to *Donnerstag* has been mixed, as samples indicate: 'Sometimes marvellously involving, sometimes intensely irritating'; 'An important twentieth-century work of art . . . deeply impressive'; 'weird mixture of cosmic imagination with juvenile smut and artistic shoddiness . . . it remains utterly fascinating as a document of a great creative mind talking to itself . . . the production achieves the astonishing along with the vulgar and banal'; 'the total effect is of a very feeble imagination with a touching (and Germanic) faith in order for its own sake'; 'more ritual than opera'. But let us note finally a positive response to the London production from Peter Heyworth in the *Observer*: 'A great artist establishes his own norm . . . At first its ludicrous aspects seize attention . . . Yet the fact remains that its music dwarfs almost everything as yet achieved in the field of opera by the generation of composers that emerged in Europe in the wake of World War II. Even as I write, the boredom and irritation I experienced at Covent Garden on Monday recede from my memory. What remains is the work's resplendent beauty.'

THE DEATH OF ORPHEUS?

Clearly, art forms must develop, so as not to stagnate and die. A Mahler symphony is far from one by Mozart. Yet it is still recognisable as a symphony and so the term serves usefully for both. Stockhausen's work makes us think again about the nature of opera as music drama, but it does not force us entirely to redefine it. However, a point may come where a destruction rather than a development takes place—or, to put it more positively, the creation of a new form instead with its own principles and viabilities. The frontiers of 'opera' are doubtless being usefully explored and extended by Stockhausen, and even perhaps Kagel. But some artists have gone even further than these.

Thus, 'Everything we do is music,' declares the veteran American John Cage (1912–). How much can we regard some of his work as music theatre? To take an extreme example, his *o'o"* (1962), a 'solo for any player', may consist merely of 'preparing and slicing vegetables, putting them in an electric blender and then drinking the juice, with the sounds of these various actions amplified throughout the hall'. His 'mixed-media event' *Musicircus* (1967) has simultaneous performances of rock music, jazz, electronic and piano and vocal music, pantomime and dance, together with films and slide shows: here the composer-director's role was simply to invite people 'willing to perform at once (in the same place and time)'. Cage has said: 'Here we are. Let us say Yes to our presence together in Chaos.' Robert Moran (1937–), a pupil of Milhaud and Berio and an exponent of 'indefinite notation', has composed works called *Bombardments, Explosions* and *L'après-midi du Dracoula*, the last work to be played by 'any instruments'. He devised a mixed-media event called *39 Minutes for 39 Autos* (San Francisco, 1968) in which the artwork consists of cars being driven around a city. Moran's *Hallelujah* (1971) used most of the 75,000 population and resources (bands, choirs, cars, lights, broadcasting stations) of Bethlehem, Pennsylvania, and he has also composed a chamber opera called *Let's Build a Nut House* (1969).

In such undertakings as these we are challenged to redefine not just opera but music itself, and that is outside the scope of this book. But it is unwise to dismiss them as wholly silly and unimportant. Rossini said that the only place to judge was in performance, and quite often artists take up positions rather short of the most *outré* ones and then come to be accepted as within a developing tradition. In the opera *Einstein on the Beach* (Paris, 1976) by the American composer Philip Glass (1937–) the music is of the kind called systematic or minimalist, the idea being to make much out of little. The work begins with nearly four minutes of the chord sequence A minor, G, and C in the key of C major repeated over and over again with changing rhythms counted out by a small chorus (whose text consists of numbers) until the entry of two women's voices, speaking not singing:

Will it get some wind for the sailboat. And it could get for it is. It could get the railroad for these workers. And it could be were it is. It could Franky it could be Franky it could be very fresh and clean. It could be a balloon. Oh these are the days my friends and these are the days my friends . . . Doo you rememberf Honz the bus driver . . . ., Well I put the red ball blue ball two black and white balls . . . Oh these are the days my friends and these are the days my friends. It could get the railroad for these workers. Itmmcould So will it get some wind for the sailboat. And it co ld get for it is [*sic*!].

The opera plays without intermission and lasts about four and a half hours, though at the New York production (1976) the audience was invited 'to leave and re-enter the auditorium quietly, as necessary'. As for Glass's musical technique, it is that of 'extending and contracting rhythmic figures in a stable diatonic framework' (article in *The New Grove*). Some of its text, compiled by Robert Wilson, suggests a mind or typist's fingers under the influence of drugs:

So Santa Claus has about red. And now the Einstine Trail is like In Einstine on the Beach. So this will. So if you know that faffffff facts. So this is what happen what I saw in. Lucy or a kite, You raced all the way up . . . [*sic*].

It is easy to be infuriated by what can seem the artistic irresponsibility of an 'anything goes' style lacking intelligence, craftsmanship and respect for an audience. Yet Glass's *Einstein on the Beach* has been given in Paris, New York, Venice and elsewhere with some success and a handsomely packaged recording has been issued by CBS. Its small print says obscurely that it was necessary 'to compress the musical material in a number of places . . . However this was achieved without any significant "cuts" to the score, so that the performance contained in these records is a complete representation of the original.'

Glass has also written *Satyagraha* (1980), on the early life of the *mahatma* Gandhi and to a sung text in Sanskrit; its title comes from two Sanskrit words meaning love (or truth) and firmness, this being the name of the *mahatma*'s philosophy of non-violent resistance. The orchestra numbers fifty-one players: strings and woodwind plus electronic organ. The mood has been described as one 'of deep spiritual serenity and composure', and the characters include other leaders besides Gandhi such as Tolstoy, Tagore and Martin Luther King. Glass's other operas are *The Photographer* (Amsterdam, 1982), *CIVIL warS* (1984), and

355

Akhnaten (Stuttgart, 1984). A new opera is expected that is to be based on a Doris Lessing novel, *The Making of the Representative for Planet 8.*

At the time of writing Glass's best known opera is his most recent one, *Akhnaten*. It tells of the Egyptian pharaoh who was married to Nefertiti and reigned from about 1379–62 BC, a religious reformer who moved towards monotheism, though his reforms were largely reversed by his successor Tutankhamen. In the opera he is shown as a controversial figure who is overthrown by the priestly class. The final scene shows a group of modern-day tourists with their guide: little remains to give evidence of Akhnaten's glory and works, but Egypt eternal is represented by the wrestlers, threshers and brickmakers who were present at the start and are still at work. The story draws from Glass music which in its endless repetitions of simple materials can create atmosphere and perhaps even change our perception of time. In the view of the critic Alexander Roth, this composer 'has tuned in to man's most primitive and elemental impulses—the beat of the human heart and the bodily cycles of breathing and movement. This is why his music produces such a visceral emotional response, why its pounding energy can be invigorating or mesmerising, sensuous, uplifting, tranquillising.' On the other hand, not everyone wants to revert to primitive impulses or to 'turn off' his mind. The critic Rodney Milnes wrote in 1985 that he was told by young people that

> the only way to get through *Akhnaten* was to have 'a really good joint first' . . . a few swift gins . . . served only to heighten my ill temper as the evening wore on . . . Mr Glass is plainly on to a good thing writing music for the unmusical . . . I am not sure what the meaning of decadence is, but suspect that anti-music written for people who have to dope themselves to be able to respond to it may come somewhere near it.

To be fair, some who have disliked *Akhnaten* have been moved by *Satyagraha*, the earlier of these two operas. But need an artist heed the critics if the public is pleased? The answer depends on one's artistic politics, élitist or otherwise, and perhaps on other factors: mischievously, one recalls what the late showbiz pianist Liberace said of hostile press comment—'I cried all the way to the bank.' And if the criticism of *Akhnaten* seems unfavourable, consider the *Times* review of the opera *Hell's Angels* (London, 1986) by Nigel Osborne (1948–), which had the same director, David Freeman of Opera Factory London. This is a two-act opera set alternately in Heaven and Earth, the present day and the Borgia Pope's court of 1494, and is a parable of plagues (syphilis and

AIDS) sent by a bored God. The *Times* critic Paul Griffiths had already found *Akhnaten* 'staggeringly boring', but here matters were even worse. He wrote of *Hell's Angels*: 'I cannot think of an evening in the theatre I have enjoyed less . . . this really was the pits . . . sheerly, utterly terrible.' The *Sunday Telegraph* wondered that when 'acres of the text are left as speech . . . how much of it needs music at all?' This libretto (also by David Freeman) has lines like God's 'Don't quote the Bible at me—I wrote it.' It was recalled that the composer himself had been quoted (in the *Observer*, 5 January 1986) as calling it 'a very unworthy piece'. Osborne is at the time of writing preparing another opera for Glyndebourne called *The Electrification of the Soviet Union*.

Writing opera has never been easy, save perhaps for a few very fluent creators. We should not seize upon works such as these by Glass and Osborne and commence a wake for opera as we understand it. Yet it is tempting to note the chosen title, *Nenia—The Death of Orpheus*, of a vocal work written in 1970 by the British composer Harrison Birtwistle (1934–). But Orpheus, that first musician of Greek legend whose story made the first surviving opera, is arguably the very spirit of music and is not so easily to be destroyed—despite the Maenads who would always tear him to shreds. And the text of the Birtwistle piece is curiously prophetic in one of its lines—'but what once happened can happen once more'. In May 1986 the English National Opera gave the première of the same composer's *The Mask of Orpheus*. 'Rich, exciting, beautiful music,' declared the *Guardian*: 'This is a score which seems to grow out of natural sound, which doesn't play musical games.'

Birtwistle was not new to opera. His first venture in this form was *Punch and Judy* (Aldeburgh, 1968). Alas, Benjamin Britten walked out of the première of this 'brutal ritualistic piece', though its forcefulness cannot be disputed. His *Orpheus* opera, which was in fact not new since it had been completed in 1977 but rejected by Covent Garden and Glyndebourne, is in three acts and had the controversial David Freeman as its first producer. The singers are mostly electronically amplified (a BBC recording had to be abandoned when a microphone failed), masks are worn, and multiple casting is used here as by Stockhausen in *Donnerstag*: thus Orpheus is played by *two* tenors plus dancer/mime, while the mezzo Eurydice and bass-baritone beekeeper Aristaeus are similar threesomes. The orchestra has no bowed strings, but large groups of woodwind and brass, three 'electric instruments', a harp and pre-recorded tape: its members also have to sing occasionally. In Act I the minstrel Orpheus is taught his art by Apollo and marries Eurydice, who is then seduced by Aristaeus, bitten by a snake and dies. Act II has his descent to the

Underworld to rescue her, his failure to refrain from looking back as she returns with him and his consequent further loss and despairing suicide. In Act III, however, he himself proves immortal, although the opera takes account of later versions of the legend, with Orpheus being destroyed by the Maenads (after which his severed head 'floated singing to Lesbos'), dying by Apollo's decree or attaining the god's forgiveness; indeed, it touches too upon the Orphic religion in which the minstrel was sometimes believed to be Apollo's son. This, wrote the critic Francis Routh (*Composer*, Summer 1986), is a work in which 'action and movement are replaced by fantasy; dramatic continuity of events (in other words, a story-line) gives way to a generalised, collective, psychological symbolism. Orpheus himself is shown as passive, a being devoid of conflict, floating in a timeless, static world.'

Though unusual in its approach, including the integration of electronic sound into the orchestra, *The Mask of Orpheus* has made a positive impression. David Freeman had already directed Monteverdi's *Orfeo* for English National Opera; and his realisation of the Birtwistle *Orpheus* was a strong presentation which for all its novelty still relates to a known tradition. It seems that the fundamental premises and motives of opera, and even its essential themes such as love, beauty and mortality—and the artist's vocation, yet again—are still with us. Freeman has also directed another more recent Birtwistle opera, *Yan Tan Tethera* (meaning *One, Two, Three* in a northern English shepherd's patois): this work is designated 'a mechanical pastoral' and has appeared (London, 1986) since *Orpheus*. With its tale of a shepherd who resists the attempt of another to steal 'his sheep, his twin sons and his wife', it is again a good-and-evil parable that could be set in ancient times as easily as in our own. Positive though this is, there is more to good opera than good intentions, and one would like to be more enthusiastic about the music itself, which in a radio performance proved, for this listener at least, crude and ultimately unendurable.

DIRECTORS AND DIRECTIONS

Who creates operas? One might answer: Mozart, Wagner and other musicians. But viewpoints change. Formerly people spoke only in these terms: of Beethoven's *Fidelio* or Wagner's *Ring*. Then *aficionados* came to prefer designating star singers or conductors: thus it was Callas's *Norma* or Karajan's *Rosenkavalier*. Today it is the director who seems to the fore, and so we talk of Zeffirelli's *Traviata* and *Otello*, or Miller's *Tosca*. Up to a point this makes sense. An opera score normally consists just of its text and music, and the process of bringing the work to staged life involves many others beyond its original authors. Who is in artistic charge? In most cases, no longer those authors, while neither a conductor nor a singer can be responsible for stage presentation. Save perhaps in the recording studio—and even here video production must be excepted—the director, who is unlikely to be a musician, may well be considered as the central figure. So has music vacated the central place in opera performance? Not, certainly, for the Musical Director of the Welsh National Opera, Richard Armstrong, who has said that 'the final responsibility must be taken by the Musical Director'.

But today's operatic directors often hold strong views of their own that may come into conflict with those of conductors and singers. These 'benevolent dictators', as Russell Davies put it in the BBC television programme *Saturday Review*, 'are seen by many as too influential, too high-handed and too well paid: in some ways they're the football managers of the arts world.' In the same programme the director Peter Hall said that 'a director wanting to make the piece hit an audience feels that he has to do something perhaps extraordinary . . . [or may say] never mind what the piece means, never mind what it says, never mind what the author wanted, what matters is what the piece does to me when I sit and let it play on my subconscious.' Some directors, of course, impose strong ideas of their own because of a fear that music may actually inhibit a theatrical experience, turning drama into a kind of costumed concert. Yet, as we know from Peter Conrad's radio documentary 'Decorators and Destroyers' (BBC Radio 3, 17 November 1985), for John Schlesinger, who came to opera from films, this form offers 'the most liberated form of theatricality . . . in a way, I think primarily, because of the music'. David Pountney of English National Opera has said that the music 'attacks always at a kind of subconscious level. It's much too heavyweight to dissect society. But what it's very good at, I think, is conjuring up broad images, broad pictures.' It is possible to present opera as a kind of dream—as in Jean Pierre Ponnelle's production of *Tristan* where he wanted to hide Isolde among the orchestra in the *Liebestod* so that she would merely be imagined by the dying Tristan, or his *Flying Dutchman* which was staged as a fantasy of the ship's steersman. On the other hand, Peter Hall fears that a too subjective director may be 'putting himself between the creator and the public'. Is doing something bizarre the only way for some directors to make their mark?

What of relations between singers and directors? Today's singers are certainly better actors than they were a generation ago. But they remain generally conservative, and at least one Wagner production in Paris was lost because its Wotan refused to wear a tuxedo instead of armour. Tradition dies hard, and star singers wield great power. For David Pountney, a singer such as the tenor Luciano Pavarotti simply needs 'a vehicle for his ability to convey a certain kind of thrill . . . and he needs a show around him built to show that off to greatest advantage. He doesn't need a director like me. I'm just redundant when he's around.' For the director Peter Brook, star singers are obsolescent: 'When brontosauruses were around, no doubt they all met in little groups and each one looked at the other and said "How well you're looking" . . . until the moment when they fell extinct.'

Yet this is not necessarily just a director's point of view, and still less is it an anti-musical stance. No good opera composer has failed to be a master dramatist also. Wagner complained about singers who produced sound without meaning and Verdi demanded a Lady Macbeth who would act the role instead of just singing it; Bellini actually told Rubini, 'You are an animal' for thinking more of his voice than his role. The tenor Robert Tear tells how Britten astonished him by saying that he was disappointed at Tear's using his role in *Curlew River* 'as a vocal exercise [instead of being] acutely conscious of the meaning of every word that he was going to sing'. It is a common directors' complaint that top singers refuse to take any risks with their voices—in spite of the fact that 'there is no drama without the risk of the actor to enter and to lose himself in the dramatic action'. The viewpoint 'I was hired to sing' is one that in the view of most directors is long overdue for change. At the same time, a singer may argue that opera is still about singing more than staging.

EPILOGUE

For musicians, it is natural to think of music first. Leaving aside professional singers, many people prefer the experience of opera on record, television or radio in domestic surroundings to the real, live, imperfect and actually-*happening* thing. But that reality remains the only thing that Monteverdi and most of his successors would recognise. In the meantime, varying kinds of experience are available and make up an economic as well as an artistic picture. Opera is a highly subsidised institution everywhere, and in that sense a cultural establishment and perhaps too a kind of cultural museum, to be preserved and cared for as such. Thus for the Italian director Franco Zeffirelli opera is a precious relic to be handled lovingly. His filmed *Traviata* has nevertheless been criticised by radicals as a 'Hollywood weepie filmed through soft focus and set in a never-never land of unbelievable and meaningless luxury'.

For such reasons as these, traditional opera is sometimes attacked as bourgeois—though not in the Soviet Union, where the Bolshoi Opera is ultra-conservative. But while East German houses have produced some powerfully Marxist approaches, these are still attempts to change opera from within and not a planned destruction of the genre.

The post-war years have seen the rebuilding of many opera houses that were destroyed, especially in Germany and Austria. There has been a gain here, however, in that such rebuilding, costly though it has been, has made them far more adaptable to modern needs in staging and lighting, while London's Covent Garden remains painfully inadequate in some facilities backstage and is currently contemplating major reconstruction. New opera houses include that of Sydney in Australia, officially opened in 1973 by Queen Elizabeth II, and costing some $100m. Its design by a Danish architect is original and compelling, with a roof featuring wing- or sail-like structures, but opera actually only occupies the smaller of its two halls, seating 1,530 people, the larger hall having originally been intended for opera but then redesigned for concert use. And it is not only such major cities that have undertaken ambitious projects of this kind: for example, in South Africa a new opera house opened in Bloemfontein in 1985. Glasgow in Scotland restored a theatre in 1976 as an opera house; on the other hand, the Scottish capital Edinburgh has no opera house as yet despite its cultural activities and the existence of the Scottish Opera Company since 1962.

British audiences for opera have increased at about the same rate as the public subsidy has declined in real terms, about ten per cent over a two-year period. It would seem that the form is thriving culturally if not financially. It has been suggested, too, that opera is also a powerful propaganda medium, drawing a wide general interest in capitalist and socialist societies alike. Large audiences in several countries seem to have enjoyed and valued the showing of the Chéreau-Boulez *Ring* on television. There is some parallel with that other leisure spectacle, sport, so that star singers like Placido Domingo and Kiri Te Kanawa are not far short of household names like sports personalities and have a similarly high earning power: such artists travel extensively by air and are in demand in all major operatic centres. This has made opera into a kind of industry, again like sport, and it has for similar reasons attracted sponsorship: thus the American oil company Amoco thought it worthwhile recently to give about a million pounds to one British company, the Welsh National Opera.

As for attendances, between 1980 and 1986 thirty-eight Covent Garden (Royal Opera House) productions have been sold out. At the

English National Opera eighteen shows have achieved the same. Average attendance at Covent Garden in the 1980–1 season was ninety-four per cent. Among modern operas, *Lulu* could fill the house in 1981 and so could *Peter Grimes* in 1984. The Welsh National Opera Company had an eighty-eight per cent attendance during the season up to January 1986; and Scottish Opera over the same period had eighty per cent. Thus the question is sometimes asked: if opera is so popular, why does it require such large subsidies? It goes without saying that you can rarely give it to the kind of numbers that fill a big sports stadium, but beyond that it must be admitted that there is still an élitist tinge to the whole operatic scene. We are as yet a long way from the situation that has favoured football, cricket and tennis, where the presence of television cameras at each major event brings large sums to the presenters. Even the Bolshoi Theatre in Moscow is far more accessible to foreign tourists than it is to the average Muscovite.

Opera takes a large part of the arts budget of every country where it plays a cultural and social role, save in the United States, where public subsidies are few and arts sponsorship comes chiefly from individuals and firms. Yet no subsidy is needed for the lighter kind of music theatre. Here we find successes and a flourishing industry—one thinks at once of the Webber-Rice works from *Joseph and the Amazing Technicolor Dreamcoat* to *Evita* and Andrew Lloyd Webber's *Cats* and *Starlight Express*— works uniformly strong in simple melody and vivid spectacle—as well as the American productions of Stephen Sondheim. Mr Lloyd Webber recently created the Really Useful Group, a British company worth several million pounds in which he and his music are the major asset and in which he currently owns thirty-eight per cent of the shares.

Even so, financial problems are endemic in this most expensive of art forms. At the beginning of 1986, the respected British Opera North company had a £230,000 deficit, but its administrator Nicholas Payne still maintained: 'If I'd just gone for a cautious artistic policy the company wouldn't have survived.' The Sadler's Wells Theatre in London, now mostly housing ballet but at one time a national opera house, only avoided a financial crisis in 1986 thanks to business sponsorship and a gift from Covent Garden of a gala performance that raised £19,000. However, France has just shown its confidence in the future of opera by building a new 'people's opera house' on the historic Bastille site in Paris, while West German opera companies receive more than twice the public subsidy enjoyed by those in Britain.

A great and still apparently increasing interest in recorded opera has allowed an enormous repertory to become available in this form. Currently the British catalogue offers in the relatively new compact disc format no fewer than four versions of *Rigoletto* and the same of *Carmen*. Today we can buy records of such comparative curiosities as Rossini's *Maometto Secondo*, Handel's *Atalanta* and Glass's *Satyagraha*. In the circumstances it seems unkind to accuse record companies of over-caution. Nevertheless the conductor Sir Colin Davis has said, 'If you want to do things and the record company thinks that it is not going to make any money out of your suggestions, then they won't put any enthusiasm behind the ideas. I had one or two victories. Nobody wanted to record *Peter Grimes* [the Jon Vickers performance]. Nobody wanted to record Tippett—they still don't! Nobody wanted to record *The Trojans*, to begin with.' But the production of video opera seems to be growing steadily, with videotapes and even the less familiar laser-read video discs which are superior in quality. The influential British magazine *Gramophone* recently began a regular opera video review: in the July 1986 issue two available versions of *Rosenkavalier* were discussed, directed respectively in Salzburg by Rudolf Hartmann (with Karajan as conductor and Schwarzkopf's Marschallin) and in London by John Schlesinger (with Solti and Te Kanawa); while other operas reviewed were *Intermezzo* in a 1983 Glyndebourne production and *Andrea Chénier* from Covent Garden (1985) with Placido Domingo in the title role. Britten's *Gloriana*, though still not conventionally recorded, recently became available on video in the English National Opera production with Sarah Walker as Queen Elizabeth I.

The opera scene has its occasional economic and artistic clouds and even catastrophes—such as the 1986 Andrei Serban production of *Fidelio* at London's Royal Opera House that was described (in the *Observer*) as 'an unmitigated disaster ... so grotesquely, scandalously inept that it calls into question the whole artistic decision-making policy of the house'. Yet the general picture is healthy. Democracy and opera are in no way opposed, for the original music theatre of ancient Greece was aimed at the widest public and so was medieval Christian music drama, and while the sixteenth-century Florentines addressed smaller groups opera soon reached its public again in Venice and elsewhere. Purcell showed with *Dido and Aeneas* that marvellous opera could be made even without an opera house and, again in London, 2000 people stood in the rain outside the Royal Opera House in Covent Garden for a recent performance of *La bohème* that was televised from the theatre on a big screen.

The operatic past is still being rediscovered in a way that keeps alive performance values and practices, or revives traditions and skills once thought lost. Over forty years ago, Professor Dent believed that to perform Handel 'a new race of singers will have to be bred up'; today Handel's operas are familiar because—save of course for *castrati*—those singers are available. Similarly in 1947 Donald Grout wrote wistfully in his *Short History of Opera* of the operatic past: 'The thought of so much buried beauty is saddening; for it is buried for the most part beyond recall.' Today much of that past is redeemed, though rightly not at the expense of the present. Of course opera still belongs largely to the more affluent industrialised countries, and here the third world presents a challenge. But where the form is vital—for us as much as for the ancient Greeks or the Renaissance Italians—our lives continue to be enhanced by the mysterious yet powerful message of the 'drama through music'.

ACKNOWLEDGEMENTS

The authors and publishers are grateful to the following for permission to reproduce copyright material: Century Hutchinson Publishing Group, *Man and His Music*, Vol. III, by W. Mellers; Victor Gollancz Ltd, *The Complete Operas of Mozart* by Charles Osborne; Andre Deutsch, *Amadeus* by Peter Shaffer; John Murray, *Gustav Mahler, Memoirs and Letters*, edited by Donald Mitchell; The Cambridge University Press, *The Life of Richard Wagner* by Ernest Newman; William Collins & Sons Ltd, *Cosima Wagner's Diaries*, Vols I and III, translated by G. Skelton; Dent & Co Ltd, *Vivaldi*, by Michael Talbot.

BIBLIOGRAPHY

Forty years ago, D. J. Grout prefaced his *Short History of Opera* with the observation, 'Volumes almost beyond counting have been written about opera.' This is a selective list of recommendations for further reading, and for a fuller bibliography the reader should turn to the booklists appended to the articles in the 1980 *New Grove* (see below). We have not included a discography because the record catalogue changes too rapidly, but for many obscure operas a recording may be the only source of information. The current *Gramophone* (UK) and *Schwann* (USA) catalogues list available records, and deleted issues may be found in libraries. The notes included with major recordings can often be informative and in some cases, such as the Janáček series on Decca with notes by John Tyrrell, represent an addition to scholarship.

For those needing information on individual operas, English National Opera (ENO) have produced, in conjunction with the Royal Opera House (ROH), a series of ENO/ROH Guides published by John Calder in the UK, and by Riverrun Press in the USA. Each guide contains the text of one opera, sometimes two, with a translation and a series of background articles. The *Cambridge Opera Handbooks* (Cambridge University Press), each devoted to a single work, are generally recommendable; they contain no libretto but have articles on the genesis, music and stage history of the opera concerned. For reviews of productions around the world and information on new operas, the British *Opera* magazine may be consulted, as may *Opera News* in the USA. *Opera Quarterly* (University of North Carolina Press) has scholarly articles on all aspects of opera and operatic history, especially in the USA. On particular composers, Dent's Master Musicians Series is generally recommendable. In the USA, Random House is publishing most of the recent books in this series in paperback.

GENERAL

THE NEW GROVE DICTIONARY OF MUSIC AND MUSICIANS (twenty volumes). Ed. *S. Sadie*, Macmillan 1980.
Contains authoritative articles on all aspects of opera, including a long article on the history of opera. Many treatments of major composers are being published separately, with new material and updated bibliographies.

THE NEW OXFORD HISTORY OF MUSIC (ten volumes). Various editors, Oxford University Press 1954–86.
Volume IX—Romanticism (1830–90) has yet to be published, but four of the available volumes contain substantial chapters on opera: V—Opera and Church Music (1630–1750), VII—The Age of Enlightenment (1745–90), VIII—The Age of Beethoven (1790–1830), and X—The Modern Age (1890–1960).

MAN AND HIS MUSIC. THE STORY OF MUSICAL EXPERIENCE IN THE WEST (four volumes). *A. Harman and W. Mellers*, Barrie and Rockliffe 1962.

SOURCE READINGS IN MUSIC HISTORY. Selected and annotated by *O. Strunk*, Norton 1950, republished in five separate paperbacks, Faber 1981.

THE ESSENCE OF OPERA. *U. Weisstein*, Macmillan (Free Press) 1964.
A collection of source documents for all periods of opera, published in USA by Norton in 1969.

A SHORT HISTORY OF OPERA. *D. J. Grout*, Columbia University Press, 1947. 2nd edition 1965.
Scholarly, and with many music examples.

A CONCISE HISTORY OF OPERA. *Leslie Orrey*, Thames and Hudson 2nd revised edition 1987.
The numerous illustrations are genuinely informative.

CONCISE OXFORD DICTIONARY OF OPERA. *H. Rosenthal and J. Warrack*, Oxford University Press. 2nd edition 1979.
Reasonably comprehensive and generally reliable.

KOBBÉ'S COMPLETE OPERA BOOK. 10th edition ed. *Earl of Harewood*, Bodley Head 1987.
A long-established authority for detailed synopses of repertory works and many less well-known operas.

OPERA AND DRAMA. *J. Kerman*, Random House 1952.
Notorious for its arrogant dismissal of Puccini and Strauss, but still valuable for insights into *Orfeo, Dido and Aeneas, Otello, Tristan, Pelléas, Wozzeck* and *The Rake's Progress*.

OPERETTA — A THEATRICAL HISTORY. *R. Traubner*, Gollancz 1984.

THE TENTH MUSE: A HISTORICAL STUDY OF THE OPERA LIBRETTO. *P. Smith*, Gollancz 1971.

PRIMA DONNA. *Rupert Christiansen*, Bodley Head 1985, Penguin Books.
An excellent history of leading female opera singers of all periods.

CHAPTER ONE: ORIGINS
CHAPTER TWO: SEVENTEENTH-CENTURY ITALY

OPERA IN PERSPECTIVE. *J. Drummond*, Dent 1980.
Useful on the distant origins of opera in the ancient world and the Middle Ages.

THE RISE OF OPERA. *R. Donington*, Faber 1981.

THE NEW MONTEVERDI COMPANION. Ed. *D. Arnold and N. Fortune*, Faber 1985.

CAVALLI. *J. Glover*, Batsford 1978.

CHAPTER THREE: FRENCH OPERA

FRENCH BAROQUE MUSIC FROM BEAUJOYEULX TO RAMEAU. *J. R. Anthony*, Batsford 2nd edition 1978.

JEAN-PHILIPPE RAMEAU: HIS LIFE AND WORK. *C. Girdlestone*, Cassell 2nd edition 1969.

OPERA BEFORE MOZART. *M. Robinson*, Hutchinson 1966.
Also useful for Chapters Four and Five below.

CHAPTER FOUR: ENGLAND AND GERMANY

NEW OXFORD HISTORY OF MUSIC, Vol. V. (See above under GENERAL)
Useful for the German composers largely neglected in English language books: see Chapter V for Keiser, Mattheson, and Telemann, Chapter II for Hasse and Graun.

A HISTORY OF ENGLISH OPERA. *E. W. White*, Faber 1983.

HENRY PURCELL AND THE LONDON STAGE. *C. Price*, Cambridge University Press 1984.

HANDEL. *P. Lang*, Faber 1966.

HANDEL AND THE OPERA SERIA. *W. Dean*, Berkeley 1969.
The most thorough and reliable source.

HANDEL AND HIS WORLD. *H. C. Robbins Landon*, Weidenfeld and Nicolson 1984.

CHAPTER FIVE: ITALIAN HIGH BAROQUE AND GLUCK'S REFORMS

MAN AND HIS MUSIC. PART TWO: LATE RENAISSANCE AND BAROQUE MUSIC. *A. Harman and A. Milner*, Barrie and Rockliff 1962.
Chapter Four examines Neapolitan opera, Scarlatti's influence and the *castrati*.

VIVALDI. *M. Talbot*, Dent (Master Musicians Series) 1978.

THE CASTRATI IN OPERA. *A. Heriot*, Calder 1956. Published in the USA by Riverrun Press.

THE GREAT SINGERS. *H. Pleasants*, Gollancz 1967.
Useful on the *castrati*, and famous singers of all periods up to about the 1930s.

C. W. VON GLUCK: ORFEO. *P. Howard*, Cambridge University Press 1981.
Contains background on Gluck's reforms.

CHAPTER SIX: MOZART AND HIS CONTEMPORARIES

THE AGE OF MOZART AND BEETHOVEN. *G. Pestelli*, Cambridge University Press 1984.
Covers many composers of *opera buffa* and *opera seria* from 1750 onwards.

HAYDN. CHRONICLE AND WORKS (five volumes). *H. C. Robbins Landon*, Thames and Hudson 1976–80.

MOZART'S OPERAS. *E. J. Dent*, Oxford University Press 2nd edition 1947.

THE MOZART COMPANION. Ed. *H. C. Robbins Landon and D. Mitchell*, Faber 1974.
The chapter on the operas is by Gerald Abraham.

THE OPERAS OF MOZART. *W. Mann*, Cassell 1977.

MOZART ON THE STAGE. *J. Liebner*, Praeger 1972.

CHAPTER SEVEN: HEROIC AND LYRICAL OPERAS IN PARIS 1760–1875

GRÉTRY AND THE RISE OF OPÉRA-COMIQUE. *D. Charlton*, Cambridge University Press 1986.

THE MEMOIRS OF HECTOR BERLIOZ. Trans. and ed. *D. Cairns*, Gollancz 1969.
This fine translation of one of the essential books of the whole Romantic period has a large glossary with long entries on Cherubini, Spontini, Meyerbeer and others.

BERLIOZ AND THE ROMANTIC CENTURY (two volumes). *J. Barzun*, Columbia University Press 3rd edition 1969.

FOLIES DE PARIS—THE RISE AND FALL OF FRENCH OPERETTA. *J. Harding*, Chappell 1979.
Also relevant to Chapter Fifteen: Later French Opera.

JACQUES OFFENBACH. *A. Faris*, Faber 1980.

GOUNOD. *J. Harding*, Allen & Unwin 1973.

BIZET. *W. Dean*, Dent (Master Musicians Series) 3rd edition 1975.

SECOND EMPIRE OPERA. *T. J. Walsh*, Calder 1981.

CHAPTER EIGHT: GERMAN ROMANTIC OPERA

THE RISE OF ROMANTIC OPERA. *E. J. Dent* revd. *W. Dean*, Cambridge University Press 1976.

THE BEETHOVEN COMPANION. Ed. *D. Arnold and N. Fortune*, Faber 1961.

Winton Dean's contribution 'Beethoven and Opera' discusses *Fidelio* and the other versions of *Léonore*.

CARL MARIA VON WEBER. *J. Warrack*, Hamish Hamilton 1968.

FOR WAGNER, see below under CHAPTER TEN.

CHAPTER NINE: ITALY IN THE PRIMO OTTOCENTO

THE NEW GROVE MASTERS OF ITALIAN OPERA. Macmillan 1983.
The most valuable of the Grove reprints for opera-lovers, containing revised articles of uniform excellence on Rossini, Donizetti, Bellini, Verdi and Puccini.

THE OPERA INDUSTRY IN ITALY FROM CIMAROSA TO VERDI. *J. Rosselli*, Cambridge University Press 1984.
A social history of Italian opera focusing on the role of the impresario.

THE LIFE OF ROSSINI by STENDHAL. Tran. *R. N. Coe*, Calder 1985.
This is at once indispensable and unreliable, but the notes in this edition point out Stendhal's grosser exaggerations.

ROSSINI. *R. Osborne*, Dent (Master Musician Series) 1986.
The author sympathetically and intelligently discusses each of Rossini's operas.

DONIZETTI AND HIS OPERAS. *W. Ashbrook*, Cambridge University Press 1982.
Comprehensive and authoritative.

VINCENZO BELLINI. HIS LIFE AND OPERAS. *H. Weinstock*, Weidenfeld & Nicolson 1971.

CHAPTER TEN: WAGNER'S MUSIC DRAMAS

THE NEW GROVE WAGNER. *J. Deathridge and C. Dalhaus*, Macmillan 1984.
This supersedes the 1980 dictionary article, as Deathridge's biographical section replaces the earlier contribution, and there is much other new material.

COSIMA WAGNER'S DIARIES, VOL. I 1869–77 and VOL. II 1878–83. Trans. *G. Skelton*, Collins 1978 and 1980.

THE LIFE OF RICHARD WAGNER (four volumes). *E. Newman*, Cambridge University Press 1933–47.
Out of date in some respects but still valuable for information on operatic life in France and Germany.

WAGNER NIGHTS. *E. Newman*, Putnam 1949, Bodley Head 1988.
Still the best synopses of the operas from *The Flying Dutchman* onwards. Issued in the USA as THE WAGNER OPERAS by Alfred Knopf.

PRO AND CONTRA WAGNER. Thomas Mann. Tran. *A. Blunden*, Faber 1985.
Contains the essay 'On the Sorrows and Grandeur of Richard Wagner' and
everything else of interest Mann wrote on the composer.

WAGNER'S *RING* AND ITS SYMBOLS. *R. Donington*, Faber 1963.

ASPECTS OF WAGNER. *B. Magee*, Alan Ross 1968.

RICHARD WAGNER. *R. Gutman*, Secker and Warburg 1968.
From an author associated with Bayreuth, the most incisive of the various
hostile views of Wagner.

RICHARD WAGNER'S MUSIC DRAMAS. *C. Dalhaus*, Cambridge University Press
1979.
Musico-dramatic studies of each opera from *The Flying Dutchman* to *Parsifal*,
assuming some technical knowledge of music.

CHAPTER ELEVEN: VERDI

THE MAN VERDI. *F. Walker*, Dent 1962.

FAMOUS VERDI OPERAS. *S. Hughes*, Robert Hale 1968.
Of the operas before *Rigoletto*, only *Nabucco* and *Macbeth* are analysed, but this
is an enjoyable armchair guide to the mature Verdi.

THE COMPLETE OPERAS OF VERDI. *C. Osborne*, Gollancz 1969.

THE VERDI COMPANION. Ed. *W. Weaver and M. Chusid*, Gollancz 1980.
There is, among many valuable articles, one by Andrew Porter guiding the
reader through the Verdi literature.

THE OPERAS OF VERDI (three volumes). *J. Budden*, Cassell 1973–81.
In addition to definitive analyses of every Verdi opera there are four chapters
on the nineteenth-century operatic scene from Rossini to Puccini.

CHAPTER TWELVE: VERISMO

NEW OXFORD HISTORY OF MUSIC. VOL. X THE MODERN AGE.
There are sections on the *verismo* period by Martin Cooper, and the post-
Puccini Italians by Mosco Carner.

PUCCINI. *M. Carner*, Duckworth 2nd edition 1974.
The best single volume on Puccini and full of information on the *verismo*
composers generally.

PUCCINI: KEEPER OF THE SEAL. *E. Greenfield*, Arrow Books 1958.
A spirited and illuminating defence.

FAMOUS PUCCINI OPERAS. *S. Hughes*, Robert Hale 1959.

As with the author's book on Verdi, an enjoyable guide paying particular attention to orchestration.

THE OPERAS OF PUCCINI. *W. Ashbrook*, Cassell 1969.

LETTERS OF PUCCINI. Ed. *G. Adami*, rev. *M. Carner*, Harrap 1974.
A selection by the librettist of *Turandot*.

CHAPTER THIRTEEN: RUSSIA

MUSSORGSKY. *M. D. Calvocoressi*, rev. *G. Abraham*, Dent (Master Musicians Series) 1974.

ENO/ROH OPERA GUIDE 11: BORIS GODUNOV. Ed. *N. John*, Calder, 1982.
Outlines the differences between Mussorgsky's versions of *Boris*.

VLADIMIR STASOV: SELECTED ESSAYS ON MUSIC. Tran. *F. Jones*, Barrie and Rockliff 1968.
Contains the essay 'Twenty-five years of Russian Art: Our Music' (1883) surveying nationalist musical achievements from Glinka to Glazunov.

TCHAIKOVSKY: A SYMPOSIUM. Ed. *G. Abraham*, Lindsay Drummond 1945.
The editor contributes a chapter on the operas.

TCHAIKOVSKY: A BIOGRAPHICAL AND CRITICAL STUDY. *D. Brown*, Gollancz 1978.
Three of the four volumes have appeared to date.

N. RIMSKY-KORSAKOV: MY MUSICAL LIFE. Tran. *J. Joffe*, Eulenberg 1974.

CHAPTER FOURTEEN: EASTERN EUROPE

SMETANA. *B. Large*, Duckworth 1970.

DVOŘÁK. *J. Clapham*, David and Charles 1979.
Contains a chronicle of Dvořák's life, list of works, and a full bibliography.

LEOŠ JANÁČEK. *J. Vogel*, Orbis 1981.
This work, translated from the 1962 Czech original, is very comprehensive.

JANÁČEK'S TRAGIC OPERAS. *M. Ewans*, Faber 1977.

LEOŠ JANÁČEK. *I. Horsbrugh*, David and Charles 1981.

MARTINŮ — THE MAN AND HIS MUSIC. *M. Šafránek*, Dobson 1946.

MARTINŮ. *B. Large*, Duckworth 1975.
Both these books are good, but neither has space for full discussion of Martinů's fourteen operas.

CHAPTER FIFTEEN: LATER FRENCH OPERA

FRENCH MUSIC FROM THE DEATH OF BERLIOZ TO THE DEATH OF FAURÉ. *M. Cooper*, Oxford University Press 1951.

CÉSAR FRANCK AND HIS CIRCLE. *L. Davies*, Barrie and Jenkins 1970.
Part three covers operas by d'Indy, Dukas, Chausson and Magnard.

EMMANUEL CHABRIER AND HIS CIRCLE. *R. Myers*, Dent 1969.

THE GALLIC MUSE. *L. Davies*, Dent 1967.
Includes studies of Fauré, Debussy, Ravel and Poulenc.

MASSENET. *J. Harding*, Dent 1970.

GABRIEL FAURÉ. *R. Orledge*, Eulenberg 1979.

MAURICE RAVEL. *H. H. Stuckenschmidt*, Calder and Boyars 1969.

ALBERT ROUSSEL. *B. Deane*, Barrie and Rockliff 1961.

CHAPTER SIXTEEN: YOUNGER NATIONAL TRADITIONS

THE STRAUSS FAMILY. *P. Kemp*, Baton Press 1985.

MANUEL DE FALLA AND THE SPANISH MUSICAL RENAISSANCE. *B. James*, Gollancz 1979.

ARTHUR SULLIVAN—A VICTORIAN MUSICIAN. *A. Jacobs*, Oxford University Press 1984.

THE ENGLISH MUSICAL RENAISSANCE. *F. Howes*, Secker and Warburg 1966.

THE MUSIC MAKERS. *M. Trend*, Weidenfeld and Nicolson 1985.

DELIUS, PORTRAIT OF A COSMOPOLITAN. *C. Palmer*, Duckworth 1976.

THE WORKS OF RALPH VAUGHAN WILLIAMS. *M. Kennedy*, Oxford University Press 1964.

THE MUSIC OF GUSTAV HOLST. *I. Holst*, Oxford University Press 3rd edition 1985.

MUSIC IN A NEW FOUND LAND: THEMES AND DEVELOPMENT IN THE HISTORY OF AMERICAN MUSIC. *W. Mellers*, Barrie & Rockliff 1964.

AMERICA'S MUSIC: FROM THE PILGRIMS TO THE PRESENT. *G. Chase*, McGraw-Hill 1955.

MUSIC IN THE UNITED STATES. *H. Wiley Hitchcock*, Prentice Hall 1969.

CHAPTER SEVENTEEN: THE EARLY TWENTIETH CENTURY: SYMBOLISM AND EXPRESSIONISM

DEBUSSY, HIS LIFE AND MIND (two volumes). *E. Lockspeiser*, Cassell 1962–65.

DEBUSSY AND WAGNER. *R. Holloway*, Eulenberg 1979.
A technical analysis of *Pelléas* and *Tristan*.

RICHARD STRAUSS: A CRITICAL STUDY OF THE OPERAS. *W. Mann*, Cassell 1964.

RICHARD STRAUSS: A CRITICAL COMMENTARY ON HIS LIFE AND WORKS (three volumes). *N. del Mar*, Barrie and Jenkins 1962–72.

THE LIFE AND MUSIC OF BÉLA BARTÓK. *H. Stevens*, Oxford University Press 2nd edition 1964.

STRAVINSKY: THE COMPOSER AND HIS WORKS. *E. W. White*, Faber 2nd edition 1979.

BUSONI THE COMPOSER. *A. Beaumont*, Faber 1985.

ALBAN BERG. *W. Reich*, Thames and Hudson 1965.
Includes Reich's adaptation of Berg's own analytical lecture on *Wozzeck*.

ORIENTATIONS — COLLECTED WRITINGS. *P. Boulez*, Faber 1986.
Reprints Boulez's essays on *Wozzeck* and the (completed) *Lulu* from his recordings, as well as his essays on *Pelléas* and on Wagner.

CHAPTER EIGHTEEN: THE LATER STRAUSS AND THE MID-TWENTIETH CENTURY

For STRAUSS, see bibliography to chapter seventeen.

HINDEMITH. *I. Kemp*, Oxford University Press 1970.
This short study gives some attention to *Cardillac* and *Mathis der Maler*.

MUSIC AND MUSICAL LIFE IN SOVIET RUSSIA 1917–70. *B. Schwarz*, Barrie and Jenkins 1972.

PROKOFIEV. *C. Samuel*, Calder and Boyars 1971.

SHOSTAKOVICH: THE MAN AND HIS MUSIC. Ed. *C. Norris*, Lawrence and Wishart 1982.
There is a chapter on the operas by Geoffrey Norris.

MEMORIES AND COMMENTARIES. *I. Stravinsky and R. Craft*, Faber 1960.
Reprints Auden's letters on *The Rake's Progress*, as well as the first scenario for the opera.

TIPPETT AND HIS OPERAS. *E. W. White*, Barrie and Jenkins 1979.

BENJAMIN BRITTEN: HIS LIFE AND OPERAS. *E. W. White*, Faber 2nd edition 1983.

THE OPERAS OF BENJAMIN BRITTEN. Ed. *D. Herbert*, Hamish Hamilton 1979. Authoritative texts of all the librettos and many illustrations of sets, costumes and first productions.

BRITTEN. *C. Headington*, Eyre Methuen 1981.

THE BRITTEN COMPANION. Ed. *C. Palmer*, Faber 1984.

CHAPTER NINETEEN: OPERA TODAY

There is naturally little published in book form on very recent opera, although *The Contemporary Composer Series* (Robson Books) includes published or forthcoming volumes on Berio, Birtwistle, Ligeti and Maxwell Davies.

INDEX

385

INDEX

INDEX